O Level

Statistics

Dean James Chalmers

CAMBRIDGE
UNIVERSITY PRESS

University Printing House, Cambridge CB2 8BS, United Kingdom

One Liberty Plaza, 20th Floor, New York, NY 10006, USA

477 Williamstown Road, Port Melbourne, VIC 3207, Australia

314–321, 3rd Floor, Plot 3, Splendor Forum, Jasola District Centre, New Delhi – 110025, India

103 Penang Road, #05-06/07, Visioncrest Commercial, Singapore 238467

Cambridge University Press is part of the University of Cambridge.

It furthers the University's mission by disseminating knowledge in the pursuit of education, learning and research at the highest international levels of excellence.

Information on this title: education.cambridge.org

First published 2009
Second edition 2015
20 19 18 17 16 15 14 13 12 11 10 9 8 7 6

Printed in Great Britain by CPI Group (UK) Ltd, Croydon CRO 4YY

A catalogue record for this publication is available from the British Library

ISBN 9781107577039 Paperback

Additional resources for this publication at www.cambridge.org/

Contents

Introduction

Statistics is a practical subject that concerns the collection, summary, display and analysis of data.

Look in your local or national newspaper, listen to your radio or watch the television, and you will find that statistical information on many aspects of everyday life is frequently being presented to you in a variety of forms.

Once data have been analysed it is possible, by looking for trends, to predict what the future may hold in store – appropriate action can then be taken.

The aim of this book is to serve as a basic introduction to the study of statistics and probability, enabling students to gain a sound understanding of their purpose, and knowledge of the elementary ideas, methods and terminology used. Chapters are arranged in a user-friendly order, beginning with topics that may be familiar and progressing, through clearly emphasised links, to topics that will be new to most students.

This second edition cover's the entire Cambridge (CIE) O Level Statistics 4040 syllabus for examinations from 2018, which has been updated to include the following: stem-and-leaf diagrams; box-and-whisker diagrams; elementary ideas of correlation; and understanding of trend and seasonal variation. It will also be of invaluable use to those studying statistics and/or probability on any other syllabus at a similar or higher level.

Table 0.1 indicates where each section in the Cambridge (CIE) O Level Statistics 4040 syllabus can be found in this book:

Table 0.1: Primary location of each section of the syllabus

Section	1	2	3	4	5.1	5.2 5.3	5.4	6	7	8	9	10	11	12
Chapter 1		•												
Chapter 2													•	
Chapter 3	•													
Chapter 4			•	•										
Chapter 5					•									
Chapter 6							•		•	•				
Chapter 7						•	•							
Chapter 8								•						
Chapter 9													•	•
Chapter 10											•			
Chapter 11												•		

1 Ungrouped Data

Learning Objectives

In this chapter you will learn:

- How to summarise and display data, and about the importance and usefulness of doing this
- How to interpret data presented in various forms and to extract useful information
- About the advantages, disadvantages and appropriateness of various forms of summary and display
- How to make relevant comparisons between the items in a set of data

Introduction

Data are facts and statistics collected together for reference or analysis. Before they are processed for use they are referred to as **raw data.** The processing of raw data may involve summarising in ordered lists and tables, or displaying in diagrams and graphs. There is never just one way of doing this – there is always a choice – and each method has its own advantages and disadvantages, which also depend on the type and subject of the data, how much of it there is, and the purpose for which the summary or display is being made. In **ungrouped** data, individual values can be seen separately from other values. Once processed in an appropriate way, calculations can be performed, and the data can be analysed.

1.1 Summary and Display of Data

When summarising or displaying data, a very important consideration is that the presentation should be clear and easy to understand. Who is it being presented to, and for what purpose is it being done?

Two-way Tables

One method of summarising data is to enter it into a table – data can be **tabulated**.

The columns and rows of a table should have headings, and totals can be included when appropriate.

Numbers and proportions (percentages, fractions and ratios) can then be compared and interpreted.

Examples

Table 1.1 shows the results of a geography test that was taken by a group of 45 students.

Table 1.1: Geography test results

	Pass	Fail	Totals
Boys	22	4	26
Girls	17	2	19
Totals	39	6	45

From Table 1.1 we can see that:

- 26 boys took the test
- 2 girls failed the test
- 39 students passed the test
- $\frac{17}{19}$ of the girls passed the test
- $\frac{1}{3}$ or 33.3% of those who failed were girls
- the ratio of passes to failures for boys was 11 : 2.

Exercise 1A

1 Table 1.2 gives information about 100 students who took an examination in physics.

Table 1.2: Physics examination results

	Pass	Fail	Totals
Boys	45	15	60
Girls	28	12	40
Totals	73	27	100

i How many students passed?
ii What fraction of the students failed?
iii What fraction of the girls passed?
iv Calculate:
  a the percentage pass rate for boys,
  b the percentage pass rate for girls.
v Which group performed better, boys or girls?

2 A woman sells red and yellow T-shirts at a market. She has small, medium and large in each colour. There are 120 T-shirts altogether, and 75 of them are red. She has 20 small red T-shirts, 14 medium yellow T-shirts and 48 large T-shirts. The ratio of large red T-shirts to large yellow T-shirts is 2 : 1.

i Copy and complete Table 1.3.

Table 1.3: T-shirt stocks

	Small	Medium	Large	Totals
Red	20			75
Yellow		14		
Total			48	120

ii Find the fraction of the T-shirts that are:
  a yellow, **b** medium.
iii What fraction of the red T-shirts are large?
iv What percentage of the small T-shirts are yellow? Answer to 1 decimal place.

3 On sports day a girl decided to sell two types of canned drinks: Cherry-Fizz and Orange-Wizz. She had 15 bottles of both types of drink in small and medium sizes. She had 13 small bottles altogether, and 7 of the medium bottles contained Orange-Wizz.

i Tabulate the data with the numbers of each of the four items.
ii What fraction of the bottles were small Cherry-Fizzes?
iii How many of the bottles were neither small nor contained Orange-Wizz?

4 At lunchtime 100 students were each asked to choose one main course from either stew or hot pot. The students were also asked to choose one dessert from either ice cream or tart. Altogether 58 chose stew, 24 chose hot pot and ice cream, and 44 chose tart. All of the students chose one main course and one dessert.

i Illustrate the data in a fully labelled table.
ii What fraction of the students chose both hot pot and tart?

5 Details about the 50 motor cars being sold by a second-hand car dealer are given in Table 1.4.

Table 1.4: Second-hand cars available

	Saloon		Hatchback	
	Petrol	Diesel	Petrol	Diesel
Manual	7	4	12	7
Automatic	5	3	9	3

i What percentage of the motor cars are automatic?
ii What fraction of the hatchbacks use diesel?
iii What percentage of the automatic saloons use petrol?
iv Which has the highest proportion of motor cars that use diesel, saloons or hatchbacks?

6 A boy has 60 discs: some are black and some are white. The discs are either plastic or wooden.

Forty percent of the discs are black, and $\frac{5}{9}$ of the white discs are plastic.

Of the wooden discs, there is one less black than white.

i Draw up a table, with headings, showing the number of each of the four types of disc.
ii What proportion of the discs is not a black plastic disc?

7 A survey gave the data shown in Table 1.5 on the numbers of adults and the numbers of employed adults in each of the households in a particular street.

Table 1.5: Adult employment numbers

	No. adults		
No. employed adults	1	2	3
0	6	3	0
1	4	5	2
2	—	5	4
3	—	—	1

i In how many households was there more than one adult?
ii In how many households were all the adults employed?
iii How many households had just one unemployed adult?
iv How many employed adults were there in all these households together?
v Explain why there are no values entered into three of the cells of Table 1.5.

8 Table 1.6 gives information about the method used by some employees to get to work today, and how they intend to get to work tomorrow.

Table 1.6: Commuting methods

		Today	Tomorrow
Bus	Male	10	8
	Female	9	10
Taxi	Male	3	3
	Female	4	3
Walk	Male	15	17
	Female	12	12

i How many employees are represented in Table 1.6?
ii How many of the employees are male?
iii How many of the employees walked to work today?
iv How many of the employees plan to take a bus to work tomorrow?
v Give details about Dora, the only female intending to travel by a different method tomorrow.
vi Explain why it is not necessarily true that only two males intend to travel by a different method tomorrow.

9 Joan wants to tabulate data showing the numbers of students that passed or failed each of the three final papers in geography at her school last year and this year. Altogether 322 students sat for each of the three papers last year, which was 23 fewer than this year. The numbers passing Papers 1, 2 and 3 last year were 310, 303 and 305, respectively. Fifteen more students failed Paper 2 this year than last year; equal numbers passed Paper 1 in both years, and three times as many students failed Paper 3 this year than last year.

i Copy and complete Table 1.7, in which these data are tabulated.

Table 1.7: Geography paper results

	Last year		This year	
	Pass	**Fail**	**Pass**	**Fail**
Paper 1	310			
Paper 2	303			
Paper 3	305			

ii What is the greatest possible number of students that failed all three papers this year?
iii What is the least possible number of students that failed all three papers last year?

10 The 124 employees at a company are classified by gender, employment status and skill. The diagram below shows, for example, that there are 25 skilled full-time females, and 6 unskilled part-time males.

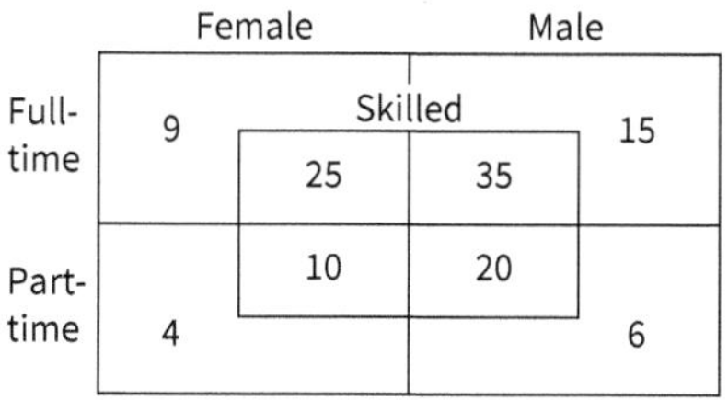

Figure 1.1: Full- and part-time employees

Find:

i the number of skilled employees,
ii the number of male employees,
iii the number of unskilled full-time female employees,
iv what fraction of the full-time employees are skilled,
v what percentage of the part-time employees are male,
vi what fraction of the skilled males work part time,
vii what percentage of the unskilled part-timers are female.

Frequency distributions

A small amount of data can be written conveniently as a list of numbers or words. We can list ten students' scores in a quiz, or the favourite colours of ten people. However, if we have to list the quiz scores of 150 students or the favourite colours of 300 people, then it would take a long time and the lists would not convey much useful information to anyone who looked at them. In cases like this, it would be more appropriate to summarise the data as a **frequency distribution**, where the data are shown in a frequency table.

A frequency distribution is ungrouped when individual values of the variable are listed.

If the variable takes numerical values then the values should be ranked, usually in ascending order.

The letter f is used to represent the **frequency**, which indicates the number of times that a particular value occurs in a set of data.

Examples

1 The frequency distribution in Table 1.8 shows the 50 values of a variable X.

Table 1.8: Values of variable X

Values of X	0	1	2	3	
Frequency of values (f)	5	10	20	15	$\Sigma f = 50$

Table 1.8 is a simple alternative to making an ordered list of the 50 values of X.

The list of 50 numbers would begin with five 0's and end with fifteen 3's.

If, for example, X represents the number of goals scored by a football team in each of its 50 games, we could see very easily that the team scored:

- 0 goals in each of 5 games
- 1 goal in each of 10 games
- 2 goals in each of 20 games
- 3 goals in each of 15 games.

So we can calculate that the team scored $(0 \times 5) + (1 \times 10) + (2 \times 20) + (3 \times 15) = 95$ goals in 50 games.

2 A survey of a particular street was made to find the number of occupants in each house. The results are displayed as a frequency distribution in Table 1.9.

Table 1.9: Frequency table for number of house occupants

Number of occupants (X)	**Number of houses(f)**	**Number of houses × number of occupants (fX)**
0	0	0
1	4	4
2	7	14
3	9	27
4	13	52
5	7	35
	$\Sigma f = 40$	$\Sigma fX = 132$

X represents the numbers of occupants, which is the variable.

f represents the number of houses, which is the frequency.

$\Sigma f = 40$ is the total number of houses.

$\Sigma fX = 132$ is the total number of occupants.

There are:

- No empty houses
- 4 houses each with 1 occupant $= 4 \times 1 = 4$ occupants
- 7 houses each with 2 occupants $= 7 \times 2 = 14$ occupants
- 9 houses each with 3 occupants $= 9 \times 3 = 27$ occupants
- 13 houses each with 4 occupants $= 13 \times 4 = 52$ occupants
- 7 houses each with 5 occupants $= 7 \times 5 = 35$ occupants.

Altogether there are 40 houses with 132 occupants.

Exercise 1B

1 The numbers of late arrivals at a certain school during each consecutive school day in June were:

5, 3, 4, 0, 1, 2, 7, 3, 3, 1, 4, 3, 3, 2, 4, 3, 0, 5, 3, 4, 2

i Show these data as an ungrouped frequency distribution in a table with three columns, as in Table 1.10. Include two totals in the last row of the table.

Table 1.10: Late arrival frequencies

Number of late arrivals (X)	Number of days (f)	fX
0	2	0

ii Explain what each of the two totals in your table represents.

iii Find:

a the most common number of late arrivals,

b on how many days there were fewer than 4 late arrivals,

c on how many days there were 5 or more late arrivals,

d on what proportion of the days there were 3 late arrivals.

Albert arrived late in June more frequently than any other student.

iv What is the greatest possible number of days on which Albert could have arrived late in June?

2 Some female doctors were asked, 'How many children do you have?' Their responses were:

2, 4, 2, 0, 1, 0, 0, 2, 1, 3, 0, 2, 5, 1, 3, 1, 0, 2, 1, 4, 1, 0, 2, 0, 3

i Show these data as an ungrouped frequency distribution in a table.

ii Copy and complete the sentence:

'These . . . female doctors have . . . children altogether.'

iii How many of the female doctors have more than 1 but fewer than 5 children?

3 The frequency table in Table 1.11 shows the ages of the members of a cycling club.

Table 1.11: Cycling club membership

Age (years)	under 12	12	13	14	15	16	17	18	over 18
Number of children (f)	0	3	5	12	7	2	0	1	0

i Find:

a the most common age of the members of the club,

b how many children are members of this club,

c the proportion of the membership that is 16 years old,

d the number of members who are under 14 years of age,

e the percentage of members who are 12 years old.

ii Find the total of the ages of the 10 youngest members.

iii Calculate the total of all the members' ages.

4 The shoe sizes of a group of children are shown in Table 1.12.

Table 1.12: Shoe sizes

Shoe size	No. children (f)
$3\frac{1}{2}$	7
4	11
$4\frac{1}{2}$	13
5	26
$5\frac{1}{2}$	31
6	22
$6\frac{1}{2}$	14
7	6

i How many children are represented in Table 1.12?
ii Find the number of children that wear:
  a sizes 4 to 5 inclusive,
  b sizes 5 to 7 exclusive.
iii What fraction of the children wear size $4\frac{1}{2}$?
iv What percentage of the children wear size 5?
v Of those that wear size 5 or larger, what fraction wear size 6 or smaller?

5 Table 1.13 shows the number of aircraft that took off from an airfield every day for 30 days.

Table 1.13: Daily flights

Number of aircraft	5	6	7	8	9	10	11	12	
Number of days (f)	2	4	7	9	4	3	0	1	Total = 30

i What is the most common number of aircraft that took off per day?
ii On how many days did more than 9 aircraft take off?
iii How many aircraft took off in these 30 days altogether?
iv On what percentage of the days did at most 6 aircraft take off?

6 Table 1.14 shows the angles that are to be used in a pie chart illustrating the number of days' sick leave taken last month by each of the employees at a computer software company. Just one employee took 6 days' sick leave.

Table 1.14: Sick leave

No. days sick leave	0	1	2	3	4	5	6	
Sector angle	189°	72°	39°	33°	15°	9°	3°	Total = 360°

i Find the number of employees that took 5 days' sick leave.
ii How many employees are there at the company?
iii What proportion of the employees took sick leave last month?
iv Show the data in a table as an ungrouped frequency distribution.
v Calculate the total number of days' sick leave that were taken.

1.2 Pictorial Representation of Data

A variety of diagrams and graphs can be used to illustrate ungrouped data.

Diagrams usually appeal to people more than lists or tables, as they impart information at a glance.

The diagrams that are frequently used are pictograms, bar charts, line graphs, pie charts and Venn diagrams.

Pictograms

Data are illustrated by the use of symbols with a key to indicate what each symbol represents.

Care must be taken when drawing symbols: if two symbols are different in shape or size, they will not represent the same item or the same number of items. Symbols with simple shapes are recommended, as it may sometimes be necessary to draw fractions of one.

Examples

Three neighbours have grown cabbages in their gardens. The pictogram in Figure 1.2 shows how many cabbages each of them grew.

	⁘ represent 4 cabbages
David	⁘ ⁘ ⁘ ⁘ ⁘ ⁘ ⁘ ⁘
Samuel	⁘ ⁘ ⁘ ⁘ ⁘ ⁘
Bonolo	⁘ ⁘ ⁘ ⁘ ⁘ ⁘ ⁚

Figure 1.2: Cabbages grown

The three neighbours grew a total of 84 cabbages.

David grew 32; Samuel grew 24 and Bonolo grew 28.

$\frac{28}{84} = \frac{1}{3}$ of the cabbages were grown by Bonolo.

i Express the number of cabbages grown by David to the number grown by Samuel as a simple ratio.

ii What percentage of the cabbages were not grown by Samuel? Give your answer correct to 1 decimal place.

Exercise 1C

1 Forty-five students were asked which sports they play. All students play at least one sport. The data were collected, and are illustrated in the pictogram in Figure 1.3.

Sport	➪ **Represents two students**
Softball	➪ ➪ ➪ ➪ ➪ ➪
Football	➪ ➪ ➪ ➪ ➪ ➪ ➪
Volleyball	➪ ➪ ➪ ➪ ➪
Table tennis	➪ ➪ ➪
Badminton	➪
Tennis	➪ ➪

Figure 1.3: Numbers playing different sports

i Find:

a the most popular sport, **b** the least popular sport,

c the fraction that play volleyball, **d** the percentage that play tennis.

ii Explain why there appear to be more than 45 students represented in Figure 1.3.

iii Express the number that play softball to the number that do not play table tennis as a simple ratio.

2 A farmer grew five different vegetables on his farm. The number of each produced is given in Table 1.15.

Table 1.15: Vegetable yields

Vegetable	**No. produced**
Cabbage	32
Carrot	64
Onion	48
Tomato	80
Potato	40

i Draw a symbol that would be suitable for showing these data in a pictogram, and state what it would represent.

ii What is the total number of vegetables produced?

iii What fraction of the total number of vegetables are onions?

iv What percentage, to 1 decimal place, are tomatoes?

v Illustrate the data in a pictogram.

3 The different types of accommodation that a number of families inhabit are illustrated in the pictogram in Figure 1.4.

	[ooo ooo] Represents 6 families
Detached house	[ooo ooo] [ooo ooo] [ooo ooo]
Semi-detached house	[ooo ooo] [ooo ooo] [ooo ooo] [ooo ooo] [ooo ooo]
Terraced house	[ooo ooo] [ooo ooo] [ooo ooo] [ooo ooo] [ooo ooo] [ooo ooo] [o o]
Bungalow	[ooo ooo] [ooo ooo] [ooo]
Flat	[ooo ooo] [ooo ooo]
Houseboat	[o]

Figure 1.4: Family housing

i Explain why you think this particular symbol was chosen to represent 6 families.
ii How many more families live in semi-detached houses than in detached houses?
iii How many fewer families live in a flat than a bungalow?
iv How many families are represented altogether?
v What fraction of the families lives in a terraced house?

Bar Charts

Bars or columns of equal width are drawn to the heights of the numbers of items, which are the frequencies. Equal-width gaps may be left between bars, and all bars should be unshaded, or all shaded in the same way – avoid using many bright colours or random patterns, as this may give a false impression of the relative size of the bars.

Advantages of displaying data in a bar chart are that most people understand them, and the frequencies are easily seen and compared. A bar chart is appropriate if there are a fairly small number of values to display, usually not more than eight.

Examples

1 A child asked each of a group of adults, 'What is your favourite drink?'

The adults' responses were: 10 tea, 7 coffee, 5 juice, 4 milk, 3 water and 1 lemonade, as depicted in Figure 1.5.

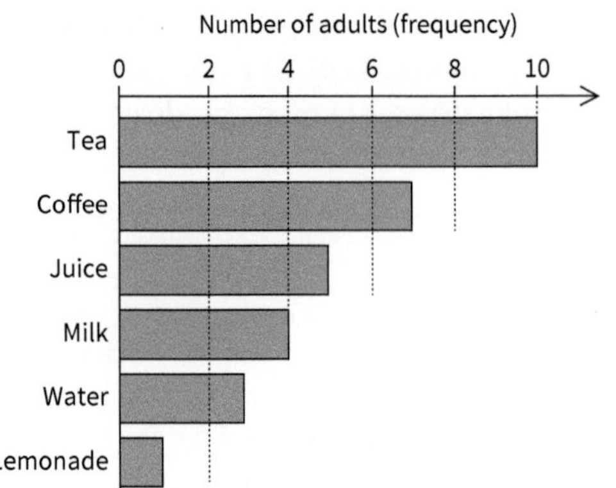

Figure 1.5: Drink preferences

i How many adults were in the group?
ii What fraction of the adults prefer coffee?
iii What percentage of the adults do not prefer water?

2 Each pupil in a class was asked to write down how many times they had checked their emails in the past week. The results are shown in the bar chart in Figure 1.6.

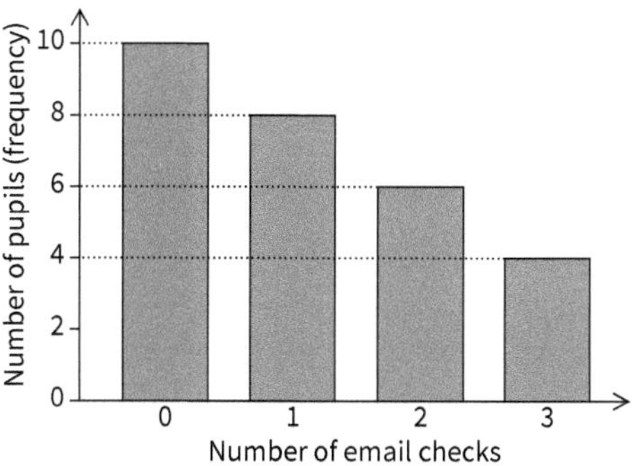

Figure 1.6: Email checking frequency

Table 1.16: Email checking frequency distribution

Number of email checks (X)	Number of pupils (f)
0	10
1	8
2	6
3	4

The data in the bar chart can be shown as a frequency distribution, as in Table 1.16.

i How many pupils are in this class?

ii How many email checks were made altogether?

iii What fraction of the pupils did check their emails?

iv What percentage of the pupils did not check their emails at all?

Exercise 1D

1 The bar chart in Figure 1.7 shows the methods of transport used by some students when travelling to school.

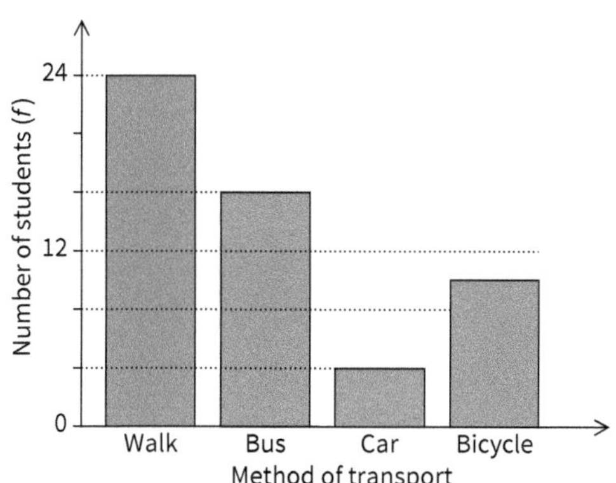

Figure 1.7: Getting to school

i Name the least common method of transport.

ii How many more students walk than use the bus?

iii Express as a simple ratio the number of students who use the bus to the number who cycle.

iv What percentage of the students travel in a car? Answer correct to 1 decimal place.

v What fraction of the students do not walk to school?

2 The owner of a shop recorded the number of bags of potatoes sold on each of five days last week, as shown in Table 1.17.

Table 1.17: Bags of potatoes sold

Day	Monday	Tuesday	Wednesday	Thursday	Friday
No. bags	40	23	31	25	47

i Illustrate the data in a bar chart.

ii How many bags of potatoes were sold last week?

iii Between which two consecutive days did the largest change in the number of bags sold occur?

iv Is it necessarily true that more potatoes were sold on Thursday than on Tuesday? Explain.

3 The bar chart in Figure 1.8 illustrates the number of goals scored by a hockey team in its 32 games last season.

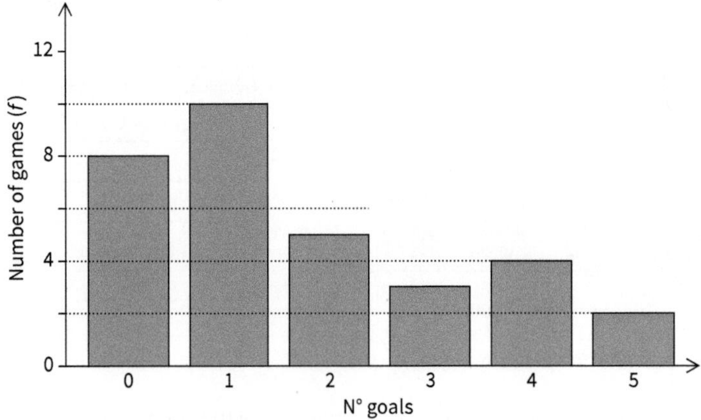

Figure 1.8: Hockey goals scored

i In how many games did the team score exactly 2 goals?
ii What was the most frequently scored number of goals?
iii In what percentage of the games did the team fail to score?
iv How many goals did the team score altogether in its 32 games last season?
v In how many games did the team score at least 4 goals?

4 The bar chart in Figure 1.9 shows how many text messages were sent today by each of the 20 children in a club.

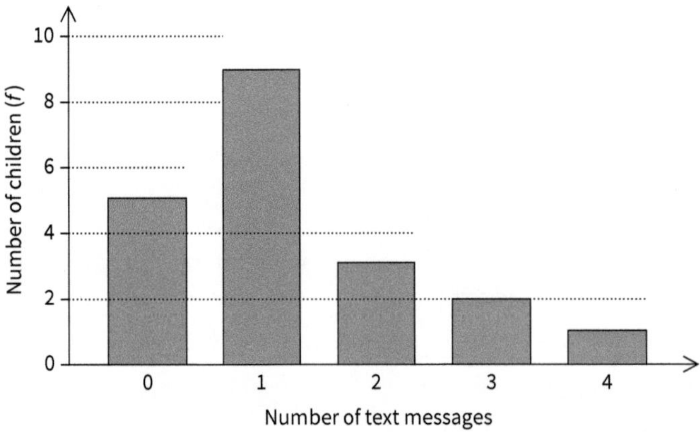

Figure 1.9: Number of text messages sent

i Illustrate the data shown in Figure 1.9 as a frequency distribution.
Use the headings given in Table 1.18.

Table 1.18: Text message frequency distribution

Number of text messages	Number of children (f)

ii Use Figure 1.9 and your table to find the total number of text messages sent by these 20 children.

5 The frequency distribution in Table 1.19 shows the number of vehicles owned by each of the families living in a particular street.

Table 1.19: Number of vehicles owned by families

Number of vehicles	0	1	2	3	4	5
Number of families (f)	1	8	7	5	3	2

i Illustrate the information given in Table 1.19 in a fully labelled bar chart.
ii How many families live in this street?
iii How many vehicles do these families own altogether?

6 Each of 66 men was blindfolded and given a ball. They were asked to throw the ball into a bucket that was placed two metres in front of them. Each man eventually threw the ball into the bucket. The numbers of unsuccessful throws are recorded in the bar chart shown in Figure 1.10.

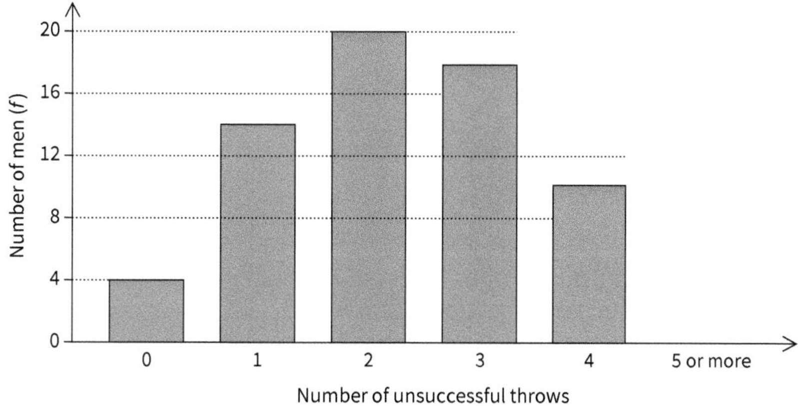

Figure 1.10: Numbers of unsuccessful throws

i Display the data in a fully labelled frequency table.
ii How many unsuccessful attempts did these 66 men make altogether?
iii Use Figure 1.10 and your table to find the number of men that:
- **a** threw the ball into the bucket on their first attempt,
- **b** threw the ball into the bucket before their fourth attempt,
- **c** needed at least three attempts to get the ball into the bucket.

Dual and Other Comparative Bar Charts

Comparative bar charts are useful if two or more sets of related data are to be compared.

A **dual** bar chart is used to show and compare *two sets* of related data. It consists of pairs of bars, with one bar in each pair for each set of data. Equal-width gaps should be left between pairs of bars, and all bars should be of equal width.

A key, in which different shading can be used, is needed to distinguish between the two sets of data.

Examples

Last month, two travel companies, TourWell and TravelSafe, organised holidays for customers at four destinations. The numbers of each are given in Table 1.20.

Table 1.20: Travel destinations

Company \ Destination	France	USA	China	South Africa
TourWell	11	9	5	7
TravelSafe	9	12	3	4

The dual bar chart in Figure 1.11 illustrates the data.

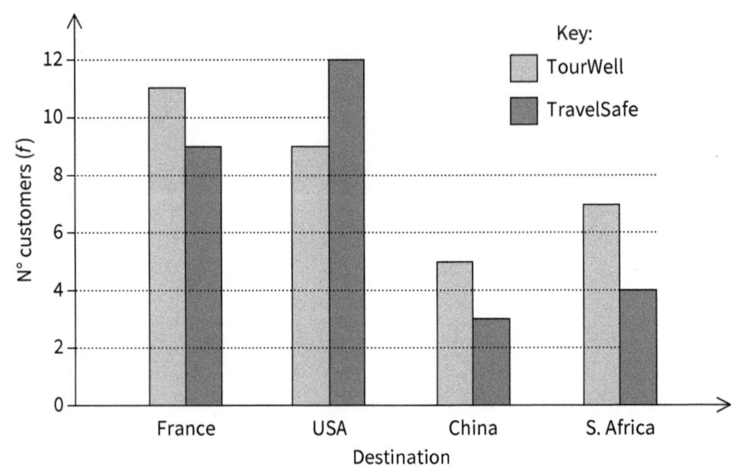

Figure 1.11: Travel destinations

i Show the data in a comparative bar chart with two groups of four bars, using one group of four bars for each travel company.

Exercise 1E

1 The results of a survey of two classes on students' favourite flavours in potato chips are shown in Table 1.21.

Table 1.21: Potato chip preferences

	Class A	Class B
Plain	6	14
Barbecue	8	6
Cheese & onion	1	0
Salt & vinegar	11	8
Hot spice	4	2

i Illustrate these data in a clearly labelled dual bar chart, showing one pair of bars for each of the five flavours.

ii What proportion of the students from class A prefer barbecue flavour chips?

iii What fraction of the students who prefer hot spice flavour are from class B?

2 The numbers of patients admitted with malaria into three hospitals over a six-week period are shown in Figure 1.12.

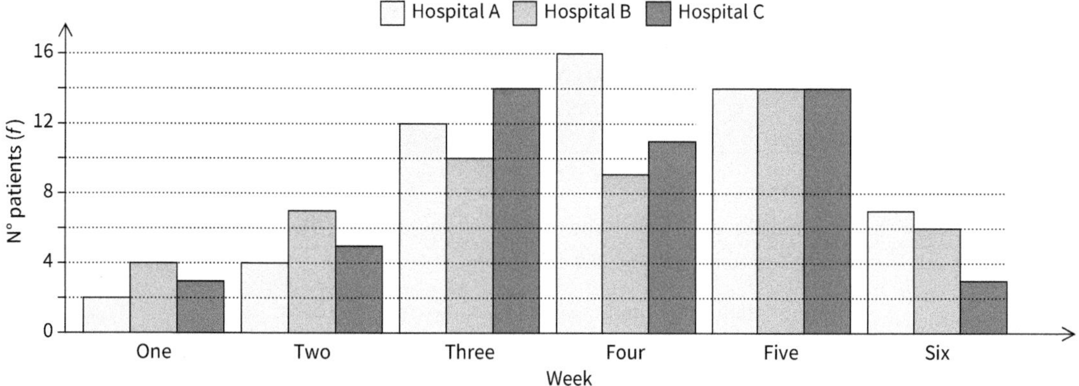

Figure 1.12: Malaria patient numbers

i Tabulate the data shown in the comparative bar chart of Figure 1.13.

ii Use Figure 1.13 and your table to find:

a how many patients were admitted with malaria to these hospitals altogether during the six weeks,

b during which week the greatest number of patients was admitted into the hospitals altogether,

c between which two consecutive weeks was the greatest change in the number of patients admitted to hospital C.

iii Express the total number of patients admitted to hospitals A, B and C as a simple ratio.

iv What percentage of the total number of patients admitted during this period were admitted to hospital B?

3 A company recorded the numbers of its full-time and part-time employees for the years 2013 to 2015, as shown in Table 1.22.

Table 1.22: Full- and part-time employees

	Year		
Type of employee	**2013**	**2014**	**2015**
Full-time	78	77	76
Part-time	24	23	22

i Illustrate the data in a dual bar chart.

ii Express, in simple form, the ratio of the two types of employee in each year.

iii In which year was the highest proportion of employees full-time?

iv During the entire three-year period, what percentage of the employees have been part-time?

4 Sixty men and eighty women applied for a job with an international aid organisation. The advertisement for the job stipulated that applicants must be fluent in at least one of Xhosa or Zulu. It was found that 55% of the male applicants and 70% of the female applicants were fluent in Xhosa, and that 60% of the male applicants and 55% of the female applicants were fluent in Zulu.

i Calculate the number of female applicants who were fluent in both Xhosa and Zulu.

ii Calculate the number of male applicants who were fluent in Zulu only.

iii Show the data in a dual bar chart with three pairs of bars showing the numbers of males and females who were fluent in Xhosa only, fluent in Zulu only and fluent in both languages.

Sectional/Composite Bar Charts

In a **sectional** bar chart, each bar represents a total and is divided into sections to show how the total is made up. These diagrams are useful for showing proportional contributions to a single total: the size of one section is fairly easy to compare with another, if there are not too many sections. However, the actual contributions to the total must be worked out by subtraction.

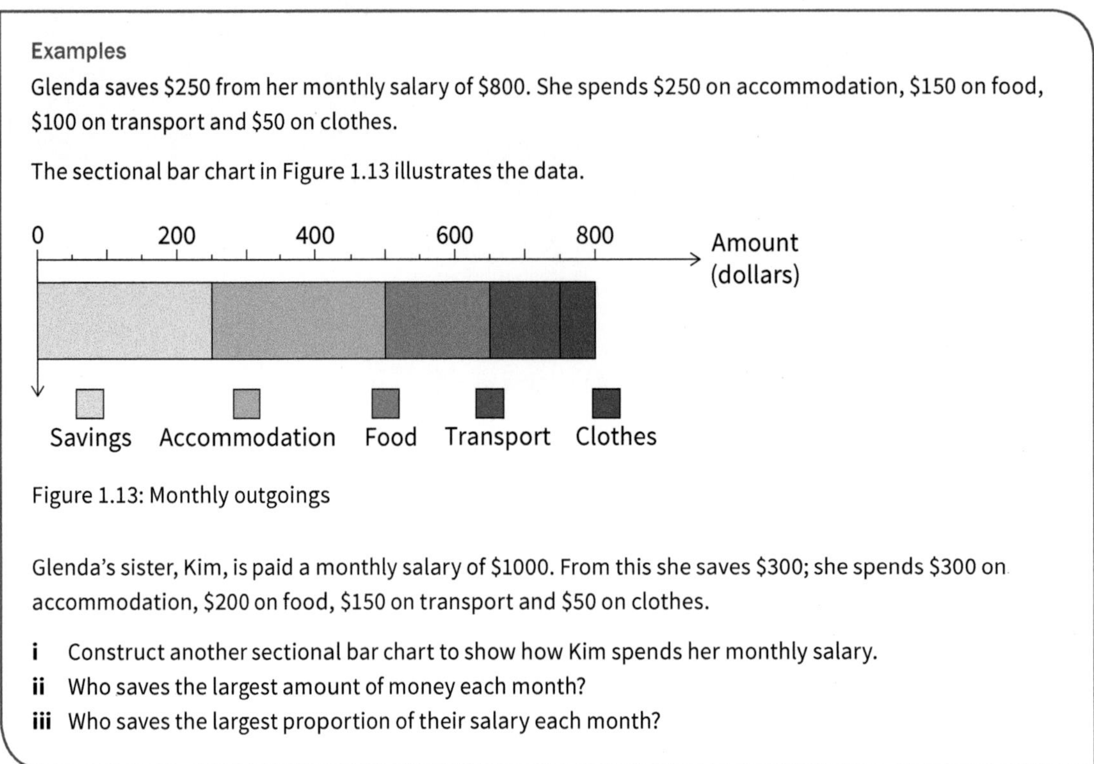

Examples

Glenda saves \$250 from her monthly salary of \$800. She spends \$250 on accommodation, \$150 on food, \$100 on transport and \$50 on clothes.

The sectional bar chart in Figure 1.13 illustrates the data.

Figure 1.13: Monthly outgoings

Glenda's sister, Kim, is paid a monthly salary of \$1000. From this she saves \$300; she spends \$300 on accommodation, \$200 on food, \$150 on transport and \$50 on clothes.

i Construct another sectional bar chart to show how Kim spends her monthly salary.
ii Who saves the largest amount of money each month?
iii Who saves the largest proportion of their salary each month?

Exercise 1F

1 The sectional bar chart in Figure 1.14 shows the number of men, women and children living in Hill Street.

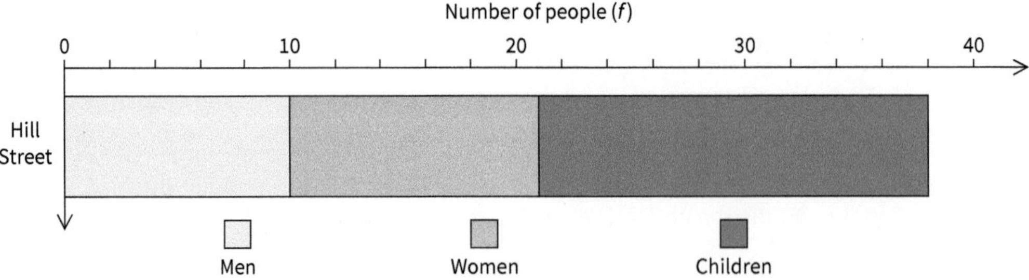

Figure 1.14: Residents of Hill Street

i Draw up a table showing the number of men, women and children that live in Hill Street.
ii Find:
  a the fraction of people living in Hill Street that are men,
  b the percentage of people living in Hill Street that are women.

Living in Valley Road, there are 15 men, 11 women and 34 children.

iii **a** Draw a sectional bar chart to illustrate the data for the people living in Valley Road.
b What percentage of the people living in Valley Road are women?
iv Which has the highest proportion of children, Hill Street or Valley Road?

2 The numbers of cars, trucks and motorbikes serviced at Mike's garage and at Jomo's garage last month are shown in the sectional bar chart in Figure 1.15.

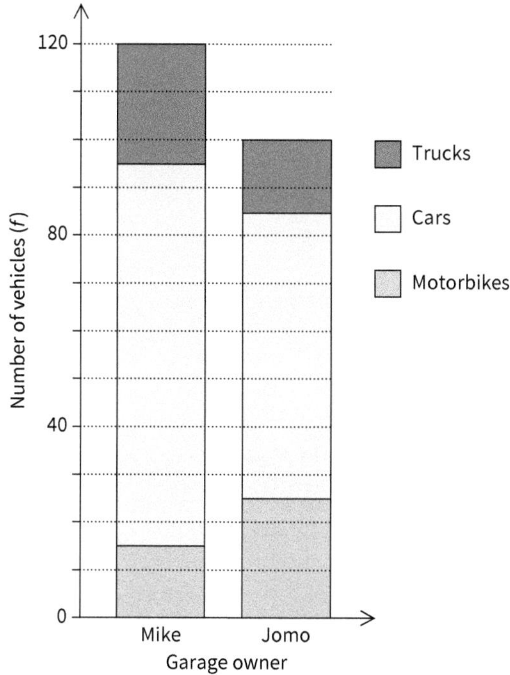

Figure 1.15: Vehicle servicing

i Tabulate the data given in Figure 1.16.
ii Showing your working, find which garage did the highest proportion of its servicing on motorbikes.

The cost of servicing each of the different types of vehicle at each of the two garages is given in Table 1.23.

Table 1.23: Servicing costs

	Mike's ($ per vehicle)	Jomo's ($ per vehicle)
Motorbike	40	50
Car	130	120
Truck	230	260

iii Calculate the total amount spent on servicing vehicles at each of the two garages last month.
iv Express the amount spent on servicing vehicles at Jomo's as a percentage of the total amount spent on servicing vehicles at the two garages together.

3 The numbers and statuses of employees at a clothing store between 2013 and 2015 are shown in Figure 1.16.

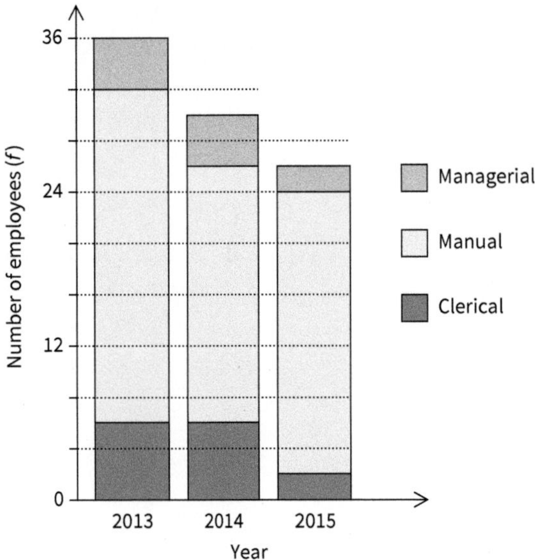

Figure 1.16: Employee status

i How many employees were there altogether in 2014?
ii How many manual employees were there in 2013?
iii How many fewer manual employees were there in 2014 than in 2013?
iv What percentage of those employed in 2013 were clerical?
v Describe the proportional change in management between 2013 and 2015.

4 In form 3A, 24 of the 40 students are boys. There are 32 students in form 3B, and 12 are girls.

i On the same diagram, construct two sectional bars with one bar for each sex.
ii In which class are there more boys?
iii Which class has the higher percentage of boys?
iv Express the number of girls in 3A to the number of girls in 3B as a simple ratio.
v Which class has the highest proportion of girls?
vi Illustrate the data in a dual bar chart showing the number of boys and the number of girls in each of the two classes.

Sectional Percentage Bar Charts

Each bar represents a total and is drawn to a height of 100%. The bars are divided into sections, and each section represents a percentage of the total. One advantage of this type of diagram is that proportional contributions are easily compared both within one bar and between bars. Actual contributions must be calculated, and this can only be done if totals are known.

Examples

A farmer used her land to grow potatoes and wheat in 2014 and in 2015.

The sectional percentage bar chart in Figure 1.17 shows the percentage of each year's income from the two crops. The data shown in the bar chart are tabulated in Table 1.24.

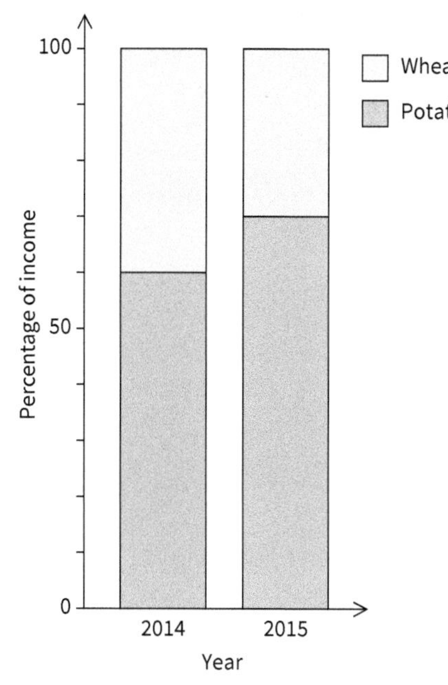

Figure 1.17: Potato and wheat income

Table 1.24: Potato and wheat income

	2014	2015
Wheat	40%	30%
Potatoes	60%	70%
Total	100%	100%

The total income represented by each bar is not indicated in Figure 1.17 or in Table 1.24. The actual income from each crop in each year is not shown. Consider these two statements, which at first sight may appear true:

a More income came from potatoes than from wheat in 2014.
b More income came from potatoes in 2015 than in 2014.

Statement (a) is *necessarily true*: 60% of 2014's income is more than 40% of 2014's income. Statement (b) is *not necessarily true*: 70% of 2015's income may be less than 60% of 2014's income. Consider two more statements, which at first sight may appear false:

c More income came from wheat than potatoes in 2015.
d More income came from wheat in 2015 than in 2014.

Statement (c) is *necessarily false*: 30% of 2015's income is not more than 70% of 2015's income. Statement (d) is *not necessarily false*: 30% of 2015's income may be more than 40% of 2014's income.

Exercise 1G

1 Table 1.25 gives the numbers of boys and girls who passed or failed a history examination last term.

Table 1.25: History examination results

	Pass	Fail
Boys	156	84
Girls	210	90

i Find the percentage of:
  a girls that failed,
  b boys that passed,
  c students that passed.

ii On the same diagram, illustrate the data with three sectional percentage bars: one for boys, one for girls and one for students.

2 Teachers at a school were asked how many siblings (brothers or sisters) they each had. The responses are summarized in Table 1.26.

Table 1.26: Teachers' siblings

Number of siblings	Number of teachers (f)
0	11
1	26
2	8
3	5
4 or more	0
	$\Sigma f = 50$

i Illustrate the data on graph paper in a sectional percentage bar chart with a key to show what each section represents.
ii What percentage of these teachers have more than one sibling?
iii How many siblings do these teachers have altogether?

3 Mrs Mafela owns three general stores in the north, south and west of town. The numbers of tins of soup, beans and tomatoes sold at each store last month are shown in Table 1.27.

Table 1.27: General store sales

	Soup	Beans	Tomatoes
North	2100	1200	150
South	1800	1650	600
West	1100	1150	250

i **a** Calculate the total number of tins of each item sold.
b What percentage of the soup was sold at the North store?
c Draw sectional percentage bar charts for the sales of soup and tomatoes at the three stores.
ii **a** Calculate the total number of tins sold at the three stores.
b What percentage of the items sold at the West store were tins of beans?
c Draw a sectional percentage bar chart for sales of the three items at the West store.

4 The percentages of students in forms 1, 2 and 3 at Castle junior school are shown in Figure 1.18.

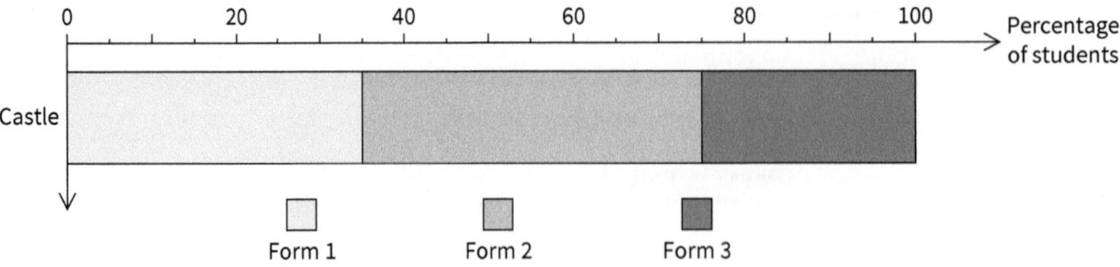

Figure 1.18: Students in each form

i If there are 320 students at Castle junior school, find the number of students in each form group.

Bishop junior school has 164 in form 1, 96 in form 2, and half of all the students are in form 3.

ii Find:

a the total number of students in forms 1, 2 and 3 at Bishop junior school,

b what percentage of the students are in form 1.

iii Draw a sectional percentage bar chart to show the data for Bishop junior school.

5 The sectional percentage bar chart in Figure 1.19 shows the proportion of total profit made from the sales of food and hardware at a general dealer's in March and in April.

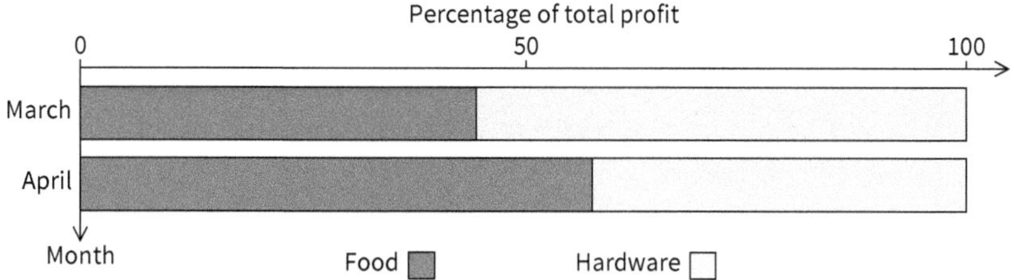

Figure 1.19: Profit in March and April

Indicate whether each of the statements below is necessarily true, not necessarily true, necessarily false or not necessarily false.

A: More profit was made from food than from hardware in April.
B: Less profit was made from hardware than from food in March.
C: Less profit was made from food in April than in March.
D: More profit was made from hardware in March than in April.

6 A man and a woman made separate journeys between Moscow and their home towns in Russia. The man took a train 45% of the distance, and the woman took a train 65% of the distance. Both of their journeys were completed by car.

Indicate whether each of the statements given below is necessarily true, not necessarily true, necessarily false or not necessarily false.

A: The man travelled further by train than the woman.
B: The woman travelled further by train than by car.
C: The man travelled a shorter distance by car than by train.
D: The woman travelled a shorter distance by car than the man.

7 The trainees at a vocational training centre take a combination of two trades. Each trainee chooses a combination of two trades from carpentry, bricklaying and mechanics. Figure 1.20 shows the percentages of first-year and second-year trainees taking each combination.

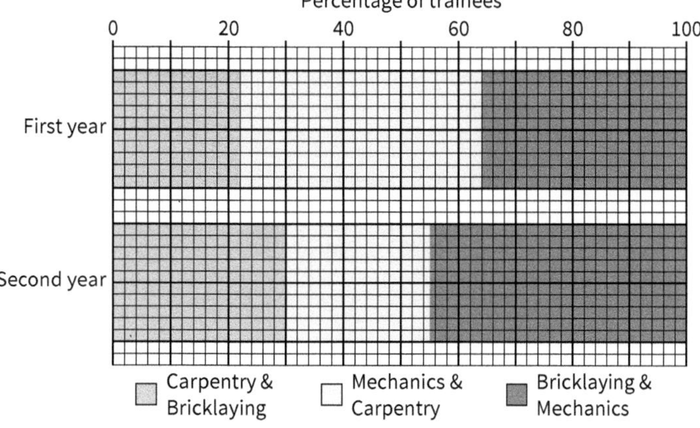

Figure 1.20: Trade combinations

There are 150 first-year trainees and 180 second-year trainees.

i Tabulate the number of trainees in each year group that take each of the three combinations.
ii Use the numbers from your table in **i** to find the number of trainees in each year group that take each of the three trades. Show these data in a table.
iii Display the data from your table in part **ii** in the form of a dual bar chart.
iv State two advantages that the dual bar chart has over the sectional percentage bar chart in Figure 1.21.

Line Graphs

There are two types of line graph that are commonly used to illustrate ungrouped data.

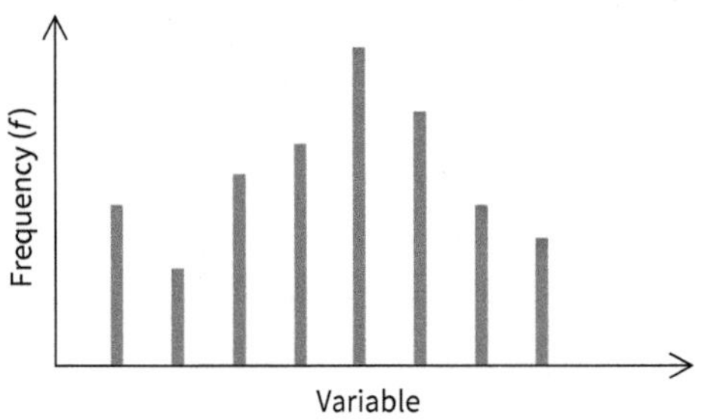

Figure 1.21: Vertical line graph

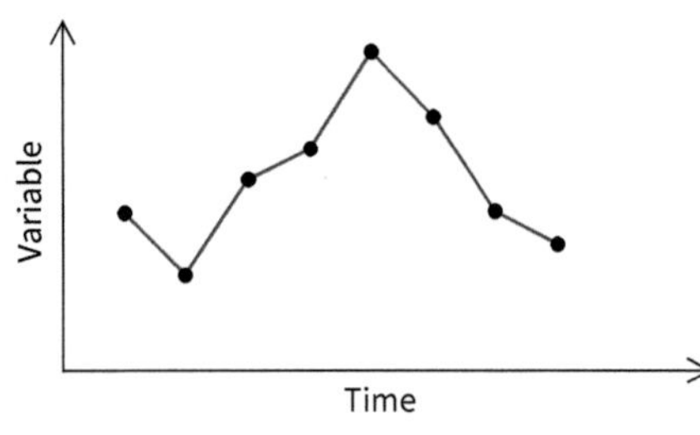

Figure 1.22: Line graph

The type of line graph shown in Figure 1.21 is essentially a bar chart with pencil-thin bars. The bar heights are drawn equal to the frequencies, which should start at zero.

The type of line graph in Figure 1.22 is especially useful if values of a variable are being measured at regular intervals of time. Points are plotted and joined with ruled lines to form a polygon. A major disadvantage is that it can be misleading if readings are taken from the lines between the points: they are drawn simply to emphasise the changes in values on the vertical axis.

The line graph in Fig 1.22 is more commonly known as a Time Series graph, which will be studied in some detail in Chapter 11.

Examples

1 The numbers of O Level passes obtained by a group of school leavers are given in Table 1.28.

Table 1.28: O Level passes

No. O Level passes	0	1	2	3	4	5	6	7	8	9	10	11
No. school leavers (*f*)	2	5	7	8	10	20	16	13	11	6	8	11

A vertical line graph is used to illustrate the data, as shown in Figure 1.23.

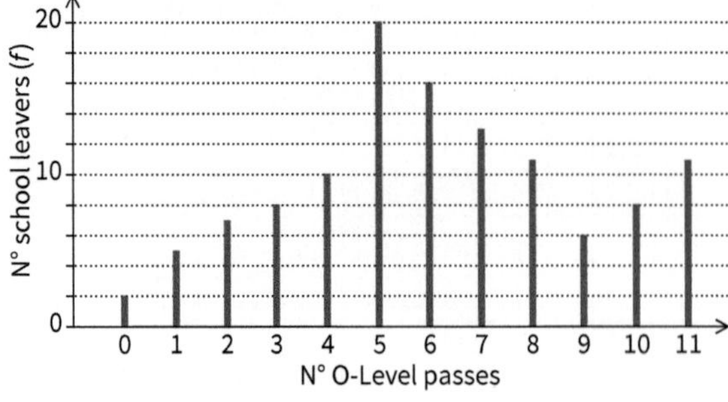

Figure 1.23: O Level passes

i How many school leavers are represented in Figure 1.23?
ii How many O Level passes did these school leavers obtain altogether?
iii What proportion of the school leavers obtained just four O Level passes?
iv What percentage of the school leavers obtained fewer than three O-Level passes?
v Of those that have more than five passes, what fraction have exactly seven passes?

Exercise 1H

1 The owner of a small shop recorded the number of loaves of bread that she sold each day last week, as shown in Table 1.29.

Table 1.29: Loaves of bread sold

Day	Mon	Tue	Wed	Thu	Fri
Number of loaves (*f*)	6	5	3	7	11

Illustrate these data in a vertical line graph.

2 The vertical line graph in Figure 1.24 shows the number of absences at a primary school for the first eight weeks of last term.

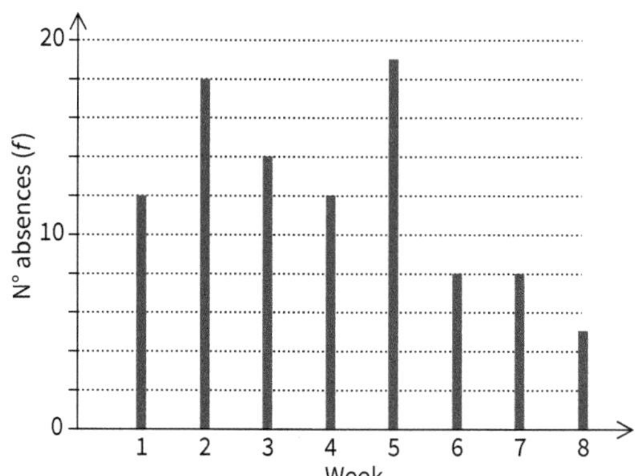

Figure 1.24: Absences per week

i Find the number of absences in week 3.
ii During how many weeks were there more than eight absences?
iii How many absences were there in this eight-week period?
iv Between which two consecutive weeks was the greatest change in the number of absences?

There were five absences in week 8. In fact, only one student was absent during that week.

v Explain how this could be the case.

3 Starting on Monday 1st August, four young men went into the forest on alternate days to collect mushrooms. At the end of each day they sold what they had collected to a man who paid them \$20 per bag. Table 1.30 shows how much money they received on each of six days.

Table 1.30: Payment for mushrooms

Day	Mon 1st	Wed 3rd	Fri 5th	Sun 7th	Tue 9th	Thu 11th
Amount received (\$)	100	140	80	120	120	100

i How many bags did they sell on Monday 1st?
ii How many fewer bags did they sell on Friday 5th than on Wednesday 3rd?
iii Illustrate the data in a vertical line graph.
iv State or estimate the amount they received for the mushrooms collected on Wednesday 10th.

4 Year-end profits, in millions of dollars, for a company are shown in Table 1.31.

Table 1.31: Year-end profits

Year	2008	2009	2010	2011	2012	2013	2014	2015
Profit (×$1 000 000)	1.000	1.025	1.075	1.075	1.100	1.050	1.150	1.175

i Illustrate the data in either type of line graph.

ii Between which two years was there a $50 000 increase in profit?

Profits increased by $25 000 between two consecutive years on three occasions during this period.

iii Express each of these as a percentage increase.

iv Express the profit made in 2015 as a percentage of the profit made in 2008.

v State one way in which you could draw a line graph to make the increases and decreases in profit appear much greater than they actually are.

Pie Charts

A pie chart shows how the whole of something is divided up, and this is done by dividing a full circle into sectors, where each sector represents a part of the whole. Each sector should be labelled with the name of the part that it represents. Sector angles and sector areas must be in the same ratio (proportional) to the size of the parts they represent.

It is not necessary or useful to write sector angles onto the chart.

Pie charts are similar to sectional bar charts in the way they display. If the percentage of the total that each sector represents is written onto or around a pie chart (which is perfectly acceptable), the pie chart will have similarities to a sectional percentage bar chart, and have similar advantages.

Examples

The numbers of students using each of four methods of transport to travel to school are shown in Table 1.32.

Table 1.32: Transport to school

Method of transport	Walking	Bus	Bicycle	Car	
Number of students (f)	276	159	75	32	Total = 542

The corresponding sector angles are given to the nearest degree and percentages to 3 significant figures in Table 1.33, and the resulting pie chart is shown in Figure 1.25.

Table 1.33: Pie chart sector angles and corresponding percentages

	Angles	Percentages
Walking	$\frac{276}{542} \times 360 = 183°$	$\frac{276}{542} \times 100 = 50.9\%$
Bus	$\frac{159}{542} \times 360 = 106°$	$\frac{159}{542} \times 100 = 29.3\%$
Bicycle	$\frac{75}{542} \times 360 = 50°$	$\frac{75}{542} \times 100 = 13.8\%$
Car	$\frac{32}{542} \times 360 = 21°$	$\frac{32}{542} \times 100 = 5.90\%$

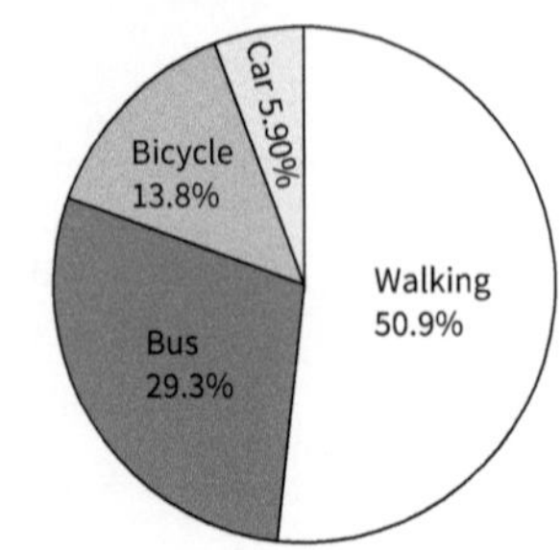

Figure 1.25: School transport pie chart

Comparative Pie Charts

Two or more sets of related data can be shown and compared using comparative pie charts. The areas of the two charts must be proportional to (in the same ratio as) the totals they represent. Care is needed when calculating the sizes of the circles: if the totals are in the ratio 1 : 2, the two radii must *not* be in the ratio 1 : 2. This is explained below:

Area of a circle $= \pi r^2$, where r is the radius of the circle.

If two pie charts with radii r and R are drawn to represent totals t and T, respectively:

Ratio of areas is $\pi r^2 : \pi R^2$, which simplifies to $r^2 : R^2$ [1]

Ratio of the two totals is $t : T$ [2]

Ratios [1] and [2] must be equal, therefore $r^2 : R^2$

$= t : T$

Cross-multiplying gives $tR^2 = Tr^2$ and so $R = \sqrt{\frac{Tt^2}{t}}$ or $R = r \times \sqrt{\frac{T}{t}}$

Examples

1 A pie chart of radius 4 cm is drawn to represent 60 vehicles.

What radius should be used to represent 135 vehicles in a comparative pie chart?

Ratio of areas is $4^2 : R^2$

Ratio of totals is 60 : 135 and these ratios must be equal, so $4^2 : R^2$

$= 60 : 135$

Cross-multiplying gives $60 \times R^2 = 135 \times 4^2$

$$R^2 = \frac{135 \times 4^2}{60}$$

$$R = \sqrt{\frac{135 \times 4^2}{60}}$$

$$R = 6\text{ cm}$$

The correct radius for a pie chart to represent 135 vehicles is 6 cm.

2 A crowd of 6400 that attended a football match on Saturday was represented in a pie chart of radius 5 cm.

Another match was played on Sunday and the crowd is to be represented in a comparative pie chart of radius 6.5 cm.

What was the size of the crowd on Sunday?

Let the size of the crowd on Sunday be T, then the two equal ratios are

$5^2 : 6.5^2$ and $6400 : T$

$5^2 : 6.5^2$

$= 6400 : T$

$5^2 \times T = 6400 \times 6.5^2$

$$T = \frac{6400 \times 42.25}{25}$$

$$T = 10\,816$$

The crowd on Sunday was 10 816.

Exercise 1I

1 There were 36 women, 21 men and 3 children in attendance at a community meeting.

i Calculate the sector angles required to construct a pie chart to illustrate these data.
ii Construct and label the pie chart using a radius of 4 cm. Include percentages on the chart.

2 Morgan's music collection consists of 34 records, 51 cassette tapes, 62 compact discs and 33 mini discs. Construct and label a pie chart using a radius of 4.5 cm. Include percentages on the chart.

3 The pie chart in Figure 1.26 illustrates the proportion of votes obtained by the Labour, SNP and Conservative parties at a by-election held in Scotland.

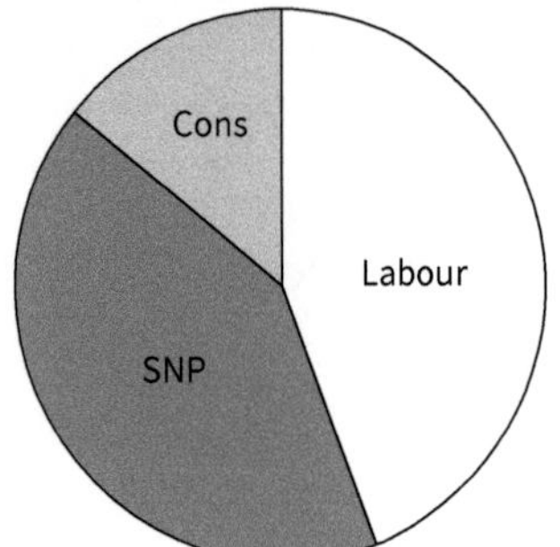

Figure 1.26: Scottish by-election votes

The sector angles used are:

Labour = 158.4°, SNP = 151.2° and Conservative = 50.4°

i What percentage of the votes was won by the party with the second highest number of votes?
ii If the Conservative party obtained 4116 votes, find:
  a the total number of votes cast,
  b by how many votes did the Labour party beat the SNP in the by-election.

4 An economics exam, for which six different grades were awarded, was taken by a group of students. The percentage of students obtaining each grade is given in Table 1.34. Grades A to E are passes and F is a failure.

Table 1.34: Economics examination results

Grades	A	B	C	D	E	F
Percentage of students	5	15	45	17.5	12.5	5

i Calculate the six sector angles needed to construct a pie chart.
ii Construct and label a pie chart to illustrate these data, using a radius of 4 cm.
iii Given that 36 students obtained grade B, find:
  a the number of students that obtained grade C,
  b the number of students that failed the exam,
  c the number of students that took the exam.

5 At Deepdale School, 400 students sat an English language examination. A pie chart was drawn to illustrate the results of these students using a radius of 6 cm. At Shallowvale School, 576 students sat the same examination.

Find the correct radius for a comparative pie chart to illustrate the results of the Shallowvale students.

6 A researcher surveyed 350 shoppers at CutPrice supermarket and 686 shoppers at SpendMor supermarket. The 350 shoppers at CutPrice were represented in a pie chart of radius 7 cm.

Calculate the correct radius to be used in a comparative pie chart to represent the shoppers at SpendMor.

7 A census was taken of the populations of the villages of Gobolale and Semojango. A pie chart of radius 8 cm was used to represent Gobolale's population of 6800, and a comparative pie chart with a radius of 10 cm was used to represent the population of Semojango. What was the population of Semojango?

8 Kay earns \$27 000 per annum. She has drawn a pie chart of radius 6.3 cm to show how she spends her salary, and her partner Joshua has drawn a comparative pie chart with a radius 5.67 cm to show how he spends his salary.

i Calculate Joshua's annual salary.
ii Calculate, correct to 3 significant figures, the correct radius for another comparative pie chart that could be drawn to show how Kay and Joshua spend their combined salaries.

9 The number of employees at a clothing manufacturer in 2015 was 19% less than in 2014. A pie chart of radius 12.5 cm was drawn to represent the employees in 2014.

i Find the radius of a comparative pie chart that could be drawn to represent the employees in 2015.
ii If there were 486 employees in 2015, how many employees were there in 2014?

10 Table 1.35 gives the number of males and the number of females who applied to join the armed forces at a recruitment office in 2005 and in 2015.

Table 1.35: Armed forces recruitment

	2005	2015
Males	423	424
Females	137	189

A pie chart drawn to represent those applying in 2015 has a sector area for females of 62 cm^2.

Using $\pi = 3.142$, find:

i the area of the pie chart used for 2015,
ii the radius of the pie chart used for 2015,
iii the correct radius to be used for a comparative pie chart to represent those who applied in 2005,
iv the area of the sector for the males that applied in 2005.

11 The favourite activities of all the girls and boys at a school are illustrated in comparative pie charts. The radius of the pie chart for girls is 4.8 cm and the radius of the pie chart for boys is 4.0 cm. The pie charts are shown in Figure 1.27, with the percentage represented by each sector indicated.

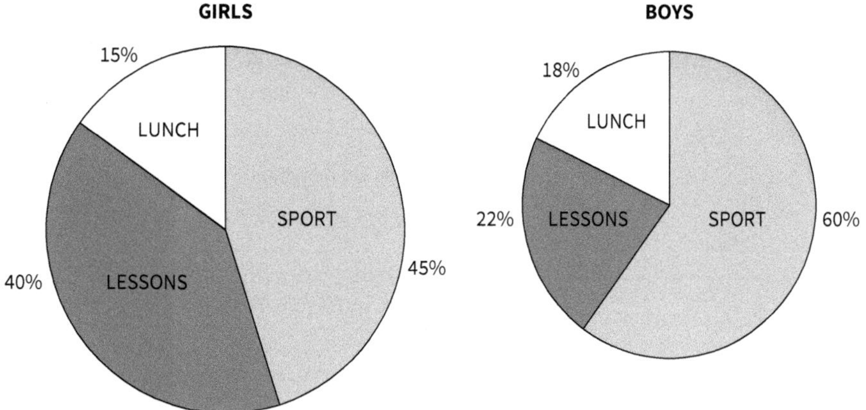

Figure 1.27: Favourite school activities

Given that lessons were the favourite activity of only 55 boys, copy and complete the frequency table in Table 1.36 by inserting the five missing numbers and the two missing totals.

Table 1.36: Favourite school activities

Favourite activity	Number of girls (f)	Number of boys (f)
Sport		
Lessons		55
Lunch		
	$\Sigma f =$	$\Sigma f =$

Venn Diagrams

Venn diagrams can be used to show numbers of items in various categories in a similar way to two-way tables.

Table 1.37: Test results

	Pass	Fail	Total
Boys	22	4	26
Girls	17	2	19
Total	39	6	45

The numbers in Table 1.37 represent 45 children who are categorised in two ways:

- each child is either a boy or a girl
- each child either passed or failed a test.

There are $2 \times 2 = 4$ categories of child.

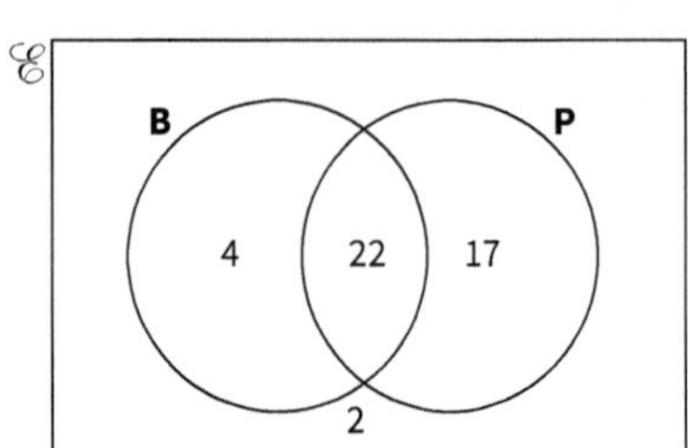

Figure 1.28: Venn diagram of test results

The Venn diagram in Figure 1.28 shows the same four categories:

Set **B** shows all 26 boys (4 failed + 22 passed).

Set **P** shows all 39 who passed (22 boys + 17 girls).

Those not in **B** are not boys, i.e. $2 + 17 = 19$ girls.

Those not in **P** did not pass, i.e. $4 + 2 = 6$ failed.

Those in **B** and in **P** are the 22 boys that passed.

Those neither in **B** nor in **P** are not boys who did not pass, i.e. they are the 2 girls that failed.

In the universal set, there are $4 + 22 + 17 + 2 = 45$ children.

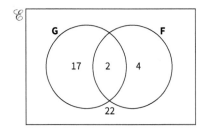

Figure 1.29: Alternative view of test results

Just as the columns and rows of a table can be swapped, so can the sets that are labelled in a Venn diagram, as in Figure 1.29.

Set **G** shows all 19 girls (17 passed + 2 failed).

Set **F** shows all 6 that failed (2 girls + 4 boys).

There are 22 who are neither girls nor failed . . . they are the 22 boys that passed.

Examples

1 Thirty adults were categorised as either 'young or old' and as either 'female or male'. The numbers are shown in Figure 1.30, where **Y** represents the set of young people and **F** represents the set of females.

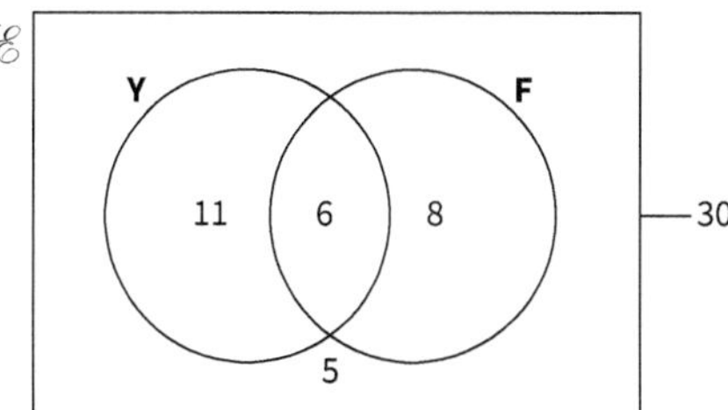

Figure 1.30: Venn diagram of adults categorised by age and gender

The numbers in these categories are:

11 young males

6 young females

8 old females

5 old males

$11 + 6 = 17$ young

$6 + 8 = 14$ females

$11 + 6 + 8 + 5 = 30$ adults altogether

2 The 32 students in a class were categorised in Figure 1.31 by whether or not they studied drama (**D**), art (**A**) and/or music (**M**). Each studied at least one of these subjects.

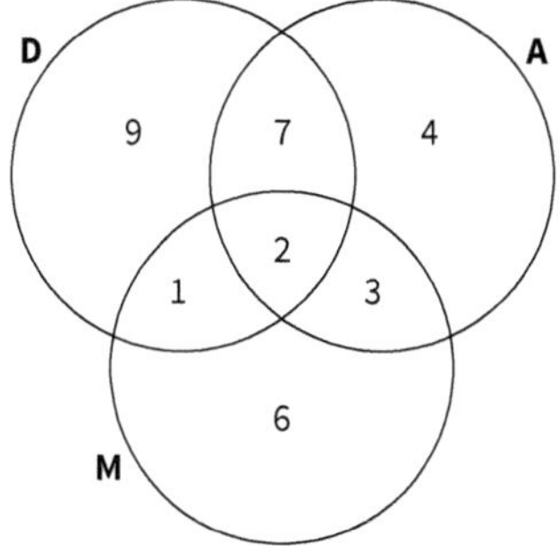

Figure 1.31: Students studying drama, art and music

9 studied drama only

4 studied art only

6 studied music only

7 studied drama and art, but not music

3 studied art and music, but not drama

1 studied drama and music, but not art

2 studied drama, art and music

Exercise 1J

1 There are 15 players in a school's chess club. Figure 1.32 shows the numbers of these who play each of the sports football and cricket.

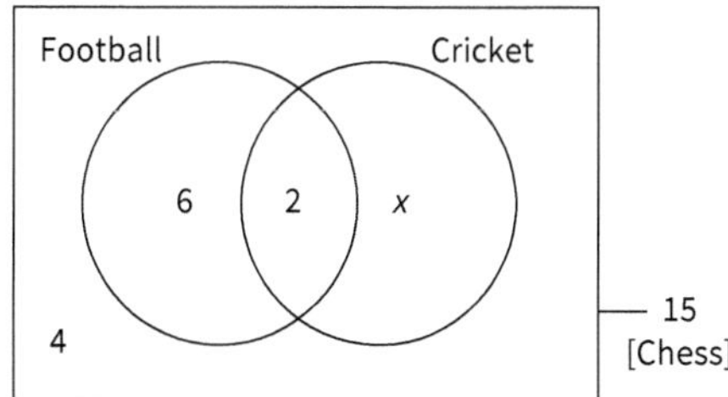

Figure 1.32: Venn diagram of chess club sporting activities

i Find the value of x.

ii How many play neither football nor cricket?

iii How many play both football and cricket?

iv What percentage of the chess club play either football or cricket, but not both?

2 In a group of 14 youths, there are 5 employed males, 2 unemployed females, and altogether 9 of the youths are employed.

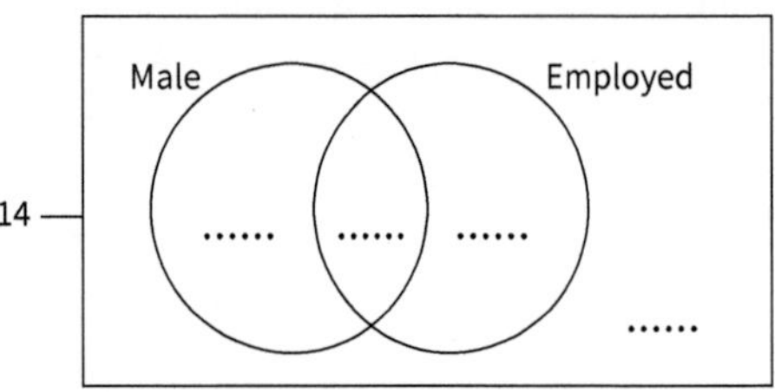

Figure 1.33: Youth employment

i Copy and complete the Venn diagram in Figure 1.33 by writing in the four missing numbers.

ii How many unemployed males are there?

3 Figure 1.34 illustrates the medium (stage, radio and television) in which 50 actors have worked during the past year.

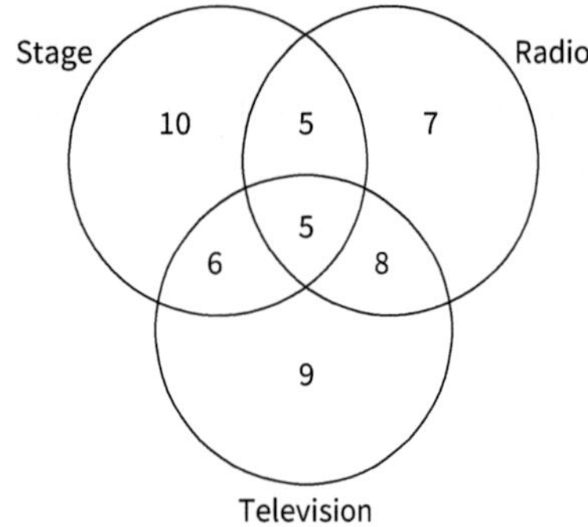

Figure 1.34: Actors' employment

i How many of the 50 actors have not worked in radio?

ii Interpret the number 8 in Figure 1.34.

iii Of those who have worked on stage, how many have not worked in television?

iv How many more actors have worked in only one of the media than have worked in two?

4 The 25 students on a first-year college course must choose to study at least one science subject from chemistry (**C**), biology (**B**) and physics (**P**). Figure 1.35 shows their choices.

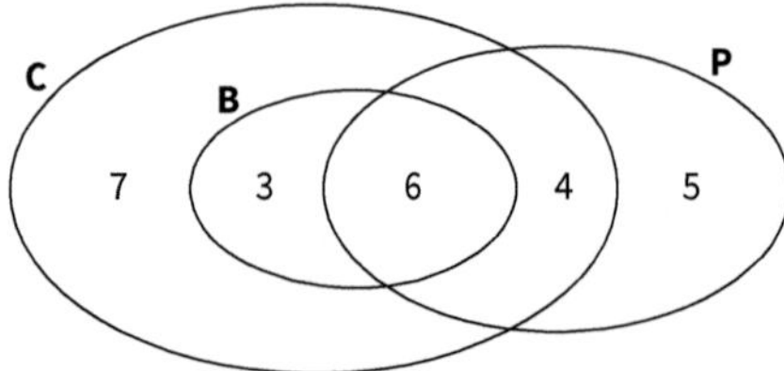

Figure 1.35: Science choices

i How many chose not to study physics?

ii Of those that chose to study physics, how many chose not to study biology?

iii What percentage of the students chose to study just two of the three sciences?

5 A school has 225 pupils. There are boys and girls who attend on a day or boarding basis. Some of the pupils attend on a scholarship. Figure 1.36 shows the number in each category.

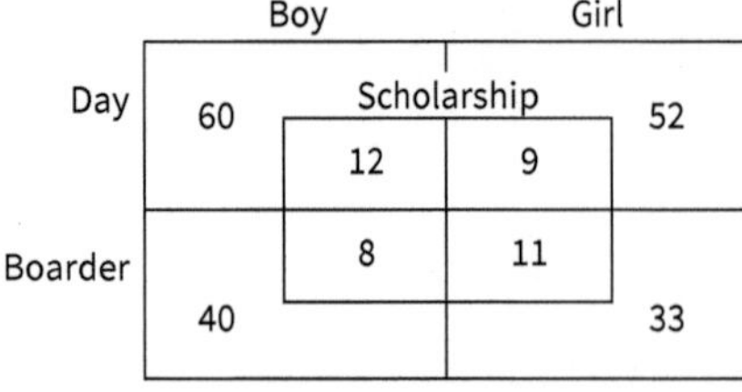

Figure 1.36: Pupil categories

i How many categories of pupil are shown?

ii How many girl boarders are there?

iii How many pupils are not on scholarships?

iv What fraction of the boys are day students?

v What percentage of the boarders are boys not on a scholarship?

6 Fifty Americans were asked which of the continents Europe (**E**), Africa (**F**) or Asia (**S**) they had visited. Their responses are illustrated in the Venn diagram in Figure 1.37.

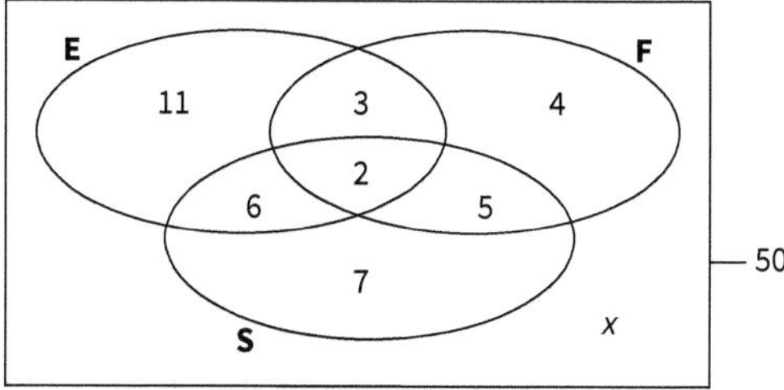

Figure 1.37: Travel destinations

i Find the value of x in Figure 1.37.

ii Show data about the numbers of these three continents visited by the 50 Americans as a frequency distribution with headings as shown in Table 1.38.

Table 1.38: Travel destinations

No. continents visited	No. Americans (f)

2 Basic Probability

Learning Objectives

In this chapter you will learn:

- How probability is measured
- How to find the probability that an event occurs and that it does not occur
- About the purpose of making single and multiple random selections
- To recognise outcomes that are equally likely
- How to calculate the number of times an event is expected to occur

Introduction

Chance plays a large part in everyone's daily life. We regularly assess probabilities to help us make decisions. How likely is it to rain this afternoon . . . shall I take a coat? How upset will my friend be if I don't call her? Although we can rarely know exactly how likely things are to happen, we use our own estimates so that we have a fairly good idea of what we can expect to happen.

2.1 Experiments, Events and Outcomes

When an **experiment** takes place it can result in a variety of **outcomes**. These outcomes may be referred to individually or in combination as an **event**.

- Rolling a normal six-sided die is an experiment.
- This experiment has six possible outcomes: 1, 2, 3, 4, 5 or 6.
- Rolling an odd number is an event and there are three outcomes favourable to this event: 1, 3 or 5.

The **probability** of any particular outcome or event occurring is measured on a scale from 0 to 1, as shown in Figure 2.1, and it can be expressed as a fraction, a decimal or a percentage. We write P(name of event) for the probability of a particular event occurring.

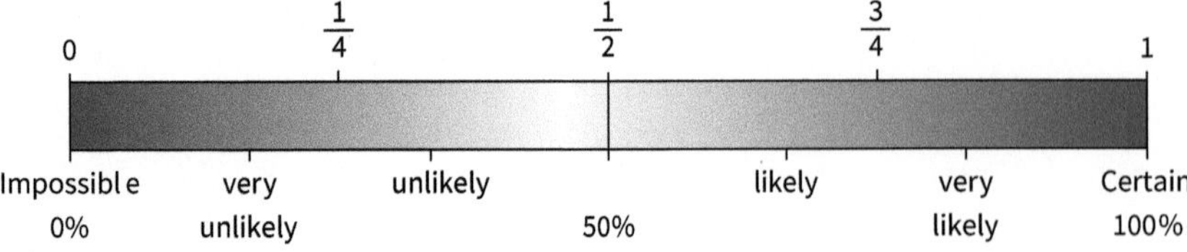

Figure 2.1: Probability is measured from 0 to 1

2.2 Equally Likely Outcomes

The outcomes of an experiment may or may not have equal chances of happening. If they do, then they are said to be **equally likely** outcomes.

Examples

1 If a normal six-sided die is rolled, there are six possible outcomes: 1, 2, 3, 4, 5, 6.
These six outcomes are equally likely and each has a probability of $\frac{1}{6}$

2 If five cards, each with a different vowel written on it, are put into a bag and one is selected, the outcomes A, E, I, O, U are equally likely, each with a probability of $\frac{1}{5}$

3 If a fair coin is tossed, there are two possible outcomes: head or tail.
These two outcomes are equally likely and each has a probability of $\frac{1}{2}$

Events can occur because of one or more than one outcome.

The probability that an event occurs is equal to the sum of the probabilities of its **favourable outcomes**.

Examples

4 The probability of rolling an even number with a normal six-sided die.
There are three favourable outcomes, 2, 4, or 6, and six possible outcomes.
P(rolling an even number) = P(2) + P(4) + P(6)

$$= \frac{1}{6} + \frac{1}{6} + \frac{1}{6} = \frac{1}{2} \quad \text{or}$$

$$\text{P(rolling an even number)} = \frac{\text{Number of favourable outcomes}}{\text{Number of possible outcomes}} = \frac{3}{6} = \frac{1}{2}$$

5 The probability of selecting a letter that is in the word DRAIN from five cards, each with a different vowel written it.
There are two favourable outcomes: A or I, and five possible outcomes.

$$\text{P(letter is in DRAIN)} = \text{P(A)} + \text{P(I)} = \frac{1}{5} + \frac{1}{5} = \frac{2}{5} \quad \text{or}$$

$$\text{P(letter is in DRAIN)} = \frac{\text{Number of favourable outcomes}}{\text{Number of possible outcomes}} = \frac{2}{5}.$$

2.3 Random Selections

Selecting objects **at random** gives each object an equal chance of being selected – there is no bias.

If one object is randomly selected from N objects, each has one chance of being selected.

In general, when randomly selecting 1 object from N objects:

$$\text{P(selecting any particular object)} = \frac{1}{N}$$

Examples

1 One student is randomly selected from a group of 11 boys and 8 girls.
The probabilities of various events are shown in Table 2.1.

Table 2.1: Student selection probabilities

Outcome	Probability
Selecting any particular student	$\frac{1}{19}$
Selecting any particular boy	$\frac{1}{19}$
Selecting any particular girl	$\frac{1}{19}$
Selecting a boy	$\frac{11}{19}$
Selecting a girl	$\frac{8}{19}$

Note that the word 'particular' specifies one object. It makes no difference whether that object or person is referred to as a boy, a girl or a student.

Each object has a $\frac{1}{19}$ chance of being selected.

2.4 Exhaustive Outcomes

A set of outcomes is said to be **exhaustive** if it contains all of the possible outcomes.

The sum of the probabilities of a set of exhaustive outcomes is equal to 1, because one of them is certain to occur.

A set of exhaustive outcomes describes 'the entire probability space', i.e. everything that can occur.

Examples of sets of exhaustive outcomes are shown in Table 2.2.

Table 2.2: Exhaustive outcomes

Experiment	Exhaustive outcomes	Probabilities
Tossing a fair coin	Head, tail	$\frac{1}{2}+\frac{1}{2}=1$
Rolling a normal die	1, 2, 3, 4, 5, 6	$\frac{1}{6}+\frac{1}{6}+\frac{1}{6}+\frac{1}{6}+\frac{1}{6}+\frac{1}{6}=1$
Spinning a square spinner numbered 5, 6, 7, 8	5, 6, 7, 8	$P(5)+P(6)+P(7)+P(8)=1$
Checking on the weather	Raining, not raining	$P(\text{rain})+P(\text{no rain})=1$
Playing a game of football	Win, draw, lose	$P(\text{win})+P(\text{draw})+P(\text{lose})=1$

For any experiment, the events *A* and *not A* are exhaustive.

$$P(A)+P(\textit{not}\,A)=1$$

Examples

1 The probability that Rathna will pass her driving test tomorrow is 0.85. Find the probability that she will not pass.

These two events, passing or not passing, are exhaustive because one of them is certain to occur.

P(Rathna passes) + P(Rathna does not pass) = 1

0.85 + P(Rathna does not pass) = 1

P(Rathna does not pass) = 1 − 0.85

P(Rathna does not pass) = 0.15

The probability that she will not pass is 0.15 or 15% or $\frac{3}{20}$

2.5 Trials and Expectation

If we know the probability that an event will happen then we can estimate the number of times it will occur when an experiment is repeated, and this will be a statement of our **expectation**.

The repeated experiment is called a **trial**.

If there are N trials then event A is expected to occur: $N \times P(A)$ times

Examples

1 A fair die is rolled 180 times. How many times can we expect to roll:

i a 6?

$P(6) = \frac{1}{6}$, so expected number of 6's $= 180 \times \frac{1}{6} = 30$

ii a square number?

P(square number) $= \frac{2}{6}$, so expected number of square numbers $= 180 \times \frac{2}{6} = 60$

iii 2 or more?

P(2 or more) $= \frac{5}{6}$, so expected number of times $= 180 \times \frac{5}{6} = 150$

2 The school netball team wins 60% of its games. How many games can it expect to win from the 25 games this season?

Expected number of wins $= 25 \times \frac{60}{100} = 15$

Exercise 2

1 A box contains ten ballpoint pens. Five of the pens write in black, three in blue and two in red.

i One pen is randomly selected from the box. Find the probability that it is:

a a black pen, **b** a red pen, **c** not a blue pen.

ii One of the black pens is removed from the box.

a How many pens remain in the box?

b If one pen is now selected at random, what is the probability that it is blue?

2 A class list contains the names of 15 boys and 20 girls. A teacher randomly selects one name from the list.

i How many names are on the list?
ii What is the probability that a particular student is selected?
iii What is the probability that a particular boy is selected?
iv Find, as a simple fraction, the probability that the teacher selects a boy.
v Is the teacher more likely to select a boy or a girl?

3 Thuso rolls a normal six-sided die. Find the probability that the number he rolls is:

i a 2 or a 3, **ii** less than 5, **iii** a multiple of 3,
iv a factor of 9, **v** 7, **vi** less than 7.

4 A card is selected at random from a normal pack of 52 playing cards. Find the probability that the selected card is:

i red, **ii** a spade, **iii** a picture card,
iv a black Jack, **v** red or a spade, **vi** a Queen or a King.

5 The probability that it rains on any particular day in Moistville is 0.66.

i What is the probability that it does not rain on any particular day?
ii On how many days is rain not expected in Moistville each year?

6 Frank has a box containing 20 red and 10 yellow buttons. In an experiment, each of his 36 classmates takes a turn at randomly selecting one of the 30 buttons.

i What is the probability that a classmate selects a red button?
ii How many of his classmates can he expect to select a yellow button?

7 Safi United's manager estimates the probability of his team winning any particular game to be $\frac{6}{11}$ and of losing any particular game to be $\frac{4}{11}$.

i What is the manager's estimate of the probability that the team will draw any particular game?
ii What is his estimate of the probability that the team will not win any particular game?
iii If the team plays 44 games in a season, find the number of these games that the manager expects his team to win, to draw and to lose.

8 A bag, which contains 12 coloured balls, is shown in Figure 2.2. There are three red, four blue and five green balls. A girl selects one ball at random from the bag.

i What is the probability that a particular ball is selected?
ii What is the probability that a particular red ball is selected?
iii Find the probability that the ball she selects is:
a red, **b** blue, **c** green,
d not red, **e** not blue, **f** not green.

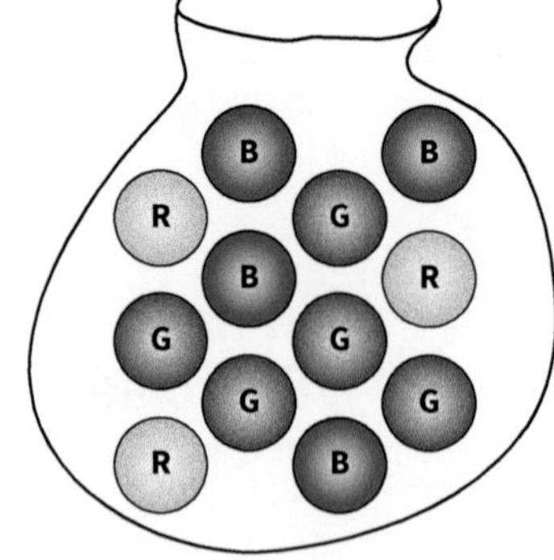

Figure 2.2: Selecting a ball from a bag

9 The ten square cards shown in Figure 2.3 are put into a box and a boy picks one card at random.

Figure 2.3: Collection of cards

i Giving your answers as percentages, find the probability that he picks:

a an A, **b** a B, **c** a C, **d** an A or a B,
e a B or a C, **f** an A or a C, **g** a D, **h** an A or a B or a C.

ii A girl picks one of the ten cards at random. If she repeated this 40 times, how many times can she be expected to select:

a a C, **b** a B, **c** a letter that is not an A?

10 The grades awarded to a group of 40 students in a mathematics examination are given in Table 2.3.

Table 2.3: Mathematics examination results

Grade	A	B	C	D	E	F
Number of students	2	8	10	9	6	5

Grades A to C are credits, grades D and E are passes and grade F is a failure. One of the 40 students is randomly selected. Write down, as a simple fraction, the probability of selecting a student who obtained:

i grade A, **ii** grade D, **iii** grade F,
iv a credit, **v** a pass.

11 Huang rolls a normal six-sided die 120 times. Find the number of times he can expect to roll:

i a 6, **ii** an odd number, **iii** a multiple of 3,
iv a number greater than 2, **v** a number that is not less than 3, **vi** a factor of 12.

12 A wheel is divided into sectors of equal size and each sector has a number painted onto it. The wheel is spun until it stops with the arrow pointing at one of the numbers, as shown in Figure 2.4.

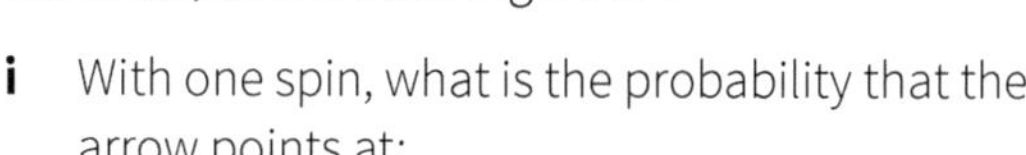

i With one spin, what is the probability that the arrow points at:

a a 5, **b** a 3, **c** an odd number?

ii Arvo plans to spin the wheel 400 times.
How many times can he expect the arrow to point at:

a a 1, **b** a 2, a 3 or a 5,
c any number except a 4?

Figure 2.4: Spin the wheel

iii How many times should he spin the wheel so that his expectation of a 4 is at least 160?

13 In a box there are black and white counters. The probability of randomly selecting a black counter is $\frac{1}{6}$.

i Find:

a the probability of randomly selecting a white counter,
b the smallest possible number of white counters in the box.

Emil took two counters out of the box and both of them were black.

ii What is the smallest possible number of white counters that could be in the box?

Emil asked each of the teachers at his school to randomly select one of the counters from the box.

iii If 25 teachers selected a white counter, estimate the number of teachers at Emil's school.

14 A teacher plans to randomly select one student from her class of 15 boys and 18 girls. What is the probability that the teacher selects:

i a particular student, **ii** a particular girl, **iii** a girl?

15 A bag contains 19 balls of the same size. There are 3 red balls, 5 blue balls and 11 pink balls. Find the probability that, if one ball is randomly selected from the bag:

i a particular red ball is selected,
ii a red ball is selected,
iii a particular blue ball is selected,
iv a blue ball is selected,
v a particular pink ball is selected,
vi a pink ball is selected.

Data Collection 3

Learning Objectives

In this chapter you will learn:

- What a census and a sample survey are, and when it is appropriate to use each of them
- How to conduct a survey
- What types of question can be asked in a survey, and what their purposes are
- How responses to a questionnaire can be analysed
- About various types of sample, and which methods can be used to select them
- Why it is important to select a representative sample
- To use random number tables in sample selection
- When and how to avoid bias in the method of sampling

Introduction

The collection of raw data is done through a survey which can be carried out to investigate people's opinions and behaviour, or to discover the characteristics and qualities of objects. Surveys are undertaken to assist national and local governments on policies and spending, for political and market research, and quality control testing in the manufacturing industry. A census targets a whole population, whereas a sample survey focuses on just part of a population. A **sample** should be representative, so that it gives an accurate picture of the opinions or characteristics of the whole population from which it has been taken.

3.1 Surveys

A survey is a means by which information or data is collected. There are two types of survey: a census and a sample survey.

Census

In a census, information is collected from an entire **population**. The word 'population' can refer to:

- all the people living in a particular country
- all the children attending a particular school
- all the bolts produced at a factory
- all the vehicles being driven in France

Conducting a countrywide census is a very large and expensive undertaking, and is only carried out regularly by governments, but usually never more than once every five or ten years.

Sample Surveys

This is where information is collected from part of a population.

It is usually preferable to carry out a sample survey because it is cheaper and less time-consuming to organise than a census and, for companies and most organisations, a census is simply not necessary.

The sample chosen to take part in a survey should be **representative** of the population from which it has been taken. This is not simple to achieve, but attempts must be made where possible to avoid **bias**.

If a representative sample has been selected, then the data or opinions obtained from the sample are used to estimate the data or opinions of the whole population.

However, there will almost always be a difference between the statistical characteristics of the sample and the population, and this difference is referred to as the **sampling error**, as in Example 2 below.

Examples

1 90% of a sample of people living in a town approves of a new road that is being built nearby.
If the sample is representative of the town's population, then we can assume that approximately 90% of the town's population approves of the new road.

2 A survey made just before an election indicated that party A would receive 20% of the votes, but at the election, party A actually received 30% of the votes.
There is a significant sampling error in this case, which may be the result of mistakes made in collecting the data, or of the sample not being representative of the population.

Once the purpose of a survey has been stated and the method of selecting the sample has been decided, the target population and the sampling units must be defined clearly.

If the target population, for example, is all the people subscribing to Go-Glow Internet Services then the sampling unit is the person subscribing to Go-Glow Internet Services.

The sampling units within a population are individually named or numbered to form a list, and this list is referred to as the **sampling frame**.

In order to conduct an effective survey, decisions on the type of data required and which questions to ask must be made.

3.2 Conducting a Survey

Surveys can take place in the street, at an interviewee's home, in the workplace or at a school.

Surveys for market research often take place in or near to a shopping complex.

The survey can involve the interviewer asking questions and noting down the interviewees' responses, or the interviewee may be given a list of questions to answer at home and later return to the person or company conducting the survey.

Whichever method is used, it involves questions being asked and responses being recorded.

A set of questions used in a survey is called a questionnaire.

Questionnaires

Surveys have a clear purpose, so the questionnaire must:

- be relevant to the purpose of the survey
- be simple to understand and easy for the interviewee to complete
- not take a long time to complete

There are two types of question that can be used in a questionnaire: open and closed.

Open and Closed Questions

Open questions allow the interviewee to respond in any way they like. Open questions may begin with phrases such as:

- 'What do you think about . . . ?'
- 'What is your opinion of . . . ?

Responses to open questions can be difficult to compile and to analyse; they often need to be interpreted, which means that they can also be misinterpreted.

Closed questions allow the interviewee to respond in a limited number of ways. Answers are restricted and some respondents may feel that none of the available answers is suitable.

Closed questions often contain phrases such as:

- 'Tick the box that . . .'
- 'Answer YES or NO to the following . . .'
- 'Do you always, sometimes or never . . .'

Responses to closed questions can be assigned a 'score' to make compiling and analysis simpler.

For example:

- Yes = 1, No = 0
- Yes = 1, Don't know = 0, No = −1
- Always = 1, Sometimes = 0, Never = −1
- Agree strongly = +2, Agree = +1, Don't know = 0, Disagree = −1, Disagree strongly = −2

Examples

1 A survey about the proposed building of a new airport was conducted amongst 1000 local residents. Their responses to the closed question 'Tick the box that best describes your attitude to the proposed airport' are shown in Table 3.1.

Table 3.1: New airport survey responses

	Disapprove	Don't know	Approve	
Assigned score	−1	0	+1	
Number of responses	180	100	720	1000
Percentages	18%	10%	72%	100%

The residents' opinions on this issue could be illustrated in an appropriate diagram, such as a pie chart, bar chart or sectional percentage bar chart.

The summed overall score for this group of 1000 residents is

$(-1 \times 180) + (0 \times 100) + (+1 \times 720) = +540$, which is equivalent to each resident responding with a score of $\frac{540}{1000} = +0.54$.

This suggests that, on average, they approve, but not strongly.

2 A questionnaire is being designed to discover the sales potential of a new chocolate bar. The designer has an open question that she has decided to make into a closed question.

The open question is, 'What do you think of the selling price of $1.75?'

She changes it to:

The selling price of $ 1.75 is: *Tick one box only*

☐ Too much ☐ About right ☐ A bargain

Exercise 3A

1 A survey investigating the sales potential of a fashionable new sports shoe is being planned.

- **i** Describe the most relevant population from which a sample should be selected to fill in the questionnaire.
- **ii** Suggest something the company could do to help the sample members fill in the questionnaire knowledgeably and honestly.
- **iii** Write three closed questions that you think would be suitable to use in the questionnaire. The questions should address the comfort, design and cost of the shoes.

2 Four hundred people filled in a questionnaire that related to the building works recently carried out at a shopping centre.

One of the questions asked them to respond to the statement 'The building works have greatly improved the shopping centre' by ticking one of three boxes marked 'Agree', 'Don't know' or 'Disagree'.

Their responses are shown in Table 3.2.

Table 3.2: Shopping centre survey results

	Males	Females	Totals
Agree	50	150	200
Don't know	140	20	160
Disagree	10	30	40
Totals	200	200	400

- **i** Illustrate the responses of the 400 people in a single percentage bar chart, with three sections.
- **ii** Illustrate the responses in a fully labelled dual bar chart, with three pairs of bars.
- **iii** Suggest a possible reason why so many males answered 'Don't know' to the question.
- **iv** Of those that were able to respond decisively to the question, write down the ratio of those that agreed to those that disagreed for:
  a the 200 males, **b** the 200 females, **c** all 400 people.

3 In response to a questionnaire investigating people's television viewing habits, responses to the question 'How often do you watch more than three hours of television per day?' gave the results shown in Table 3.3.

Table 3.3: Television viewing habits

	Never	Rarely	Sometimes	Often	Everyday	Totals
Adults	129	20	15	10	6	180
Children	21	24	30	45	60	180
Totals	150	44	45	55	66	360

A pie chart illustrating the responses of all 360 people is to be drawn with a radius of 17 cm.

i In the pie chart, what would the angle of the smallest sector be?
ii What percentage of the area of the largest sector could be attributed to the responses of the adults?
iii Calculate the correct radius of a comparative pie chart that could be drawn to show the responses of the children only.

4 The first five questions on a questionnaire were all closed and asked respondents to tick one of two boxes that were labelled 'Yes' and 'No'.

For analysis, a 'Yes' response was coded as +1, a 'No' response was coded as −1.

i Draw one conclusion from the information given about the responses to each of these five questions. In this part of the question, assume that each respondent ticked one box.
  a For a group of 10 people, the summed overall score on Question 1 was +10.
  b For a group of 20 people, the summed overall score on Question 2 was 8.
  c For a group of 30 people, the summed overall score on Question 3 was 0.
  d The summed overall score for a different group of people on Question 4 was −15.
  e On Question 5 at least 26 people in a group of 30 ticked 'Yes'.

ii The last question on this questionnaire asked people to respond by ticking one of three boxes labelled 'Always', 'Sometimes', 'Never'.

The three possible responses were coded +1, 0 and −1 in the same order as written.

The summed overall score for a group of 50 people was 0.

Four statements are given below. Decide which *could* be true and which *must* be true.

A All 50 people said 'Sometimes'.
B 25 people said 'Always' and 25 people said 'Never'.
C An equal number said 'Always' as said 'Never'.
D Nobody answered this question.

5 A sample of 2000 people living in the same area were asked to select one of five possible answers to the closed question 'What do you think about the local transport services in your area?' Their responses and the scores assigned to them are shown in Table 3.4.

Table 3.4: Local transport survey results

Response	Very good	Fairly good	Average	Quite poor	Very poor
Assigned score	+5	+3	+1	−1	−4
Number of responses	674	502	265	365	194

i Suggest a reason why the response 'Average' has been assigned a positive score.
ii Work out the summed overall score for the 2000 people.
iii Interpret your answer to part **ii** by writing a sentence describing the opinion of the average resident in this sample.
iv **a** Find the new overall summed score if the assigned scores are changed to +5, +3, 0, −3 and −5.

b Would this new summed score give you sufficient reason to change your response to part **iii**? Give a reason for your answer.

3.3 Types of Sample

There are several ways in which a sample can be chosen to represent a population. Each of the different methods attempts to be fair by not disadvantaging any member of the population.

As far as possible, every member of the population should have an equal chance of being selected for the sample. If this can be achieved, then the sampling method is fair or unbiased.

Sample surveys are quite common and, provided that they are well managed, they are useful to businesses, education and health establishments, governments, and society as a whole.

Before the survey can take place, the type of sample required must be decided upon.

There are several different types of sample that can be used.

Simple Random Samples

The sample is chosen at random, so that all members of the population have an equal chance of being selected.

Some methods of obtaining a random sample of people are:

- Writing names on pieces of paper, and randomly selecting the required number of pieces of paper.
- Selecting every 25th person leaving a post office.
- Using random sampling numbers (from tables or a calculator) to select from a numbered list.

By using the SHIFT and Ran# (or similar) keys, calculators can generate three-digit random numbers, such as 0.345, 0.870, 0.009 and 0.112. The first zero and the decimal point are ignored, giving 345, 870, 009 and 112.

These digits may be regrouped into a set of two-digit random numbers: 34, 58, 70, 00, 91 and 12.

Any random number that is too large or too small for a population can simply be ignored.

Examples

1 The numbered list in Table 3.5 gives the first names, in random order, of the 30 students in a class.

Table 3.5: Student names

00	John	*m*	10	Harriet	*f*	20	Rahmin	*m*
01	Lucy	*f*	11	Peter	*m*	21	Daisy	*f*
02	Angela	*f*	12	Brian	*m*	22	Violet	*f*
03	Mike	*m*	13	Thomas	*m*	23	Jane	*f*
04	Mary	*f*	14	James	*m*	24	Robert	*m*
05	Rose	*f*	15	Ruby	*f*	25	Rebecca	*f*
06	David	*m*	16	Dolly	*f*	26	Sally	*f*
07	Shuyi	*f*	17	Sara	*f*	27	Faida	*f*
08	Simon	*m*	18	George	*m*	28	Hilda	*f*
09	Joy	*m*	19	Paula	*f*	29	William	*m*

A simple random sample of five students is required.
With a calculator, we generate the random numbers 0.982, 0.124, 0.130, 0.704.
These need to be regrouped as two-digit numbers, so we have 98, 21, 24, 13, 07 and 04.
Note that 98 will be discarded because it is too large for the population.
The students with these numbers are selected: Daisy (21), Robert (24), Thomas (13), Shuyi (07) and Mary (04).
Note that the sample contains some girls and some boys.

2 The random two-digit numbers in Table 3.6 are to be used to select various random samples from a list of 60 names that have been numbered from 00 to 59.

The names from 00 to 29 are males, and the names from 30 to 59 are females.

Table 3.6: Two-digit random number table

73	15	34	65	15	41	55	02	48	42
49	20	66	35	13	57	84	13	57	03

The first row is used to select a simple random sample of four: 15, 34, 41, 55 are selected.
Note that 73 and 65 are too large for the sample, and that the second 15 is ignored; nobody can be selected more than once for the sample. The sample consists of 1 male and 3 females.
The second row is used to select a random sample of 10% of the population. We require a sample of size 6, so 49, 20, 35, 13, 57 and 03 are selected. The sample consists of 3 males and 3 females.

Systematic Samples

A systematic sample is obtained by selecting at regular intervals from a numbered list.

The list is divided into equal-sized groups, and one item from each group is selected for the sample.

Examples

1 A systematic sample of 4 from a list of 100 names is needed.
The list is divided into 4 groups with 25 names in each group.
One name is randomly selected from the first group of 25 names on the list, then every 25th name after that is selected.
If number 07 is selected from the first group, the sample will consist of the names with the numbers 07, 32, 57 and 82.

To take a systematic sample of S names from a population of P names:

- List the names and divide them into S groups with N names in each group: $N = \frac{P}{S}$
- Randomly select one from the first group and then select every Nth name on the list.

Examples

2 From the previous numbered list of 30 students, a systematic sample of five students is required.
Divide the population into five groups of six. The groups are: 00–05, 06–11, 12–17, 18–23 and 24–29.
Randomly select one member from the first group (to do this we could roll a die and subtract 1).
One less than the number on the die selects the first member of the sample.
Every sixth successive name on the list is also selected.
The possible samples given by this method are shown in Table 3.7.

Table 3.7: Random samples of students

No. on die – 1	0	1	2	3	4	5
Students selected for the sample	00 John 06 David 12 Brian 18 George 24 Robert	01 Lucy 07 Shuyi 13 Thomas 19 Paula 25 Rebecca	02 Angela 08 Simon 14 James 20 Rahmin 26 Sally	03 Mike 09 Joy 15 Ruby 21 Daisy 27 Faida	04 Mary 10 Harriet 16 Dolly 22 Violet 28 Hilda	05 Rose 11 Peter 17 Sara 23 Jane 29 William
Composition of the sample	5 boys 0 girls	1 boy 4 girls	3 boys 2 girls	1 boy 4 girls	0 boys 5 girls	2 boys 3 girls

Notice the composition of these six systematic samples.
Sample 0 and sample 4 are clearly unrepresentative of the population in terms of gender.
This may or may not be of concern – it depends on the purpose of the survey for which the sample is being taken.

3 A systematic sample of 20 people is required from the population of a village.
The interviewer decides to use a local doctor's list of recent patients to obtain his sample.
Although the doctor's list could be used to obtain a systematic sample, the village population would not be well represented by the sample. Young, healthy villagers would have little or no chance of being selected.

Stratified Random Samples

One method that can be used to try avoiding unrepresentative samples is to select a stratified random sample.

Populations consist of distinct *strata* or groups. Human populations are often stratified by:

- gender
- employment status
- age group
- income group

A stratified random sample aims to fairly represent each group or stratum in the population. The size of each group in the sample should be proportional to the size of each group in the population. Sample members are selected at random from each group.

Examples

1 From the previous list of 30 students' names, a random sample of five, stratified by gender, is required.
The numbered list consists of 12 boys and 18 girls.
The sample of five should consist of boys and girls in the same ratio as in the population.

$\frac{12}{30}$ of the population are boys, so for the sample of five we need $\frac{12}{30} \times 5 = 2$ boys.

$\frac{18}{30}$ of the population are girls, so for the sample of five we need $\frac{18}{30} \times 5 = 3$ girls.

A sample of 2 boys and 3 girls will represent the population fairly by gender.
Two boys will be randomly selected from the 12 boys.

Three girls will be randomly selected from the 18 girls.

Note that each particular student has an equal chance of being selected, whether they are referred to as a student, a boy, or a girl.

$$\text{P (a particular student is selected)} = \frac{5}{30} = \frac{1}{6}$$

$$\text{P (a particular boy is selected)} = \frac{2}{12} = \frac{1}{6}$$

$$\text{P (a particular girl is selected)} = \frac{3}{18} = \frac{1}{6}$$

Quota Samples

A data collector may be asked to interview a certain number of males and a certain number of females.

She or he may also be asked to interview equal numbers of people under 40 and people who are 40 or more (40+), but he or she can choose who to include in the sample from the given quota of numbers and types of people.

The sample, as described above, would consist of the four types shown in Table 3.8.

Table 3.8: Interviewee sample categories

	Male	**Female**
Under 40	Males under 40	Females under 40
40+	Males 40+	Females 40+

Quota sampling is similar to stratified sampling and is often used in market research, but the interviewer actually chooses the people for the sample. One advantage of quota sampling is that a numbered list of names is not required, i.e. quota sampling does not require a **sampling frame**.

Bias in Sampling

If a sample is not representative of the population from which it is selected then the sampling method used is very likely to be biased.

Unrepresentative samples, which are a major cause of sampling error, should be avoided, if possible.

There should be no bias towards any member or group in the population.

Random and systematic sampling may accidentally produce unrepresentative samples: either could select all males, for example.

Stratified sampling is fairer, but it is impossible to take account of each and every group in a population.

A sample of people must be selected carefully, as it is common for one person to be biased towards certain types of people. Quota sampling is often biased because of the data collector's own prejudices. If asked to interview 100 people from each of the four groups in the previous table, some might ignore smokers, people wearing dirty clothes, women who are chewing gum, men with beards, and so on.

Examples

1 A committee of five boys and two girls was randomly selected from a class of 12 boys and 16 girls. The committee of seven is not well stratified.
The selected committee is unrepresentative, as the boys are over-represented and the sampling method used was, therefore, biased.
To be fairly stratified by gender, the committee of seven should consist of three boys and four girls.

2 A student wants to find the average number of books read each month by the students in her school. She visits the library each afternoon for a week to collect data for her calculations.
The student's sample will be unrepresentative of the population.
In the library she is likely to find students who read more than the average number of books.

Exercise 3B

1 The two-digit random numbers in Table 3.9 are to be used to select a simple random sample of five from a list of 40 names that have been numbered from 00 to 39.

Table 3.9: Two-digit random number table

34	41	55	67	04	70	82	26	92	23
12	09	38	27	09	27	12	09	38	12
57	61	24	50	94	17	02	31	24	36

i Explain why the first row of numbers cannot be used to select the sample.
ii Explain why the second row of numbers cannot be used to select the sample.
iii Use the third row to select the required sample, and write down the numbers of those selected.

2 A list of the names of 50 adults has been made and they have been numbered from 00 to 49.
The two-digit random numbers in Table 3.10 are to be used to select various samples.

Table 3.10: Two-digit random number table

21	50	10	72	35	84	93	47	62	18
30	17	41	17	29	30	41	51	06	43
85	94	72	15	08	22	69	38	12	46

Starting at the left and moving along each row, use:

i the first row to select a simple random sample of size 5,
ii the second row to select a simple random sample of size 6,
iii the third row to select a systematic sample of size 5.

3 Various samples are to be selected from a list of the names of 25 boys and 35 girls. The boys are numbered from 00 to 24, and the girls are numbered from 25 to 59. The two-digit random numbers in Table 3.11 are to be used to select the samples.

Table 3.11: Two-digit random number table

07	63	77	20	07	68	94	37	63	22
41	67	03	26	19	24	80	13	71	37
03	28	67	43	11	70	34	49	25	73

Starting at the left and moving along a row, use:

i the first row to select a simple random sample of four children,
ii the second row to select a simple random sample of two boys and three girls,
iii the third row to select a systematic sample of six children.

4 The random two-digit numbers in Table 3.12 are to be used to select a sample of five individuals from a population of 80 adults, of whom 47 are women and 33 are men.

The women have been numbered from 00 to 46, and the men have been numbered from 47 to 79.

Table 3.12: Two-digit random number table

13	36	81	45	06	27	22	58	34	55	71	20	97	45	77
78	62	18	51	03	99	31	57	29	46	16	92	10	23	56
04	17	82	90	48	37	23	38	48	17	21	89	19	77	84

i The first row of random two-digit numbers, reading from left to right, is to be used to select a simple random sample from the population.
a Which of the numbers in the first row cannot be used to select members for the sample?
b Write down the numbers of the five individuals that will be selected for the sample.
c Explain in what way the sample obtained in **b** could be considered unrepresentative.

ii The first individual for a systematic sample of five is to be chosen by randomly selecting an appropriate number from the second row.
a Which of the numbers in the second row would be appropriate for selecting the first person for the sample?
b Find the number of women and the number of men in each of the systematic samples that would be obtained.

iii Give a detailed explanation of how the third row of random numbers could be used to select a random sample stratified by gender, indicating which of the numbers would be selected.

5 A travel agency published 60 holiday brochures last year. Of these, 30 were about beach holidays, 20 were about cruises and 10 were about weekend city breaks.

Your company has been asked to undertake a survey by taking a sample of six of these brochures.

i Express the sample size as a percentage of the population size.
ii If you are told that the purpose of the survey is not related to the different types of holiday, how might this affect your choice of which method of sampling to use?

Two-digit numbers have been allocated to the brochures as follows:

- 00–29 for the beach holiday brochures,
- 30–49 for the cruise holiday brochures,
- 50–59 for the weekend city break brochures.

The two-digit random numbers in Table 3.13 are going to be used to select various samples. Numbers outside the allocated range are to be ignored, and no brochure may appear more than once in any one sample.

Table 3.13: Two-digit random number table

20	51	13	28	92	51	07	18	42	47
14	11	73	80	27	05	43	66	39	97
56	53	07	33	26	68	12	09	84	47

iii **a** Starting at the beginning of the first row of the table, and moving along the row, select a simple random sample of the required size.

b State, giving reasons, which two of the first six numbers in the first row have been ignored.

iv A systematic sample is to be selected.

a Write down the smallest possible and largest possible two-digit numbers of the first brochure selected.

The systematic sample is to be selected by starting at the beginning of the second row of the table, and moving along the row.

b Write down the numbers of the six selected brochures.

v A sample stratified by type of holiday is to be selected.

a How many brochures about each type of holiday would be selected for this type of sample?

b Starting at the beginning of the third row, and moving along the row, select a sample stratified by type of holiday. Use every number if the type of holiday to which it relates has not yet been fully sampled.

6 **i** The three-digit random numbers in Table 3.14 were used to select a simple random sample of five children from the list of 36 names in Table 3.15, which are numbered from 00 to 35.

Table 3.14: Three-digit random number table

0.182	0.904	0.889	0.335	0.060

Table 3.15: Population of children for sampling

00	Kerry	*f*	12	Donna	*f*	24	George	*m*
01	Brian	*m*	13	Matthew	*m*	25	Debbie	*f*
02	Ahmed	*m*	14	Dorian	*m*	26	Karen	*f*
03	Stella	*f*	15	Chloe	*f*	27	Jip	*f*
04	Pierre	*m*	16	Rudy	*m*	28	Kirtesh	*m*
05	Molly	*f*	17	Fifi	*f*	29	Yash	*m*
06	Dodi	*m*	18	Ayanda	*m*	30	Lisa	*f*
07	Tefo	*m*	19	Beryl	*f*	31	Bontle	*f*
08	Eric	*m*	20	Clara	*f*	32	Len	*m*
09	Nazeem	*m*	21	Victor	*m*	33	Julia	*f*
10	Opelo	*f*	22	Susan	*f*	34	Fred	*m*
11	Wei Jie	*m*	23	Theo	*m*	35	Vijay	*m*

a List the names of the five children who were selected, and explain briefly how these were obtained.

b In what way could this sample be considered to be unrepresentative?

ii From the list of 36 names, a systematic sample is to be selected. Write down the names of the children selected if the systematic sample contains:

a four children and Tefo is the first name to be selected,

b three children and Lisa is the third name to be selected,

c six children and Victor is the fourth name to be selected.

7 The three-digit random numbers in Table 3.16 are to be used to select various samples from a population of hospital patients. The sampling frame consists of 640 units numbered 000 to 639.

Table 3.16: Three-digit random number table

0.718	0.406	0.089	0.222	0.711	0.405	0.003	0.904	0.637	0.253
0.336	0.582	0.818	0.040	0.317	0.429	0.945	0.605	0.026	0.333

i How many of the random numbers in the first row cannot be used to sample the population?
ii Write down the numbers of the first and last person selected in a simple random sample of six using the first row of the table.

The second row of Table 3.16 is to be used to select a systematic sample of size 16.

iii Write down the numbers of the 1st, 10th and 16th names to be selected for this sample.

8 George wants to find the most popular types of music among the students in his year group by interviewing a stratified sample of 30 students. His year group has 368 students, and 205 of them are girls. Find the number of girls and the number of boys to be interviewed, if his sample is to be representative in terms of gender.

9 In a certain country, 12 million vehicles are registered on the Ministry of Transport's central computer, which are each classified as one of three types.

There are 6 325 400 cars, 3 867 200 goods transporters and the remainder are public transport vehicles.

The Ministry wishes to test the roadworthiness of a sample of 1800 vehicles, stratified by type.

i How many of each type of vehicle should the Ministry include in its sample?
ii Suggest a method that could be used to select these 1800 vehicles.

10 At an international athletics meeting there are male and female competitors from five continents in track events, and in field events. Table 3.17 gives the numbers of each.

Table 3.17: Athletics competitors

	Track M / F	Field M / F
Africa	20 / 25	16 / 14
Asia	32 / 26	15 / 12
America	86 / 72	45 / 60
Australia	14 / 10	4 / 8
Europe	52 / 40	36 / 30

A researcher wants to select a sample of size 50, stratified by gender and type of event, to find out whether the athletes are involved in education in their local communities.

i How many female athletes should be in the sample?
ii How many track-event athletes should be in the sample?
iii Show, in tabular form, the composition of the sample of 50 athletes.
iv Why is it not possible to state how many African athletes should be in the sample?

11 A fruit juice manufacturer suspects that the sugar added during production last month was infected by harmful bacteria. Each litre of fruit juice had 5 grams of sugar, randomly selected from a bag containing 50 kilograms, added to it.

Last month the manufacturer produced and sold 10 000 litres of fruit juice, in half-litre containers, to three supermarkets A, B and C, as shown in Table 3.18.

Table 3.18: Fruit juice sales

	No. half-litre containers	
	Apple juice	Orange juice
A	1000	2800
B	2500	4700
C	1500	7500

It was decided to test a random sample of 250 litres from the juice sold to the supermarkets.

An employee was sent to get the sample and took 250 containers of apple juice from supermarket A.

i What percentage of the population did the manufacturer intend to select for the sample?

ii What mistake(s) did the employee make in selecting the sample?

iii Advise the employee, showing calculations where necessary, on how to improve the sample selection.

12 A youth club has four categories of membership. There are 17 junior boys, 13 junior girls, 38 senior boys and 32 senior girls. The club coordinator has the chance take 20 people to a special event.

i If 20 members are chosen at random from the club membership to attend the event, find the probability that a particular junior boy is chosen.

The coordinator decides that the group of 20 should consist of 4 staff and 16 club members, and that an equal number of club members should be randomly selected from each of the four categories.

ii Find the probability that a particular junior boy will be selected.

iii Explain why this system is unfair to the senior members of the club.

iv Calculate the number that should be chosen from each of the four categories of membership, if the coordinator takes into account the sizes of the four categories in the club's membership.

13 At a university, there are equal numbers of male and female students. To get a sample of students, a researcher decides to toss a coin.

If it comes up heads, she will randomly select 100 male students.

If it comes up tails, she will randomly select 100 female students.

In answer to the question 'Would this sample be representative of the population? Explain your reasoning', four people wrote the following:

A: No, it would not be representative. The coin might be biased, which would make one gender more likely to be picked.

B: Yes, it would be representative. The coin toss ensures that the selected sample would be random.

C: No, it would not be representative. Regardless of the result of the coin toss, the sample will be of only one gender.

D: Yes, it would be representative. The sample would contain male students and female students with equal probability.

Comment on each of the four answers given above. Indicate clearly which of them you agree with and which of them you disagree with.

14 At a certain school there are 720 students, 392 of whom are boys. A sample of five students is required by the Deputy Head to attend a meeting with parents.

i **a** Find the number of boys and girls to be selected, if the sample is to be representative in terms of gender.

b State the name of this type of sample.

Each of the 720 students has a four-figure admission number.
The girls have consecutive odd admission numbers starting at 2001.
The boys have consecutive even admission numbers starting at 2002.

ii Write down the largest admission number issued to:
a a girl, **b** a boy.

The school Head used a calculator to generate some random numbers to select the students.

The numbers that he obtained were 0.143, 0.673, 0.772, 0.081, 0.219 and 0.5.

iii After some thought, he realises that just one of his six random numbers cannot be used to select the members for his sample.
a State which one of the six numbers cannot be used, and explain why.
b Write down the admission numbers of the five students that will be selected.

15 A student wishes to conduct a survey to find out the average amount of money that a person living in his village spends on petrol each month. He decides to interview a sample of 300 people.

Explain why the student would not obtain a representative sample if he interviewed 300 randomly selected car drivers to get data for his calculations.

4 Grouped Data

Learning Objectives

In this chapter you will learn:

- To distinguish between quantitative and qualitative variables, and between discrete and continuous variables
- To appreciate the advantages and disadvantages of grouping data
- To use a variety of methods of grouping data
- To understand why continuous data is naturally grouped
- About class measures and the consequences of approximation
- How to summarise, display and interpret grouped data
- To use appropriate techniques for comparison and estimation in grouped data.

Introduction

In Chapter 1, ways of summarising and displaying ungrouped data were studied; here we take this a step further by investigating how data can be grouped, summarised and displayed. One of the main purposes of grouping is to categorise or classify the data, which is appropriate when specific values do not need to be known. The differences between discrete and continuous variables are particularly important: we may choose whether or not to group discrete data, but for continuous data we have no choice . . . they are naturally grouped whether we like it or not! Data collected from a census and most surveys would be grouped before being analysed – the opinion of each individual is rarely considered important, but the opinion of a large number of individuals is.

When data are displayed grouped in a table or diagram, individual values of the variable are usually not seen. Values are put together with others, so various ranges of values are displayed instead (an exception to this is a stem-and-leaf diagram).

The way in which grouped data are analysed and interpreted depends on whether the variable is discrete or continuous.

Discrete variables and continuous variables can be either quantitative or qualitative.

4.1 Types of Variable

Any particular **variable**, which is something that can change or take different values, can be categorised as one of four types: quantitative or qualitative and discrete or continuous.

Quantitative and Qualitative Variables

Quantitative variables can be measured, counted or observed. They have numerical values and can be ranked (ordered from smallest to largest or vice versa).

Qualitative variables have qualities or characteristics, and are described by words rather than numbers.

Generally they can only be ranked alphabetically.

Examples

1 Quantitative variables include:
- *Masses* of the students in a class
- *Examination marks* obtained by a group of students
- *Numbers of pens* owned by the students in a school.

2 Qualitative variables include:
- *Colours* of the shoes worn by various women
- *Types of food* eaten by the animals at a zoo
- *Surnames* of the teachers at a school.

Discrete and Continuous Variables

Discrete *variables* are those that can take only certain specific values within a given range, and the number of possible values is countable. There is always a 'gap' between one possible value and the next – see Figure 4.1.

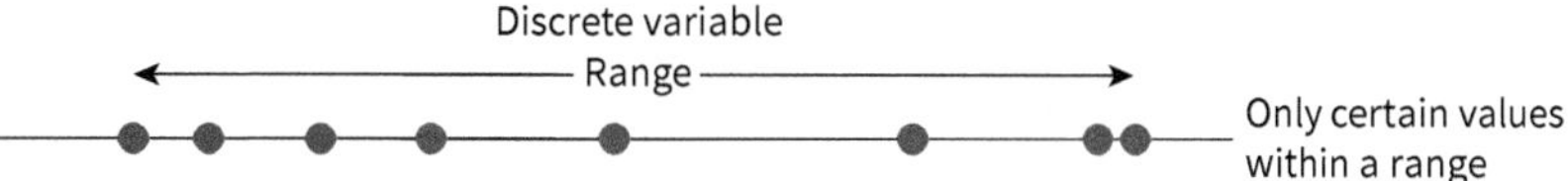

Figure 4.1: Discrete variable

Example

1 Between 1 and 10 inclusive, the following discrete quantitative variables have a countable number of possible values.

i The *number of people* travelling on buses through a town.
There are 10 possible values: 1, 2, 3, 4, 5, 6, 7, 8, 9, 10.

ii The *number of sides* that a polygon can have.
There are 8 possible values: 3, 4, 5, 6, 7, 8, 9, 10.

iii The *shoe sizes* that people wear.
There are 19 possible values: $1, 1\frac{1}{2}, 2, 2\frac{1}{2}, \ldots, 8\frac{1}{2}, 9, 9\frac{1}{2}, 10$.

Discrete quantitative variables can take values other than integers, as part **iii** in Example 1 shows.

The values may appear at regular or irregular intervals within a range.

Example

2 Within a given range or ranges, the following discrete qualitative variables have a countable number of possible qualities or characteristics.

i The *surnames* of policemen are specific and, therefore, countable.

ii The *manufacturers* of newly purchased cars.

iii The *days of the week* on which a supermarket can open.

Continuous *variables* are those that can take any value within a given range or ranges, as shown in Figure 4.2. Values of continuous variables are generally measured, and the number of possible values within a range is uncountable. Because measurement is required, values of a continuous variable can only be given to a certain degree of accuracy. It is, therefore, not possible to give an exact value for a continuous variable.

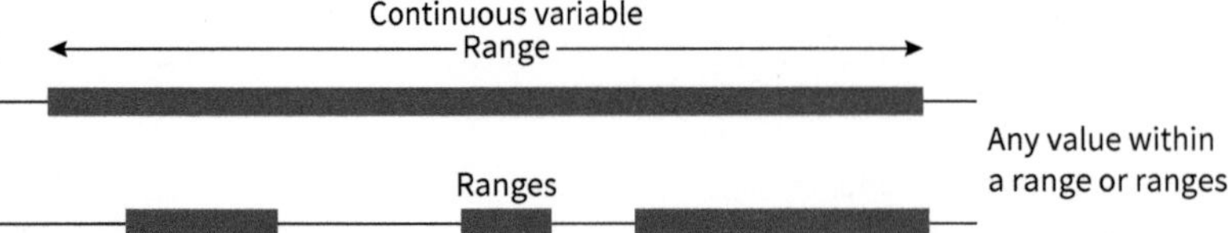

Figure 4.2: Continuous variable

Examples

3 All of the following continuous quantitative variables have an uncountable number of possible values.

- **i** The *heights* of people who, to the nearest metre, are 2 m tall.
  Any value in the range $1.5\,\text{m} \leq \text{height} < 2.5\,\text{m}$.
- **ii** The *ages* of adults who, to the nearest 10 years, are 30 years old.
  Any value in the range $25 \leq \text{age} < 35$ years.
- **iii** The *masses* of objects which, correct to 1 decimal place, are 7.3 kg.
  Any value in the range $7.25\,\text{kg} \leq \text{mass} < 7.35\,\text{kg}$.

4 Within a given range or ranges, all of the following continuous qualitative variables have an uncountable number of possible qualities or characteristics.

- **i** The *eye colours* of green- or brown-eyed people.
  There are an uncountable number of shades of green or brown.
- **ii** The *textures* of rough carpets.
  There are an uncountable number of degrees of roughness.
- **iii** The *feelings* of happy people.
  These can be described in an uncountable number of ways.

Although we commonly say things like, 'The pencil is 9 cm long', what we really mean is, 'To the nearest whole number, the pencil is 9 cm long'. What may appear to be an exact value is actually one that has been rounded to a certain degree of accuracy. Any such rounded value represents a range with an uncountable number of values in it.

A variable must be able to take more than one value, otherwise it is a constant.

- The *number of letters* in the word 'JUPITER' is a constant with a value of 7.
- The *number of letters* in the words of the phrase 'THE PLANET JUPITER' is a discrete quantitative variable with values 3, 6, and 7.

Exercise 4A

1 Some variables are: shapes, heights, prices, altitudes, volumes, attitudes, duration and hairstyles.

- **i** Which of these variables are qualitative?
- **ii** Which of the quantitative variables in the list are continuous?

2 Freddy rolls a normal six-sided die. Are his possible scores discrete or continuous?

3 **i** Emily records the number of pets that each student in her class has. Are her data discrete or continuous?

ii Jed records the heights of ten friends to the nearest centimetre. Are his data discrete or continuous?

4 Four variables W, X, Y and Z are defined:

W = {the possible number of lions seen on drives in a game park}
X = {all integers between 3 and 9, inclusive}
Y = {any number such that $3 < Y < 9$}
Z = {all possible shoe sizes}
State whether each of the variables is discrete or continuous.

5 A group of students sat a mathematics test that was marked as a whole number out of 40. The teacher converted the marks to percentage scores. Are the set of percentage scores discrete or continuous?

6 State which three of the following are not discrete quantitative variables, and in each case give a reason.

A: the types of food eaten by Mr Patel's cat.
B: the possible number of broken eggs in boxes containing one dozen eggs.
C: the number of white cars purchased in Johannesburg last month.
D: the heights of all the buildings in a city.

7 State any differences and/or similarities between each pair of variables given below.

i *C*: the number of leaves on the trees in a park, and *D*: the lengths of the leaves on these trees.
ii *E*: the colours in a rainbow, and *F*: the official colours on Ghana's flag.

8 **i** Write down the three values of the qualitative variable *medal awarded* in each final race at the Olympic Games.

ii Name two continuous quantitative variables that your answers in part **i** are related to.

9 How many values are there between 1 and 10 inclusive, if these values represent:

i the possible score when you double the number rolled with a normal die?
ii the possible lengths of time, in minutes, that a person takes to brush their teeth?
iii the possible number of interior angles of a regular polygon?
iv the possible width, in metres, of a road?
v the number of factors of all the integers from 8 to 12, inclusive?

10 Eight items, A to H, are given.

A: The possible length of a person's right thumb
B: The possible colour of the sky
C: The number of windows in your present room
D: The number of windows in the rooms of your present building
E: The length of your left foot
F: The texture of your fingernails
G: Your friends' cell phone numbers
H: The number of novels you plan to read this month.
Copy Table 4.1 and write each letter into the region that best describes it.

Table 4.1: Variable categories

	Discrete	Continuous
Quantitative		
Qualitative		
Not a variable		

4.2 Grouped Discrete Data

Grouping data is convenient if a variable has many values or if the total frequency is large, although some information about the variable will be lost, because values will not be shown individually.

Grouped discrete data can be tabulated as a frequency distribution, or displayed in a variety of diagrams.

Frequency Distributions

Data is represented as a frequency distribution in a table by grouping values of a variable into classes.

The number of values in each class (the frequency, f) is also shown.

There are many occasions when it is appropriate to group discrete data. A long list of numbers, especially if they are not ordered, gives no clear overall picture of the values in a distribution. One purpose of grouping is to be concise, which is advantageous if the finer details of the data are of no great importance. One disadvantage of grouping data is that we lose the original information.

Class Measures

A **class** is a group or set of values. For classes of discrete data, a 'gap' will always appear between one class and the next. Each class has the following measures associated with it:

Lower **limit** and upper limit: these are the lowest and highest actual values that exist in a class.

Lower **boundary** and upper boundary: these are the two values in the middle of the gaps between a class and those on either side of it: they are found half-way between the upper limit of one class and the lower limit of the next class.

Class interval: this is the difference between a class's upper boundary and lower boundary.

Class mid-value: this is the value that is half-way between the limits of a class, and for grouped discrete data, is the same as the value that is half-way between the boundaries of a class.

Examples

A poultry farmer recorded the number of eggs laid by each of her 40 hens last week:

10, 11, 1, 4, 13, 9, 11, 8, 14, 8, 1, 11, 9, 6, 14, 12, 3, 6, 9, 13, 12, 5, 0, 7, 10, 4, 6, 9, 13, 9, 10, 2, 11, 3, 12, 13, 9, 14, 13, 7

By grouping the values, the data can be summarised and the 40 hens classed by their productivity – see Table 4.2.

Table 4.2: Numbers of eggs laid

Number of eggs	0–2	3–5	6–8	9–11	12–14
Number of hens (f)	4	5	7	13	11

Note: The data are discrete, and there are no values in the 'gaps' between the classes.

- Lower class limits are 0, 3, 6, 9, 12
- Upper class limits are 2, 5, 8, 11, 14
- Class boundaries are –0.5, 2.5, 5.5, 8.5, 11.5, 14.5
- The interval of each of the five classes is 3: they have equal intervals
- Class mid-values are 1, 4, 7, 10, 13.

The grouped discrete data can be shown in an appropriate diagram, such as a bar chart or a pie chart, as shown in Figure 4.3.

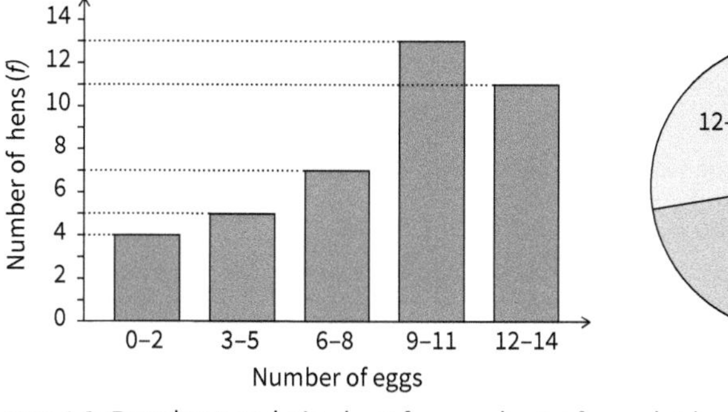

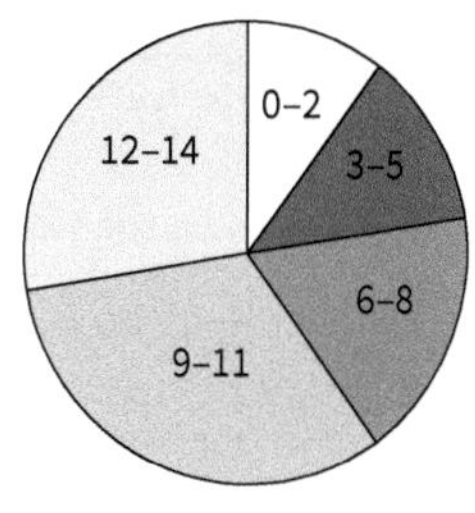

Figure 4.3: Bar chart and pie chart for numbers of eggs laid

i How many hens laid 8 or fewer eggs?

ii How many hens laid at least 6 eggs?

iii What percentage of the hens laid more than 2 but fewer than 9 eggs?

If the data in the example above were shown as an ungrouped frequency distribution, the table would have 15 columns or rows (for 0 to 14 eggs) with frequencies from 1 to 6 only.

Approximation and Rounding

Discrete data also become grouped when values are rounded off to a certain degree of accuracy.

Suppose you counted the number of crisps in each of ten packets, and the numbers you found were: 15, 18, 20, 22, 25, 27, 31, 32, 33 and 34.

If these values are rounded off to the nearest 10, the data becomes grouped into two classes: 4 packets containing 20 crisps and 6 packets containing 30 crisps, as shown in Table 4.3.

Table 4.3: Contents rounded to the nearest 10

Number of crisps (nearest 10)	20	30
Number of packets (*f*)	4	6

The first class value of 20 represents 15 to 24 crisps, inclusive, and the second class value of 30 represents 25 to 34 crisps, inclusive, as shown in Table 4.4.

Table 4.4: Actual contents

Actual number of crisps	15–24	25–34
Number of packets (*f*)	4	6

- lower class limits are 15 and 25
- upper class limits are 24 and 34
- lower class boundaries are 14.5 and 24.5
- upper class boundaries are 24.5 and 34.5
- Both classes have an interval of 10 crisps
- class mid-values are 19.5 and 29.5.

A number line with the values shown on it explains this – see Figure 4.4.

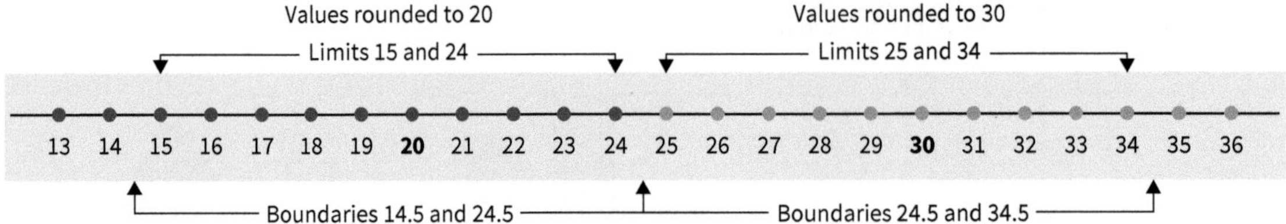

Figure 4.4: Number line showing crisp number classes

Examples

The numbers of people in the crowds at 20 football matches played on Saturday afternoon are given to the nearest 1000 in Table 4.5.

Table 4.5: Football match attendance

Number of people (nearest 1000)	8000	9000	10 000–15 000
Number of football matches (f)	5	11	4

Each of the numbers in the top row of Table 4.5 represents a class of values.
Each class has a lower limit and an upper limit, as shown in Table 4.6.
The class boundaries, which are not shown in Table 4.6, are 7499.5, 8499.5, 9499.5 and 15499.5.

Table 4.6: Actual football match attendance

Actual number of people	7500–8499	8500–9499	9500–15 499
Number of football matches (f)	5	11	4

The smallest possible number of people in the crowds at all of these 20 matches was $(5 \times 7500) + (11 \times 8500) + (4 \times 9500) = 169000$.

The largest possible number of people in the crowds at all of these 20 matches was $(5 \times 8499) + (11 \times 9499) + (4 \times 15499) = 208980$.

Exercise 4B

1 Forty students wrote a test that was marked as a whole number out of 20. Their scores were:

9	6	2	14	0	13	4	9	15	19	3	11	12	7	8	10	16	20	11	9
14	11	5	6	12	1	2	16	13	14	10	6	7	6	4	19	1	5	17	5

i Illustrate these data as a grouped frequency distribution with seven classes. The first class should be for 0–2 marks, the second class for 3–5 marks, and so on.

ii Use your table to find:

a the number of students who scored less than 9 marks,

b the probability that a randomly selected student scored at least 12 marks,

c the percentage of students that scored 6 or more marks, but less than 15 marks.

2 The ungrouped frequency table in Table 4.7 shows the 52 values of a discrete variable X.

Table 4.7: Values of variable X

X	2	3	4	5	6	7	8	9	10	11	12	13	14	15	16	17	18	19	20	
f	1	2	3	5	2	1	5	7	2	0	1	3	5	1	1	2	5	5	1	$\Sigma f = 52$

i Illustrate these data in a table as a grouped frequency distribution in four classes with equal frequencies.
ii State the upper limit of each of these classes.

3 Attendances at 760 football matches played in the English Premier League in the last two seasons are summarised in Table 4.8.

Table 4.8: Premier League match attendances

Attendance	21 000–25 999	26 000–34 999	35 000–49 999	50 000–67 499
No. matches (*f*)	45	544	134	37

i Write down the lower and upper boundary values of the class containing 544 matches.
ii Calculate the mid-value of each of the four classes.
iii Find the least possible total attendance at all 45 matches in the first class.
iv Calculate the greatest possible total attendance at these 760 matches.
v Find the smallest possible number of different people that attended these 760 matches.

4 A survey was made to find the months of birth of the 400 pupils at a school. The data were grouped, and are shown in the bar chart in Figure 4.5.

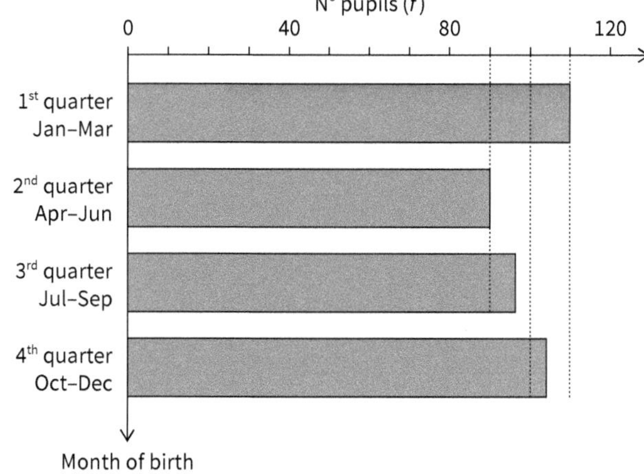

Figure 4.5: Birth months

i If 96 pupils were born in the 3rd quarter of the year, how many were born in the 4th quarter?
ii Express the number born in the 3rd quarter to the number born in the 4th quarter as a simple ratio.
iii What percentage of the pupils was not born in the 2nd quarter?
iv State one disadvantage of grouping these data.

5 Twenty children were asked, 'How many trips abroad have you made?' Their responses were:

1, 15, 9, 6, 0, 7, 9, 8, 5, 4, 2, 10, 8, 11, 3, 9, 7, 5, 6, 4

i Copy and complete the grouped frequency table in Table 4.9.

Table 4.9: Numbers of trips abroad

No. trips abroad	0–3	4–7	8–11	12–15
No. children (*f*)				1

ii Find:
  a the interval of each class, by first considering the class boundaries,
  b the class mid-values.

iii Illustrate the grouped data in a bar chart.

6 The grouped frequency table in Table 4.10 shows how many games each of 90 badminton players won last year.

Table 4.10: Badminton victories

Number of games won	0–4	5–9	10–14	15–19	20–24	25–29
Number of badminton players (*f*)	25	19	15	21	8	2

i Why is it not possible to find the number of players who won 10 games last year?
ii State the mid-value of the class with the second largest number of players in it.
iii Regroup the 90 players into two equal interval classes and illustrate these in a pie chart with a radius of 5 cm.

Seventy percent of these badminton players' partners play tennis.

iv If you were asked to construct a comparative pie chart showing how many games each of the partners won last year, what should its radius be?

7 Ravinthra said that 40 people came to his party. If this number is correct to the nearest 10, find:

i the smallest possible number of people that came to his party,
ii the largest possible number of people that came to his party.

8 According to official figures, 13 000 new full-time jobs have been created in Klumpton. If this figure is correct to the nearest 1000, find:

i the smallest possible number of new full-time jobs created,
ii the largest possible number of new full-time jobs created.

9 Correct to the nearest \$100, everyone working at Mobitech computers earns \$1100 per week.

i What is the minimum possible amount that an employee earns in a week?
ii If there are 10 people working at Mobitech, find:
  a the minimum possible amount that they could earn per week in total,
  b the maximum possible amount that they could earn per week in total.

10 To the nearest ten, the numbers of people entering 25 different banks between 9 a.m. and 10 a.m. are summarised in Table 4.11.

Table 4.11: Bank customers

No. people (nearest 10)	30–40	50–60	70–80	90–100
No. banks (*f*)	8	12	1	4

i What is the smallest possible number of people that entered any one of these banks?
ii What is the largest possible number of people that entered any one of these banks?
iii Write down the lower boundary and the upper boundary of the class containing the largest number of people.
iv Between 9 a.m. and 10 a.m., calculate:
  a the smallest possible number of people that could have entered all of these 25 banks,
  b the largest possible number of people that could have entered all of these 25 banks.

11 Correct to the nearest hundred, the numbers of pupils attending ten different schools are given in Table 4.12.

Table 4.12: School sizes

No. pupils (nearest 100)	100–300	400–600	700–900
No. schools (*f*)	3	5	2

Of these ten schools, Westdale has the smallest number of pupils.

i What is the smallest possible number of pupils attending Westdale?

Of these ten schools, Highport has the greatest number of pupils.

ii What is the greatest possible number of pupils attending Highport?
iii Write down the interval and the mid-value of the class of schools with 400–600 pupils.
iv Calculate the largest possible number of pupils at these ten schools altogether, if no school has the same number of pupils as any other.

Stem-and-leaf Diagrams (Stemplots)

These are used to illustrate discrete data in equal interval classes. They are useful for displaying small to medium amounts of data, and they allow us see the original (raw) values after grouping. There are no restrictions on the class intervals used, but they must be equal. A useful feature is that two sets of related data can be shown *back-to-back*, for the purpose of making comparisons.

The diagram appears similar to a bar chart. The bars are made from the final digit of each piece of quantitative data (the leaves), and the stem is made from the remaining digits, which can be in ascending or descending order. A key must be included to explain what the values in the diagram represent.

Examples

1 The test scores, in percentages, of 30 male students in a physics exam are given in below.

43, 31, 23, 37, 58, 61, 72, 70, 77, 68, 82, 39, 67, 53, 61, 55, 45, 59, 91, 52, 83, 27, 61, 45, 30, 64, 46, 59, 62, 41

The scores are classified and ranked in equal interval groups: 20–29, 30–39, 40–49, and so on. For these test scores, the 10's digits appear in the stem, and the units digits are attached as the leaves, as shown in Figure 4.6. A key explains the data.

	Males (30)
2	3 7
3	0 1 7 9
4	1 3 5 5 6
5	2 3 5 8 9 9
6	1 1 1 2 4 7 8
7	0 2 7
8	2 3
9	1

Key: **2** | 3 represents a score of 23% for a male

Figure 4.6: Stem-and-leaf diagram for male results

Note that the leaves are aligned vertically so as to produce a bar-chart-like shape.
If we now consider the scores of 30 female students in the same exam, given below we can show them back-to-back (Figure 4.7), so that the performances of the two groups can be compared.

73, 51, 86, 40, 61, 64, 75, 73, 80, 71, 85, 86, 70, 79, 64, 58, 48, 62, 94, 55, 83, 30, 88, 58, 82, 78, 97, 62, 65, 74

Females (30)		Males (30)
	2	3 7
0	**3**	0 1 7 9
8 0	**4**	1 3 5 5 6
8 8 5 1	**5**	2 3 5 8 9 9
5 4 4 2 2 1	**6**	1 1 1 2 4 7 8
9 8 5 4 3 3 1 0	**7**	0 2 7
8 6 6 5 3 2 0	**8**	2 3
7 4	**9**	1

Key: 4 | **9** | 1 represents a score of 94% for a female and 91% for a male

Figure 4.7: Stem-and-leaf diagram comparing males and females

The females' scores range from 30 to 97, and the males' scores range from 23 to 91.
The group with the highest frequency for females is 70–79, but for males it is 60–69.
By locating the 'bulges' on the diagram, which correspond to the highest frequencies in a bar chart, we are likely to conclude that the females performed better on average than the males.

2 The numbers of days on which it rained in each of 12 consecutive months were:

6, 19, 13, 12, 11, 8, 4, 5, 16, 9, 11, 14

The data can be grouped into four classes with equal intervals: 0–4, 5–9, 10–14 and 15–19, and depicted as shown in Figure 4.8.

0	4
0	5 6 8 9
1	1 1 2 3 4
1	6 9

Key: **0** | 4 represents 4 days of rain

Figure 4.8: Stem-and-leaf diagram for rainfall

Exercise 4C

1 The stem-and-leaf diagram in Figure 4.9 shows the number of employees at each of 20 companies.

1	0 8 8 8 8 9 9
2	0 5 6 6 7 7 8 9
3	0 1 1 2 9

Key: **2** | 5 represents 25 employees

Figure 4.9: Employees at 20 companies

i What is the most common number of employees?
ii How many of the companies have fewer than 25 employees?
iii What percentage of the companies have more than 30 employees?

iv Using class limits, write down the class that contains.

a the smallest number of companies, **b** the smallest number of employees.

2 A survey was conducted among 20 people leaving a theatre. They were asked, 'How many times have you attended the theatre in the past year?' Their responses were:

6, 2, 4, 1, 8, 11, 3, 4, 16, 7, 20, 13, 5, 15, 3, 12, 9, 13, 26, 10

i Construct a stem-and-leaf diagram for these data.

ii How many people in the survey had attended the theatre, on average, more than once per month?

iii What percentage of these people had attended the theatre not more than six times in the year?

3 Over a two-week period, Frank collected data on the number of passengers travelling on two ferries, *P* and *Q*. He has presented his results in the back-to-back stem-and-leaf diagram in Figure 4.10.

Ferry *P* (14)					Ferry *Q* (14)					
	8	7	6	**2**						
7	6	4	0	**3**	0	5	8			
8	6	5	3	**4**	3	4	5	7	7	7
	5	3	3	**5**	0	2	6	6	9	

Key: 3 | **4** | 3 represents 43 passengers on ferry *P* and 43 passengers on ferry *Q*

Figure 4.10: Comparison of ferry passenger numbers

i How many more passengers travelled on ferry *Q* than on ferry *P* during this period?

Frank says he observed the two ferries carrying the same number of passengers on just one of the 14 days.

ii Decide which of these phrases applies best to Frank's observation, giving a reason for your choice:

A: it is necessarily true *B*: it is not necessarily true

C: it is necessarily false *D*: it is not necessarily false.

4 The numbers of runs scored by two batsmen, *P* and *Q*, in their cricket matches last season are given in Table 4.13.

Table 4.13: Runs scored

Batsman *P*	53	41	57	38	41	37	59	48	52	60	47	36	37	44	61
Batsman *Q*	56	48	31	64	24	52	45	36	57	68	77	23	42	51	71

i Illustrate these data in a back-to-back stem-and-leaf diagram.

ii Giving a reason for each of your answers, decide which of the two batsmen has:

a performed better, **b** performed more consistently.

5 The back-to-back stem-and-leaf diagram in Figure 4.11 shows the percentage scores of the students who were the 25 best performers in an examination.

Girls (12)					Boys (13)					
		4	1	**8**	2					
	8	6	6	**8**	5	9				
3	2	1	0	**9**	0	1	3	3	4	4
	8	7	7	**9**	5	6	6	9		

Key: 1 | **8** | 2 represents a score of 81% for a girl and 82% for a boy

Figure 4.11: Top-performing pupils

i Calculate the total marks obtained by:

a the three lowest-scoring girls, **b** the five highest-scoring boys.

The 25 students are arranged in a line in the order of their scores.

ii Find the greatest possible number of boys that could be standing between two other boys.

Cumulative Frequency Distributions

Another way in which values of a variable can be grouped is if they are gathered together one at a time.

Here we are accumulating more and more values, and the frequencies of these groups are called **cumulative frequencies** (abbreviated to *cf*). Adding frequencies together one by one from an ordered list or frequency distribution gives a set of 'running totals' for groups of values in the data.

One of the purposes of forming data into a cumulative frequency distribution is so that we can easily see how many values of the variable are less than or more than a particular value. Conversely, the frequencies of the original values are found by looking at differences between cumulative frequencies.

Examples

1 30 children wrote a short essay and each was given a mark out of 10. Their marks were:

6, 9, 5, 7, 2, 8, 4, 7, 6, 5, 3, 6, 9, 6, 7, 4, 6, 6, 8, 5, 6, 7, 3, 7, 6, 5, 8, 6, 8, 4

These marks can be tabulated as an ungrouped frequency distribution, as in Table 4.14.

Table 4.14: Ungrouped frequency distribution of essay marks

Mark	No. children (f)
2	1
3	2
4	3
5	4
6	9
7	5
8	4
9	2
	$\Sigma f = 30$

By gathering together the frequencies, we can show the marks as a cumulative frequency (*cf*) distribution, as in Table 4.15.

Table 4.15: Cumulative frequency distribution of essay marks

Marks	Adding frequencies	*cf*
2 or less	1	1
3 or less	1+2	3
4 or less	1+2+3	6
5 or less	1+2+3+4	10
6 or less	1+2+3+4+9	19
7 or less	1+2+3+4+9+5	24
8 or less	1+2+3+4+9+5+4	28
9 or less	1+2+3+4+9+5+4+2	30

The cumulative frequency distribution shows us how many students scored a particular mark or less.

'Marks' could also be written 'less than 3', 'less than 4', . . ., 'less than 10', with the same cumulative frequencies.

Note that the final cumulative frequency value (30) is the same as the sum of the frequencies, as everyone scored 9 or less.

2 A farmer recorded the numbers of maize cobs produced by each of 100 maize plants, as summarised in Table 4.16.

Table 4.16: Numbers of maize cobs

No. cobs (X)	No. plants (f)
0	5
1	12
2	22
3	55
4	6
	$\Sigma f = 100$

A cumulative frequency table is drawn up (Table 4.17), with three different ways of writing the numbers of maize cobs.

Table 4.17: Cumulative frequency table of maize cob numbers

No. maize cobs (X)			Adding frequencies	cf
≤ 0	0	< 1	5	5
≤ 1	1 or fewer	< 2	$5 + 12$	17
≤ 2	2 or fewer	< 3	$5 + 12 + 22$	39
≤ 3	3 or fewer	< 4	$5 + 12 + 22 + 55$	94
≤ 4	4 or fewer	< 5	$5 + 12 + 22 + 55 + 6$	100

Exercise 4D

1 A shop assistant was asked to prepare forty 2 kg bags of potatoes to be sold at a supermarket.

The number of potatoes that he put into each bag was recorded in Table 4.18.

Table 4.18: Numbers of potatoes in bags

Number of potatoes	Number of bags (f)
7	2
8	8
9	11
10	16
11	3

i How many potatoes did he put into the 40 bags altogether?

ii Draw up a cumulative frequency table with columns headed, 'No. potatoes' and 'No. bags (cf)'. The first entry in the first column should be, 'Fewer than 7'.

iii Find the number of bags into which the assistant put:

a 10 or fewer potatoes,

b more than 9 potatoes,

c more than 8, but not more than 10 potatoes.

2 Twenty-four students sat a test in science. Their marks out of 10 were:

8	6	7	3	5	6	3	8	7	7	6	5
6	5	6	4	5	9	8	4	5	6	7	4

i Illustrate these data in a table as an ungrouped frequency distribution.

ii How many students scored 5 or fewer marks?

iii Draw up a cumulative frequency table to illustrate the data.

iv If one student is selected at random, find the probability that they scored:

a more than 6 marks, **b** at least 6 marks.

3 When examination certificates were collected, 55 ex-students were asked, 'How many credits did you obtain?' Their responses are given in the cumulative frequency table shown in Table 4.19.

Table 4.19: Cumulative frequency distribution of examination credits

No. credits (X)	$X \leq 0$	$X \leq 1$	$X \leq 2$	$X \leq 3$	$X \leq 4$	$X \leq 5$	$X \leq 6$	$X \leq 7$	$X \leq 8$	$X \leq 9$
No. ex-students (cf)	0	1	6	17	31	41	47	52	54	55

i Copy and complete the frequency table shown in Table 4.20.

Table 4.20: Frequency table for examination credits

No. credits (X)	0	1	2	3	4	5	6	7	8	9
No. ex-students (f)	0	1	5							1

ii Find the number of students who obtained:
a 7 or more credits, **b** more than 1 but fewer than 5 credits.

iii If a student who obtained 3 or more credits is selected at random, find the probability that they obtained fewer than 6 credits.

4 Each woman in a group was asked to state the number of days on which she listened to the midday news on the radio last week. Their responses are illustrated in the bar chart in Figure 4.12.

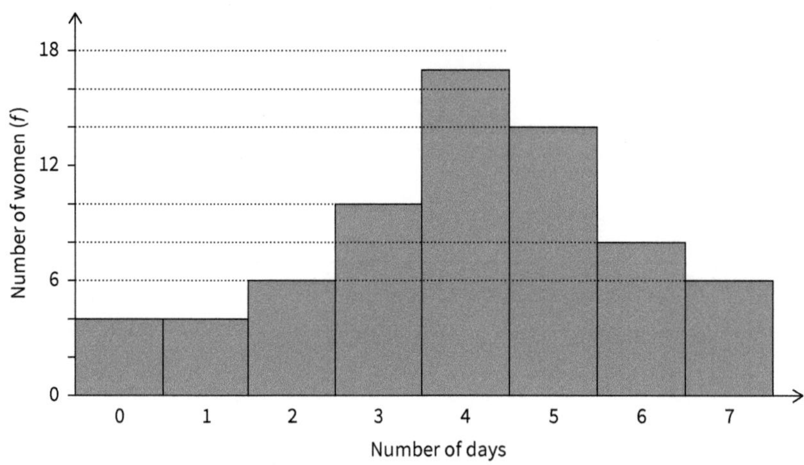

Figure 4.12: Radio news listening

i How many women are represented in the bar chart?
ii How many of the women listened to the midday news on over half of the days of last week?
iii Show the data from the bar chart in a table as a cumulative frequency distribution.
iv What is the greatest possible number of these women that listened to the midday news at the weekend only?
v Calculate, correct to 1 decimal place, the percentage of these women that listened to the midday news on at least 6 days last week.
vi Is it necessarily true that four of these women did not listen to the news at all last week? Explain your answer.

5 Each of 50 children was shown a map of Africa on which the countries were not named. The children were each given a coin and asked to place it on Uganda. If the first coin was incorrectly placed, a second coin was given and the child asked to try again. Each child was allowed up to five attempts. The frequency table in Table 4.21 shows the number of unsuccessful attempts made by the children.

Table 4.21: Unsuccessful attempts at country identification

Number of unsuccessful attempts (u)	0	1	2	3	4	5
Number of children (f)	3	5	8	10	11	13

i Copy and complete the cumulative frequency table in Table 4.22.

Table 4.22: Cumulative unsuccessful attempts at country identification

Number of unsuccessful attempts (u)	$u \leq 0$	$u \leq 1$	$u \leq 2$	$u \leq 3$	$u \leq 4$	$u \leq 5$
Number of children (cf)						

ii How many of the children:

a located Uganda on their first attempt?

b failed to locate Uganda?

c needed 3 or 4 attempts to locate Uganda?

6 A bag contains 4 red balls and 4 green balls. Forty people were asked to randomly select 5 balls from the bag when it had all 8 balls in it. Table 4.23 shows the number of red balls that the people selected.

Table 4.23: Number of red balls selected

Number of red balls	0	1	2	3	4	5
Number of people (f)	—	5	15	14	6	—

i Suggest a reason why there are two dashes in the table, rather than two zeros.

ii Draw up a cumulative frequency table for the data.

iii How many people selected more than 1 but not more than 3 red balls?

7 A piece of music was played to 30 adults, and each was asked to name the composer. If the first name given was wrong, the adult was allowed to try again. Each adult was allowed to try no more than six names.

The cumulative frequency table in Table 4.24 shows the number of incorrect names, I, given by each of the adults. For example, 18 adults gave 2 or fewer incorrect names before getting the name of the composer correct.

Table 4.24: Incorrect composer identification

Number of incorrect names (I)	$I \leq 0$	$I \leq 1$	$I \leq 2$	$I \leq 3$	$I \leq 4$	$I \leq 5$	$I \leq 6$
Number of adults (cf)	1	10	18	21	23	24	30

i How many adults named the composer correctly:

a on their first attempt?

b before their 5th attempt?

c on their 2nd or 3rd attempt?

ii Find, as a percentage, the probability that a randomly selected adult failed to name the composer.

4.3 Continuous Data

Data for continuous variables are, by their nature, grouped. This is simply because values for a continuous variable are measured, and we can only do this to a certain degree of accuracy. Exact values cannot be given, so they have to be **approximated** or *rounded off*.

Examples

A boy's mass is given as 47 kg to the nearest kilogram.

There are an uncountable number of masses that would be rounded to the nearest kilogram as 47 kg, and the boy's actual mass could be any of these – see Figure 4.13.

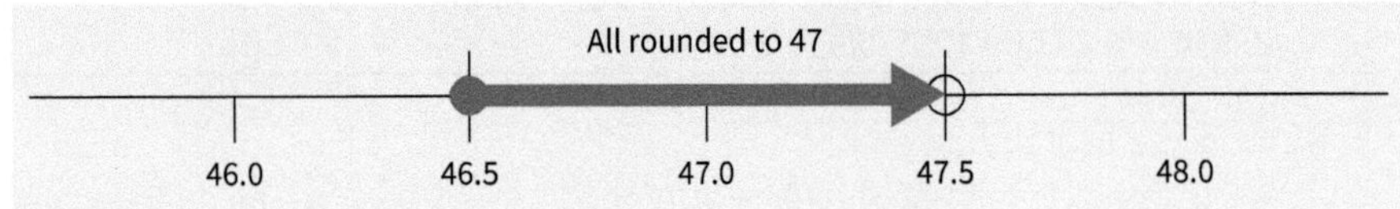

Figure 4.13: Rounding of continuous data

His actual mass must be in the range from 46.5 kg up to, but not including, 47.5 kg.

The rounded mass of 47 kg represents the class 46.5 kg ≤ mass < 47.5 kg.

Class Measures

Continuous data often appear discrete because values have to be rounded off. Rounded values of such data always represent classes of values. Each class of values has a lower boundary, an upper boundary, a class interval and a class mid-value.

Approximation and Rounding

When continuous data are rounded to the nearest R units, then generally:

$$\text{Actual lower boundary} = \text{Rounded lower boundary} - \frac{1}{2}R$$

$$\text{Actual upper boundary} = \text{Rounded upper boundary} + \frac{1}{2}R$$

Example

1 The heights of all the students in a class are given as 150–170 cm.

This range means that, correct to the nearest 10 cm, all the students' heights are 150, 160 or 170 cm.

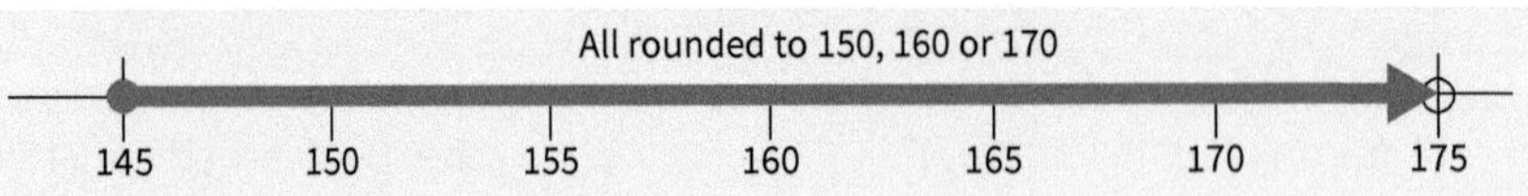

Figure 4.14: Rounding of heights

The actual lower boundary is $150 - \frac{1}{2} \times 10 = 145$ cm.

The actual upper boundary is $170 + \frac{1}{2} \times 10 = 175$ cm.

Heights given as 150–170 cm represent the class 145 cm ≤ height < 175 cm.

Class boundaries are 145 cm and 175 cm, as shown in Figure 4.14; the class interval is 30 cm, and the class mid-value is 160 cm.

When values have been rounded off, 'gaps' are created between classes. These gaps are closed when the classes are written using their actual boundary values.

Example

2 Precious stones are classed by mass in grams, correct to 2 significant figures, as shown in Table 4.25.

Table 4.25: Precious stone classes

Mass (mg)	2.9–3.0	3.1–3.2	3.3–3.4	3.5–3.6

Masses are naturally continuous and, because they have been rounded, there appear to be gaps of 0.1 g between classes, so $R = 0.1$ g.
To find the actual lower boundaries, subtract half of 0.1 g from each rounded lower boundary, as shown in Table 4.26.
To find the actual upper boundaries, add half of 0.1 g to each rounded upper boundary.

Table 4.26: Actual masses in precious stone classes

Rounded Masses (mg)	2.9–3.0	3.1–3.2	3.3–3.4	3.5–3.6
Actual masses (mg)	$2.85 \leq m < 3.05$	$3.05 \leq m < 3.25$	$3.25 \leq m < 3.45$	$3.45 \leq m < 3.65$

Class mid-values are 2.95 g, 3.15 g, 3.35 g and 3.55 g, and each class has an interval of 0.2 g, not 0.1 g as appeared originally.

Actual boundaries are most commonly found using the previously described '$\pm\frac{1}{2}R$ rule', but there are numerous exceptions, as illustrated by the following examples.

Examples

3 A group of children is classed by their age in completed years as 4, 5 or 6–9, as shown in Table 4.27.

Table 4.27: Age groups

Age in completed years	4	5	6–9
Actual age (A years)	$4 \leq A < 5$	$5 \leq A < 6$	$6 \leq A < 10$

Their actual ages are *rounded down* to the nearest whole number.
Class mid-values are 4.5, 5.5 and 8. Class intervals are 1, 1 and 4 years.

4 A company hires out cars. Customers pay $25 per full day and also per part day, no matter how short. The classes are shown in Table 4.28.

Table 4.28: Hire charges

Days paid for	4	5	6–9
Actual days' hire (D days)	$3 < D \leq 4$	$4 < D \leq 5$	$5 < D \leq 9$

All actual days' hire are *rounded up* to the nearest whole number.
Class mid-values are 3.5, 4.5 and 7 days. Class intervals are 1, 1 and 4 days.

Exercise 4E

1 The heights of 40 boys were measured to the nearest centimetre, and are summarised in Table 4.29.

Table 4.29: Boys' heights

Height (X cm)	150–159	160–169	170–179
No. boys (f)	10	18	12

Write down:

i the actual upper boundary of the second class,
ii the actual lower boundary of the first class,
iii the actual interval of the third class,
iv the mid-value of each of the three classes.

2 Table 4.30 shows how long, to the nearest 10 minutes, it takes 200 students to walk to school.

Table 4.30: Time taken to walk to school

Time taken (t minutes)	10–30	40–60	70–100
No. students (f)	42	126	32

Write down:

i the true lower limit of the first class,
ii the true upper limit of the third class,
iii the mid-value of the second class,
iv the true interval of each of the three classes.

3 The heights of 50 mountains are summarised in Table 4.31.

Table 4.31: Mountain heights

Height (metres)	2500–3200	3300–4000	4100–4800	4900–6000
No. mountains (f)	3	17	24	6

Write down:

i the degree of accuracy used to round the heights,
ii the smallest possible height of a mountain that is in the 4100–4800 m class,
iii the upper boundary height of the 50 mountains,
iv the mid-value of the class containing a mountain that is $3\frac{1}{4}$ km high.

4 A quality control officer measured the lengths of 4000 screws that were produced to make furniture. The results are shown in Table 4.32.

Table 4.32: Lengths of screws

Length (X cm)	2.5–2.9	3.0–3.4	3.5–3.9	4.0–4.8
No. screws (f)	258	2045	1555	142

i Write down:
  a the true upper boundary of the class that contains the greatest number of screws,
  b the lower boundary of the class that contains the least number of screws,
  c the interval of the class that contains 6.45% of the screws.

Only screws with lengths in the range $2.7\text{ cm} \le X < 4.4\text{ cm}$ can be used for making the furniture.

ii Calculate an estimate of:
  a the number of screws that can be used,
  b the percentage of screws that cannot be used.

5 The heights of 50 buildings in a town were measured correct to the nearest 0.5 metres.

For the class recorded as 6.5–12.5 metres, write down:

i the actual class boundaries, **ii** the class interval, **iii** the class mid-value.

6 The age, in completed years, of the 32 children attended to by a doctor this week are tabulated in Table 4.33.

Table 4.33: Ages of child patients

Age in completed years	2	3	4–11
No. children (f)	10	13	9

Write down:

i the actual lower boundary of the class given as 2, **ii** the actual interval of the class given as 3,
iii the mid-value of the class 4–11.

7 i State, for each of the following variables, whether it is discrete or continuous:

a the distances run, to the nearest kilometre, by 30 baseball players during a game,
b the number of children attending each of Alice's picnics,
c the ages, in completed years, of all the children living in a village.

The variables described above are each grouped into consecutive classes as 0–6, 7–13, 14–18.

ii State the true lower and upper class limits of the 7–13 class for:
a the variable described in **i a**, **b** the variable described in **i b**,
c the variable described in **i c**.

8 i In a grouped frequency distribution, three consecutive classes are 20–30, 40–60 and 70–90.

Write down the actual class mid-value of the 40–60 class, if the values are:

a the number of times a normal dice has to be rolled, to the nearest 10, to score a total of 90,
b the times taken, to the nearest 10 minutes, for students to solve a mathematics problem,
c the daily number of parcels delivered, to the nearest 10, by a team of couriers.
ii For each of the variables described above, state whether it is discrete or continuous.

9 Describe the most likely situation in which the following might not be considered to be a variable:

i the numbers of goals scored by the 22 football players in a particular game,
ii the ages of the youngest child of each player in a netball team,
iii the admission price paid by each person visiting an art exhibition on any particular day.

10 On 1 November 2015, a boy had completed 7 years. His sister's age, to the nearest year, was 5.

Find the earliest and latest possible dates on which each of these two children could have been born.

4.4 Representation of Continuous Data

Continuous data are always grouped. If there appear to be gaps between the boundary values of consecutive classes, then the values have been rounded off. These gaps must be 'closed' by finding the actual boundaries, and the actual classes of values are what should be shown when illustrating the data in any type of diagram. The process is shown in Figure 4.15.

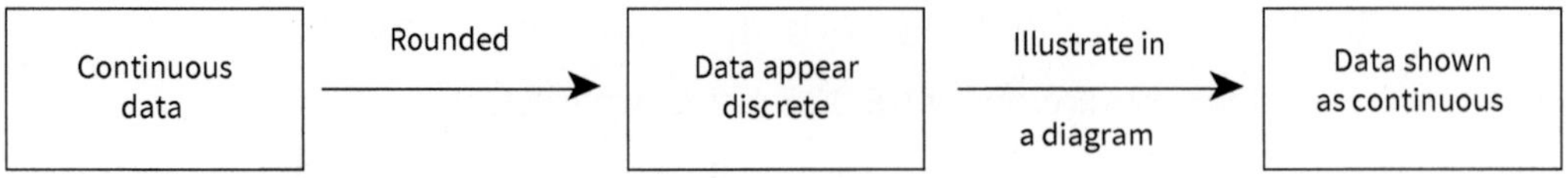

Continuous data	Rounded →	Data appear discrete	Illustrate in a diagram →	Data shown as continuous

Figure 4.15: Representing continuous data

The diagrams most suited to illustrating continuous data are histograms, frequency polygons and cumulative frequency diagrams.

When illustrating continuous data in a histogram or frequency polygon, it is very important to check whether the class intervals are all equal or not; diagrams for equal and unequal class intervals are not constructed in the same way.

Histograms and Frequency Polygons for Equal Class Intervals

In a ***histogram***, column areas are used to represent class frequencies, and there should be no gaps between any two columns.

- The variable axis is labelled as a continuous number line and the width of each column is equal to the class interval.
- The vertical axis is labelled from 0 up to the highest frequency, and each column is drawn to a height equal to its class frequency.

For each class, column area and class frequency are **proportional** (in the same ratio). This is sometimes written: *column area* α *class frequency*.

Because column area is so important in a histogram, and because gaps are not allowed between columns, exact class intervals must be known and there should be no gaps between them. For these reasons, histograms are best suited to illustrating continuous data. Grouped discrete data is more suited to illustration in a bar chart (although you will sometimes see histograms used).

Frequencies can easily be seen and compared in a histogram for equal class intervals, and so it is a fairly straightforward task to find what proportion of the total is in each class.

As with all continuous data, we are only able to give exact numbers of items between the class boundaries; at values that fall between class boundaries, we can only calculate estimates, by assuming that the values in all classes are spread evenly over the whole interval.

Examples

1 The speeds of 210 vehicles passing a school are summarised in equal class intervals in Table 4.34 and in the histogram in Figure 4.16.

Table 4.34: Vehicle speeds

Speed (km/h)	No. vehicles (*f*)
0–20	20
20–40	60
40–60	80
60–80	50

Column area (base × height)	Column blocks	Ratio of frequency : area : blocks
400	8	5 : 100 : 2
1200	24	5 : 100 : 2
1600	32	5 : 100 : 2
1000	20	5 : 100 : 2

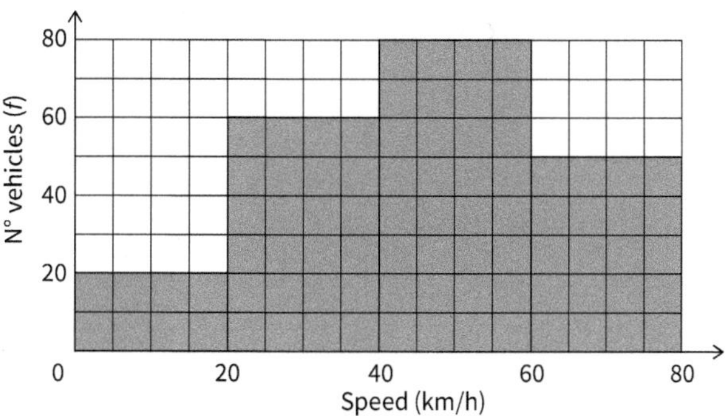

Figure 4.16: Histogram of vehicle speeds

In the histogram, 5 vehicles are represented by 2 blocks, so each block represents 2.5 vehicles. We can use this 'scale' to make estimates about the speeds of the vehicles.
Estimate the number of vehicles that were being driven at:

i under 30 km/h,

All of the first class + half of the second class (20 blocks) = 50 vehicles

ii 50 km/h or more,

Half of the third class + all of the fourth class (36 blocks) = 90 vehicles

iii between 30 km/h and 50 km/h.

Half of the second class + half of the third class (28 blocks) = 70 vehicles

2 The heights of 80 young trees growing at a nursery are tabulated in Table 4.35 and shown in a histogram in Figure 4.17.

Table 4.35: Heights of trees

Height (cm)	No. trees (*f*)
30–40	24
50–60	40
70–80	16

The gaps of 10 cm between the classes mean the measurements are given to the nearest 10 cm. Actual boundaries are 25, 45, 65 and 85.

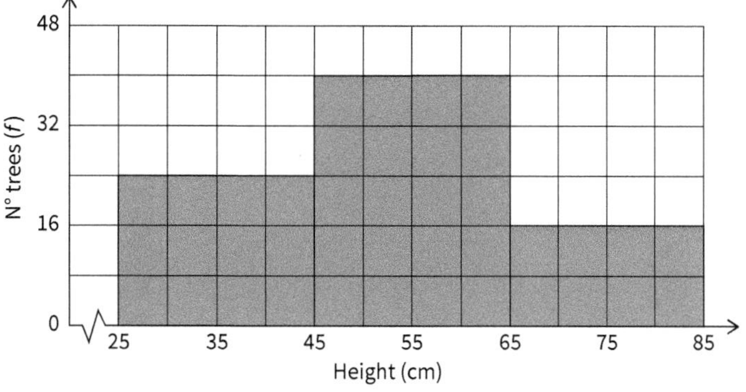

Figure 4.17: Histogram of tree heights

The variable axis can be concertinaed, if it is not necessary to start numbering from 0.

In the histogram, 1 block represents 2 trees.
We assume the heights of the trees are evenly distributed between the boundaries in each class to calculate estimates.
Estimate the number of trees with heights

i under 35 cm,

Half of the first class (6 blocks) = 12 trees

ii under 55 cm,

All of the first class + half of the second class (22 blocks) = 44 trees

iii between 55 cm and 75 cm.

Half of the third class + half of the fourth class (14 blocks) = 28 trees

3 Fundraisers organised an event where 40 hairdressers shaved the heads of volunteers.

The numbers of heads that were completely shaved in 10 minutes are shown in Table 4.36.
Table 4.36: Shaved heads

No. completely shaved heads (*h*)	5	6	7	8	9	10
No. hairdressers (*f*)	6	10	12	6	4	2

Figure 4.18 shows the volunteers that Pamela shaved in those 10 minutes.

Figure 4.18: New hairstyle

How many heads has she shaved? . . . Let us say 5.97.
But how many heads has she *completely* shaved? . . . Only 5! The value 5.97 is rounded down to 5.
The actual classes are $5 \le h < 6$, $6 \le h < 7$, $7 \le h < 8$, $8 \le h < 9$, $9 \le h < 10$, $10 \le h < 11$, and the histogram in Figure 4.19 illustrates the data using the actual boundaries.

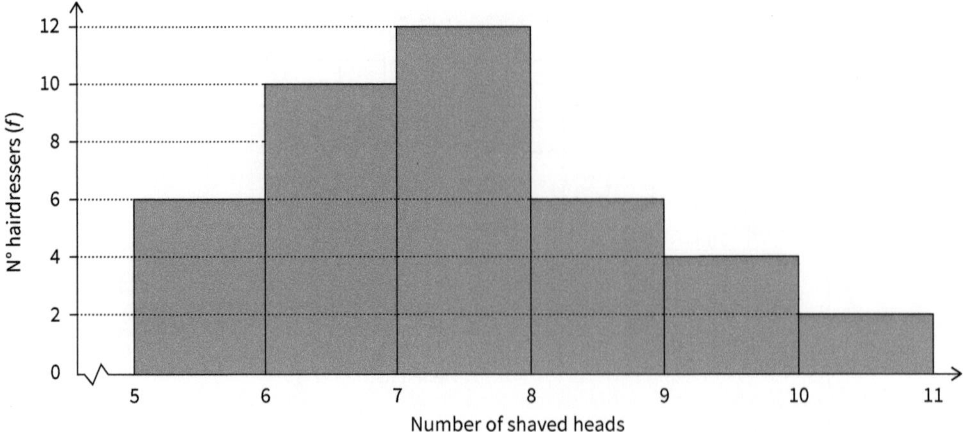

Figure 4.19: Histogram of heads shaved

When counting 'completed' items, the actual class boundaries must be considered carefully. Calculate an estimate of the number of hairdressers that actually shaved:

i fewer than $7\frac{1}{2}$ heads,

All of the first class + all of the second class + half of the third class

$= 6 + 10 + \left(\frac{1}{2} \times 12\right) = 22$ hairdressers.

ii $8\frac{1}{2}$ or more heads,

Half of the fourth class + all of the fifth class + all of the sixth class

$= \left(\frac{1}{2} \times 6\right) + 4 + 2 = 9$ hairdressers.

iii between $7\frac{3}{4}$ and $9\frac{3}{4}$ heads.

One-quarter of the third class + all of the fourth class + three-quarters of the fifth class

$= \left(\frac{1}{4} \times 12\right) + 6 + \left(\frac{3}{4} \times 4\right) = 12$ hairdressers.

Frequency polygons are a type of line graph that are especially useful for comparing two sets of data.

- The variable axis is marked as a continuous number line and the frequency axis from 0 up to the highest frequency.
- Points are plotted at (M, f), where M and f are the mid-value and frequency of each class.
- Consecutive points are joined by ruled lines to form a polygon which can be closed at the mid-values of two additional equal interval classes, one on each side of the data, both with zero frequency.

Frequency polygons are also best suited to illustrating continuous data. It is important to remember that each plotted point represents the frequency of a class, not of a particular value. The ruled lines simply give 'shape' to the diagram; these lines provide no useful information other than to emphasise changes in class mid-values and frequencies. Extracting correct information from a histogram is generally much simpler than from a frequency polygon, so it often helps if you can *see* the histogram behind the polygon.

Examples

1 Table 4.37 and the frequency polygon in Figure 4.20 illustrate the masses, in kilograms, of 40 babies. A histogram illustrating the same data is shown behind the polygon in Figure 4.20.

Table 4.37: Babies' masses

Mass (kg)	No. babies (f)
2.5–3.0	8
3.0–3.5	12
3.5–4.0	14
4.0–4.5	6

Points are plotted at the class mid-values of 2.75, 3.25, 3.75 and 4.25 at the corresponding frequencies.

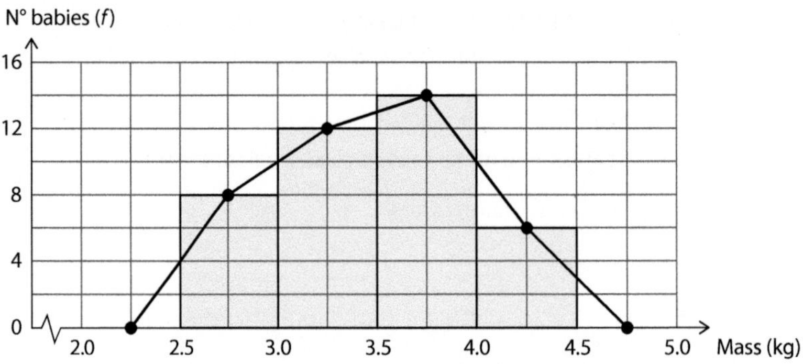

Figure 4.20: Frequency polygon for babies' masses

The polygon is closed at the points (2.25, 0) and (4.75, 0).

The point on the line at (4.0, 10) does *not* tell us that there are 10 babies each with a mass of 4.0 kg.

2 The heights of 100 eight-year-old children at a primary school were recorded. The data are summarised for the 50 boys and the 50 girls separately in Table 4.38.

Table 4.38: Children's heights

Height (*h* metres)	No. boys (*f*)	No. girls (*f*)
$1.00 \le h < 1.10$	3	5
$1.10 \le h < 1.20$	9	15
$1.20 \le h < 1.30$	16	13
$1.30 \le h < 1.40$	13	10
$1.40 \le h < 1.50$	9	7
	$\Sigma f = 50$	$\Sigma f = 50$

Both sets of data can be shown on a single diagram for comparison, as in Figure 4.21. A key is included to distinguish the two polygons. Points are plotted at the mid-value of each class and its corresponding frequency.

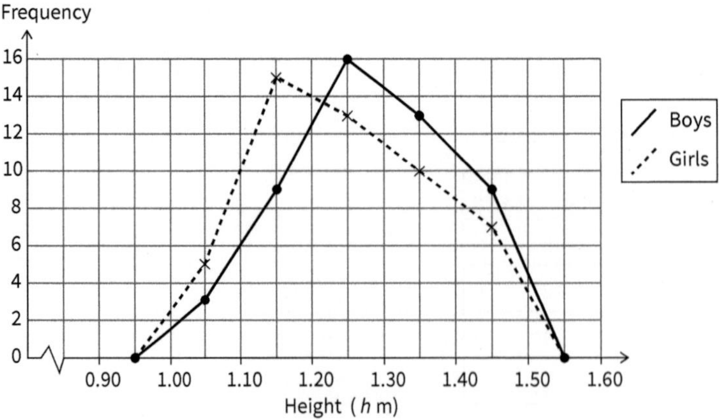

Figure 4.21: Frequency polygon for children's heights

The heights of the boys and girls have similar ranges, but the shorter children tend to be girls, while the taller children tend to be boys. We might conclude that, on average, these boys are taller than these girls.

Exercise 4F

1 The histogram in Figure 4.22 shows the masses, in kilograms, of the parcels received at a post office last week.

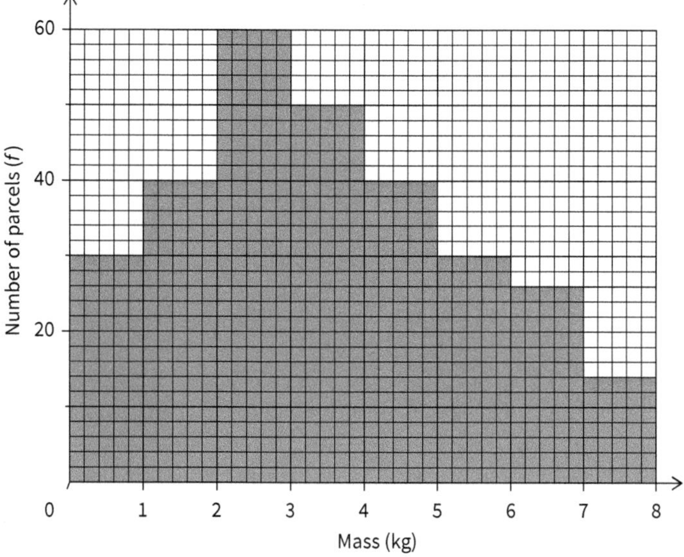

Figure 4.22: Parcel masses

- **i** How many parcels were less than 2 kg?
- **ii** What is the interval of each class?
- **iii** Find the mid-value of the class that contains the largest number of parcels.
- **iv** How many parcels were received at the post office altogether last week?
- **v** What percentage of the parcels had a mass of 5 kg or more?
- **vi** Find a calculated estimate of the number of parcels with masses of 5.5 kg or more.
- **vii** Find the lower boundary of the heaviest 40 parcels.

2 Passengers at a railway station were asked how long they had been waiting for their trains. Their waiting times are summarised in Table 4.39.

Table 4.39: Waiting times

Waiting time (minutes)	under 10	10–20	20–30	30–40	40–50	50–60
No. passengers (*f*)	35	55	65	60	20	15

- **i** Illustrate the data in a fully labelled histogram.
- **ii** Find:
  - **a** the number of passengers that had waited for less than half an hour,
  - **b** the number of passengers that had waited for 20 minutes or more,
  - **c** an estimate of the number of passengers that had waited for less than 35 minutes,
  - **d** an estimate of the number of passengers that had waited for three-quarters of an hour or more.

3 The times taken in seconds for 80 women to run a 400-metre race are given in Table 4.40.

Table 4.40: 400 m times

Time taken (seconds)	60–	65–	70–	75–	80–	85–	90–95
No. women (*f*)	1	6	15	29	20	7	2

i Label an axis for 'Time taken (seconds)' from 57.5 to 97.5, using 2 cm to represent 5 seconds, and construct a fully labelled closed frequency polygon.

ii Find:

a the number of women that took less than 85 seconds,

b the number of women that took 1.25 minutes or more,

c an estimate of the number of women that took less than 82.5 seconds,

d the number of women whose average speed was more than 5 m/s.

4 **i** Construct a fully labelled histogram that illustrates the best jumps of 40 boys in a long jump competition, as shown in Table 4.41. Label the 'Best jump' axis from 150 cm to 450 cm, using 2 cm to represent 50 cm.

Table 4.41: Top long jump distances

Best jump (cm)	180–220	230–270	280–320	330–370	380–420
No. boys (f)	7	14	12	5	2

ii Find:

a the number of boys whose best jump was less than 275 cm,

b an estimate of the number of boys whose best jump was at least 3 metres,

c an estimate of the percentage of boys who jumped 4 metres or more.

iii Construct a closed frequency polygon onto the histogram that you have drawn.

5 The heights above sea level of 116 mountains are given to the nearest hundred feet in Table 4.42.

Table 4.42: Heights of mountains

Height (nearest 100 ft)	1200–1700	1800–2300	2400–2900
Number of mountains (f)	32	48	36

i Illustrate these continuous data in a histogram.

Geology experts have recently decided that any land mass that is 2000 feet or more above sea level is a mountain, otherwise it is a hill.

ii Calculate an estimate of the percentage of these 'mountains' that are now classified as 'hills'.

A team of mountaineers wants to climb a mountain that is between 2500 and 2800 feet above sea level.

iii Calculate an estimate of the number of these mountains from which they can choose.

6 The numbers of full 30-litre pots of soup prepared in a kitchen in the last two months are given in Table 4.43.

Table 4.43: Full 30-litre pots of soup prepared

No. full 30-litre pots of soup	3–5	6–8	9–11
No. days (f)	18	24	20

i Write down the actual upper limit of the second class and find the interval of this class.

ii Illustrate the data in a closed frequency polygon.

iii Calculate an estimate of the number of days on which the kitchen staff prepared:

a less than 135 litres,
b 225 litres or more,
c less than 150 litres,
d between 135 and 315 litres.

7 Records were kept in regions A and B of the number of hours of sunshine each day in August last year.

Neither region had more than 8 hours of sunshine per day. The data are shown in the histograms in Figure 4.23.

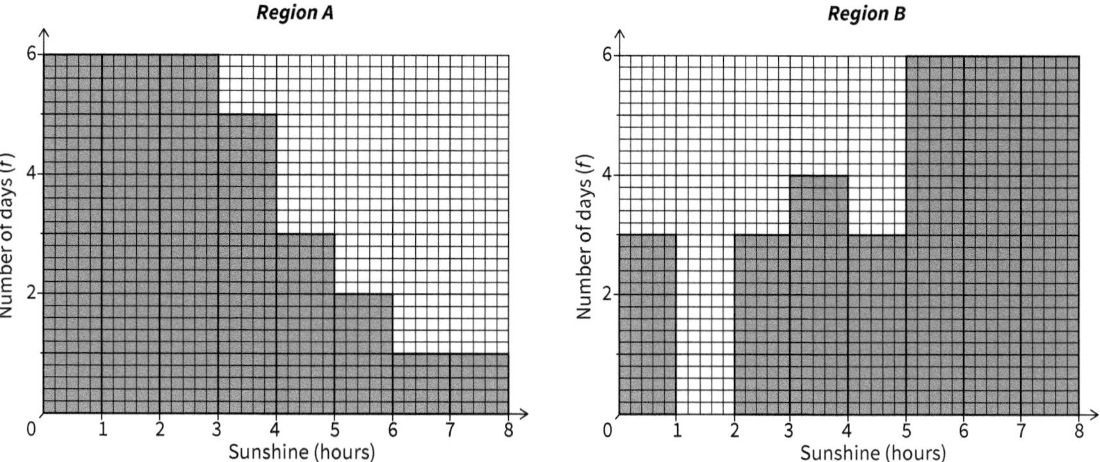

Figure 4.23: Days of sunshine in regions A and B

i For which region has information been omitted for one day in August? Explain your reasoning.

ii After studying the histograms, three students made the following observations:

Paul: 'There was more sunshine in region A than region B during the first two weeks of August.'
Jane: 'During the whole month there was less sunshine in region A than region B.'
Biki: 'There were 3 days on which the two regions had the same amount of sunshine.'

Decide which of the students has made a necessarily true statement and explain your reasoning.

8 The masses of all of a farmer's animals are shown in the frequency polygon in Figure 4.24.

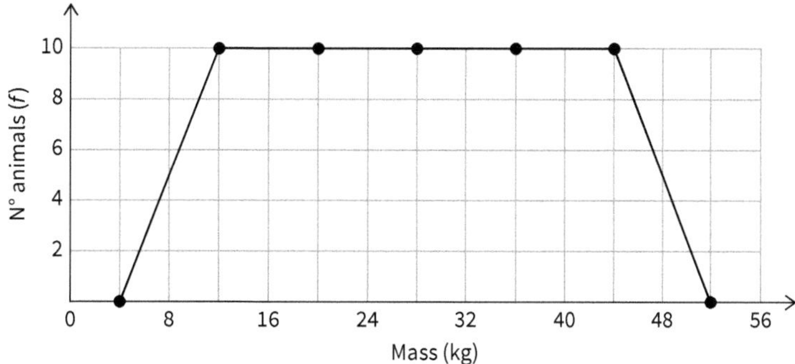

Figure 4.24: Animal masses

i How many animals does she have?
ii Write down the upper boundary of the masses of all her animals.
iii Explain how you know that the farmer has no chickens.
iv Draw up a frequency table for these data.

9 To reduce the number of infections by a winter virus, 400 people were treated with a new vaccine.

Unfortunately, it was found that the vaccine had no effect on the infection rate when winter came.

However, effects were noticed in the amount of undisturbed sleep that the vaccinated people had, and it was also noticed that the vaccine appeared to affect people's masses.

The data have been illustrated in two pairs of frequency polygons in Figure 4.25.

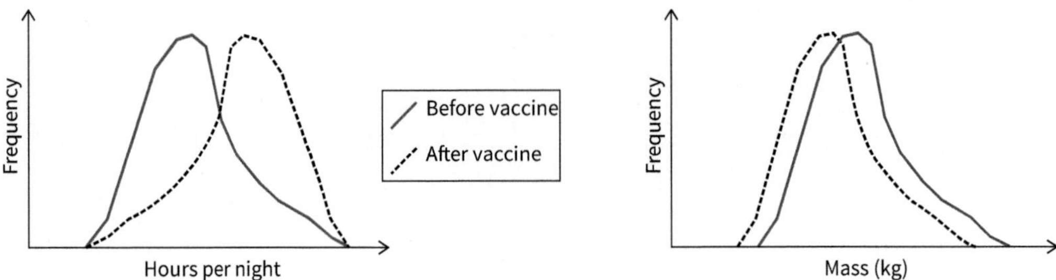

Figure 4.25: Vaccine side effects

Use the two diagrams to explain in detail the effects the vaccine had on those that took it.

Histograms and Frequency Polygons for Unequal Class Intervals

The process of constructing these diagrams for unequal class intervals is quite different than for equal class intervals, as some calculations and new units are required.

The principle of using column area to represent class frequency in a histogram still holds, but the widths of the columns are not all equal, so column heights cannot be equal to class frequencies.

- The variable axis is labelled as a continuous number line and the width of each column is equal to the class interval.
- The vertical axis is labelled 'frequency density'.
- Frequency densities must be calculated to ensure that area is proportional to frequency for each class.

A simple way of doing this is to ensure that: Column area = Class frequency

The numbers and units for frequency density are calculated as: Frequency density $= \frac{\text{Class frequency}}{\text{Class interval}}$

For example, a class with a frequency of 150 children and an interval of 25 minutes has a frequency density of $\frac{150 \text{ children}}{25 \text{ minutes}} = 6$ children per minute.

This ensures that the area of the column is equal to 150 children.

Again, the advantage of a histogram over a frequency polygon is that class boundaries are clear to see. It is also far simpler to calculate estimates using a histogram because areas within different sections of the columns are all rectangular in shape.

Examples

1 Twenty objects are divided into two classes according to their masses in grams, as shown in Table 4.44.

Table 4.44: Objects classified by mass

Mass (g)	No. objects (*f*)
0–2	10
2–3	10

The class intervals are 2 g and 1 g.
The class frequencies are equal (10 objects), so the two columns of the histogram must have equal areas. If frequencies are used for column heights:

the first column will have an area of $2 \times 10 = 20$,

the second column will have an area of $1 \times 10 = 10$.

Areas will not be equal, so frequencies cannot be used for the column heights. The correct height of each column must be calculated; this is referred to as the *frequency density* (or just *density*). Numbers and units for frequency density are calculated so that column area = class frequency.

First column: width × height = frequency

$2\,\text{g} \times \text{density} = 10 \text{ objects}$

$\text{density} = 5 \text{ objects per gram}$

Second column: width × height = frequency

$1\,\text{g} \times \text{density} = 10 \text{ objects}$

$\text{density} = 10 \text{ objects per gram}$

The column heights are 5 and 10, and the units of density are 'objects per gram' or 'objects/gram'. The correct histogram is shown in Figure 4.26.

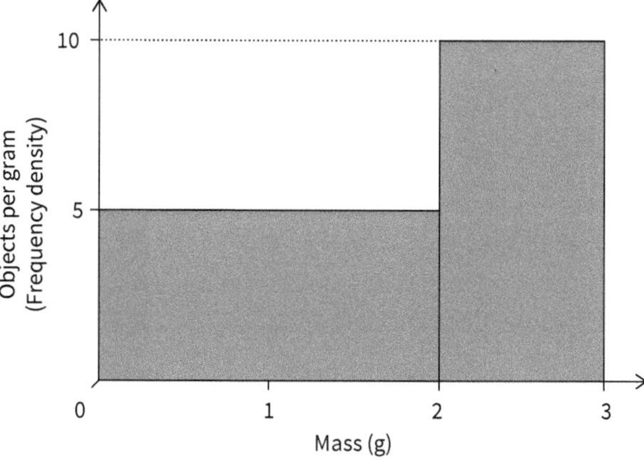

Figure 4.26: Histogram of objects organised by mass

Note that each column area in Figure 4.27 is equal to the frequency of the class that it represents.

2 The numbers of megabytes (Mb) used for storing documents on 339 computers at a college are given in Table 4.45, and densities are calculated in Table 4.46.

Table 4.45: Storage space

Storage used (Mb)	No. computers (f)
0–10	51
10–30	84
30–60	96
60–100	108
	$\Sigma f = 339$

Density = class frequency ÷ class interval

Table 4.46: Densities for storage space classes

Class	Frequency	Interval	Density
0–10	51	10	$51 \div 10 = 5.1$
10–30	84	20	$84 \div 20 = 4.2$
30–60	96	30	$96 \div 30 = 3.2$
60–100	108	40	$108 \div 40 = 2.7$

The histogram in Figure 4.27 represents the data.

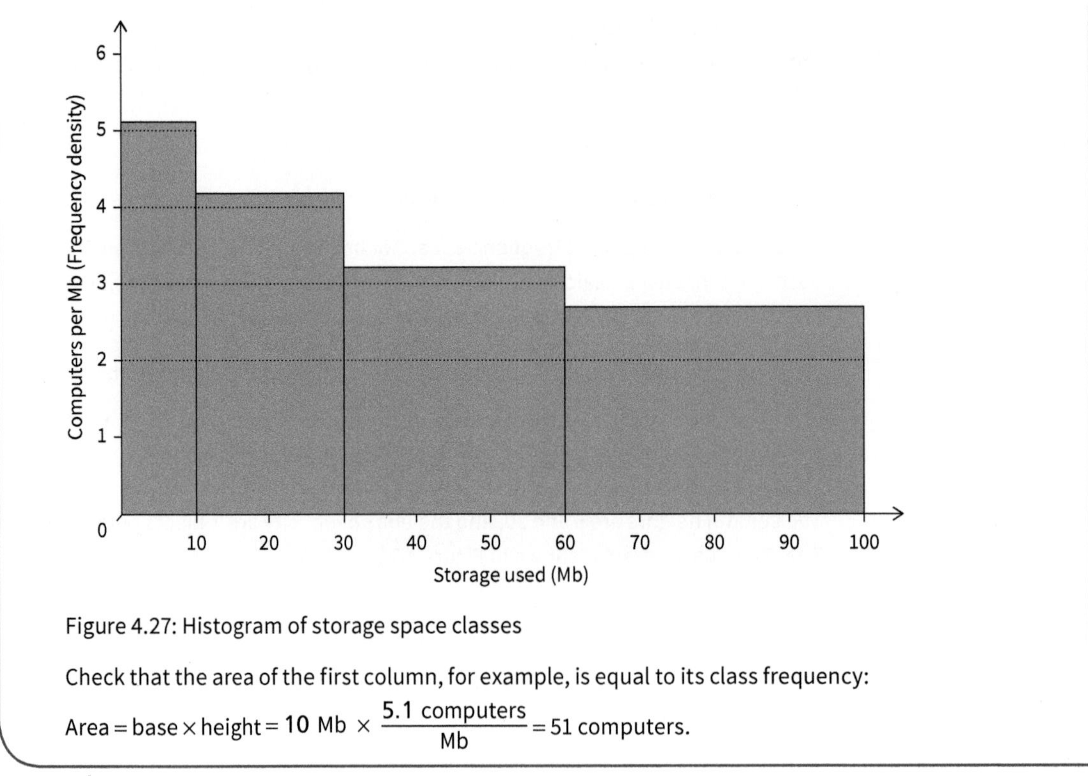

Figure 4.27: Histogram of storage space classes

Check that the area of the first column, for example, is equal to its class frequency:

Area = base × height = 10 Mb × $\frac{5.1 \text{ computers}}{\text{Mb}}$ = 51 computers.

For unequal class intervals, *frequency polygons* are constructed so that the area under the closed polygon is proportional to the total frequency of the data. Again, a simple way of doing this is to ensure that the area under the polygon and the total frequency are equal.

- Axes are labelled in the same way as for a histogram.
- All unequal class intervals are subdivided into a number of identical **standard intervals**, each with the same frequency density as the class to which it belongs.
- Points are plotted at (mid-value, density) for each standard interval, and joined by ruled lines.
- The polygon is closed at the mid-value of an additional standard interval class on each side of the data with zero density.

Each plotted point represents a standard interval class and its frequency density.

Densities are calculated as: Frequency density $= \frac{\text{Class frequency}}{\text{Class interval}}$, which will ensure that: Area under closed frequency polygon = total frequency of the data

Example

1 The grouped frequency table in Table 4.47 shows the amount of extra time played in 65 football matches last season.

Table 4.47: Extra time played

Extra time (minutes)	No. matches (f)
0–3	12
3–4	9
4–6	16
6–10	28

Densities are calculated as in Table 4.48.

Table 4.48: Densities of classes for extra time

Class	Frequency	Interval	Density
0–3	12	3	$12 \div 3 = 4$
3–4	9	1	$9 \div 1 = 9$
4–6	16	2	$16 \div 2 = 8$
6–10	28	4	$28 \div 4 = 7$

An appropriate 'standard' interval is chosen. It is sensible to use the highest common factor of the class intervals which, in this case, is 1 minute. Only three of the classes need to be subdivided, as shown in Table 4.49.

Table 4.49: Densities using standard interval

Standard interval classes	Density
0–1, 1–2, 2–3	4
3–4	9
4–5, 5–6	8
6–7, 7–8, 8–9, 9–10	7

Points are plotted at the mid-values of all standard interval classes at the appropriate density, as shown in Figure 4.28.

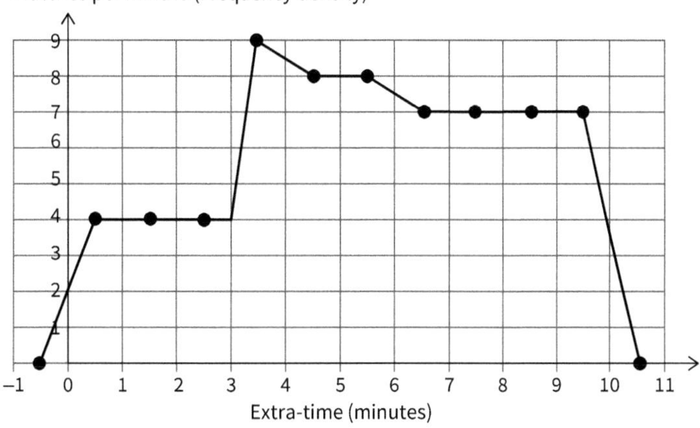

Figure 4.28: Frequency polygon for extra time

The polygon is closed at the mid-values of two additional standard interval classes (–0.5, 0) and (10.5, 0), ensuring that the area under the frequency polygon is equal to 65 matches.

Calculated estimates from histograms and frequency polygons with unequal class intervals can still be made by finding areas of part-columns, or area under the polygon, between the required values.

Example

2 The histogram and frequency polygon in Figure 4.29 show the times taken by emergency services to arrive at the scenes of 185 road-traffic accidents.

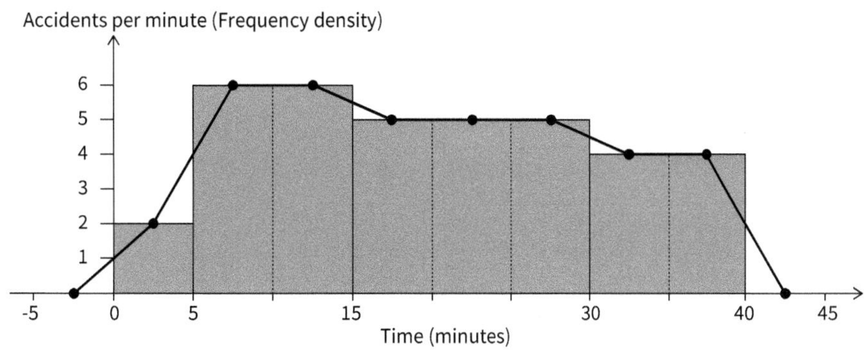

Figure 4.29: Emergency service response times

By calculating the areas of various sections of the histogram or the frequency polygon, a frequency table for these data can be drawn up, as shown in Table 4.50.

Frequency density $= \dfrac{\text{class frequency}}{\text{class interval}}$, so class frequency = frequency density × class interval.

Table 4.50: Frequency table for response times

Class	Interval (minutes)	Density $\left(\dfrac{\text{accidents}}{\text{minute}}\right)$	Frequency (accidents)
–5–0	5	0	$0 \times 5 = 0$
0–5	5	2	$2 \times 5 = 10$
5–15	10	6	$6 \times 10 = 10$
15–30	15	5	$5 \times 15 = 75$
30–40	10	4	$4 \times 10 = 40$
40–45	5	0	$0 \times 5 = 0$
			$\Sigma f = 185$

The two classes with zero frequency do not need to be included in the table.
We can calculate estimates using either the diagram itself or the frequency table.
How many accidents did emergency services arrive at after:

i 20 minutes or more,

Area to the right of a vertical line at 20 minutes, which is $(5 \times 10) + (4 \times 10) = 90$ accidents

ii less than $12\frac{1}{2}$ minutes.

Area to the left of a vertical line at $12\frac{1}{2}$ minutes, which is $(2 \times 5) + (6 \times 7\frac{1}{2}) = 55$ accidents.

Exercise 4G

1 The masses of 37 watermelons were recorded and are summarised in the grouped frequency table in Table 4.51.

Table 4.51: Watermelon masses

Mass (kg)	No. watermelons
0–1	6
1–3	16
3–6	15

i Calculate the correct densities and the correct density units that can be used for each of the three classes.

ii Illustrate the data in a histogram.

iii Calculate an estimate of the number of watermelons that have a mass of:

a less than 0.5 kg,

b 4 kg or more.

2 The times taken by the mechanic at Bullet Motors to fully service 44 vehicles are given in Table 4.52.

Table 4.52: Vehicle service times

Time taken (hours)	0–	1–	3–7
No. vehicles (f)	4	16	24

i Calculate the correct densities and the correct density units that can be used for the three classes.

ii Illustrate the data in a histogram.

iii Calculate an estimate of the number of vehicles that were serviced in:

a less than 2 hours,

b 5 hours or more.

3 The lengths of a sample of 540 objects were recorded and are summarised in Table 4.53.

Table 4.53: Lengths of objects

Length (cm)	0–4	4–6	6–8	8–12
No. objects (*f*)	120	120	140	160

i Illustrate these data in a frequency polygon using a standard interval of 2 cm.

ii Calculate an estimate of:

a the number of objects that are less than 7 cm,

b the number of objects that are 5 cm or more,

c the number of objects that are less than 3 cm,

d the percentage of the objects that are 9 cm or more.

4 The histogram in Figure 4.30 illustrates the maximum speeds of some working tractors.

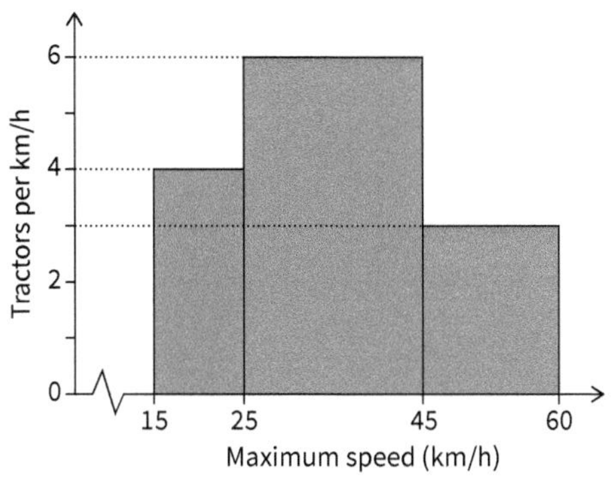

Figure 4.30: Tractor maximum speeds

i How many tractors are represented in the histogram?

ii Illustrate the data in a grouped frequency table.

iii Calculate an estimate of the number of tractors with a maximum speed of:

a less than 35 km/h,

b 49 km/h or more,

c between 20 km/h and 30 km/h.

One of the tractors is chosen at random.

iv Estimate the probability that its maximum speed is:

a under 20 km/h,

b 50 km/h or more.

5 The body temperatures of 500 patients who were admitted to a hospital over a six-month period are given in Table 4.54.

Table 4.54: Patient body temperatures

Temperature (t °C)	$36.0 \le t < 36.5$	$36.5 \le t < 36.8$	$36.8 \le t < 37.0$	$37.0 \le t < 37.4$
No. patients (*f*)	50	210	120	120

i Illustrate the data in a histogram.

ii Calculate an estimate of the number of patients whose temperatures were:

a under 36.9 °C, **b** 36.7 °C or more.

iii Calculate an estimate of the percentage of patients with temperatures such that $36.9\text{ °C} \le t < 37.1\text{ °C}$

6 The frequency polygon in Figure 4.31 summarises the values of a variable, X, in three classes.

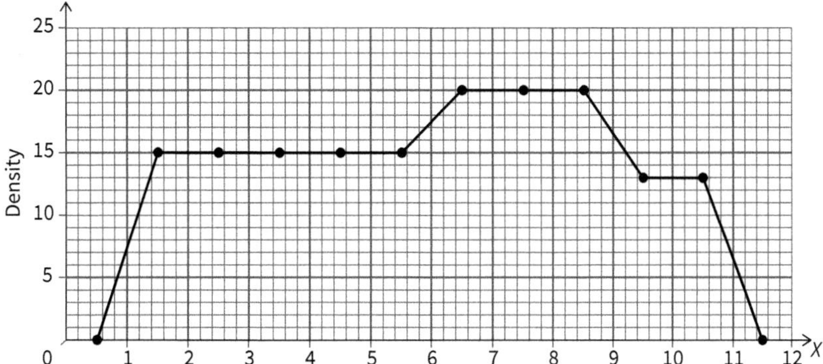

Figure 4.31: Frequency polygon for values of X

The first class, $1 \leq X < 6$ contains 75 values of X.

i Find the total number of values of X shown in the frequency polygon.
ii Estimate the number of values of X in the range $7.5 \leq X < 10$.

7 The frequency table in Table 4.55 gives the heights h in metres of 150 men who applied to join the army.

Table 4.55: Heights of army applicants

Height (h m)	$1.68 \leq h < 1.76$	$1.76 \leq h < 1.84$	$1.84 \leq h < 1.96$	$1.96 \leq h < 2.08$
No. men (f)	24	24	60	42

i Write down the interval of the first class in metres.
ii Write down the interval of the second class in centimetres.
iii Illustrate the data in a histogram. Use density units of 'men per metre' or 'men per centimetre'.
iv If the minimum height for a man to be considered for recruitment into the army is 170 cm, calculate an estimate of the number of men who were rejected because of their height.
v Calculate an estimate of the lower boundary of the height of the tallest 57 of these 150 men.

8 The heights of a group of 130 children are given in Table 4.56.

Table 4.56: Children's heights

Height (cm)	**No. children (f)**
110–120	40
130–160	60
170–190	30

i Show the data in a histogram with heights from 100 cm to 200 cm.
ii What percentage of the children are less than 1.65 m tall?
iii Estimate how many children are less than 118 cm tall.
iv Using a standard interval of 10 cm, construct a closed frequency polygon onto your histogram.

9 A biologist planted 684 seeds and recorded the times taken for the seeds to germinate – see Table 4.57.

Table 4.57: Seed germination times

Time taken (hours)	21–24	25–28	29–33	34–39	40–47	48–50
No. seeds (f)	120	160	130	84	160	30

i Explain why the class containing 120 seeds has an interval of 4 hours.
ii Illustrate the data in a histogram.
iii Calculate an estimate of:
- **a** the number of seeds that germinated in less than 31 hours,
- **b** the number of seeds that germinated in less than 26 hours,
- **c** the percentage of seeds that took between 1 and 2 days to germinate.

10 The lengths of a sample of 300 bolts produced at a factory are summarised in Table 4.58.

Table 4.58: Lengths of bolts

Length (x mm)	12	13–14	15	16–19
No. bolts (f)	35	120	85	60

i Write down the lower and upper boundaries of the first class of bolts.

ii Illustrate the data in a frequency polygon using a standard interval of 1 mm.

iii Calculate an estimate of the number of bolts with lengths of:

a less than 13.5 mm, **b** 17.5 mm or more, **c** in the range $13.5 \text{ mm} \le x < 17\,5 \text{ mm}$.

iv If bolts with lengths in the range $12.3 \text{ mm} \le x < 15\,3 \text{ mm}$ are considered acceptable, calculate an estimate of the percentage of these 300 bolts that are considered unacceptable.

11 The departure delay times of some buses last weekend are represented in the histogram in Figure 4.32.

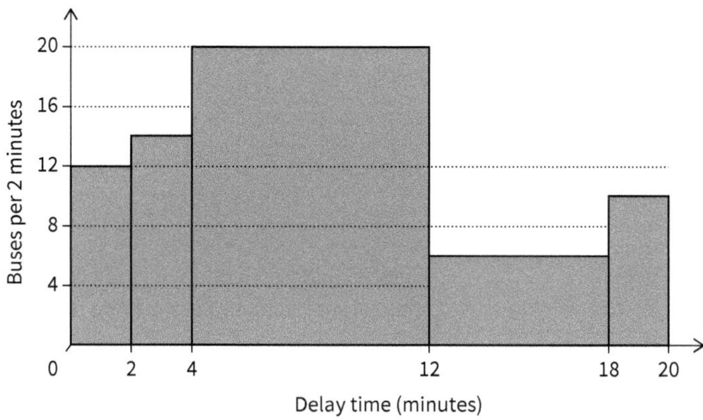

Figure 4.32: Bus delay times

i How many buses are represented?

ii Calculate an estimate of the percentage of these buses that departed:

a less than 10 minutes late, **b** at least a quarter of an hour late.

iii Explain what the manager meant when he said that only 36 of these buses departed at 'a reasonable time'.

12 A police patrol unit was equipped with a speed gun for measuring the speeds of passing vehicles. Table 4.59 shows the speeds of 440 vehicles that passed the unit in a period of 6 hours.

Table 4.59: Vehicle speeds

Speed (km/h)	30–60	70–90	100–110	120–130	140–180
No. vehicles (f)	80	96	124	100	40

i Illustrate the data in a histogram.

ii Calculate an estimate of the number of vehicles that were being driven at under 75 km/h.

The police unit was patrolling to enforce a speed limit of 120 km/h in the area, and drivers who were travelling in excess of the speed limit were fined $50 each.

iii Calculate an estimate of the total amount that offenders were fined during these 6 hours.

13 A group of 154 children is split into two groups, first by mass then by their age in completed years. When grouped by mass, there are 100 in the 40–48 kg group, and 54 in the 48–60 kg group. The data are to be shown in a histogram where the column for the larger group of children has a height of 10 cm.

i Calculate the correct height for the column representing the smaller group of children.

When grouped by age, the column for the 9–13 group has a height of 15.2 cm, and the column for the 14–17 group has a height of 11.8 cm.

ii How many children are in each group?

14 The grouped frequency table in Table 4.60 summarises the value of one euro (€1) in Singapore dollars (S$), to the nearest cent, for the 365 days of 2014 [S$1 = 100 cents].

Table 4.60: Euro to Singapore dollar equivalence

Value of 1 euro (€1) in Singapore dollars (S$)	Number of days (f)
1.61–1.62	83
1.63–1.68	66
1.69–1.73	120
1.74–1.76	96

The lower boundary of the first class is S$1.605.

i Write down the upper boundary of the first class.

ii **a** On graph paper, draw a horizontal axis for the value of €1 in Singapore dollars from S$1.605 up to S$1.765, using 1 cm to represent S$0.01.

b Draw a column of height 8.3 cm for the first class.

c Complete the histogram.

iii Use the histogram and Table 4.60 to calculate an estimate of the number of days on which €40 was worth at least S$68.

15 The frequency polygon in Figure 4.33 illustrates the times taken by competitors to be eliminated from a competition.

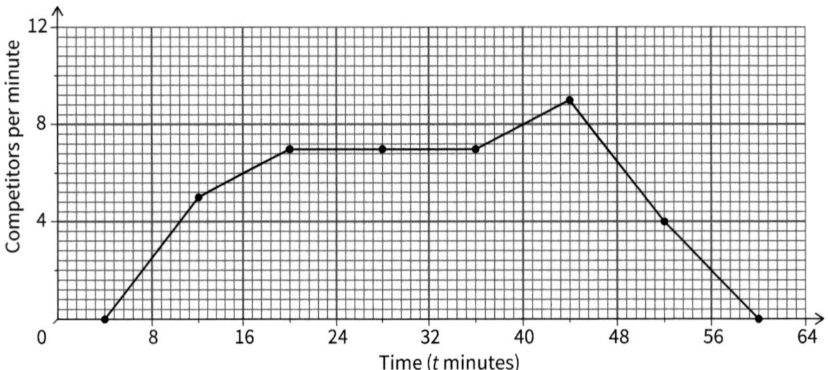

Figure 4.33: Competition elimination times

i By first drawing up a frequency table, or otherwise, find:

a the total number of eliminated competitors represented,

b the greatest possible length of time between the first and last of these competitors being eliminated.

ii Calculate an estimate of the number of competitors who were eliminated:

a in under 20 minutes,

b in three-quarters of an hour or more,

c after 15 to 30 minutes.

16 The distances run, in metres, by 120 athletes in 6 minutes are summarised in Table 4.61.

Table 4.61: Distances run in six minutes

Distance (metres)	No. athletes (f)	Height of column (units)
1750 to under 1850	8	4
1850 to under 2000	15	5
2000 to under 2050	18	a
2050 to under 2150	27	b
2150 to under 2300	33	c
2300 to under 2550	19	d
	$\Sigma f = 120$	

The distances are to be illustrated in a histogram, in which the 1750 to under 1850 class will be represented by a column of height 4 units, and the 1850 to under 2000 class will be represented by a column of height 5 units.

i Calculate the values of a, b, c and d, the heights of the columns representing the other four classes.
ii If the last two classes were combined into a single 2150 to under 2550 class, calculate the correct height of the column that would represent it.

17 The times taken, to the nearest minute, for a group of interviewees to complete an aptitude test are given in Table 4.62.

Table 4.62: Aptitude test completion times

Time (minutes)	No. interviewees (f)	Height of column (units)
1–3	6	2
4–5	8	4
6–9	p	3.5
10–14	q	5
15–20	r	3
21–T	10	2.5
	$\Sigma f = 24 + p + q + r$	

The times are to be illustrated in a histogram, in which a column of height 2 units for the 1–3 class represents 6 interviewees, and a column of height 4 units for the 4–5 class represents 8 interviewees.

i Calculate the values of p, q, and r, the numbers of interviewees in each of the next three classes.
ii Find the value of T, the rounded upper limit of the times for the last class of 10 interviewees.

18 Figure 4.34 illustrates the wind speed, in knots, at a number of locations around the coast of Australia, taken at 9 a.m. on a particular morning in September.

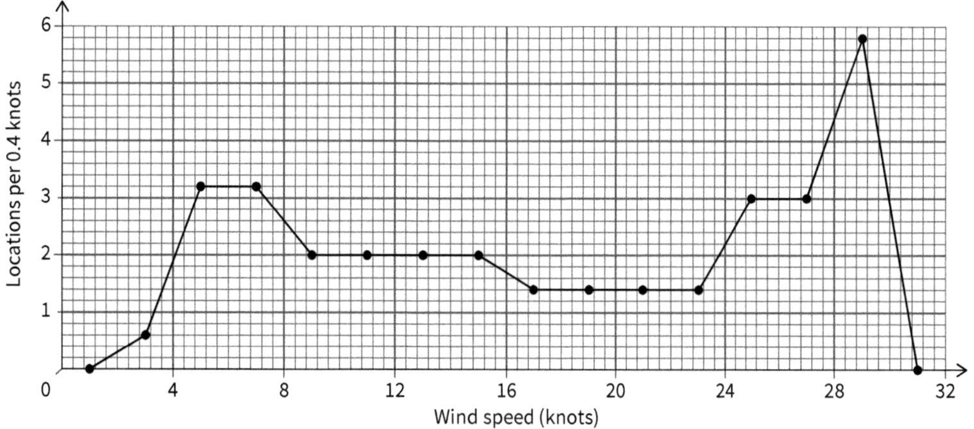

Figure 4.34: Coastal wind speeds

A standard interval of 2 knots has been used to construct the frequency polygon.

i Copy and complete the frequency table in Table 4.63, showing the six classes of wind speeds, their densities and their frequencies.

Table 4.63: Frequency table for wind speeds

Wind speed (knots)	Locations per 0.4 knots (density)	Number of locations (frequency)
2–4	0.6	
4–8		
8–16	2.0	40
		30
		$\Sigma f =$

ii Calculate an estimate of the number of locations where the wind speed was:

a less than 12 knots, **b** in the range 7 knots ≤ wind speed < 13 knots.

Warnings of strong winds were issued by the coastguards at 47 of these locations.

iii Calculate an estimate of the wind speeds required for the warning to be issued.

Cumulative Frequency Diagrams

A cumulative frequency diagram is a graph obtained by plotting points for classes of grouped data. Each class is represented by a point plotted using its upper class boundary and its corresponding cumulative frequency value.

When class intervals are equal, points are plotted at regular intervals along the variable axis, but when class intervals are unequal, points are plotted at irregular intervals along the variable axis. Points can be joined by ruled lines or by a smooth curve.

Examples

The diameters of 800 cylindrical pipes, x cm, are summarised in the grouped frequency table shown in Table 4.64. The class intervals are unequal, being of widths 5 cm or 10 cm.

Table 4.64: Pipe diameters

Diameter (x cm)	$0 \leq x < 5$	$5 \leq x < 10$	$10 \leq x < 20$	$20 \leq x < 30$	$30 \leq x < 35$	$35 \leq x < 35$
No. pipes (f)	50	150	320	200	60	20

A cumulative frequency table is drawn up, as in Table 4.65.

Table 4.65: Cumulative frequency table for pipe diameters

Diameter (x cm)	$x < 0$	$x < 5$	$x < 10$	$x < 20$	$x < 30$	$x < 35$	$x < 40$
No. pipes (cf)	0	50	200	520	720	780	800

A cumulative frequency polygon and curve, drawn through seven points, are shown on the same diagram in Figure 4.35.

The point at (30, 720), for example, tells us that there are 720 pipes whose diameters are less than 30 cm.

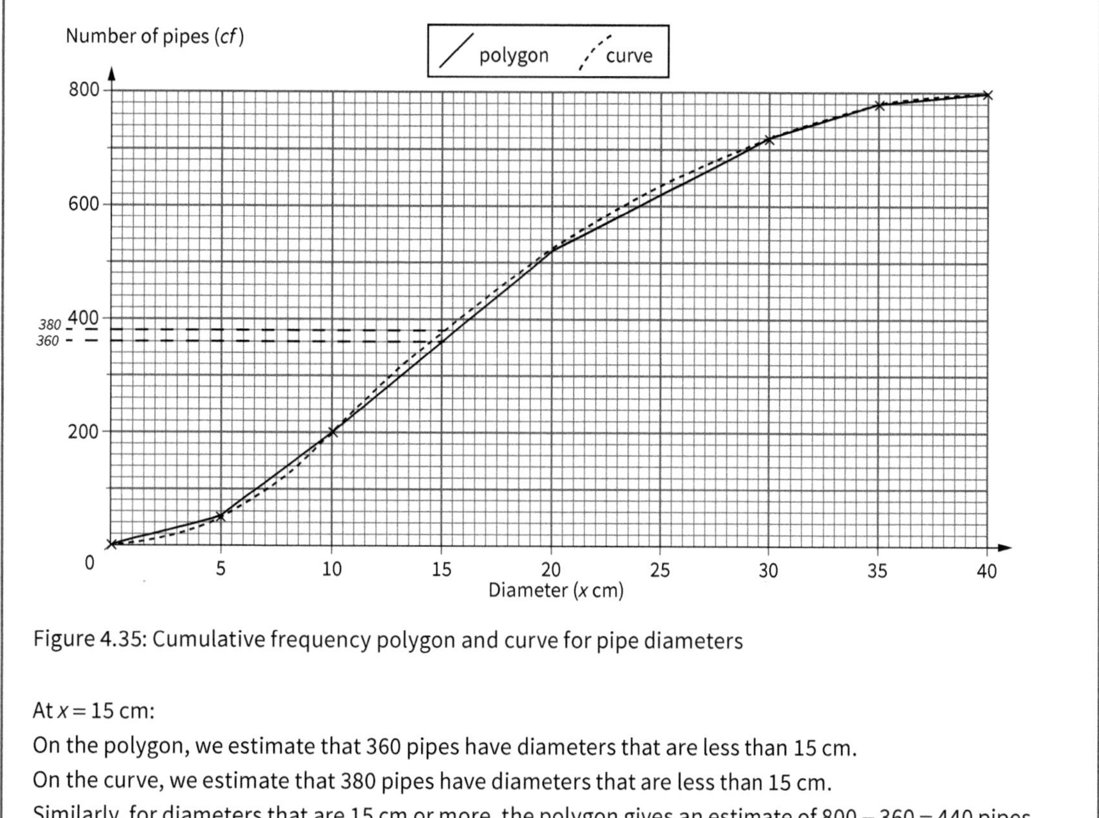

Figure 4.35: Cumulative frequency polygon and curve for pipe diameters

At $x = 15$ cm:

On the polygon, we estimate that 360 pipes have diameters that are less than 15 cm.

On the curve, we estimate that 380 pipes have diameters that are less than 15 cm.

Similarly, for diameters that are 15 cm or more, the polygon gives an estimate of $800 - 360 = 440$ pipes, and the curve gives an estimate of $800 - 380 = 420$ pipes.

Estimates from a polygon and a curve will not be exactly the same, as their only common points are those plotted from the cumulative frequency table.

Exercise 4H

1 A market gardener produced 1600 tomatoes last year, and she recorded the mass of each. Her results are displayed in the cumulative frequency polygon in Figure 4.36.

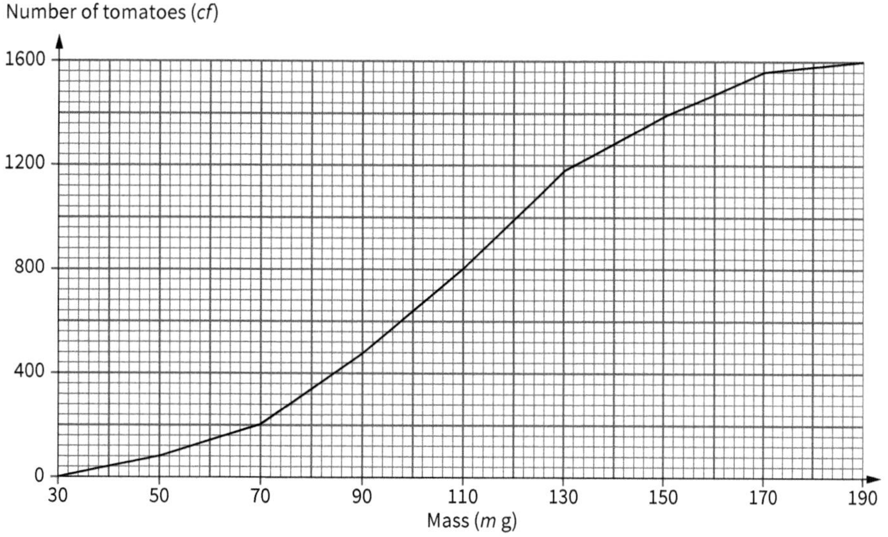

Figure 4.36: Tomato masses

Use the diagram to estimate the number of tomatoes that had masses of:

i less than 98 g, **ii** 98 g or more, **iii** less than 126 g,
iv 126 g or more, **v** 98 g or more, but less than 126 g.

2 The lengths of 80 objects are recorded in the cumulative frequency polygon in Figure 4.37.

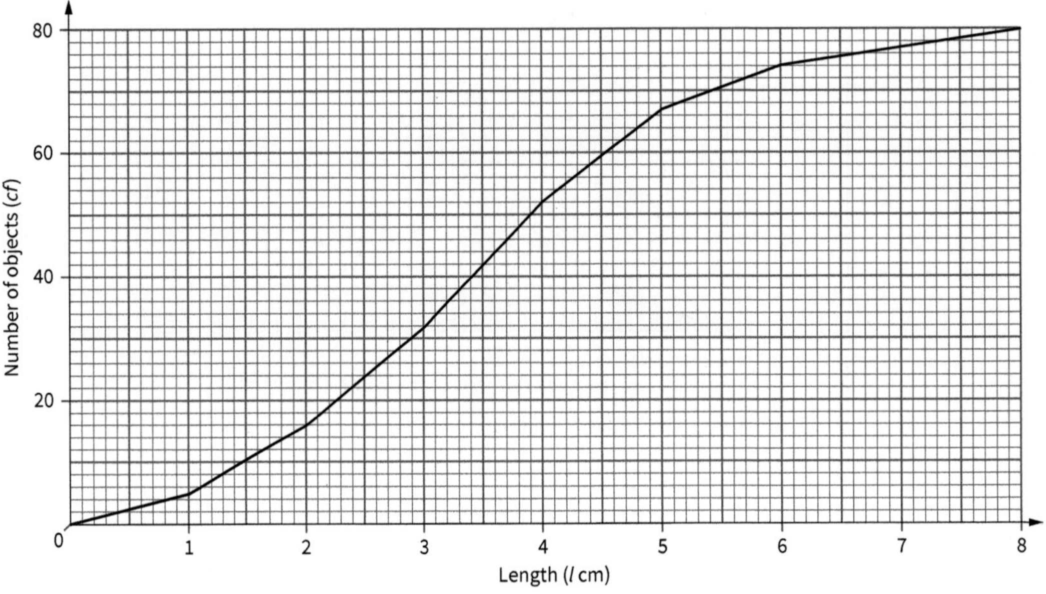

Figure 4.37: Object lengths

i Use the diagram to estimate the number of objects with lengths that are:
a less than 4 cm, **b** 4 cm or more, **c** less than 3.8 cm,
d 3.8 cm more, **e** less than 5.3 cm,
f 3.8 cm or more, but less than 5.3 cm.

3 The cumulative frequency curve in Figure 4.38 illustrates the lengths of some pieces of rope at a sailing supply shop.

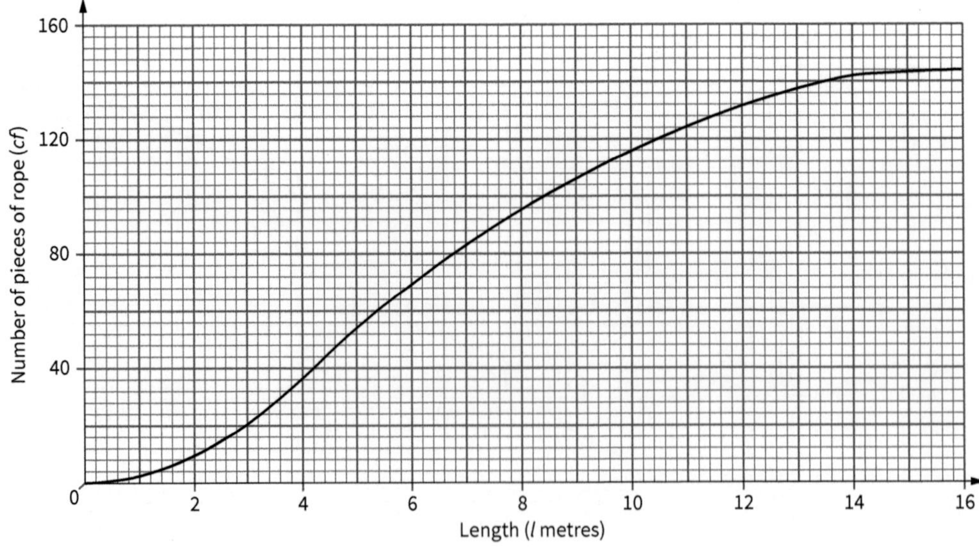

Figure 4.38: Lengths of rope

i How many pieces of rope are represented in the diagram?

ii Find the values of a, b, c and d used in the cumulative frequency table in Table 4.66.

Table 4.66: Cumulative frequency table for rope lengths

Length (l metres)	$l<0$	$l<2.4$	$l<4$	$l<6$	$l<a$	$l<b$	$l<12$	$l<16$
No. pieces of rope (cf)	0	18	c	69	90	110	d	144

iii Use the diagram and table to find:

a the frequency of the group $4\,\text{m} \leq l < 6\,\text{m}$,

b the frequency density of the group $2.4\,\text{m} \leq l < 4\,\text{m}$.

4 Seventy adults entered a 50-metre sprint competition. The cumulative frequency table in Table 4.67 shows the times taken by the competitors.

Table 4.67: Sprint times

Time (seconds)	under 5	under 6	under 7	under 8	under 9	under 10	under 11	under 12
No. competitors (cf)	0	3	12	28	48	60	66	70

i On graph paper, show this data in a cumulative frequency polygon.

Number the horizontal axis from 5 to 12 using 2 cm to represent 1 second.

Number the vertical axis from 0 to 70 using 1 cm to represent 5 adults.

Plot points at (5, 0), (6, 3), (7, 12), (8, 28), . . ., (12, 70) and join consecutive points by ruled lines.

ii Use your polygon to estimate the number of adults that took:

a less than 7.5 seconds,
b 7.5 seconds or more,
c less than 9.5 seconds,
d 9.5 seconds or more,
e between 7.5 and 9.5 seconds.

5 A gardener weighed all of the 180 mangoes from the trees in her garden. Their masses are given in the cumulative frequency table in Table 4.68.

Table 4.68: Mango masses

Mass (m g)	$m<150$	$m<200$	$m<250$	$m<300$	$m<350$	$m<400$	$m<450$	$m<500$
No. mangoes (cf)	0	8	30	70	130	160	174	180

i On graph paper, show these data in a cumulative frequency curve.
Number the horizontal axis from 150 to 500 using 2 cm to represent 50 g.

Number the vertical axis from 0 to 180 using 1 cm to represent 10 mangoes.

Plot points at (150, 0), (200, 8), (250, 30), (300, 70), . . ., (500, 180) and join consecutive points with a smooth curve.

ii Use your curve to estimate the number of mangoes that were:

a less than 270 g,
b 270 g or more,
c less than 425 g,
d 425 g or more,
e 270 g or more, but less than 425 g.

6 The cumulative frequency table in Table 4.69 illustrates the duration h hours, of 216 sporting events.

Table 4.69: Sporting event durations

Duration (h hours)	$h<1.0$	$h<2.0$	$h<4.0$	$h<6.5$	$h<7.0$	$h<8.0$
No. events (cf)	36	72	108	144	180	216

The data are to be illustrated in a cumulative frequency polygon.

i Explain why the polygon could be constructed by plotting seven points, rather than just six points.

ii Between which two values of h will the polygon be:

a steepest, **b** shallowest?

iii Without drawing the polygon, estimate the number of events that lasted for less than 3 hours.

7 The lengths of time that 200 office employees spent on social networking websites during working hours last week are shown in Table 4.70.

Table 4.70: Times spent on social networking

Time (t hours)	**No. employees (f)**
$0 \le t < 2$	14
$2 \le t < 4$	64
$4 \le t < 6$	47
$6 \le t < 8$	40
$8 \le t < 10$	26
$10 \le t < 12$	9
	$\Sigma f = 200$

i Copy and complete the cumulative frequency table shown in Table 4.71.

Table 4.71: Cumulative frequency table for social networking times

Time (t hours)	**No. employees (cf)**
$t<0$	0
$t<2$	
$t<4$	
$t<6$	
$t<8$	
$t<10$	
$t<12$	200

ii Use your tables to state whether you consider each of the following to be a good estimate, a bad estimate, a true statement or a false statement:

a 7 employees spent less than 1 hour on social networking sites,

b 78 employees spent less than 4 hours on social networking sites,

c 75 employees spent 8 hours or more on social networking sites,

d 57 employees spent 7 hours or more on social networking sites.

8 The cumulative frequency table in Table 4.72 shows the 114 values of a variable X.

Table 4.72: Values of X

X	$X<0$	$X<10$	$X<20$	$X<30$	$X<40$	$X<50$	$X<60$
cf	0	14	30	48	68	90	114

i Calculate the missing frequency values a, b, c and d in the frequency table shown in Table 4.73.

Table 4.73: Frequency table for X

X	frequency (f)
$0 \leq X < 10$	14
$10 \leq X < 20$	a
$20 \leq X < 30$	b
$30 \leq X < 40$	c
$40 \leq X < 50$	d
$50 \leq X < 60$	24
	$\Sigma f = 114$

ii Use the two tables that you have to estimate the frequency for the following values of X:
a $X < 15$ and $X \geq 15$, **b** $X < 25$ and $X \geq 25$, **c** $X < 35$ and $X \geq 35$,
d $X < 45$ and $X \geq 45$, **e** $X < 55$ and $X \geq 55$.

9 The frequency table for values of a variable Y is shown in Table 4.74.

Table 4.74: Values of Y

Y	$0 \leq Y < 8$	$8 \leq Y < 16$	$16 \leq Y < 24$	$24 \leq Y < 32$	$32 \leq Y < 40$
f	10	16	30	20	14

i Use the frequency table to draw up a cumulative frequency table.
ii On graph paper, show these data in a cumulative frequency polygon.

Number the horizontal axis from 0 to 40 using 2 cm to represent 5 units.

Number the vertical axis from 0 to 90 using 2 cm to represent 5 units.

Plot the points from your cumulative frequency table and join consecutive points by ruled lines.

iii Use your polygon to estimate the number of values of Y such that:
a $12 \leq Y < 24$, **b** $4 \leq Y < 20$, **c** $14 \leq Y < 30$.

10 Values of a particular variable are divided into four unequal interval classes.

The class boundaries are 0, 5, 11, 18 and 26, and the variable has 60 values that are less than 5.

When the five points are plotted from the cumulative frequency table and joined, a straight line is obtained.

i Explain why the frequency of the class 5–11 must be equal to 72.
ii Find the number of values of the variable that are less than 26.

11 Subscribers to a television network were given 4 hours, starting at 1 p.m., in which to text the answer to a simple multiple-choice question, whose possible answers were A, B or C. Four prize winners were randomly selected from those that got the answer correct. The numbers of texts received during this four-hour period are shown in the cumulative frequency table in Table 4.75.

Table 4.75: Cumulative frequency table of numbers of texts received

Time	up to 2 p.m.	up to 3 p.m.	up to 4 p.m.	up to 5 p.m.
Numbers of texts received (*cf*)	1000	1500	1800	2500

i Copy and complete Table 4.76 showing how many of each answer were received during each hour.

Table 4.76: Answers received

	A	B	C	**Totals**
1–2 p.m.		800	50	
2–3 p.m.	80		30	
3–4 p.m.		210		
4–5 p.m.	85		75	
Totals			175	2500

ii During which two 1-hour periods were the largest number of texts received? Suggest reasons for this.

iii If the correct answer was B, find the probability that a particular subscriber who got the answer correct actually won a prize.

Measures of Central Tendency 5

Learning Objectives

In this chapter you will learn:

- How to find the measures of central tendency for ungrouped data
- How to calculate estimates of the measures of central tendency for grouped data
- About the ways in which sets of related data can be compared using average values
- Why one measure may be more or less appropriate to use than the others
- To select the most appropriate measure to represent the values in a set of data

Introduction

Averages are in everyday use, and this is the most common word used to refer to the measures of central tendency. There are three measures to choose from when deciding what the average value of a set of data is. One of the measures will often be more appropriate to use than the others. The measure chosen as the average should be typical of the values in the set of data and fairly central to it. Depending on how the data are presented, we can find or estimate the chosen measure by calculation, by ordering the values, by reading from a graph or by simple observation.

5.1 Measures of Central Tendency for Ungrouped Data

Mean

The **mean** is calculated by dividing the sum of all the values in a distribution by the number of values. It is often referred to as the arithmetic mean.

For a list of N values of a variable X:

$$\text{Mean value, } \overline{X} = \frac{\Sigma X}{N}$$

Example

1 The eight values 34, 67, 43, 71, 92, 67, 39 and 13 have a sum of 426.

The arithmetic mean $= \frac{426}{8} = 53.25$

For values of a variable X with frequencies f:

$$\text{Mean value, } \overline{X} = \frac{\sum fX}{\sum f}$$

Example

2 The frequency distribution of a variable X has 25 values, as shown in Table 5.1.

A column is added to the table to find the sum of these 25 values, and is headed 'fX'.

Table 5.1: Frequency distribution of X

Variable (x)	Frequency (f)	fx
20	2	$2\times20=40$
21	3	$3\times21=63$
22	5	$5\times22=110$
23	6	$6\times23=138$
24	9	$9\times24=216$
	$\sum f=25$	$\sum fx=567$

There are 2 values of 20, 3 values of 21, 5 values of 22, 6 values of 23 and 9 values of 24.

The 25 values of X have a sum of 567, so the arithmetic mean is $\frac{567}{25}=22.68$

The mean of two (or more) sets of data is found from the sum of the combined values and the total number of values in the two sets of data.

Examples

3 A and B are two sets of numbers.

The total of the 20 values in set A is 500.

The total of the 30 values in set B is 840.

Mean of set $A=\frac{500}{20}=25$.

Mean of set $B=\frac{840}{30}=28$

The combined sets have $20+30=50$ values with a sum of $500+840=1340$.

Mean of the combined sets is $\frac{500+840}{20+30}=\frac{1340}{50}=26.8$.

Note that the mean of the combined sets is *not* $\frac{25+28}{2}$.

4 The mean mass of 20 cakes is 80g, and the mean mass of 10 biscuits is 50g.

Total mass of the 20 cakes is $20\times80=1600$ g.

Total mass of the 10 biscuits is $10\times50=500$ g.

Combining the cakes and biscuits, we have 30 items with a total mass of $1600+500=2100$g.

Mean mass of the combined items is $\frac{1600+500}{20+10}=\frac{2100}{30}=70$ g.

Mode

The **mode**, or modal value, is the value that appears most frequently in a distribution. There may be more than one mode.

Examples

1 In the distribution 3, 4, 3, 4, 6, 4, 8, 5, 2, the value 4 appears more frequently than the others, so the mode is 4.

2 In the distribution 17, 19, 14, 17, 15, 14, 20, the values 14 and 17 appear more frequently than the others, so the modes are 14 and 17.

3 The frequency distribution of the variable Y is shown in Table 5.2.

Table 5.2: Frequency distribution of Y

Variable (Y)	40	41	42	43	44
Frequency (f)	9	6	5	3	2

From Table 5.2, $Y = 40$ appears most frequently (9 times), so the modal value is 40.

Median

The **median** is the middle value when all values in a distribution are arranged in order (ranked). The values can be ranked from smallest to largest (ascending), or largest to smallest (descending).

For a list of N values, the median is halfway between the 1st and Nth values.

$$\text{The median is the } \left(\frac{N+1}{2}\right)\text{th value}$$

Examples

1 The distribution 5, 9, 13, 18, 19, 24, 30 is ranked in ascending order.

There are 7 values, so the median is the $\left(\frac{7+1}{2}\right)$th $=$ 4th value, which is 18.

2 The distribution 56, 37, 55, 74, 46, 38 must first be ranked.

In ascending order, we have: 37, 38, 46, 55, 56, 74.

There are 6 values, so the median is the $\left(\frac{6+1}{2}\right)$th $= 3\frac{1}{2}$th value, i.e. between the 3rd and 4th.

The 3rd value is 46 and the 4th value is 55.

Median $=$ mean of the two middle values $= \frac{46 + 55}{2} = 50.5$

For a variable, X, with a total frequency of Σf:

$$\text{The median is the } \left(\frac{[\Sigma f]+1}{2}\right)\text{th value}$$

Example

3 The distribution of X shown in Table 5.3 has 25 values, and their positions are shown in a third column.

Table 5.3: Frequency distribution of X

Variable (X)	Frequency (f)	Positions
30	9	1st to 9th
31	6	10th to 15th
32	5	16th to 20th
33	3	21st to 23rd
34	2	24th to 25th
	$\Sigma f = 25$	

Median is the $\left(\frac{25+1}{2}\right)$th = 13th value, which is 31.

Exercise 5A

1 Find the mean, median and mode of each of the following distributions.

i 12, 17, 17, 39, 41, 44, 54, 67, 87
ii 123, 115, 98, 107, 115, 109, 113, 98
iii 3.5, 1.0, 17.9, 38.3, 1.0, −34.2, 27.8, 48.8, −11.4
iv $-1\frac{1}{4}, 1\frac{1}{2}, -1\frac{3}{4}, 1\frac{1}{4}, 1\frac{3}{4}, -1\frac{1}{2}$
v See Table 5.4.

Table 5.4: Frequency distribution of X

X	10	11	12	13	14	15
Frequency (f)	9	6	4	3	2	1

vi See Table 5.5.

Table 5.5: Frequency distribution of Y

Y	15	16	17	18	19
Frequency (f)	99	99	99	99	99

vii See Table 5.6.

Table 5.6: Frequency distribution of T

T	Frequency (f)
36	8
37	11
38	13
39	16
40	37

viii See Table 5.7.

Table 5.7: Frequency distribution of P

P	Frequency (f)
5.6	8
5.7	87
5.8	40
5.9	35
6.0	21

2 The mean mass of 20 apples is 150g, and the mean mass of 30 bananas is 170g. Find:

i the total mass of the 20 apples,
ii the total mass of the 30 bananas,
iii the total mass of all 50 pieces of fruit,
iv the mean mass of all 50 pieces of fruit.

3 The mean length of 10 pencils is 11.4cm. The mean length of these pencils and 15 crayons combined is 9.3cm. Find:

i the total length of all 25 items,
ii the total length of the 15 crayons,
iii the mean length of the 15 crayons.

4 In a science quiz, 15 boys scored a mean mark of 62%, and 17 girls scored a mean mark of 70%.

i Calculate the total percentage marks obtained by all 32 students.
ii Calculate the mean percentage mark of all 32 students.

5 Martin recorded all the scores out of 10 that he obtained in mathematics quizzes at school, as shown in Table 5.8.

Table 5.8: Mathematics quiz scores

Score (X)	0	1	2	3	4	5	6	7	8	9	10
Frequency (f)	3	5	12	25	31	40	47	25	7	3	2

i Write down Martin's modal score.
ii For how many mathematics quizzes has Martin recorded his score?
iii Find his median score.
iv Calculate:
  a the total of the scores that Martin obtained,
  b his mean score per quiz.

6 A list of N numbers has a sum of 312 and a mean of 20.8. Find the value of N.

7 The mean value of 42 numbers is 3.25. Find the sum of the numbers.

8 The mean value of 13, 19, 27, 42 and q is 30. Find the value of q.

9 The mean length of 7 poles is 2.31m, and the mean length of the shortest 6 of these is 2.25m. Find the length of the longest pole.

10 Three men have masses of 74.9kg, 80.5kg and 88.2kg. When they are joined by a fourth man their mean mass increases by 3.6kg. Find the mass of the fourth man.

11 The mean duration of five movies is 1 hour and 42 minutes, and the mean duration of the longest three of these is 1 hour and 54 minutes. Find the duration of each of the shortest two movies, given that one is 10 minutes longer than the other.

12 During rush hour, Cosmo counted the number of occupants in all the vehicles that passed through a set of traffic lights. His results are shown in Table 5.9.

Table 5.9: Numbers of vehicle occupants

Number of occupants	1	2	3	4	5
Number of vehicles (f)	43	38	x	12	3

Given that the mean number of occupants per vehicle was 2.152, find the value of x.

13 A variable has nine values: 4, 11, 25, 37, 11, 26, 35, 11 and p.

- **i** **a** Which measure of central tendency can be found without knowing the value of p?
  - **b** Write down the value of this measure.
- **ii** If it is known that p is more than 30:
  - **a** which other measure of central tendency can be found?
  - **b** write down the value of this measure.
- **iii** If the remaining measure of central tendency is 22, find the value of p.

14 The bar chart in Figure 5.1 shows the number of sisters that each of the students in a class has.

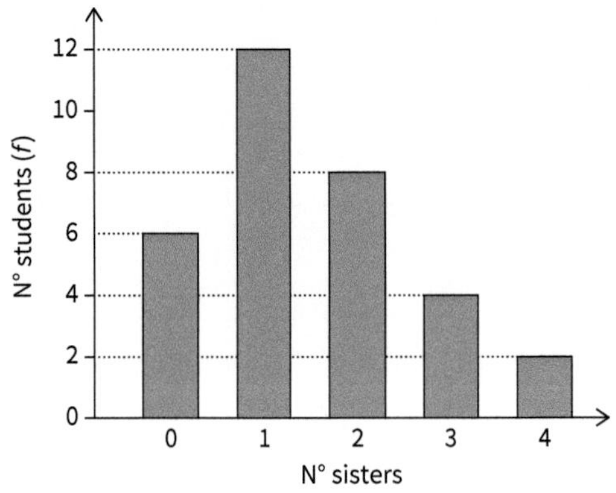

Figure 5.1: Number of sisters for each student

- **i** Tabulate the data shown in the bar chart. Use the headings 'No. sisters (X)' and 'No. students (f)'.
- **ii** Write down the modal number of sisters.
- **iii** Find the median number of sisters.
- **iv** Calculate the mean number of sisters.

15 A survey was made of the number of occupants of each house in a particular street. The results were illustrated in the bar chart shown in Figure 5.2, but one of the bars has been partly erased.

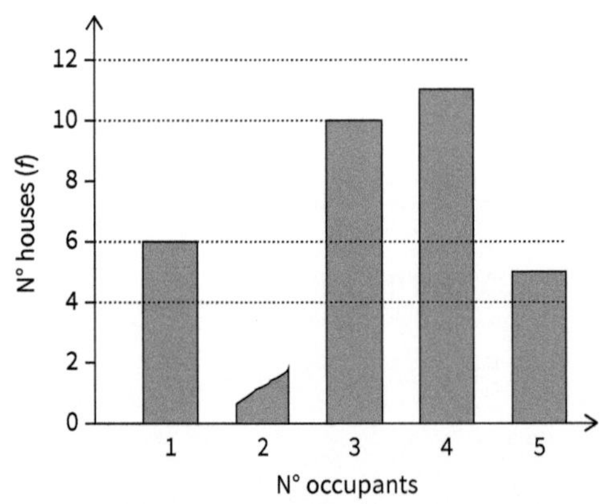

Figure 5.2: Numbers of house occupants

Given that the mean number of occupants per house was exactly 3, find:

- **i** the total number of houses that were surveyed,
- **ii** the total number of occupants in all the houses.

16 The stem-and-leaf diagram in Figure 5.3 shows the number of books on each of the shelves in a school library.

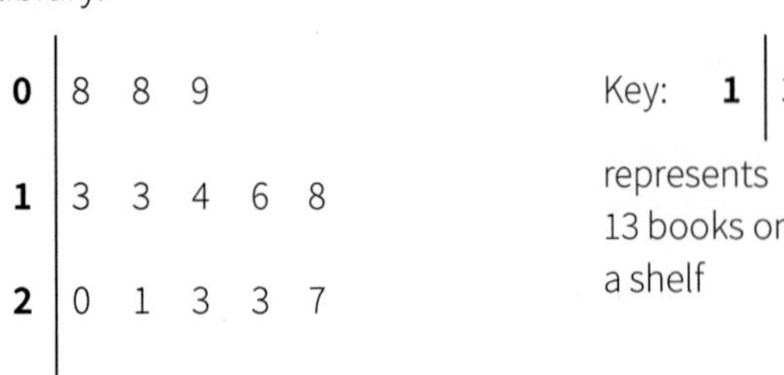

Figure 5.3: Number of books on shelves

- **i** Write down the modal number of books per shelf.
- **ii** Find the median number of books per shelf.
- **iii** Calculate, correct to 1 decimal place, the mean number of books per shelf.

17 The back-to-back stem-and-leaf diagram in Figure 5.4 shows the percentage scores of the students who were the 25 best performers in an examination.

Girls (12)		Boys (13)
4 1	**8**	2
8 6 6	**8**	5 9
3 2 1 0	**9**	0 1 3 3 4 4
8 7 7	**9**	5 6 6 9

Key: 1 | **8** | 2 represents 81% for a girl and 82% for a boy

Figure 5.4: Top examination performers

i State the median score for:

a the 12 girls, **b** the 13 boys.

The 25 students are to be given awards. Before the presentation, they will be lined up in order according to their marks.

ii Describe the student who will stand in the middle of the line.

18 The variable X shown in Table 5.10 has a mean of 9.6.

Table 5.10: Frequency distribution of X

X	Frequency (f)
7	2
8	7
9	11
10	9
11	p
12	$p-3$

Find the value of p.

19 The numbers of books read in the past month by each of a group of children are shown in Table 5.11.

Table 5.11: Numbers of books read

Number of books	0	1	2	3
Number of children (f)	10	8	6	x

i If the mean number of books read is exactly 1, find x.

ii If the modal number of books read is 0, find the largest possible value of x.

iii If the median number of books read is 2, find:

a the smallest possible value of x,

b the largest possible value of x.

20 The frequency distribution of a discrete variable Q is shown in Table 5.12.

Table 5.12: Frequency distribution of Q

Q	1	2	3	4
Frequency (f)	x	$2x$	$3x$	$4x$

i Given that $x \neq 0$, state the modal value of Q.

ii Find the median.

iii Calculate the mean.

iv What type of number must x be for these calculations to be valid?

21 In the distribution of the variable W shown in Table 5.13, p is a positive integer.

Table 5.13: Frequency distribution of W

W	p	$p+1$	$p+3$	$p+5$
Frequency (f)	$p+5$	$p+3$	$p+1$	p

i State the modal value of W.
ii Find the median value of W.

22 The numbers 7, 13, 18, 26 and y are ranked in ascending order, and the mean is equal to the median. Find the value of y.

5.2 Measures of Central Tendency for Grouped Data

Because individual values and their frequencies are usually not shown in grouped data, we are unable to calculate the measures of central tendency exactly, but we are able to calculate **estimates**.

Calculating an Estimate of the Mean

For classes with mid-values M and frequencies f, a calculated estimate of the mean, $\overline{X}$, is given by:

$$\overline{X} = \frac{\Sigma fM}{\Sigma f}$$

Examples

1 The masses of 75 sacks of potatoes are given in Table 5.14.

Table 5.14: Masses of sacks of potatoes

Mass (kg)	No. bags (f)
115-165	15
165-215	37
215-265	23
	$\Sigma f = 75$

Mid-value (M)	fM
140	$15 \times 140 = 2100$
190	$37 \times 190 = 7030$
240	$23 \times 240 = 5520$
	$\Sigma fM = 14650$

Correct to 1 decimal place, an estimate of the mean mass of the sacks of potatoes is

$$\overline{X} = \frac{\Sigma fM}{\Sigma f} = \frac{14\,650}{75} = 195.3\,\text{kg}$$

2 The ages, in completed years, of 50 athletes are given in Table 5.15.

Table 5.15: Athletes' ages

Age (completed years)	17	18	19	20
Number of athletes (f)	6	12	18	14

The 17-year-olds are all aged from 17 up to but not including 18 years, i.e. $17 \le \text{age} < 18$.

The mid-values of the classes are 17.5, 18.5, 19.5 and 20.5.

Estimate of the mean age $= \frac{(17.5 \times 6) + (18.5 \times 12) + (19.5 \times 18) + (20.5 \times 14)}{(6 + 12 + 18 + 14)} = \frac{965}{50} = 19.3$ years.

Lengths given to the nearest centimetre as 3-6cm actually represent 2.5 cm ≤ length < 6.5 cm, but the class mid-value of 4.5cm can be calculated using either: $\frac{3+6}{2} = \frac{2.5+6.5}{2} = 4.5$. Sometimes, as in the example above, using rounded boundaries in the calculations will give a set of wrong mid-values.

- Whenever values have been **approximated**, true class mid-values should be carefully checked using the actual class boundary values.

Modal Class

For a grouped frequency distribution, the **modal class** is the class with the highest **density**. The modal class has the highest frequency per standard interval.

For equal class intervals, the class with the highest frequency is also the class with the highest density.

In all histograms, the modal class has the greatest column height.

Example

The waiting times of 180 train passengers are given in the frequency table in Table 5.16, which is extended to include density calculations.

Table 5.16: Waiting times

Waiting time (minutes)	Number of passengers (f)	Density (passengers per minute)
0–15	75	$75 \div 15 = 5$
15–25	60	$60 \div 10 = 6$
25–30	45	$45 \div 5 = 9$

The modal class is 25-30 minutes, which contains the greatest number of passengers per minute.

Exercise 5B

1 **i** Calculate an estimate of the mean value of V, W, X, Y and Z shown in the frequency distributions in Tables 5.17–5.21.

a Table 5.17: Frequency distribution of V

Length (V cm)	f
$0 < V < 10$	19
$10 \le V < 20$	22
$20 \le V < 30$	19

b Table 5.18: Frequency distribution of W

Mass (W kg)	f
$12 \le W < 20$	13
$20 \le W < 28$	20
$28 \le W < 36$	11

c Table 5.19: Frequency distribution of X

Speed (X km/h)	f
$10 \le X < 25$	64
$25 \le X < 40$	109
$40 \le X < 55$	116
$55 \le X < 70$	111

d Table 5.20: Frequency distribution of Y

Time (Y seconds)	f
10–19	7
20–29	18
30–39	31
40–49	19

Table 5.21: Frequency distribution of Z

e

Height (Z cm)	200–500	600–1000	1100–1300	1400–1700	1800–2100
f	40	50	42	24	44

ii State the modal class of each of the five variables, V, W, X, Y and Z.

2 The lengths, Lcm, of a sample of 'sausages' from a moporoto tree are given in Table 5.22.

Table 5.22: Moporoto fruit lengths

Length (L cm)	$20 \le L < 45$	$45 \le L < 60$	$60 \le L < 70$	$70 \le L < 90$
f	100	75	60	60

i Calculate an estimate of the mean length.

ii Find the modal class.

3 The histogram in Figure 5.5 shows the mean number of people voting per hour at polling stations on Election Day.

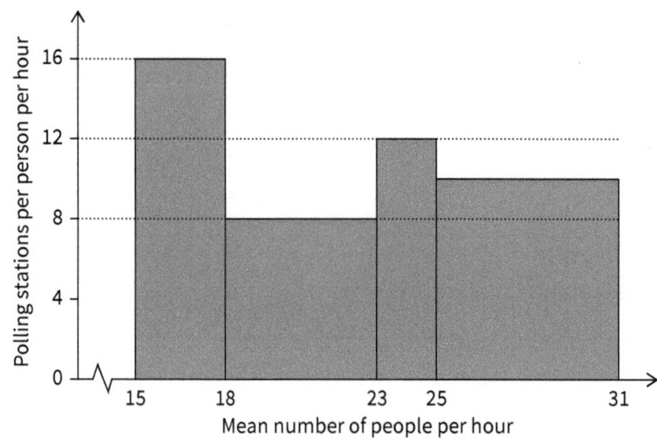

Figure 5.5: Voters per hour

i Find the total number of polling stations that are represented in the histogram.

ii Draw up a grouped frequency table for these data.

iii Calculate an estimate of the mean number of people voting per hour per polling station.

iv Given that each polling station opened from 7.00a.m. to 11.00p.m. on Election Day, calculate an estimate of the total number of people that voted at these polling stations.

4 The 60 members of a rowing club competed in an endurance race. The grouped frequency distribution in Table 5.23 shows the times they took to complete the race.

Table 5.23: Race times

Time taken (t hours and minutes)	Number of rowers (f)
40 m ≤ t < 50 m	4
50 m ≤ t < 1hr 00 m	28
1h 00 m ≤ t < 1hr 05 m	10
1h 05 m ≤ t < 1hr 10 m	12
1h 10 m ≤ t < 1hr 18 m	6

i Write down, in minutes, the mid-value of the class of times that contains 10 rowers.

ii Calculate an estimate of the mean time taken by the rowers, giving your answer in minutes and seconds.

iii Briefly explain why the modal class is 50 m ≤ t < 1hr 00 m.

5 The histogram in Figure 5.6 illustrates the distribution of a variable Y.

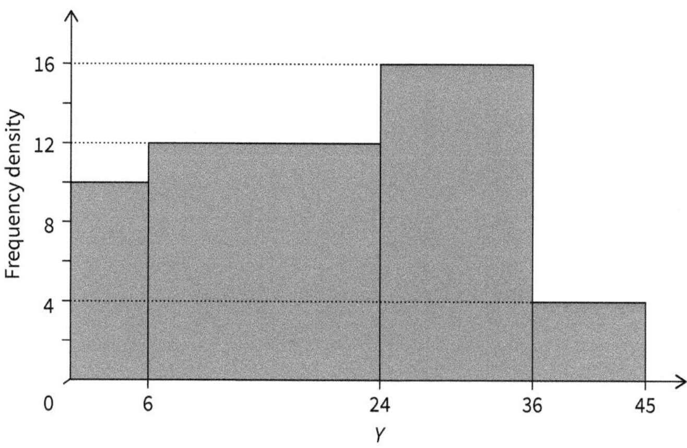

Figure 5.6: Distribution of Y

i State the class with the greatest density.

ii State the class with the greatest frequency.

iii Calculate an estimate of the mean value of Y.

6 Pupils organised a sponsored run in which they ran as many complete laps of the school's track as possible in 20 minutes. The numbers of complete laps run by the pupils are shown in Table 5.24.

Table 5.24: Numbers of complete laps

Number of complete laps	1–4	5–7	8–9	10–12
Number of pupils (f)	56	80	48	16

i Explain why the mid-value of the first class is equal to 3 laps.

The pupils' sponsors donated $2 per completed lap to a local charity.

ii Calculate an estimate of:

a the total amount of money raised,

b the mean number of laps run per pupil.

7 The same novel was given to 5 boys and 7 girls. After reading for 30 minutes, all 5 boys were on the 12th page and all 7 girls were on the 15th page. Calculate an estimate of the mean number of pages that had been read by:

i the 5 boys,

ii the 7 girls,

iii all 12 children.

Estimating the Median From a Cumulative Frequency Diagram

A cumulative frequency diagram illustrates a grouped distribution where points are plotted using upper class boundaries against their cumulative frequency values. Each plotted point indicates how many of the items are less than a particular value.

These diagrams can be used to estimate values in any position within a distribution, including the median. It should be noted that a polygon and a curve are unlikely to give identical estimates.

To locate the median, divide the total frequency by 2. The $\left(\frac{\Sigma f}{2}\right)$th value is used in order to arrive at the same point on the cumulative frequency axis whether working down from the top or up from the bottom.'

For a cumulative frequency distribution with a total frequency Σf

$$\text{The median is the } \left(\frac{\Sigma f}{2}\right) th \text{ value}$$

Examples

1 The cumulative frequency curve in Figure 5.7 shows the lifetimes of a sample of 144 AAA batteries.

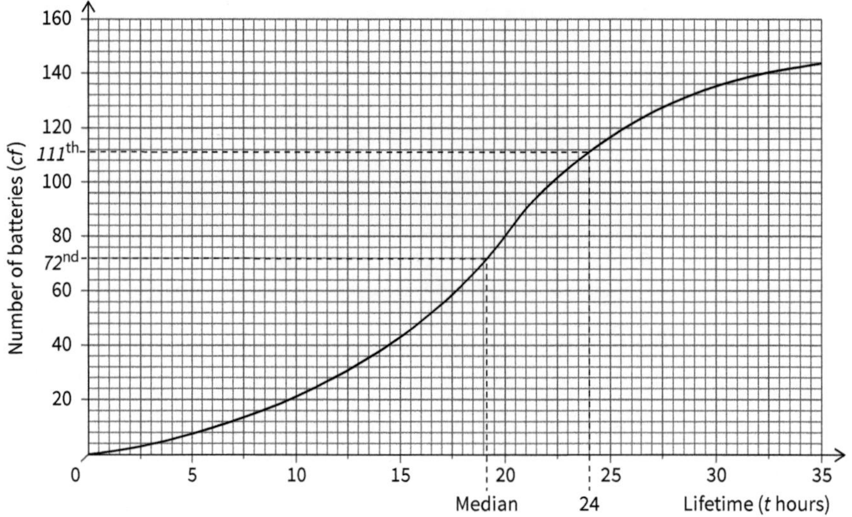

Figure 5.7: Battery lifetimes

As $\Sigma f = 144$, the median will be the lifetime of the $\left(\frac{\Sigma f}{2}\right)$th $= 72$nd battery, which is shown by a dotted line on the diagram to be approximately 19.2 hours.

The second dotted line allows us to make an estimate of the number of batteries that have lifetimes of:

i under 24 hours, which is approximately 111 batteries,

ii 24 hours or more, which is approximately $144 - 111 = 33$ batteries.

2 The body temperatures of 176 patients admitted to a hospital are given in Table 5.25.

Table 5.25: Body temperatures

Body temperature (t°F)	$96 \le t < 98$	$98 \le t < 100$	$100 \le t < 102$	$102 \le t < 104$	
No. patients (f)	94	46	28	8	$\Sigma f = 176$

A cumulative frequency table can now be drawn up, as in Table 5.26.

Table 5.26: Cumulative frequency table of temperatures

Body temperature (t°F)	$t < 96$	$t < 98$	$t < 100$	$t < 102$	$t < 104$
No. patients (cf)	0	94	140	168	176

Points are plotted at (96, 0), (98, 94), (100, 140), (102, 168) and (104, 176).

A cumulative frequency polygon is shown in Figure 5.8.

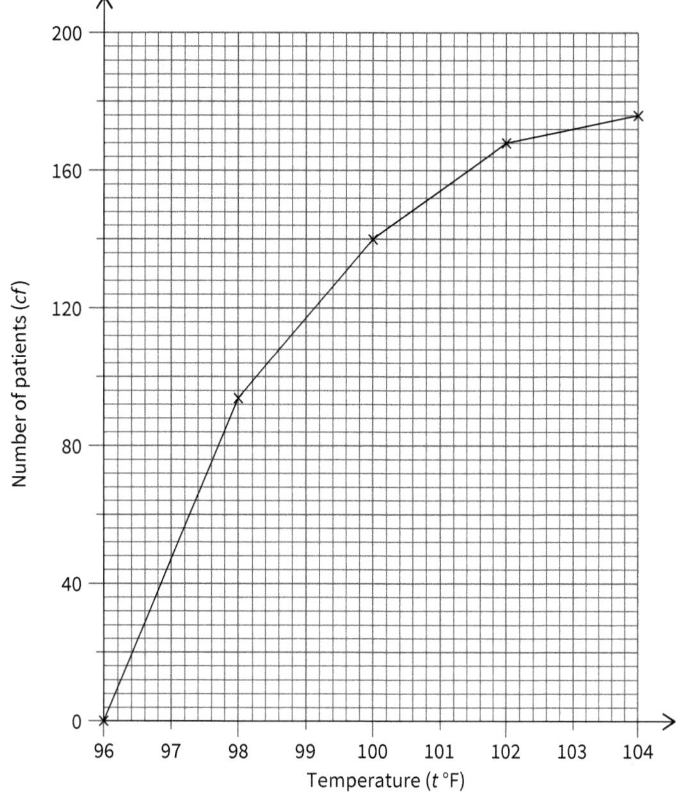

Figure 5.8: Cummulative frequency polygon for temperatures

The median is the $\left(\frac{\Sigma f}{2}\right)$th $= \left(\frac{176}{2}\right)$th $= 88$th value.

Use the polygon to estimate:

i the median temperature,

ii the number of patients with temperatures less than 101°F,

iii the number of patients with temperatures of 101°F or more.

In cases where rounded data are given, points must be plotted at the actual upper class boundaries.

Example

3 An outdoor catering company produced 480 circular pizzas last week.

Data about the pizzas' diameters, to the nearest centimetre, are given in the frequency table in Table 5.27.

Table 5.27: Pizza diameters

Diameter (nearest cm)	No. pizzas (f)
10–19	36
20–29	78
30–49	102
50–79	216
80–99	48
	$\Sigma f = 480$

Table 5.28: Cumulative frequencies for pizza diameters

Diameter (d cm)	No. pizzas (cf)
$d < 9.5$	0
$d < 19.5$	36
$d < 29.5$	114
$d < 49.5$	216
$d < 79.5$	432
$d < 99.5$	480

Before attempting to draw up a cumulative frequency table, the gaps of 1cm between classes must be accounted for by finding the actual class boundaries. These are as shown in the cumulative frequency table in Table 5.28.

Points for a cumulative frequency diagram should be plotted at (9.5, 0), (19.5, 36), . . ., (99.5, 480).

Suppose the points were incorrectly plotted at (9, 0), (19, 36), . . ., (99, 480).

i How would this error affect the shape of the curve or polygon?
ii How would this error affect the position of the curve or polygon?
iii Compare the two different readings that you would obtain for the median diameter of the pizzas.

Exercise 5C

1 The cumulative frequency polygon in Figure 5.9 shows the heights, in centimetres, of 100 adults.

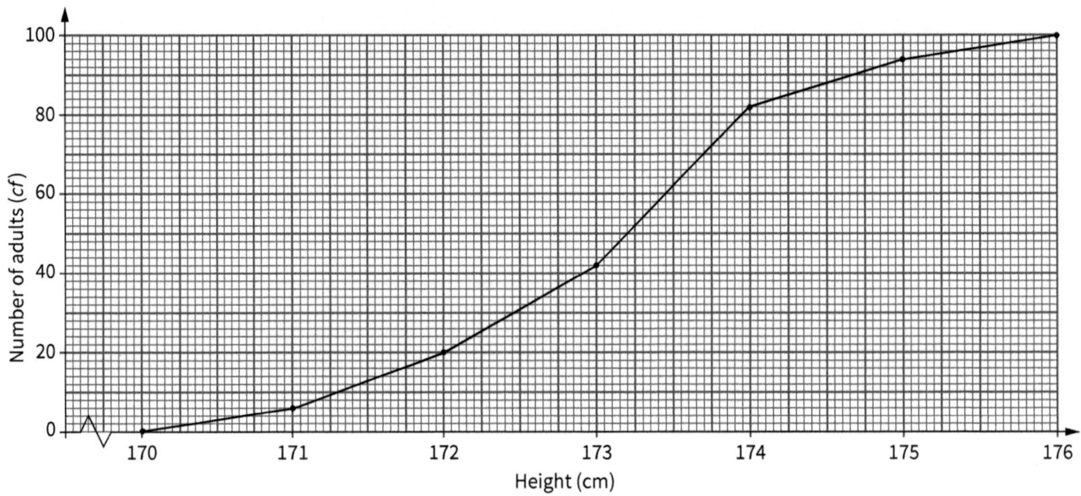

Figure 5.9: Adult heights

Use the polygon to find:

i the number of adults that are less than 172cm,
ii an estimate of the median height,
iii the number of adults that are 175cm or more.

2 Table 5.29 shows values of a continuous variable φ.

Table 5.29: Values of φ

φ	*cf*
$\varphi < 0$	0
$\varphi < 1$	20
$\varphi < 2$	45
$\varphi < 3$	55
$\varphi < 4$	62
$\varphi < 5$	72
$\varphi < 6$	74
$\varphi < 7$	78
$\varphi < 8$	80

i On graph paper, draw and label axes for φ from 0 to 8 using 2cm to represent one unit, and for cumulative frequency from 0 to 80 using 2cm to represent ten units.
ii Plot the nine points from the table, and join consecutive points by ruled lines.
iii Use your cumulative frequency polygon to estimate, to 1 decimal place, the median value of φ.
iv Estimate the number of values of φ that are:
a under 4.5, **b** 2.5 or more.

3 The masses, m grams, of 180 apples are illustrated in the cumulative frequency in Table 5.30.

Table 5.30: Apple masses

Mass (m g)	$m < 154$	$m < 156$	$m < 158$	$m < 160$	$m < 162$	$m < 164$	$m < 166$	$m < 168$	$m < 170$
No. apples (cf)	0	10	22	42	64	104	148	174	180

i On graph paper, draw and label axes for mass from 154 g to 170 g using 1 cm to represent 1 gram, and for cumulative frequency from 0 to 180 using 1 cm for 10 apples.

ii Plot the 9 points from the table, and join consecutive points by ruled lines.

iii Use your polygon to estimate, to 1 decimal place, the median mass of the apples.

iv Estimate the number of apples that are:

a under 163 g, **b** 167 g or more, **c** in the class $159\text{ g} \le m < 161\text{ g}$.

4 The cumulative frequency curve in Figure 5.10 shows the amount earned last month by all of the women employed at a large insurance company.

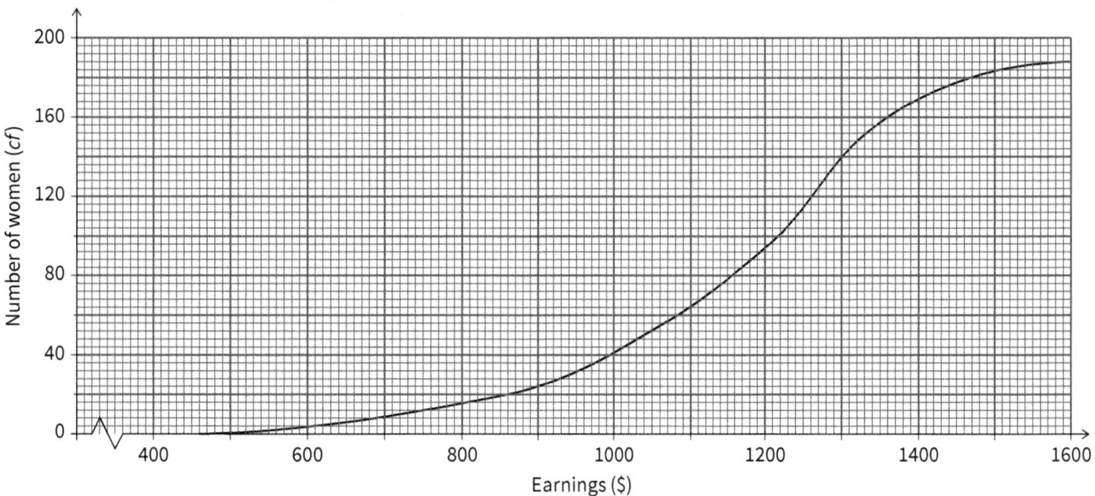

Figure 5.10: Earnings last month

i For last month, write down:

a the number of women that were employed at this company,

b the smallest possible amount earned by any one of these women.

ii From the curve, estimate:

a the median amount earned, **b** the number of women that earned less than \$800,

c the number of women that earned \$1000 or more.

5 The lifetimes of a sample of 320 light bulbs were recorded in Table 5.31.

Table 5.31: Light bulb lifetimes

Lifetime (X hours)	No. light bulbs (cf)
$X < 400$	0
$X < 500$	28
$X < 650$	92
$X < 850$	276
$X < 1000$	300
$X < 1200$	320

i On graph paper, draw and label axes for lifetime from 400 to 1200 hours using 1 cm to represent 50 hours, and 1 cm to represent 20 light bulbs.

ii Construct a cumulative frequency curve.

iii Use the curve you have drawn to estimate:

a the median lifetime of the light bulbs,

b the number of light bulbs with lifetimes of less than 600 hours,

c the number of light bulbs with lifetimes of 950 hours or more.

6 Students investigated the departure times of 200 commercial aircraft. They recorded the number of minutes by which each aircraft's departure was delayed, and their results are shown in Table 5.32.

Table 5.32: Aircraft delay times

Delay time (t minutes)	No. aircraft (f)
$0 \le t < 10$	48
$10 \le t < 20$	98
$20 \le t < 30$	46
$30 \le t < 40$	8
	$\Sigma f = 200$

i Draw up a cumulative frequency table with headings, 'Delay time (t mins)' and 'No. aircraft (cf)'. The first entry in the first column should be $t < 0$, followed by $t < 10$.

ii On graph paper, draw and label suitable axes for delay time and for number of aircraft and, by plotting the points from your table, construct a cumulative frequency polygon.

iii Use the polygon to estimate:

- **a** the median delay time,
- **b** the number of aircraft that were delayed by less than 8 minutes,
- **c** the number of aircraft that were delayed by 25 minutes or more,
- **d** the percentage of aircraft that were delayed by at least 17 minutes,
- **e** the number of aircraft whose delay time was in the range $15 \le t < 25$ minutes

7 Table 5.33 illustrates the heights of the 87 trees in a public park.

Table 5.33: Tree heights

Height (m)	2–5	6–9	10–13	14–17	18–21	22–25	26–29
No. trees (f)	4	6	14	26	25	7	5

i Write down the actual lower boundary and the actual upper boundary of the class that contains 4 trees.

ii Construct a cumulative frequency table to illustrate these data.

iii On graph paper, draw and label axes using 1cm for a height of 2 metres, and 2cm for 10 trees.

iv Construct a cumulative frequency polygon for these data.

v From your polygon, find an estimate of:

- **a** the median height of the trees,
- **b** the number of trees with heights of less than 15.5m,
- **c** the number of trees with heights of at least 24.3m.

vi If there are 30 trees with heights of less than X metres, estimate the value of X.

vii If one-third of the trees have heights of at least Y centimetres, find an estimate of the value of Y.

8 The frequency distribution of a continuous variable, Q, is illustrated in the histogram in Figure 5.11.

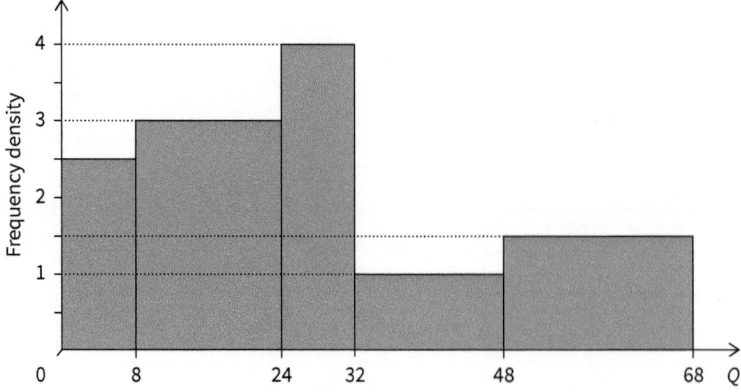

Figure 5.11: Frequency distribution of Q

Given that the class $0 \le Q < 8$ contains 20 values of Q, by constructing a cumulative frequency polygon, or otherwise, find an estimate for the median value of Q.

9 Car batteries have a nominal voltage of 12 volts. A manufacturer tested a sample of 160 batteries, and her results are given in Table 5.34.

Table 5.34: Battery voltages

Voltage (V)	11.8–12.0	12.1–12.3	12.4–12.6	12.7–13.1	13.2–13.4	13.5–13.7
No. batteries (f)	18	26	12	78	18	8

i State the actual lower boundary and the actual upper boundary of the class containing 78 batteries.

ii Construct a cumulative frequency table for the battery voltages.

iii On graph paper, draw and label axes for voltage using 4cm to represent 0.5 volts, and 2cm to represent 20 batteries. Construct a cumulative frequency polygon to illustrate these data.

iv Use the polygon to estimate:

a the median voltage,

b the number of batteries producing less than 12.4 volts,

c the number of batteries producing 13 volts or more.

10 i There are 800 people living on Ascotta Island and their ages to the nearest year are given in Table 5.35.

Table 5.35: Islanders' ages

Age (X years)	$X < 10$	$X < 15$	$X < 25$	$X < 40$	$X < 50$	$X < 65$	$X < 80$
No. people (cf)	48	96	540	660	710	774	800

a Draw and label axes with 2cm representing 10 years, and 2cm representing 100 people.

b Construct a cumulative frequency polygon for the data.

c Use your polygon to estimate the median age in years and months.

ii The neighbouring island of Zollora also has a population of 800 people. On Zollora the median age is 45. There are 200 people under 29 years, 600 people under 69 years, and everyone living on Zollora is less than 80 years of age.

a Use the data given above to plot points onto the same sheet of graph paper, and construct a cumulative frequency polygon to illustrate the age distribution of the people living on Zollora.

Label the polygons A and Z.

The inhabitants of Zollora have challenged the inhabitants of Ascotta to a game of football.

b Which team do you think is most likely to win the game? What evidence do the diagrams give to support your answer?

11 A batch of 520 computer processors was tested for the time taken to delete 100 megabytes of data.

The results are presented in Table 5.36.

Table 5.36: Deletion times

Time taken (t seconds)	$t < 0$	$t < 0.05$	$t < 0.15$	$t < 0.40$	$t < 0.65$	$t < 0.80$
No. processors (cf)	0	120	250	400	490	520

i On graph paper, label a horizontal axis for time taken, using 1cm to represent 0.05 seconds, and a vertical axis for cumulative frequency, using 1cm to represent 20 processors.

ii Use the table to plot six points and draw a cumulative frequency curve.

iii Use your curve to estimate the number of processors satisfying each of these inequalities,

a $t < 0.30$, **b** $t \geq 0.60$, **c** $0.320 \leq t < 0.525$.

The slowest 5% of these processors failed the test.

iv Estimate the time limit allowed for a processor not to fail the test.

5.3 Features of the Measures of Central Tendency

When selecting a measure of central tendency as the average value in a distribution, some thought should be given to the appropriateness of each measure. Depending on the type of data and their context, the characteristics of one measure are likely to make it more suitable than the others. A selection of their features and characteristics are given in Table 5.37.

Table 5.37: Features of the measures of central tendency

Mode	Useful to manufacturers Unlikely to be affected by **extreme values** The only measure that can be used for qualitative variables Ignores most values in the data No use in any calculations
Median	Can be found if extreme values are unknown Not affected by extreme values Ignores most values in the data No use in any calculations Can only be used for quantitative variables
Arithmetic mean	The most commonly understood average Makes use of all the values in a distribution Can be used in further calculations Can be affected by extreme values All values must be known

Exercise 5D

1 Which measure of central tendency is the most useful to a shoemaker? Give a reason for your answer.

2 For each sentence below, indicate which measure of central tendency the word 'average' refers to:

A: The average car being driven in Namibia is white.
B: Most people living in New York have more than the average number of fingers.

C: The average number of children in the eight classes at a primary school is 23.25.
D: Half the students scored less than the average number of marks in a history examination.

3 If you were asked to find the average height of all the students in your class, which measure of central tendency could you find by measuring the heights of, at most, two students?

4 Thirty unskilled workers and one highly paid manager are employed at a factory. A government official wants to know the average weekly earnings of those employed at the factory.

Which of the three measures of central tendency is likely to give the least representative average? Explain your answer.

5 Sam has recorded the favourite colours of his 25 classmates. Which measure(s) of central tendency will he be able to find for his data?

6 A factory produces small glass ornaments which are checked before being sent to retailers.

Table 5.38 shows Y, the number of damaged ornaments found per day for a period of 100 days.

Table 5.38: Numbers of damaged ornaments

No. damaged ornaments (Y)	0	1	2	3	4	5	6 - z
No. days (f)	33	18	15	12	9	8	5

i Find the median number of damaged ornaments found per day.
ii State the mode and explain why, in this case, it is not a good measure of central tendency.

An estimate of the mean value of Y is calculated to be exactly 2 damaged ornaments per day.

iii Find the upper boundary, z, which has been used in the calculation.

7 By very careful measurement, Anne has calculated the mean mass of her two cats to be 3.87315kg. Explain why this is an estimate.

6 Weighted Averages

Learning Objectives

In this chapter you will learn:

- How to calculate a weighted average of two sets of related data
- To appreciate the importance of index numbers
- How to calculate price relatives
- About the meaning, significance and limitations of index numbers in relation to prices, costs and expenses
- How to calculate crude and standardised rates for mortality, fertility and accidents
- How to interpret crude and standardised rates, and to understand their limitations

Introduction

The task of dealing with a single set of data is usually not too complicated, but what happens when two (or more) sets of related data are combined? Are the sets equally important or is one more significant than the other? When sets of data are combined, measures such as averages are *weighted* in some way.

Crude data, such as numbers of births, deaths and accidents, all need to be recorded and analysed by governments so that they can plan such things as education and healthcare.

6.1 Combining Sets of Data

The most commonly known average is the mean. It is calculated by dividing the sum of a set of values by the number of values.

However, the mean of two sets of combined data can only found by taking the average of the means of the original sets if the original sets carry equal **weight**.

The simplest weights are frequencies.

For example, a 40-year-old man has 10-year-old twins. The mean of their ages is *not* $\frac{40+10}{2} = 25$, but $\frac{(1\times40)+(2\times10)}{3} = 20$. The ages 40 and 10 have weights of 1 and 2, respectively.

Examples

1 Two boys have 12 sweets each, and three girls have 22 sweets each.

If all of the children and all of the sweets are combined for sharing, then five children have $(2 \times 12) + (3 \times 22) = 90$ sweets to share. On average, they have $\frac{90}{5} = 18$ sweets each.

The combined average of 18 is *not* $\frac{12+22}{2}$.

2 In a test taken by 4 boys and 6 girls, the boys obtained a mean score of 35% and the girls obtained a mean score of 75%.

For all 10 students:

$$\text{Mean score} = \frac{\text{total score of all students}}{\text{total number of students}} = \frac{\text{total score of boys} + \text{total score of girls}}{\text{number of boys} + \text{number of girls}}$$

$$= \frac{(4 \times 35) + (6 \times 75)}{6 + 4} = \frac{590}{10} = 59\%$$

There are more girls than boys, so the girls' mean score of 75% has a weight of 6, and the boys' mean score of 35% has a weight of 4 - see Figure 6.1.

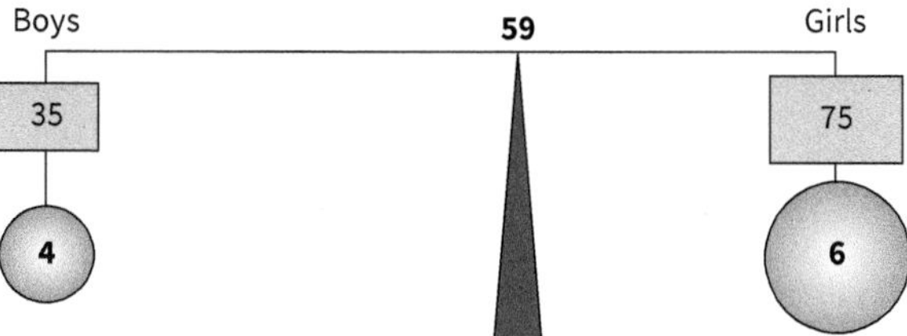

Figure 6.1: Weighted test scores

The combined mean score of all ten students is 59%.

This combined mean score is a **weighted average**.

For a set of weighted numbers:

$$\text{Weighted average} = \frac{\sum[\text{weight} \times \text{number}]}{\sum[\text{weights}]}$$

Examples

3 Find a weighted average of 64 and 40, using weights of 5 and 7, respectively.

$$\text{Weighted average} = \frac{(5 \times 64) + (7 \times 40)}{5 + 7} = \frac{600}{12} = 50$$

Exercise 6A

1 Find the weighted average of 16 and 21 using weights of 3 and 2, respectively.

2 Use weights of 11 and 14, respectively, to find a weighted average of 2.4 and 3.8.

3 In a business studies examination, which was taken by 382 boys and 418 girls, the boys obtained a mean score of 45% and the girls obtained a mean score of 62%. Calculate, to 1 decimal place, the mean score of all the students who took the examination.

4 A group of 134 girls and 166 boys sat an English literature examination. The boys obtained a mean score of 68.5% and the mean score for all the students was 64.35%. Calculate the mean score for the girls.

5 Students sat two mathematics papers, A and B. The teacher decided that paper B was twice as important as paper A, so he calculated the students' overall average scores by assigning a weight of 1 to paper A, and a weight of 2 to paper B.

Table 6.1 shows some of the scores of four students.

Table 6.1: Mathematics examination scores

Name	Score on paper A	Score on paper B
Daniel	62	47
Eva	38	77
Aesop		60
Rina	55	

i Find the weighted average score awarded to:
a Daniel, **b** Eva.
ii Aesop was awarded a weighted average score of 56. Find his score on paper A.
iii Rina was awarded a weighted average score of 85. Find her score on paper B.

6 A boy made a journey on foot and then by bicycle. He walked for 1 hour 30 minutes at an average speed of 6 km/h and then cycled 12 km at 16 km/h.

i How far did he walk?
ii For what length of time did he cycle?
iii Calculate his average speed for the whole journey.

7 **i** A chemist mixed two non-reacting powders, *A* and *B*, during an experiment. She mixed 7.2 g of *A*, which had a volume of 6 cm^3, with 4 g of *B*, which had a volume of 8 cm^3.
a Write down the total mass and the total volume of the mixture.
b Hence, find the density of the mixture.

ii During another experiment, a chemist melted and mixed two metals *P* and *Q*, which had densities of 2.7 g/cm^3 and 3.1 g/cm^3, respectively, to make an alloy. She mixed 4 cm^3 of *P* with 49.6 g of *Q*.
a Find the mass of *P* and the volume of *Q* that she used.
b Calculate the density of the alloy.

8 A weighted average of 17.5 has been calculated for the values 13 and 21. Given that 21 had a weight of 9, find the weight that was used for 13.

6.2 Index Numbers

Index numbers are used to show proportional changes in values and costs over a period of time. They are used in relation to:

- prices of goods and services
- cost of living
- costs involved in running a business
- values of stocks and shares.

Price relatives

Price **relatives** are index numbers showing proportional changes in the prices of items between years.

An index number of 100 is assigned to the price of an item in a chosen base year, and all past and future prices for that item are given index numbers relative to 100.

- The price relative of an item and its price are always in the same proportion.
- Price relatives show the percentage change in the price of an item since the base year.

$$\frac{\text{Price relative in year } A}{\text{Price in year } A} = \frac{100}{\text{Price in base year}}$$

$$\text{Price relative in year } A = \frac{\text{Price in year } A}{\text{Price in base year}} \times 100$$

Examples

1 A bottle of shampoo cost \$4.00 in 2015. In 2016 the price had increased to \$4.60. Find the price relative for 2016, based on the price in 2015.

The base year price of \$4.00 is assigned an index number of 100.

$$\frac{\text{price relative in 2016}}{\text{price in 2016}} = \frac{\text{price relative in 2015}}{\text{price in 2015}}$$

$$\frac{\text{price relative in 2016}}{4.60} = \frac{100}{4.00}$$

$$\text{Price relative in 2016} = \frac{4.60}{4.00} \times 100 = 115$$

The price relative of 115 shows that the price of the item increased by 15% between 2015 and 2016.

2 In 2014 the cost of a one-way flight from Bombay to Ouagadougou was \$500. In 2015 the cost was \$485 and the price relative for 2016, based on the 2014 price, is 108.

Find:

i the price relative in 2015 based on the 2014 price,

ii the price in 2015.

An index of 100 is assigned to the price in 2014 (the base year).

The data is simplified if it is tabulated, as shown in Table 6.2.

Table 6.2: Flight costs

Year	Cost (\$)	Price relative
2014	500	100
2015	485	a
2016	b	108

i $\frac{a}{485} = \frac{100}{500}$

$a = \frac{485}{500} \times 100$

$a = 97$

A decrease of 3%

ii $\frac{b}{108} = \frac{500}{100}$

$b = \frac{500}{100} \times 108$

$b = 540$

The price in 2016 is \$540

Exercise 6B

1 The prices of some items are given in dollars for last year and this year in Table 6.3.
Find the price relative of each item this year, using last year as the base year in each case.

Table 6.3: Item prices

	Last year		This year	
	Price ($)	Price relative	Price ($)	Price relative
A	8.00	100	10.00	
B	15.00	100	16.50	
C	3.60	100	5.40	
D	21.50	100	43.00	
E	20.00	100	19.00	
F	16.40	100	16.81	

2 Calculate last year's price for each of the five items *P* to *T* shown in Table 6.4.

Table 6.4: Relative prices

	Last year		This year	
	Price ($)	Price relative	Price ($)	Price relative
P		100	21.00	105
Q		100	18.90	108
R		100	46.40	145
S		100	20.24	92
T		100	12.95	87.5

3 A coat cost $80 in 2014. The price relatives, based on the 2014 price, were 110 in 2015 and 115 in 2016.
Find the price of the coat in:

i 2015, **ii** 2016.

4 Table 6.5 shows the prices of a particular computer from 2013 to 2015.

Table 6.5: Computer prices

Year	2013	2014	2015	2016
Price ($)	1000	1050	910	

i Using 2013 as the base year, find:
a the price relative for 2014, **b** the price relative for 2015.

Using 2013 as the base year, the price relative for the computer in 2016 is 87.5.

ii What is the price of the computer in 2016?

5 Some of the prices in dollars of two items, A and B, are given for the years 2014 to 2016 in Table 6.6.

Table 6.6: Prices of A and B

Item	2014	2015	2016
A	60.00	58.80	68.70
B	80.00		85.12

i Using 2014 as the base year, find the price relative of item A in:
a 2015, **b** 2016.

The price relative of item B in 2015, based on the 2014 price, was 112.

ii What was the price of item B in 2015?
iii Find the price relative of item B in 2016, using 2015 as the base year.

6 The price relatives of three types of fuel are given for the years 2006, 2011 and 2016 in Table 6.7.

Table 6.7: Fuel prices

Fuel	2006	2011	2016
Petrol	100	112.5	135
Diesel	100	109	109
Paraffin	100	105	106

i What is the significance of the three 100s in the column for 2006?
ii What is the significance of the two price relatives of 109 in the row for diesel?
iii One unit of paraffin cost $2.00 in 2006. How much did one unit of paraffin cost in 2011?
iv One litre of petrol cost $0.81 in 2011. How much did one litre of petrol cost in 2006?
v Calculate the cost of 5 litres of petrol in 2016.

Simple combined index numbers

A simple combined index of weighted items, which is sometimes called a *cost of living index*, can be calculated to compare the cost of items in one year with the cost of the same items in a base year:

$$\text{Simple combined index for year A} = \frac{\text{Total cost in year A}}{\text{Total cost in base year}} \times 100$$

The index will indicate the percentage change in the total cost of the items. This will only be relevant if exactly the same items are bought in those two years.

Examples

An average school student used 25 pens, 12 pencils and 6 erasers per year in 2015.

In 2015 these items cost 80 cents, 35 cents and 25 cents, respectively.

In 2016 these same items cost 95 cents, 45 cents and 30 cents, respectively.

Calculate a simple combined index for these three weighted items.

Table 6.8: Stationery costs

Item	2015	2016	Average number purchased/Weight
Pen	80	95	25
Pencil	35	45	12
Eraser	25	30	6

The numbers are tabulated in Table 6.8. The quantities of items purchased in the base year act as the weights.

Based on 2015 costs, a combined index for 2016 $= \dfrac{\text{total cost in 2016}}{\text{total cost in base year}} \times 100$

$$= \frac{(25\times95)+(12\times45)+(6\times30)\text{ cents}}{(25\times80)+(12\times35)+(6\times25)\text{ cents}} \times 100$$

$$= \frac{3095}{2570} \times 100 = 120.4 \text{ (The index has no units)}$$

The index of 120.4 shows that the total cost of the items will increase by 20.4%, but only if the same quantity of each item is bought in 2016 as in 2015.

Exercise 6C

1 Peter is a keen sports fan. Every year he pays to attend 10 football matches and 8 cricket matches.

The cost of attending each match is given for last year and this year in Table 6.9.

Table 6.9: Sports match prices

	Cost last year ($)	Cost this year ($)
Each football match	40.00	50.00
Each cricket match	25.00	27.50

By calculating the total cost for both years, find a simple combined index for this year's costs based on last year's costs.

2 Every year Joyce attends a monthly yoga class and a weekly pilates class. The cost of each class is shown for last year and this year in Table 6.10.

Table 6.10: Exercise class costs

	Cost last year ($)	Cost this year ($)
Each yoga class	30.00	32.00
Each pilates class	8.00	9.50

By calculating the total cost for both years, find a simple combined index for this year's costs based on last year's costs.

3 Last year Tsaone kept 3 tortoises, 7 cats and 25 tropical fish at her house as pets. The annual cost of feeding a tortoise was $800, a cat was $350 and a tropical fish was $10.

i Calculate how much it cost her to feed all of her pets last year.

This year the annual cost of feeding a tortoise is $1000, a cat is $400 and a tropical fish is $15.

ii Calculate the amount that you would expect Tsaone to spend on food for her pets this year.

iii Find a simple combined index, to 1 decimal place, for the costs this year, based on last year's costs.

iv What assumptions have you made in calculating the index?

4 An average family buys 150 kg of potatoes, 60 kg of cabbages and 85 kg of onions per year.

Table 6.11: Vegetable costs

Item	2014	2015	2016
Potato	0.28	0.34	0.40
Cabbage	0.18	0.22	0.25
Onion	0.32	0.35	0.38

The price of 1 kg of each of these three items is given in dollars ($) for 2014, 2015 and 2016 in Table 6.11.

i Giving the answers exactly, and using 2014 as the base year, find a simple combined index for these items in:

a 2015, **b** 2016.

ii Find a simple combined index for the items in 2016, using 2015 as the base year.

The predicted simple combined index for 2017, using 2014 as the base year, is 150. For 2017, the predicted cost for 1 kg potatoes is $0.46, and for 1 kg cabbage it is $0.28.

iii Calculate, in dollars to 2 decimal places, the predicted cost of 10 kg of onions in 2017.

Weighted Aggregate Index Numbers

Costs are made up of spending on a combination of items.

An **aggregate** index is a weighted average of the price relatives of a combination of items.

Suitable weights can be found from base year quantities or from base year expenditure.

An aggregate index for any chosen year will be accurate only if the base year weights are valid in the chosen year.

$$\text{Aggregate index} = \frac{\Sigma[\text{weight} \times \text{price relative}]}{\Sigma[\text{weights}]}$$

Examples

Talula runs her business from a small office. Last year her business costs were:

- Office rental at $150 per month
- 2400 units of electricity at $0.50 per unit
- 7500 telephone units at $0.40 per unit.

This year:

- Office rental has increased by $9 per month
- Electricity prices have increased to $0.55 per unit
- Telephone usage prices increased by $0.02 per unit.

To calculate an aggregate index for Leslie's costs this year based on last year's costs, we need:

i Suitable weights for the three items,

ii Price relatives for the three items.

i Weights based on expenditure are:

Office rental $= \$150 \times 12 \quad = \$1800$
Electricity $= \$0.50 \times 2400 = \$1200$
Telephone $= \$0.40 \times 500 \quad = \$3000$

Weights are $1800:1200:3000 = 3:2:5$.

ii Price relatives are:

Office rental: $\frac{159}{150} \times 100 = 106$

Electricity: $\frac{55}{50} \times 100 = 110$

Telephone: $\frac{42}{40} \times 100 = 105$

Price relatives are $106:110:105$.

$$\text{Aggregate index} = \frac{(3 \times 106) + (2 \times 110) + (5 \times 105)}{(3+2+5)} = 106.3$$

The aggregate index suggests that Talula's costs will be 6.3% higher this year than last year. This may not be accurate, as the weights were calculated using last year's costs. Talula may move to a different office or use a different number of electricity and telephone units this year.

Exercise 6D

1 Calculate, correct to 2 decimal places, an aggregate index using:

i Price relatives of 116, 103 and 96 with weights of 15, 7 and 8, respectively.
ii Price relatives of 112.5, 88.75 and 146 with weights of 11, 23 and 16 respectively.
iii Price relatives of 92, 105.5, 117 and 98 with weights of 25, 40, 23 and 12, respectively.

2 The three price relatives 104, 107.5 and 118 produce an aggregate index of 112.5 when weights of 13, 20 and x, respectively, are applied to them. Calculate the value of x.

3 The prices of three items, A, B and C, in 2015 and 2016 are shown in Table 6.12.

Table 6.12: Item prices

	Price ($) in year	
Item	**2015**	**2016**
A	10.00	12.00
B	8.50	9.52
C	6.00	5.76

i Calculate the price relative for each item in 2016 using 2015 as the base year.
ii Using a weight of 5 for item A, 11 for item B, and 4 for item C, calculate an aggregate index for 2016 using 2015 as the base year.

4 During 2015 a small school's budget was spent on salaries, equipment and maintenance materials. The amounts spent were \$100 000, \$25 000 and \$12 500, respectively.

i Suggest suitable simplified expenditure weights that could be used to calculate an aggregate index for the cost of running the school.

In 2016 all school staff received a salary increase of 9%, the cost of equipment rose by 13% and the cost of maintenance materials decreased by 2%.

ii Write down the price relatives for the three items in 2016, based on 2015 prices.
iii Calculate an aggregate index for running the school in 2016, using 2015 as the base year. Give your answer correct to 2 decimal places.
iv The cost of running the school in 2015 was \$137 500. Use the index that you have calculated to find an estimate of the cost of running the school in 2016.
v Suggest two reasons why the index may not give an accurate estimate for the costs in 2016.

5 To run her business last year, a woman spent \$1200, \$1250 and \$1200 on items A, B and C.

The costs per unit of these three items were \$6, \$5 and \$4, respectively.

i Suggest suitable weights that could be used to calculate an aggregate index for her costs based on:
a last year's expenditure, **b** quantities purchased last year.

ii Given that the unit costs of these three items are \$5.70, \$5.15 and \$4.10, respectively this year, find:
a price relatives for the three items this year based on last year's prices,
b an aggregate index for this year based on last year's expenditure, correct to 1 decimal place,
c an aggregate index for this year based on last year's quantities, correct to 1 decimal place.

6 In order to calculate an aggregate cost of housing index, a woman used her housing expenses in 2015 as the base for her calculations. In 2015 she spent the following:

- \$480 on maintenance,
- \$280 per month on mortgage repayments,
- 1280 units of electricity at \$0.75 per unit.

i Calculate the amount that she spent on:
a mortgage repayments in 2015, **b** electricity in 2015.

ii Use the information given and your answers to **i** to suggest, in simplified form, suitable weights that the woman could use to calculate an aggregate cost-of-housing index.

From 2015 to 2016 the cost of each maintenance job increased by 12%, her monthly mortgage repayments decreased by \$8.40, and the cost of one unit of electricity increased to \$0.81.

iii Calculate the price relatives for maintenance, mortgage repayments and electricity in 2016, using 2015 as the base year.
iv Use the weights and price relatives in **ii** and **iii** to find an aggregate cost-of-housing index for 2016.
v If the woman used only 1250 units of electricity in 2016, and if the index that you have calculated is actually correct, what were her maintenance costs in 2016?

7 The prices of the three items of expenditure incurred by a businesswoman in 2014 and 2016 are given in Table 6.13.

Table 6.13: Business expenses

Item	2014 prices (\$)	2016 prices (\$)
A	48.00	49.92
B	30.00	32.20
C	28.50	27.36

During 2014 the businesswoman spent:

- \$2400 on item A,
- \$1350 on item B,
- \$228 on item C.

i Calculate the price relatives for each of the three items in 2016 based on prices in 2014.
ii Find suitable simplified weights based on quantities purchased by the woman in 2014.
iii Use the price relatives and weights to find, to 5 significant figures, an aggregate business index for 2016 based on 2014.
iv Calculate the expected average annual percentage increase in the businesswoman's costs.

8 To find an aggregate cost-of-motoring index, a man based his calculations on his expenses in 2015.

In 2015 he spent:

- \$46 per month on tax and insurance,
- \$480 on maintenance,
- 1824 litres of fuel, costing \$0.75 per litre.

i Using the man's expenditure in 2015, suggest suitable simplified weights that he could use to calculate an aggregate cost-of-motoring index.

By 2016, this man's tax and insurance costs had increased to \$62.10 per month; he spent only \$420 on maintenance, and the price of fuel had increased by \$0.18 per litre.

ii Calculate the price relatives for the three items in 2016, using 2015 as the base year.
iii Calculate, to 2 decimal places, an aggregate cost-of-motoring index for 2016, based on costs in 2015.
iv Give one reason why the index you have calculated in **iii** may not give a true reflection of the change in the man's motoring costs between 2015 and 2016.

6.3 Crude and Standardised rates

A rate includes the measurement of at least two quantities, and one of these is commonly a length of time or the size of a population.

All societies benefit greatly from the calculation of rates, especially in areas such as public health, policing and employment; such knowledge assists governments and local authorities to direct their resources where they are most needed.

Examples of rates that can be calculated are:

- Deaths per thousand of the population per year (mortality rate)
- Incidents of malaria per ten thousand of the population per year
- Unemployment per hundred of the working-age population
- Fatal road accidents per million kilometres of driving
- Births per thousand of the female population per year (fertility rate)
- Defective items per thousand items produced at a factory

Crude rates

These are simple rates that give the total number of events occurring in a population without reference to the individuals or subgroups (strata) within the population.

Crude death rates and birth rates, for example, measure the number of deaths and births per thousand (‰) of the population, with no reference to the ages of those in the population.

$$\text{Crude birth / mortality rate} = \frac{\text{Number of births}}{\text{Original population size}} \times 1000‰$$

$$\text{Crude birth / fertility rate} = \frac{\text{Number of births}}{\text{Original population size}} \times 1000‰$$

[Note that a crude birth rate may be calculated per thousand of the female population]

Assuming no immigration and no emigration:

New population = Original population + Number of births – Number of deaths

A teacher could calculate a crude absence rate for two classes over a period of 20 days as:

$$\text{Crude absence rate} = \frac{\text{Number of absences per class in 20 days}}{\text{Class size} \times 20} \times 100\%$$

This would give a rate of absence per student per class over a period of 100 days.

Using such rates to compare the classes' dedication to their education would be of little use because the reasons for absence such as genuine illness, truancy, family commitments, the weather and available transport have not been taken into account.

Accident rates are associated with dangerous activities such as sport, driving and working in heavy industries.

In general, crude rates cannot be used to compare one population with another, unless the populations are identical.

Examples

1 At the start of the year the population of a city was 125 000, and there were 1425 deaths during the year.

$$\text{Crude death rate} = \frac{1425}{125\,000} \times 1000 = 11.4‰.$$

2 A town with a population of 68 000 in January had a crude birth rate of 9.75‰.

$$9.75 = \frac{\text{Number of births}}{68\,000} \times 1000$$

$$\text{Number of births} = \frac{9.75 \times 68\,000}{1000} = 663$$

3 Last year, 3498 people died in a city where the crude death rate was 8.25‰.

$$8.25 = \frac{3498}{\text{Original population}} \times 1000$$

$$\text{Original population} = \frac{3498}{8.25} \times 1000 = 424\,000$$

4 Last year the 35 vehicles belonging to a delivery company were driven 6 800 000 miles and, during this time, they were involved in 26 accidents.

The accident rate can be measured in accidents per million miles:

$$\text{Accident rate} = \frac{\text{Number of accidents}}{\text{Number of miles driven}} \times 1\,000\,000$$

$$= \frac{26}{6\,800\,000} \times 1\,000\,000$$

$$= 3.82 \text{ accidents per million miles}$$

Or the accident rate can be measured per thousand vehicles per year:

$$\text{Accident rate} = \frac{\text{Number of accidents}}{\text{Number of vehicles}} \times 1000$$

$$= \frac{26}{35} \times 1000$$

$$= 743 \text{ accidents per thousand vehicles per year}$$

5 The 400 employees at Brickbuild Construction Ltd. suffered a total of 19 accidents last year.

The accident rate, measured per 1000 employees per year $= \frac{19}{400} \times 1000 = 47.5‰$ per year.

Exercise 6E

1 The population of a small village was 4400, and during the year 33 people died. Find the crude death rate.

2 Last year, in a small town whose population numbered 20 000, the mortality rate was 5.6‰. How many people died in this town during the year?

3 In a location where the crude death rate was 7.44‰ there were 125 deaths last year. Find, to the nearest hundred, the population of the location at the beginning of last year.

4 Last year, the crude death rate of a city in which 5100 died was 8‰. The crude birth rate for the city's entire population was 12‰.

i Find the population of the city at the beginning of last year.
ii Assuming there was no migration in or out of the city, find the population at the end of last year.

5 A transport company's 85 vehicles had an accident rate of 16 accidents per million miles driven last year. If the company's vehicles had been driven a mean distance of 75 000 miles, calculate the number of accidents last year.

6 There were 72 accidents amongst the 144 workers at a steel plant last year. Each worker at the plant worked for 40 hours per week, and for 50 weeks per year. Find the accident rate measured in accidents per worker per 100 000 hours of work.

7 MacTar is a company engaged in the road-building industry. During the last 12 months, its 25 site supervisors suffered 2 accidents and its 313 manual workers suffered 31 accidents. Calculate a crude accident rate, in accidents per 1000 employees, for its:

i site supervisors, **ii** manual workers, **iii** site supervisors and manual workers combined.

8 A steel fabrication plant employs 83 fitters, 17 administrators and 20 drivers.

Table 6.14 shows the number of personal accidents suffered at the plant last year.

Table 6.14: Steel plant accident numbers

	Fitters	Administrators	Drivers
Total number of accidents	31	1	2
Number of non-serious accidents	27	1	1

i For each of the three classes of employee, calculate, to the nearest whole number, the crude accident rate per 1000 employees.
ii Which of the three classes of employee suffered the highest crude serious accident rate? Give evidence to support your answer.

9 The crude fertility rate in a certain town last year was 60‰ of the female population.

The crude mortality rate for the town's entire population was 30.2‰.

Given that females made up 52% of the town's population at the beginning of the year, calculate the percentage change in the town's population from the beginning to the end of the year.

10 Table 6.15 shows information about the three classes of employees at two chemical companies, Fertilog and Drainmaster, last year. Crude accident rates are measured per 1000 people.

The crude accident rates for class C employees at the two companies were identical.

Table 6.15: Chemical company accident rates

	Fertilog			Drainmaster		
Class	No. employees	No. accidents	Crude accident rate	No. employees	No. accidents	Crude accident rate
A	10	a	100	b	3	150
B	24	2	c	55	11	d
C	64	4	e	f	8	e

Calculate the exact values of a, b, c, d, e and f in Table 6.15.

Standardised Rates

A rate becomes **standardised** when the crude values used in its calculation are weighted. In the case of births and deaths, this is done to take account of the different age groups in the population. The weights are called standard population figures, and they reflect the proportion of each age group in the entire population.

Standardised death rates, for example, give measures that can be used to compare the healthiness of different environments. There is a better chance of a long and healthy life in a location where the standardised death rate is low.

$$\text{Standardised rate} = \frac{\Sigma[\text{Standard population} \times \text{Group crude rate}]}{\Sigma[\text{Standard population}]}$$

Examples

1 Table 6.16 gives information about the population of the village of Adumela.

The standard population figures refer to the whole country in which Adumela is located.

Find the crude and standardised death rates, measured per 1000 of the population.

Table 6.16: Population of Adumela

Age group	Group population	No. deaths	Group crude death rate (‰)	Standard population
Under 20	6000	36	6	30%
20 to 60	7000	56	8	50%
Over 60	2000	34	17	20%
Totals	15000	126		100%

$$\text{Crude death rate} = \frac{\text{total number of deaths}}{\text{total population}} \times 1000 = \frac{126}{15000} \times 1000 = 8.4‰$$

$$\text{Standardised death rate} = \frac{\Sigma[\text{standard population} \times \text{group crude death rate}]}{\Sigma[\text{standard population}]}$$

$$= \frac{(30 \times 6) + (50 \times 8) + (20 \times 17)}{(30 + 50 + 20)} = \frac{920}{100} = 9.2‰$$

2 Table 6.17 gives information about the three groups of employee at a construction company last year. Standard population figures refer to the entire construction industry.

Find the crude and standardised accident rates, measured per 1000 employees.

Table 6.17: Construction company accident rates

Group	Group population	No. accidents	Group crude accident rate (‰)	Standard population
Manual	350	105	300	85%
Clerical	15	0	0	10%
Managerial	12	3	250	5%
Totals	377	108		100%

$$\text{Crude accident rate} = \frac{\text{total number of accidents}}{\text{total population}} \times 1000 = \frac{108}{377} \times 1000 = 286.5‰$$

$$\text{Standardised accident rate} = \frac{\Sigma[\text{standard population} \times \text{group crude accident rate}]}{\Sigma[\text{standard population}]}$$

$$= \frac{(85 \times 300) + (10 \times 0) + (5 \times 250)}{(85 + 10 + 5)} = \frac{26\,750}{100} = 267.5‰$$

Exercise 6F

1 **i** Calculate a standardised death rate using crude death rates of 7.8‰ and 10.2‰ with standard population values of 60% and 40%, respectively.

ii Calculate a standardised birth rate using crude birth rates of 52‰ and 13‰ with standard population values of 30% and 70%, respectively.

iii Calculate a standardised accident rate using crude accident rates of 17.8‰ and 9.6‰ with standard population values of 81.5% and 18.5%, respectively.

2 **i** Table 6.18 gives information for the population of the town of Westwood.

Table 6.18: Westwood population

Age group	Group population	No. deaths	Group crude death rate (‰)	Standard population
Under 20	10000	45	p	25%
20–40	8000	48	6	30%
40–60	15000	135	9	35%
Over 60	12000	150	12.5	10%

a What is the total population of Westwood?

b How many people died in Westwood?

c Calculate the crude death rate for Westwood.

d Find the value of p.

e Calculate a standardised death rate for Westwood.

ii Information about the population of Eastside, which is near to Westwood, is given in Table 6.19.

Table 6.19: Eastside population

Age group	Group population	No. deaths	Group crude death rate (‰)	Standard population
Under 20	14 000	49	x	25%
20–40	16 000	y	5.5	30%
40–60	z	77	11	35%
Over 60	8000	164	20.5	10%

a Find the values of x, y and z.
b Calculate the crude death rate for Eastside.
c Numerically, what do the towns of Westwood and Eastside have in common?
d Calculate a standardised death rate for Eastside.
e Giving your reason, state which town appears to offer a better chance of a long and healthy life.

3 Table 6.20 gives information on the populations of two towns, Northside and Southlake.

Table 6.20: Northside and Southlake populations

	Northside		Southlake		
Age group	Population	No. deaths	Population	Group death rate (‰)	Standard population
0–20	24 500	196	18 000	9	30%
20–50	19 500	234	22 000	11	30%
50–75	16 500	231	11 500	14	25%
Over 75	9000	147	18 000	$15\frac{2}{3}$	15%

i Calculate the crude death rate for Northside.
ii Calculate a standardised death rate for Southlake.
iii Calculate the crude death rate for Southlake.
iv Calculate a standardised death rate for Northside.
v Giving a reason, state which of the two towns appears to be a healthier place in which to live.

4 The neighbouring towns of Redville and Greenwood have death rates per 1000 as shown in Table 6.21.

Table 6.21: Death rates in Redville and Greenwood

	Crude death rate	Standardised death rate
Redville	14.2	9.1
Greenwood	6.4	9.1

i What do the identical standardised death rates suggest about the healthiness of the two towns?
ii What do the figures suggest about the ages of the populations of the two towns?

5 The death rates, per thousand of population, of the towns Blueflat and Pinkerton are given in Table 6.22.

Table 6.22: Death rates in Blueflat and Pinkerton

	Crude death rate	Standardised death rate
Blueflat	8.3	10.6
Pinkerton	8.3	7.2

i Which town do the figures suggest is the healthier place in which to live?
ii What do the figures suggest about the ages of the populations of the two towns?

6 The data in Table 6.23 relate to the coastal towns of Blymouth and Mounton last year.

Fertility rates are given per thousand of the entire population of each town.

Table 6.23: Fertility rates in Blymouth and Mounton

	Blymouth			Mounton	
Age group	**Population**	**No. births**	**Fertility rate (‰)**	**Population**	**Standard population**
0–19	11 000	99	a	8000	42%
20–29	b	450	60	7000	25%
30 and over	5500	c	12	5000	33%

i Find each of the numbers represented by the letters a, b and c.
ii Calculate the crude fertility rate of Blymouth.
iii Calculate a standardised fertility rate for Blymouth.

The crude fertility rate for the population of Mounton is twice that of Blymouth.

iv Calculate the total number of births that occurred in Mounton.
v Calculate a standardised fertility rate for Mounton, where the under-20 fertility rate is 18.0‰ and there were 756 births in the under-30 age group.

7 Table 6.24 gives information about the female population and age group fertility rates, which are measured per thousand females, in the town of Kavumbo last year.

Table 6.24: Female population of Kavumbo

Age group of females	Population of females in age group	No. births	Age group fertility rate	Standard population of females (%)
Under 20	3750		60	17%
20–29	5200		210	24%
30–39	6850		140	28%
Over 39	9500		18	31%

i Show that the standardised fertility rate for Kavumbo is 105.38‰.
ii By calculating the number of births in each of the four age groups, find the total number of births in Kavumbo last year.
iii Hence, calculate last year's crude fertility rate.

There are equal numbers of males and females in Kavumbo and in the standard population. The crude and standardised mortality rates for the town were 15.0 and 12.0 per thousand of the population, respectively.

iv Use one of these values to find the change in the size of the town's population due to births and deaths, from the beginning to the end of last year.

8 The manager of a goods transportation company, Megahaul, has recorded data on the mechanical breakdowns suffered by the company's vehicles during the past year. Her findings are presented in Table 6.25, where the breakdown rates are measured per 1000 vehicles, and the standard population values refer to the proportion of class A, B and C vehicles in the whole of the goods transportation industry.

Table 6.25: Megahaul breakdown figures

Vehicle type	Number of vehicles	Number of breakdowns	Crude breakdown rate	Standard population
Class A	25	3	a	15%
Class B	60	b	250	45%
Class C	c	12	80	d

i Calculate the values of a, b, c and d in the table.

ii Find the crude breakdown rate for Megahaul, giving your answer to the nearest whole number.

iii Calculate the exact value of the standardised breakdown rate for Megahaul.

Grab-a-Line is Megahaul's local competitor in the goods transporting industry.

The crude breakdown rate and the standardised breakdown rate for Grab-a-Line are 138 and 150, respectively.

iv The manager at Megahaul issues all the mechanics who service the company's vehicles with a warning, saying that, 'Your performance is worse than the performance of the mechanics at Grab-a-line.'

  a State the main assumption that the manager is making here.

  b If her assumption is actually correct, is she justified in warning the mechanics or not. Explain your reasoning.

You have been elected by the mechanics to speak to the manager in their defence.

v Write a sentence in which you should suggest at least one important point that the manager has not taken into account when she interpreted the data.

9 Goldstock Mineral is a company that operates two mines, A and B, in the same region. It has collected data about the accidents that its workers have been involved in at these mines during the past year. The accident rates are given in Table 6.26 per 1000 workers.

Table 6.26: Mining accidents

	Mine A			Mine B		
Worker group	Population	Number of accidents	Crude accident rate	Population	Number of accidents	Crude accident rate
Mine-face	1680	146	a	p	170	84.8
Surface	642	38	b	q	17	56.1
Foundry	97	13	c	84	r	131.0
Transport	41	1	d	35	s	28.6
Totals	2460	198				

i Calculate, correct to 1 place of decimals, a, b, c and d, the crude rate for each of the four groups of workers at mine A.

ii Find, correct to 1 decimal place, the crude accident rate for mine A.

The group crude accident rates for mine B are given in the table correct to 1 place of decimals.

iii By finding the values of p, q, r and s in Table 6.26, calculate the crude accident rate for mine B.

In the whole of the mining industry in the country where mine A and mine B are located, the number of mine-face, surface, foundry and transport workers is in the ratio 30 : 6 : 3 : 1.

iv Calculate, correct to 1 place of decimals, the standardised accident rate at mine A and at mine B.

Krassimir, Ivan and Petko are planning to apply for work at one of Goldstock Mineral's mines.

- Krassimir is a qualified worker and will only accept a position in a foundry.
- Ivan is only interested in working at the mine surface.
- Petko will happily accept any job that he is offered.

v At which mine would you advise Krassimir and Ivan to apply for work? Justify your answers.
vi Assuming that Petko is equally likely to be offered a position in any of the four worker groups, advise him on which mine you think he should apply to work at. Justify your answer.

10 Worldwide it is estimated that there are 27 000 extreme sports enthusiasts.

A week-long extreme sports event is held annually and is attended by some of these enthusiasts.

Table 6.27 gives details of the numbers of enthusiasts participating in the different types of extreme sports at the event, along with some information about the accidents that occurred at the event last year and this year. Accident rates are measured per thousand participants.

Table 6.27: Extreme sports accident rates

	Event held last year			Event held this year		
Extreme sport	**Number of participants**	**Number of accidents**	**Crude accident rate**	**Number of participants**	**Number of accidents**	**Crude accident rate**
Land-based	240		50		11	40
Air-based	60		$33\frac{1}{3}$		7	$66\frac{2}{3}$
Water-based	150		40		6	37.5
Totals	450				24	

i Calculate the total number of accidents that occurred at the event held last year.
ii Calculate the total number of participants at the event held this year.
iii Hence, calculate the crude accident rate for the event held last year and for the event held this year.

Table 6.28 gives the primary activities of the 27 000 extreme sports enthusiasts.

Table 6.28: Extreme sports participants

Type of extreme sport	Number of enthusiasts
Land-based	12 555
Air-based	8100
Water-based	6345

iv Use this table to calculate appropriate standard population values for the three types of extreme sports.
v Use your answers to **iv** to calculate the standardised accident rates at the event for last year and this year.

A team of Health and Safety experts have studied the data about the event held in the last two years.

Their report contains following two sentences:

- 'The same . . . of participants were involved in accidents in both years.'
- 'It appears that the organisers' attention to health and safety issues has . . . since last year's event.'

vi Suggest two words that would be appropriate to complete the sentences, based on the answers that you have obtained in previous parts of this question. Justify your choice of the second word.

The extreme sports governing body claims that only the first of these sentences is necessarily true.

vii Give a reason why the governing body is perfectly justified in making this claim.

7 Measures of Dispersion

Learning Objectives

In this chapter you will learn:

- To use a variety of techniques for finding or calculating estimates of the measures of dispersion for ungrouped data, grouped data and combined sets of data
- How to select an appropriate measure of dispersion to represent the spread of a set of data
- To use a measure of dispersion to describe a set of data, and to make comparisons between two sets of related data

Introduction

A distribution is not described fully by a measure of central tendency alone. Knowing that the average monthly earnings in a country are $2000 gives us no information on how varied those earnings are. To get a clearer picture of a distribution, we need to know how spread out the values are, and this is the purpose of finding measures of dispersion. There are various measures that can be used, and once an appropriate one has been found, extreme values can be identified, and we will have another measure that can be used to compare two sets of related data.

How well does a measure of central tendency alone describe a set of data? Can it give a clear picture of the values in the data?

Examples

A boy and girl went fishing on Saturday, and each caught five fish with a mean mass of 2 kg.

From this information, we may think that the children returned home with identical catches. This may not be the case, as Figure 7.1 shows.

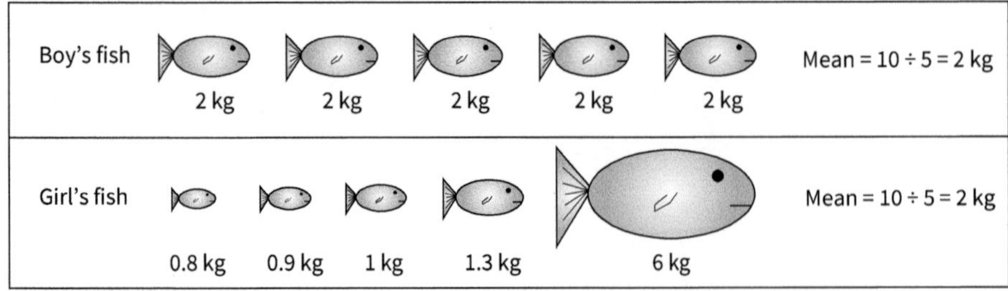

Figure 7.1: Fish caught

The boy's fish have equal masses; the masses are not dispersed.
The girl's fish do not have equal masses; the masses are dispersed.

Measures of **dispersion** commonly used to describe the spread of the values in a set of data are: range, interquartile range, and standard deviation.

7.1 Range

This is the simplest measure of dispersion and is in everyday use. The **range** is the difference between the largest and smallest possible values in a distribution.

Examples

1 At a school, the numbers of students in the six classes are: 22, 21, 24, 28, 26 and 23.
The range of the numbers of students is $28 - 21 = 7$.

2 At a company, 12 people earn \$4.50 per hour, five people earn \$8.75 per hour and two people earn \$15.25 per hour.
The range of hourly rates is $\$15.25 - 4.50 = \$10.75$ per hour.

3 The lengths of 30 pencils are given in the grouped frequency table in Table 7.1.

Table 7.1: Pencil lengths

Length (l cm)	$8 \le l < 9$	$9 \le l < 11$	$11 \le l < 13$	$13 \le l < 17$
No. pencils (f)	7	12	6	5

In this case, we cannot find the range exactly, because the actual lengths are not given.
The boundaries of the first and last classes are used to find the lower limit and the upper limit of the range.
Lower limit of the range $= 13 - 9 = 4$ cm
Upper limit of the range $= 17 - 8 = 9$ cm
So, $4\text{ cm} < \text{range} < 9\text{ cm}$; i.e. the range is between 4 cm and 9 cm.

Exercise 7A

1 Find the range of the following sets of numbers:

i 4, 7, 7, 9, 13, 21, ii 23, 15, 28, 22, 13, 21, iii −3, 5, 18, 24, 29, 37.

2 The frequency distributions of three variables, X, Y and Z, are given in Tables 7.2–7.4. State the range of each.

i Table 7.2: Frequency distribution of X

X	f
10	5
11	7
12	9
13	4

ii Table 7.3: Frequency distribution of Y

Y	f
7	0
9	15
11	20
13	14

iii Table 7.4: Frequency distribution of Z

Z	f
60	17
65	23
70	28
75	59
80	21
85	12

3 Table 7.5 shows the numbers of brothers and the numbers of sisters that each of 25 children has.

Table 7.5: Numbers of siblings

		Brothers					
		0	**1**	**2**	**3**	**4**	**5**
Sisters	**0**	1	2	1	0	0	0
	1	2	2	2	1	1	0
	2	1	3	4	0	0	1
	3	3	0	2	1	0	0

Find the range of the number of:

i brothers,
ii sisters,
iii siblings.

4 To the nearest minute, the times taken between entering and leaving the school dining hall at lunchtime by 50 students are given in Table 7.6.

Table 7.6: Eating times

Time taken (minutes)	20–21	22–24	25–30
No. students (f)	6	39	5

Find the lower limit and the upper limit of the range of the times taken.

5 **i** Fifty girls are all classed as being 140 cm to 160 cm tall, correct to the nearest 10 cm. Find the upper limit of the range of their heights.
ii House sparrows are reported to have masses, correct to the nearest gram, from 22 g to 30 g. Find the upper limit of the range of their masses.
iii This season, a top athlete ran all her 100-metre races in times from 10.4 to 10.9 seconds. Find the upper limit of the range of these times.

6 The grouped frequency table shown in Table 7.7 gives details of the amounts spent in dollars by 250 customers at a fuel station.

Table 7.7: Amounts spent

Amount spent (\$$x$)	$5 \leq x < 15$	$15 \leq x < 25$	$25 \leq x < 40$	$40 \leq x < 100$
No. customers (f)	35	66	108	41

Given that the lower limit of the range of the amounts spent is \$25.01, find the upper limit of the range of the amounts spent.

7.2 Interquartile Range

If a distribution contains even one extreme value, then the range will not be very representative of the spread of the majority of the values. The range can, therefore, be misleading.

The **interquartile range** is the measure of dispersion that gives the range of the middle half (middle 50%) of the values, and so it is not affected by extreme values.

The interquartile range is the difference between the upper **quartile** and the lower quartile of a distribution.

The median divides a distribution into two equal parts, with an equal number of values in each part.

The lower quartile divides the *lower half* into two equal parts, and the upper quartile divides the *upper half* into two equal parts.

In effect, the median and quartiles divide a distribution into four equal parts, as can be seen in Figure 7.2.

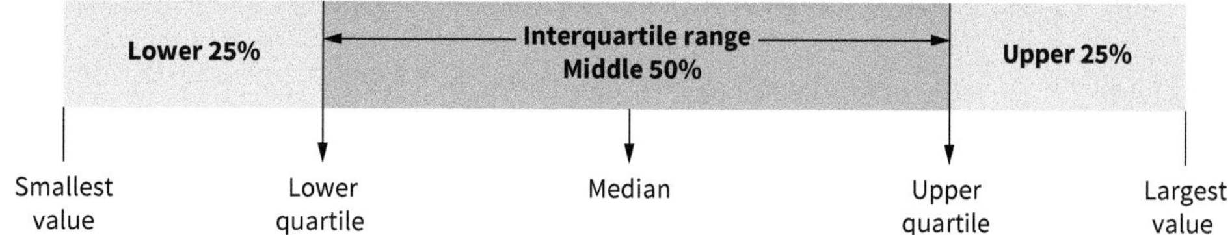

Figure 7.2: Quartiles of a distribution

Interquartile Range for Ungrouped Data

Finding the interquartile range is fairly straightforward when there are eight values, as there will simply be two values in each of the four parts. But how can we divide seven or ten values into four parts with an equal number of values in each?

In the following examples the lower quartile, median and upper quartile are represented by Q_1, Q_2 and Q_3, respectively. The values in the distribution must first be arranged in order.

Examples

1 For the set of numbers 3, 5, 6, 8, 11, 14, 17:

Figure 7.3 shows the distribution.

$N = 7$	1st		2nd		3rd		4th		5th		6th		7th
	3		5		6		8		11		14		17
			Q_1				Q_2				Q_3		

Figure 7.3: Distribution of seven numbers

Lower quartile, Q_1 is $\frac{1}{4}(N+1) = 2\text{nd} \rightarrow 5$

Median, Q_2 is $\frac{1}{2}(N+1) = 4\text{th} \rightarrow 8$

Upper quartile, Q_3 is $\frac{3}{4}(N+1) = 6\text{th} \rightarrow 14$

2. For the set of numbers 2, 3, 5, 9, 15, 17, 19, 20, 25:

Figure 7.4 shows the distribution.

$N = 9$	1st		2nd		3rd		4th		5th		6th		7th		8th		9th
	2		3	↑	5		9		15		17		19	↑	20		25
				Q_1					Q_2					Q_3			

Figure 7.4: Distribution of nine numbers

Lower quartile, Q_1 is $\frac{1}{4}(N+1) = 2.5\text{th} \rightarrow \frac{3+5}{2} = 4$

Median, Q_2 is $\frac{1}{2}(N+1) = 5\text{th} \rightarrow 15$

Upper quartile, Q_3 is $\frac{3}{4}(N+1) = 7.5\text{th} \rightarrow \frac{19+20}{2} = 19.5$

Interquartile range $= Q_3 - Q_1 = 19.5 - 4 = 15.5$

Summarising for odd N, we have the positions shown in Table 7.8.

Table 7.8: Quartile positions for odd N

Lower quartile (Q_1)	Median (Q_2)	Upper quartile (Q_3)
$\frac{1}{4}(N+1)$	$\frac{1}{2}(N+1)$	$\frac{3}{4}(N+1)$

It is acceptable to find the quartiles in the positions given above for any value of N, but there is a slight discrepancy when a distribution has an even number of values, as the following examples show.

Examples

3 For the set of numbers 13, 18, 22, 29, 35, 36, 43, 50:

Figure 7.5 shows the distribution.

$N=8$	1st		2nd		3rd		4th		5th		6th		7th		8th
	13		18	↑	22		29	↑	35		36	↑	43		50
				Q_1				Q_2				Q_3			

Figure 7.5: Distribution of eight numbers

Lower quartile, Q_1 is $\frac{1}{4}(N+2)=2.5\text{th} \rightarrow \frac{18+22}{2}=20$

Median, Q_2 is $\frac{1}{2}(N+1)=4.5\text{th} \rightarrow \frac{29+35}{2}=32$

Upper quartile, Q_3 is $\frac{1}{4}(3N+2)=6.5\text{th} \rightarrow \frac{36+43}{2}=39.5$

Interquartile range $= Q_3 - Q_1 = 39.5 - 20 = 19.5$

4 For the set of numbers 4, 6, 7, 11, 14, 16:

Figure 7.6 shows the distribution.

$N=6$	1st		2nd		3rd		4th		5th		6th
	4		6		7	↑	11		14		16
			Q_1			Q_2			Q_3		

Figure 7.6: Distribution of six numbers

Lower quartile, Q_1 is $\frac{1}{4}(N+2)=2\text{nd} \rightarrow 6$

Median, Q_2 is $\frac{1}{2}(N+1)=3.5\text{th} \rightarrow \frac{7+11}{2}=9$

Upper quartile, Q_3 is $\frac{1}{4}(3N+2)=5\text{th} \rightarrow 14$

Interquartile range $= Q_3 - Q_1 = 14 - 6 = 8$

Summarising for even N, we have the positions shown in Table 7.9.

Table 7.9: Quartile positions for even N

Lower quartile (Q_1)	Median (Q_2)	Upper quartile (Q_3)
$\frac{N+2}{4}$	$\frac{N+1}{2}$	$\frac{3N+2}{4}$

The actual positions of Q_1 and Q_3 depend on whether there are an odd or an even number of values. The position of the median is not affected though: it is always the $\frac{1}{2}(N+1)$th value.

More often than not, we will be finding the difference between Q_1 and Q_3 (the interquartile range), so it rarely makes a great difference whether we use the positions for odd N or the positions for even N.

As a rule, be consistent.

Example

5 The frequency distribution of a variable X is shown in Table 7.10.

Table 7.10: Frequency distribution of X

X	1	2	3	4	5	6	
f	10	14	18	17	14	6	$\Sigma f = 79$
Positions	1st–10th	11th–24th	25th–42nd	43rd–59th	60th–73rd	74th–79th	

The 79 values of X are ranked in ascending order in the table.

We must look at the positions of these values, so that we can locate the quartiles:

Q_1 is the $\frac{79+1}{4} = 20$th value, which is 2.

Q_3 is the $\frac{3(79+1)}{4} = 60$th value, which is 5.

The interquartile range is $5 - 2 = 3$.

Exercise 7B

1 For each of the following sets of numbers, find:

a the lower quartile, **b** the upper quartile, **c** the interquartile range.

i 20, 6, 28, 34, 16

ii 6, 13, 2, 20, 9, 25, 31

iii 5, 8, 11, −7, 0, 14, 23, 19, −2, 10, −5

iv 8, 2, 22, 30, 4, 14

v 120, 92, 74, 88, 104, 58, 50, 62

vi 15, 25, 29, 37, 71, 43, 17, 15, 7, 14

2 Values of the variable P are shown in Table 7.11.

Table 7.11: Values of P

P	10	20	30	40	50	60	
Frequency	2	13	5	11	13	15	$\Sigma f = 59$

i State the position of the lower quartile and of the upper quartile.

ii Find the interquartile range of the values of P.

3 A student kept a record of her scores in weekly science assignments during three years at school, as shown in Table 7.12.

Table 7.12: Science assignment scores

Score	0	1	2	3	4	5	6	7	8	9	10
Frequency	1	6	9	10	18	27	11	9	5	2	1

i For how many assignments has she recorded her scores?

ii Find her lower and upper quartile scores and, hence, find the interquartile range.

4 Values of the discrete variable Q are shown in Table 7.13.

Table 7.13: Values of Q

Q	1.0	1.1	1.2	1.3	1.4	1.5	1.6	1.7	1.8	1.9	2.0	
Frequency	8	11	13	17	22	27	11	7	6	5	2	$\Sigma f = 129$

i State the position of the lower quartile and the upper quartile.
ii Find the lower and upper quartile values of Q.
iii State the interquartile range.

5 The shoe sizes of a randomly selected sample of 49 women are illustrated in Table 7.14.

Table 7.14: Women's shoe sizes

Shoe size	3	$3\frac{1}{2}$	4	$4\frac{1}{2}$	5	$5\frac{1}{2}$	6	
Number of women (f)	5	6	9	10	7	7	5	$\Sigma f = 49$

i Find the lower quartile and the upper quartile of their shoe sizes.
ii One of the women is selected at random. Find the probability that her shoe size is:
  a less than the lower quartile,
  b greater than the upper quartile,
  c not outside the interquartile range.

6 Table 7.15 shows the number of sons and the number of daughters that each of 259 men has.

Table 7.15: Numbers of offspring

		Sons				
		0	1	2	3	Totals
Daughters	0	4	41	19	7	71
	1	31	58	11	5	105
	2	22	19	10	6	57
	3	7	8	7	4	26
Totals		64	126	47	22	259

i Find the interquartile range of the number of:
  a daughters,
  b sons.

ii **a** Draw up a frequency table showing how many children (sons and daughters) these men have.
  b How many children do these 259 men have altogether?
  c Find the interquartile range of the number of children.

Interquartile Range for Grouped Data

Most methods of summarising and displaying grouped data do not show individual values of the variable. For this reason, we are usually only able to calculate estimates of the measures of dispersion. However, stem-and-leaf diagrams do allow us to calculate exact values rather than estimates, because individual values of the variable can be seen.

Stem-and-leaf Diagrams

Stem-and-leaf diagrams show ranked discrete data in equal interval classes.

Examples

The test scores, in percentages, of 27 female students and 28 male students in a physics examination are given in the back-to-back stem-and-leaf diagram shown in Figure 7.7.

						Females (27)		Males (28)						
							2	3	7					
							3	0	1	7				
					8	0	**4**	1	3 *	5	5	6		
				8	5	1	**5**	2	3	5	6 *	8		
		4	4	2	<u>2</u>	1	**6**	1	1	1	2	4	7 * 9	
9	8	5	4	<u>3</u>	2	1	0	**7**	0	2	5			
	8	6	6	5	<u>3</u>	2	0	**8**	2	3				
					7	4	**9**	1						

Key: 4 | 9 | 1 represents 94% for a female and 91% for a male

Figure 7.7: Physics examination scores

Females $N = 27$:

Lower quartile Q_1 is $\frac{1}{4}(N+1) = 7$th value, which is 62%.

Median Q_2 is $\frac{1}{2}(N+1) = 14$th value, which is 73%.

Upper quartile Q_3 is $\frac{3}{4}(N+1) = 21$th value, which is 83%.

These three measures are underlined in Figure 7.7.

Males $N = 28$:

Lower quartile Q_1 is $\frac{1}{4}(N+2) = 7\frac{1}{2}$th value, which is 44%.

Median Q_2 is $\frac{1}{2}(N+1) = 14\frac{1}{2}$th value, which is 57%.

Upper quartile Q_3 is $\frac{1}{4}(3N+2) = 21\frac{1}{2}$th value, which is 68%.

These three measures are marked * in Figure 7.7.

Table 7.16: Dispersion measures for physics examination results

	Median	Range	Interquartile range
Females	73%	97 − 40 = 57%	83 − 62 = 21%
Males	57%	91 − 23 = 68%	68 − 44 = 24%

The measure of central tendency and the two measures of dispersion shown in Table 7.16 allow us to make comparisons between the two groups of students.

On average, the females performed better than the males, and the females' scores were less dispersed than the males' scores.

Box-and-whisker Diagrams

These diagrams, also called *boxplots*, are most effectively drawn on graph paper. They show two measures of dispersion (the range and interquartile range) and one measure of central tendency (the median). The diagram takes the form shown in Figure 7.8, where Q_1 and Q_3 represent the quartiles, and Q_2 the median.

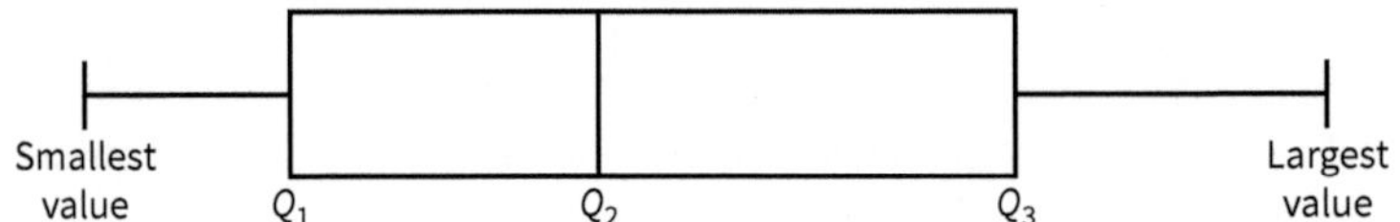

Figure 7.8: Box-and-whisker diagram

The smallest and largest values in the data are placed at the start and end of a range line - the *whisker*.

The quartiles, Q_1 and Q_3, form a rectangular *box* which is split by the median, Q_2.

These five values must be placed in the correct positions relative to each other.

The whisker is not drawn through the box, and the scale used should be indicated on the diagram.

Examples

Data for two distributions, *A* and *B*, are given in Table 7.17.

Table 7.17: Dispersion measures for *A* and *B*

	Smallest value	Largest value	Lower quartile	Median	Upper quartile
A	1.0	5.7	2.0	3.0	4.4
B	1.2	5.0	2.3	3.5	4.5

The data for each distribution are shown on separate box-and-whisker diagrams in Figure 7.9. The scale applies to both.

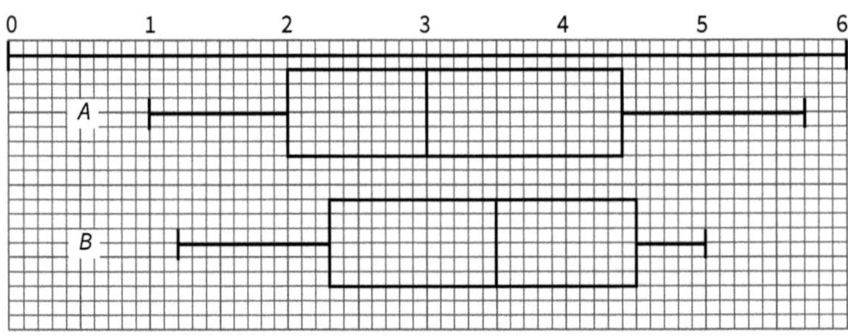

Figure 7.9: Box-and-whisker diagrams for *A* and *B*

The diagrams show that:

- *A* has a range of 4.7 and an interquartile range of 2.4,
- *B* has a range of 3.8 and an interquartile range of 2.2.

Comparison of the medians suggests that, on average, the values in *A* are lower than in *B*.

Comparison of the ranges and interquartile ranges suggests that the values in *A* are more dispersed than in *B*.

Exercise 7C

1 The stem-and-leaf diagram in Figure 7.10 shows the percentage scores of 43 candidates in a university exam.

2	3 3 5 9
3	0 4 4 6 7 7 8 9
4	0 0 1 5 6 7 7
5	1 3 4 6 7 9
6	2 5 7 9 9 9
7	2 2 7 8 8
8	3 5 6 6
9	0 1 8

Key: **8** | 3 represents a score of 83%

Figure 7.10: University exam results

Find:

i the range of the scores, **ii** the median score, **iii** the interquartile range of the scores.

2 The stem-and-leaf diagram in Figure 7.11 illustrates the number of patients visiting a dentist's surgery each day for a period of 15 days.

1	6 6 7 8 9
2	0 1 2 3 5 7 9
3	0 0 2

Key: **1** | 6 represents 16 patients

Figure 7.11: Patient numbers

i Find the median number of patients per day.
ii Find the lower quartile and upper quartile, and state the interquartile range.

3 A new movie was shown every night for four weeks at a cinema. The back-to-back stem-and-leaf diagram in Figure 7.12 shows the numbers of men and women in the audience each evening.

Men (28)		Women (28)
	17	0 0
	16	1 3 6 8
3	**15**	2 4 5 7 8 8 9 9
1 0	**14**	3 4 6 7 8 8
3 0	**13**	2 3 5 7
6 3 1	**12**	5 7 9
7 5 4 4 2	**11**	2
7 5 1 1 1 1 0	**10**	
9 7 7 6 4 3 3 2	**9**	

Key: 1 | **12** | 5 represents 121 men and 125 women

Figure 7.12: Movie audiences

i Find the median for the men and for the women.

ii Given that the lower and upper quartiles for the men are 98 and 122, find the interquartile range for the women.

iii Compare the attendance of the men with the attendance of the women.

4 The monthly amounts of money spent on clothes by 30 people are listed below to the nearest \$10.

220	90	130	220	230
80	110	70	90	150
70	160	80	120	120
50	60	70	120	60
110	140	80	110	160
50	180	60	240	70

i Show the data on spending in a stem-and-leaf diagram.

ii What was the lowest possible amount spent?

iii Why is it not necessarily true that \$240 was the greatest amount spent?

iv Estimate the median amount spent.

v Given that the upper quartile is \$150, find an estimate of the interquartile range.

5 The mean numbers of beds sold per fortnight during the past year at two branches, *A* and *B*, of a furniture store are listed in Table 7.18.

Table 7.18: Beds sold per fortnight

Branch *A*:	15	12	19	21	26	17	8	14	19	22	27	33	25
	18	11	23	30	14	17	17	8	14	20	18	21	16
Branch *B*:	11	21	33	20	13	13	12	11	14	35	34	10	26
	39	12	25	7	12	11	30	17	11	36	8	13	11

i Illustrate these data in a back-to-back stem-and-leaf diagram.

ii Find three measures of central tendency for the number of beds sold at each branch.

The owner of these two furniture stores is planning to close one of them down.

iii Advise the owner on what he should find out before he decides which store to close.

6 For each of the box-and-whisker diagrams shown in Figure 7.13, work out:

a the range, **b** the interquartile range.

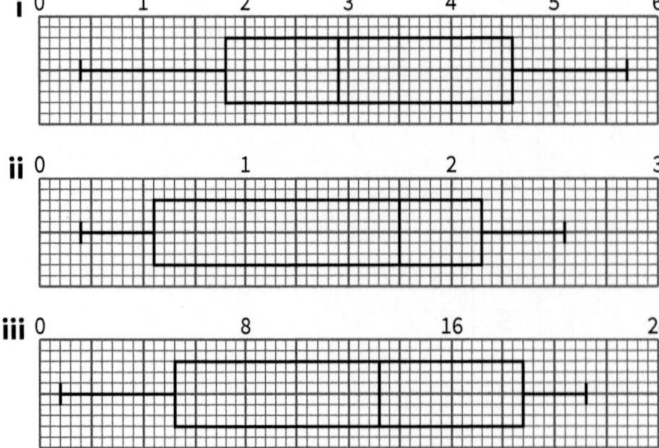

Figure 7.13: Box-and-whisker diagrams

7 The box-and-whisker diagrams in Figure 7.14 show the average morning temperatures at two weather stations, A and B, recorded over a period of three months.

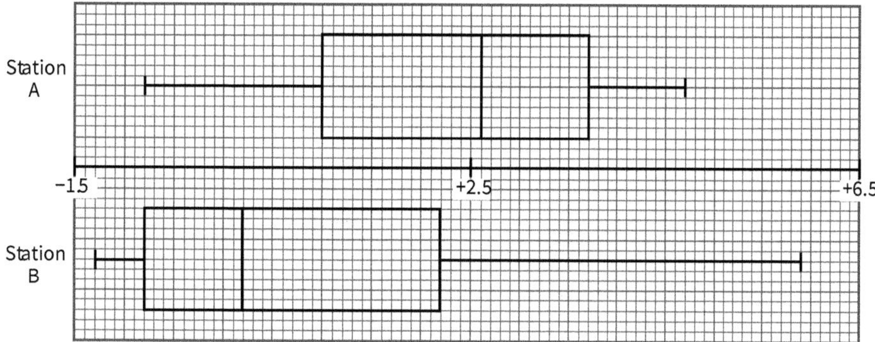

Figure 7.14: Average morning temperatures

i Copy and complete the table shown in Table 7.19, showing seven measures for each of the weather stations.

Table 7.19: Measures for morning temperatures

	Minimum	Maximum	Lower quartile	Median	Upper quartile	Range	IQR
Station *A*							
Station *B*							

ii Which weather station do you consider to have been the more pleasant during this period? Support your answer with two pieces of statistical evidence.

8 On graph paper, construct a box-and-whisker diagram for the data given in each of Tables 7.21-7.24. Use the scales given.

i Use 1 cm to represent 1 unit of the variable in Table 7.20.

Table 7.20: Measures

Smallest value	Largest value	Lower quartile	Median	Upper quartile
8	22	11	13	17

ii Use 1 cm to represent 2 units of the variable in Table 7.21.

Table 7.21: Measures

Smallest value	Largest value	Lower quartile	Median	Upper quartile
21	51	27	36.6	43

iii Use 1 cm to represent 4 units of the variable in Table 7.22.

Table 7.22: Measures

Smallest value	Largest value	Lower quartile	Median	Upper quartile
7.5	69.5	38.3	48.3	55.9

iv Use 1 cm to represent 5 units of the variable in Table 7.23.

Table 7.23: Measures

Smallest value	Range	Interquartile range	Median	Upper quartile
3.8	77.5	37.5	46.3	77.3

9 The smallest value in a distribution is 7 and the range is 14. The lower quartile is 11, the upper quartile is 16 and the median is 13. Show this information in a box-and-whisker diagram, using 1 cm to represent 1 unit.

10 The largest value in a distribution is 570 and its range is 600. The upper quartile is 440, the median is 330 and the interquartile range is 220. Show this information in a box-and-whisker diagram, using 1 cm to represent 50 units.

11 The stem-and-leaf diagram in Figure 7.15 shows the marks out of 50 scored by 25 adults on the theory section of their driving test.

1	3 5 6 6
2	0 7 7 7 8 9 9
3	1 2 2 5 5 5 6 7 9
4	0 0 3 4 5

Key: **1** | 3 represents a score of 13 out of 50

Figure 7.15: Driving test theory scores

i Write down the range. **ii** Find the interquartile range of the marks.
iii Show these data in a box-and-whisker diagram, using 1 cm to represent 2 marks.

12 In a laboratory storeroom, there are 23 different chemicals. The densities of these chemicals are given in g/cm^3 correct to 2 places of decimals.

0.70 0.48 0.35 0.56 0.40 0.52 0.43 0.77 0.45 0.67 0.36 0.47
0.65 0.66 0.74 0.32 0.57 0.62 0.50 0.42 0.34 0.44 0.56

i Display the data in a stem-and-leaf diagram.
ii Find: **a** the median, **b** the interquartile range.
iii Display the data in a box-and-whisker diagram, using 1 cm to represent 0.05 g/cm^3 of density.
iv Explain why the greatest possible range of the densities is actually 0.46 g/cm^3.

13 A traffic survey counted the number of vehicles turning at a certain junction every hour for 57 consecutive hours. The results are shown in Figure 7.16.

7	1 4 7 7 8
6	0 5 5 5 6 7 7 9
5	1 3 4 4 6 7 7 8 9 9
4	2 2 3 4 4 5 5 5 6 7 7 8 8 9
3	0 0 1 2 5 7 8 8
2	0 1 1 3 7 9
1	0 3 4 5
0	2 6

Key: **5** | 1 represents 51 vehicles per hour

Figure 7.16: Vehicles turning at a junction

i Find:

a the median number of vehicles per hour,

b the interquartile range.

ii Construct a box-and-whisker diagram to illustrate the data, and indicate the scale used.

14 The annual salaries of a group of 35 females and 35 males are given in dollars in the back-to-back stem-and-leaf diagram in Figure 7.17.

Females (35)		Males (35)
7 0	**18**	5 6
7 6 5 2	**19**	0 4 7
8 7 5 4 3 3 3 2	**20**	2 6 8
9 8 8 6 6 5 4 3 1	**21**	3 5 5 7 8 8
7 6 5 3 2 2 1 0	**22**	0 1 3 5 6 7 7 9
6 4 2	**23**	3 4 5 6 7 8 9 9
0	**24**	3 5 7 7 8

Key: 1 | **21** | 3 represents a salary of \$21,100 for a female and \$21,300 for a male

Figure 7.17: Annual salaries

i Find the median salary for:

a the females, **b** the males.

ii Given that the lower and upper quartiles for the males are \$21,300 and \$23,700, find the lower and upper quartiles for the females.

iii Show the data in separate box-and-whisker diagrams on the same sheet of graph paper. Use 1 cm to represent \$500.

iv Compare the salaries of the two groups, using values from your box-and-whisker diagrams to support what you write.

7.3 Cumulative Frequency Diagrams

Estimates for values at certain positions within a distribution (median, lower and upper quartiles, etc.) can be read from a cumulative frequency diagram. By estimating the quartiles, we can also obtain an estimate for the interquartile range of a distribution.

Quartiles, Deciles and Percentiles

As well as estimating the quartiles from a cumulative frequency diagram, we can estimate deciles and percentiles. The position of a **decile** is any number of tenths, and a **percentile** is any number of hundredths, of the total frequency.

For a distribution of N values, these measures are found in the positions given in Table 7.24.

Table 7.24: Quartiles, deciles and percentiles

	Lower quartile (Q_1)	Median (Q_2)	Upper quartile (Q_3)	Dth decile	Pth percentile
	$\frac{N}{4}$	$\frac{N}{2}$	$\frac{3N}{4}$	$\frac{D}{10}\times N$	$\frac{P}{100}\times N$
Midway between:	0th and median	0th and Nth	Median and Nth		

N is identical to Σf in a frequency distribution, and to the highest *cf* value in a cumulative frequency distribution.

- Lower quartile ≡ 25th percentile ≡ 2.5th decile
- Median ≡ 50th percentile ≡ 5th decile
- Upper quartile ≡ 75th percentile ≡ 7.5th decile

Examples

1 A grouped distribution contains 280 readings, which have been ranked from smallest to largest.

The 4th decile is the 112th reading, as $\frac{4}{10} \times 280 = 112$.

The 45th percentile is the 126th reading, as $\frac{45}{100} \times 280 = 126$.

2 The masses of 140 watermelons are illustrated in the cumulative frequency table (Table 7.25), frequency table (Table 7.26) and cumulative frequency polygon (Figure 7.18).

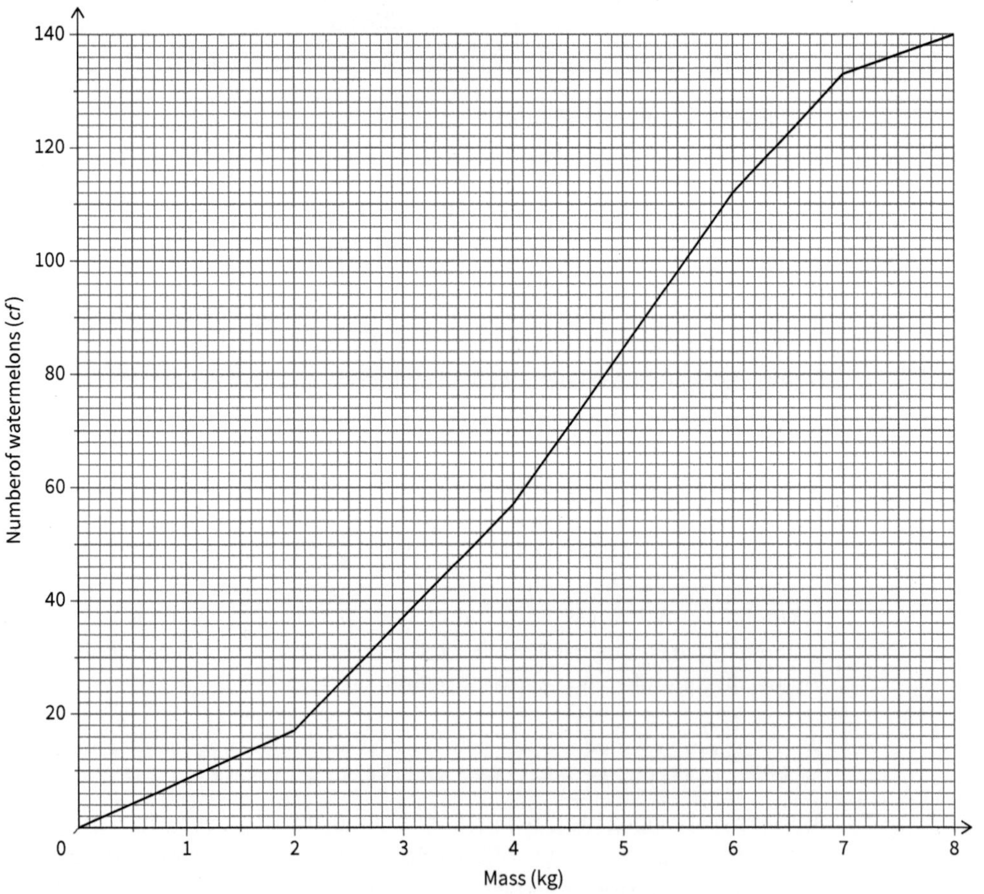

Figure 7.18: Cumulative frequency polygon for watermelon masses

Table 7.25: Cumulative frequency table of watermelon masses

Mass (M kg)	*cf*
$M < 0$	0
$M < 2$	17
$M < 4$	57
$M < 6$	112
$M < 7$	133
$M < 8$	140

The classes and their frequencies are shown in Table 7.26.

Table 7.26: Frequency table for watermelon masses

Mass (M kg)	f
$0 \le M < 2$	$17 - 0 = 17$
$2 \le M < 4$	$57 - 17 = 40$
$4 \le M < 6$	$112 - 57 = 55$
$6 \le M < 7$	$133 - 112 = 21$
$7 \le M < 8$	$140 - 133 = 7$
	$\Sigma f = 140$

For $\Sigma f = 140$:

i Lower quartile, Q_1 is the $\left(\frac{140}{4}\right)$th $=35$th value, which is approximately 2.90 kg.

ii Upper quartile, Q_3 is the $\left(\frac{3 \times 140}{4}\right)$th $=105$th value, which is approximately 5.93 kg.

iii Interquartile range $= Q_3 - Q_1 = 5.93 - 2.90 = 3.03$ kg.

iv 95th percentile is the $\left(\frac{95}{100} \times 140\right)$th $=133$rd value, which is exactly 7 kg.

v 7th decile is the $\left(\frac{7}{10} \times 140\right)$th $=98$th value, which is approximately 5.50 kg.

Example

4 The cumulative frequency diagram in Figure 7.19 shows the masses, in grams, of 60 fruit stones.

i To obtain an estimate for the range of the middle 70% of the masses, we must find the difference between the 15th and 85th percentiles.

The 15th percentile has a cumulative frequency value of $0.15 \times 60 = 9$.
It is the mass in the 9th position, which is 1.6 g.
The 85th percentile has a cumulative frequency value of $0.85 \times 60 = 51$.
It is the mass in the 51st position, which is 3.6 g.
Dotted lines in Figure 7.20 show the 15th and 85th percentiles.
The range of the middle 70% of masses is $3.6\,\text{g} - 1.6\,\text{g} = 2.0\,\text{g}$.

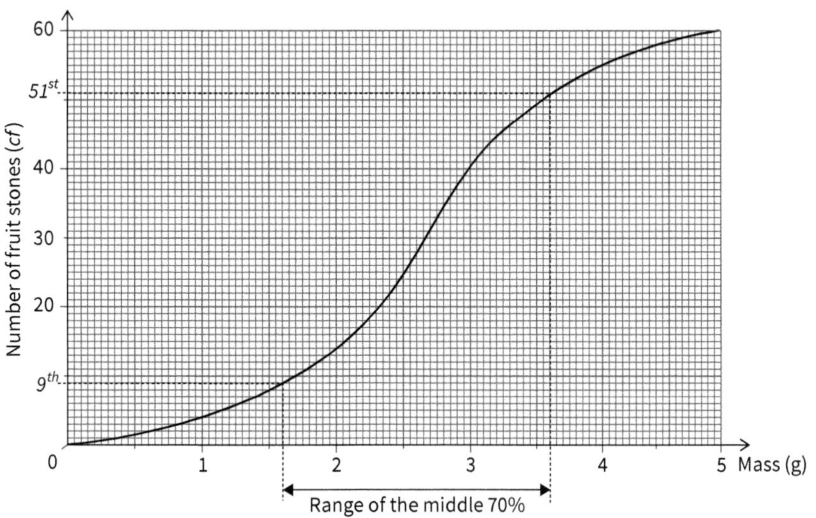

Figure 7.19: Fruit stone masses

Exercise 7D

1 The cumulative frequency polygon in Figure 7.20 illustrates the number of hours of sunshine recorded in the southern hemisphere town of Punta Stella on 360 days of last year.

i Use the polygon to find, correct to 1 decimal place, an estimate of:

a the lower quartile,
b the upper quartile,
c the interquartile range,
d the 90th percentile.

ii Estimate the number of days on which there was less than 9.4 hours of sunshine.

iii Calculate an estimate of the proportion of days on which the sun shone for 35% of the day or more.

iv Find the interquartile range for these data.

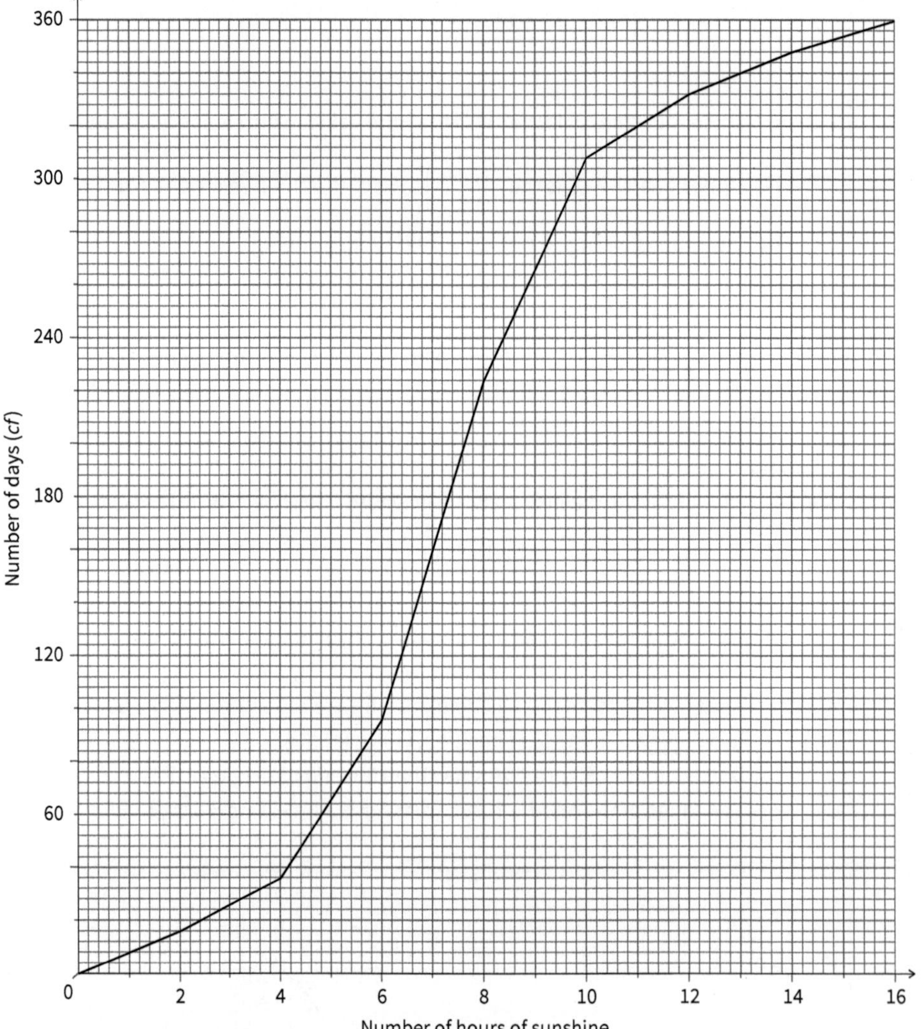

Figure 7.20: Hours of sunshine

2 i On graph paper, construct and label a cumulative frequency diagram (polygon or curve) for the distributions of the variables X, Y and Z given in Tables 7.27-7.29. Use the scale given for each.

a 1 cm to represent 1 unit of X, as shown in Table 7.27.
b 2 cm to represent 5 units of Y, as shown in Table 7.28.
c 4 cm to represent 5 units of Z, as shown in Table 7.29.

Table 7.27: Distribution of X

X	cf
$X < 0$	0
$X < 2$	5
$X < 4$	15
$X < 6$	35
$X < 8$	70
$X < 10$	90
$X < 12$	95
$X < 14$	98
$X < 16$	100

Table 7.28: Distribution of Y

Y	cf
$Y < 0$	0
$Y < 5$	34
$Y < 10$	65
$Y < 15$	78
$Y < 20$	82
$Y < 25$	84
$Y < 30$	92
$Y < 35$	106
$Y < 40$	120

Table 7.29: Distribution of Z

Z	cf
$Z < 45$	0
$Z < 48$	6
$Z < 50$	14
$Z < 51$	20
$Z < 54$	49
$Z < 59$	83
$Z < 62$	100
$Z < 63$	113
$Z < 65$	116

ii For each variable X, Y and Z, find an estimate of:

a the interquartile range, **b** the 85th percentile.

3 The best throws, x metres, of 98 athletes in a javelin competition are summarised in Table 7.30.

Table 7.30: Javelin throws

Best throw (x m)	$x < 15.0$	$x < 16.0$	$x < 17.5$	$x < 19.0$	$x < 20.5$	$x < 22.0$	$x < 23.0$
No. athletes (cf)	0	6	22	45	71	86	98

i On graph paper, draw and label a horizontal axis from 15.0 to 23.0 using 2 cm to represent 1 metre.

ii Plot the seven points given in the table and construct a cumulative frequency polygon.

iii Use the polygon to estimate:

a the interquartile range, **b** the 72nd percentile.

Forty-eight athletes achieved a best throw that was less than Roberta's best throw.

iv Find:

a an estimate of Roberta's best throw,

b the statistical name given to Roberta's best throw in the context of this question.

Athletes that achieved the ten best throws qualified for the next stage of the competition.

v Find the minimum distance that was needed to qualify for the next stage of the competition.

vi Find the number of best throws in the following classes:

a $16.0\text{ m} \leq x < 17.5\text{ m}$, **b** $19.0\text{ m} \leq x < 20.5\text{ m}$.

4 The lengths, in centimetres, of a sample of 400 bolts are summarised in Table 7.31.

Table 7.31: Bolt lengths

Length (cm)	3.50–	3.55–	3.70–	3.80–	3.85–3.90
No. bolts (f)	28	256	96	12	8

i Construct a cumulative frequency table to illustrate these data.

ii On graph paper, draw and label a horizontal axis from 3.50 to 3.90 using 4 cm to represent a length of 0.1 cm, and a vertical axis for cumulative frequency using 1 cm to represent 20 bolts.

iii Plot six points, and draw a cumulative frequency polygon.

iv Use the polygon to estimate:

a the median length,

b the interquartile range,

c the probability that a randomly selected bolt is less than the upper quartile length,

d the number of bolts with lengths of 3.83 cm or more,

e the range of the lengths of the middle 80% of the bolts, correct to 2 decimal places.

5 The times taken, to the nearest minute, by 84 girls to complete a jigsaw puzzle were recorded and are presented in Table 7.32.

Table 7.32: Jigsaw puzzle completion times

Time taken (minutes)	25–29	30–34	35–39	40–44	45–49	50–54	55–59	60–64
No. girls (f)	2	3	7	14	23	23	9	3

i Construct a cumulative frequency table for the data.

ii On graph paper, label a horizontal axis starting at 24.5 minutes, using 2 cm to represent 5 minutes.

iii Construct a cumulative frequency polygon.

iv Use the polygon to estimate:

a the interquartile range,

b the 40th percentile.

Forty-one girls took less time than Jenny.

v Estimate the time that Jenny took.

A group of boys completed the puzzle with a median time of 50 minutes and an interquartile range of 8 minutes.

vi Describe how the times taken by the girls and by the boys differed.

6 The ages, in completed years, of 126 representatives at a conference are given in Table 7.33.

Table 7.33: Conference representatives' ages

Age (completed years)	18–25	26–29	30–33	34–37	38–41	42–49
No. representatives (f)	8	11	14	28	38	27

i Write down the actual limits of the first class.

ii Construct a cumulative frequency table to illustrate the data.

iii Using 1 cm for 2 units horizontally, construct a cumulative frequency polygon on graph paper.

iv Use your polygon to estimate, to 1 decimal place:

a the median age,

b the interquartile range,

c the 35th percentile,

d the number who, to the nearest year, are not yet 44 years old.

7 After milking his cows each day, a dairy farmer pours all the milk into five-litre containers. The numbers of completely full containers that he obtained each day during the last three months are given in Table 7.34.

Table 7.34: Full 5-litre milk containers

No. full five-litre containers	28–30	31–33	34–36	37–40	41–43
No. days (f)	5	9	22	45	11

By constructing a cumulative frequency curve for the data, find an estimate of the interquartile range of the daily volume of milk produced by the dairy farmer's cows.

8 The histogram in Figure 7.21 illustrates the annual rainfall at various locations in India last year.

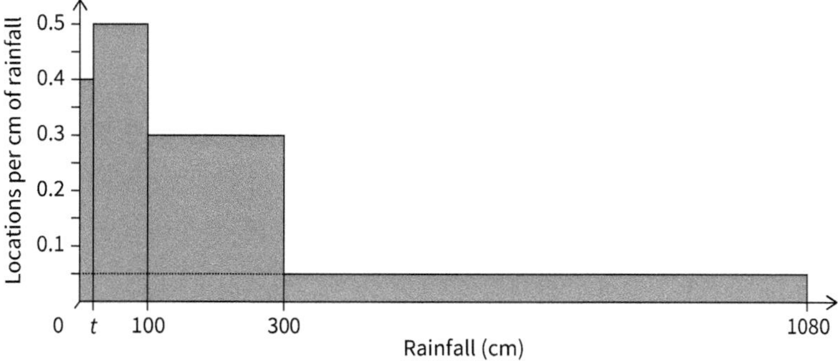

Figure 7.21: Rainfall in India

i If the first column represents 8 locations, find:

  a the upper boundary, t, of the first class,

  b the total number of locations represented.

ii Use the histogram to draw up a cumulative frequency table for the data.

iii Construct a cumulative frequency polygon and use it to find:

  a an estimate of the interquartile range,

  b the value of X, given that the Xth percentile is equal to 10 metres.

9 A text message was sent to 120 different mobile devices. The cumulative frequency curve in Figure 7.22 shows the time taken, t seconds, for the message to be received.

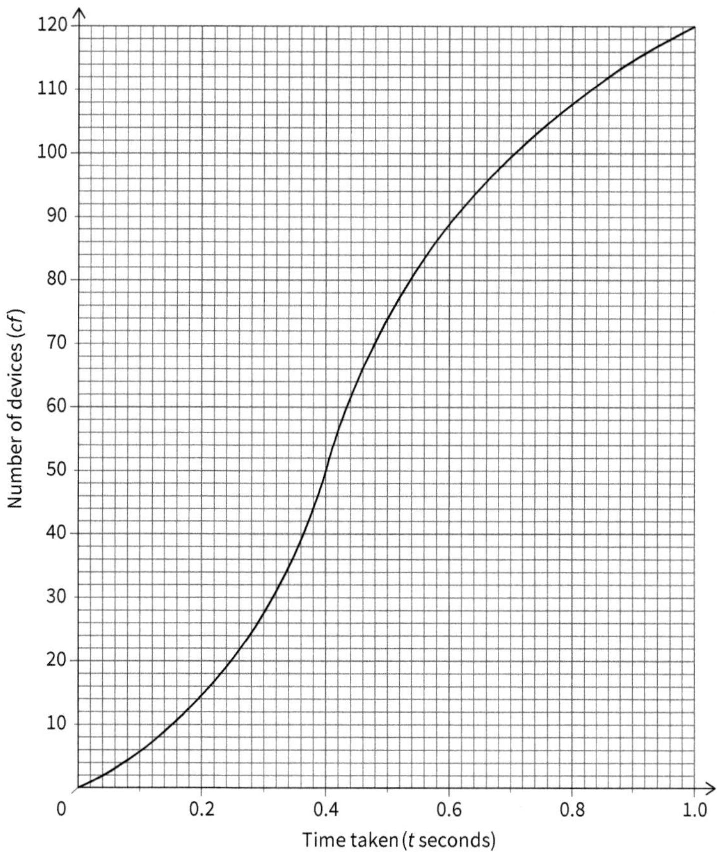

Figure 7.22: Text message transmission times

i Giving answers correct to 2 decimal places, use the diagram to estimate:

a the interquartile range of the times.

b the 35th percentile.

c the 8th decile.

The manufacturers of the fastest 35% of the devices were commended with certificates.

ii Find the minimum time required for the manufacturer of a device to be commended.

iii Find the range of times taken by the middle 30% of the devices.

10 The cumulative frequency diagram in Figure 7.23 shows the distribution of a variable, X.

i Explain why the range of X is 20.5.

ii Show that the interquartile range is 5.5.

iii Display the data for X in a box-and-whisker diagram. Indicate the scale used on your diagram.

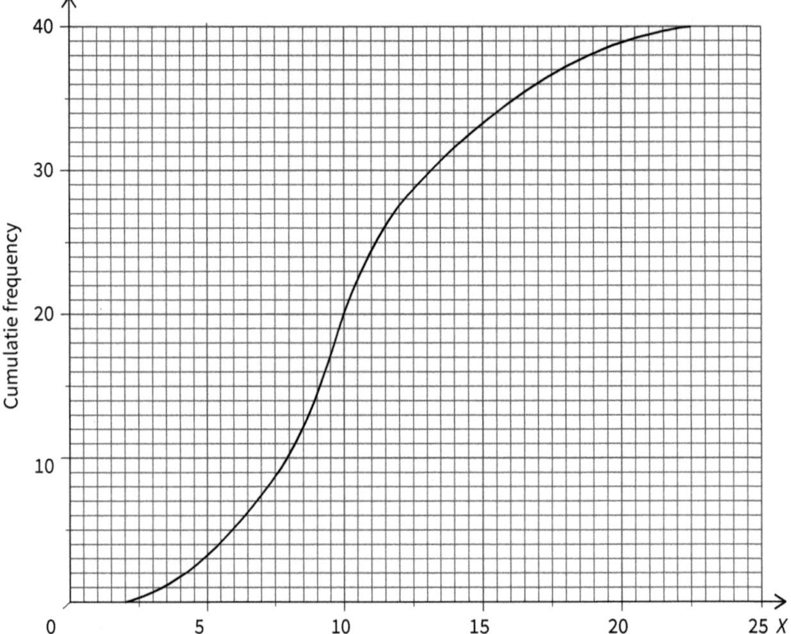

Figure 7.23: Distribution of X

11 A survey was carried out to investigate the lengths of time that adults spent watching television in an average week. The results, for a randomly selected sample of men and women, are illustrated in the cumulative frequency diagrams in Figure 7.24.

i How many adults took part in the survey?

ii Use the diagram to estimate how much longer the average man spends watching television than the average woman.

iii Giving two pieces of statistical evidence to support your answer, within which group of adults are the lengths of time spent watching television less varied?

iv The frequency distribution in Table 7.35 refers to the adults who claimed to watch less than 20 hours of television per week.

Table 7.35: Viewers of less than 20 hours

Number of hours	2.5 up to 5	5 up to 10	10 up to 15	15 up to 20	
Number of adults	p	q	r	s	$\Sigma f = t$

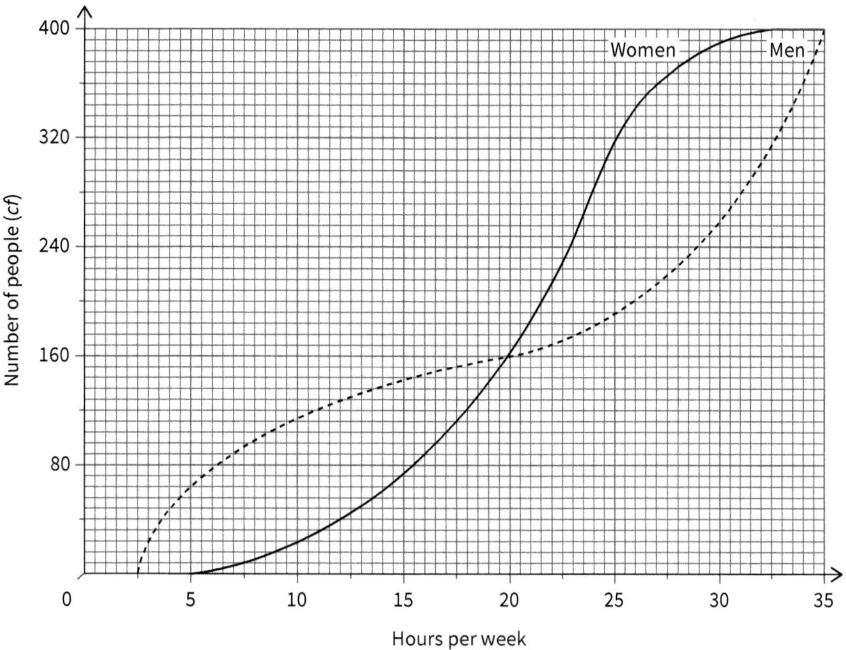

Figure 7.24: Television viewing times

a Find the values of p, q, r, s and t.
b State which of the four classes in Table 7.35 is the modal class.

7.4 Linear Interpolation from a Cumulative Frequency Table

Linear interpolation is a method used to calculate an estimate of a value in any particular position in a distribution, such as the median and the quartiles.

For any given position, an estimate of the value in that position can be calculated.

For any given value, an estimate of its position can be calculated.

Linear interpolation will give exactly the same value or position as you would obtain from a perfectly drawn and perfectly read cumulative frequency polygon.

For a data set with a total frequency Σf:

- Median value is the $\left(\frac{\Sigma f}{2}\right)$th, i.e. *cf* value $= \frac{\Sigma f}{2}$
- Lower quartile is the $\left(\frac{\Sigma f}{4}\right)$th, i.e. *cf* value $= \frac{\Sigma f}{4}$
- Upper quartile is the $\left(\frac{3\Sigma f}{4}\right)$th, i.e. *cf* value $= \frac{3\Sigma f}{4}$.

The *cf* value of a decile or percentile is found by taking the appropriate tenth or percentage of Σf.

Examples

1 Passengers at a bus station were asked how long their journeys home usually took.

Their responses are summarised in the cumulative frequency table in Table 7.36.

Table 7.36: Journey times

Time taken (t mins)	No. passengers (cf)
$t<0$	0
$t<3$	15
$t<8$	40
$t<15$	70
$t<18$	88
$t<20$	92

i Calculate an estimate of the median time.

Let the median be M.

M is the $\frac{92}{2}=46$th value, which lies between 8 and 15; the class interval is $15-8=7$.

Class boundaries have cf values 40 and 70, so class frequency is $70-40=30$.

$$\frac{M-8}{15-8}=\frac{46-40}{70-40}$$

$$\frac{M-8}{7}=\frac{6}{30}$$

$$M=8+\frac{6}{30}\times 7$$

$$M=9.4$$

$$M=9\,\text{min}\ 24\,\text{sec}$$

The cf-axis from 40 to 70 is aligned with the t-axis from 8 to 15, as shown in Figure 7.25.

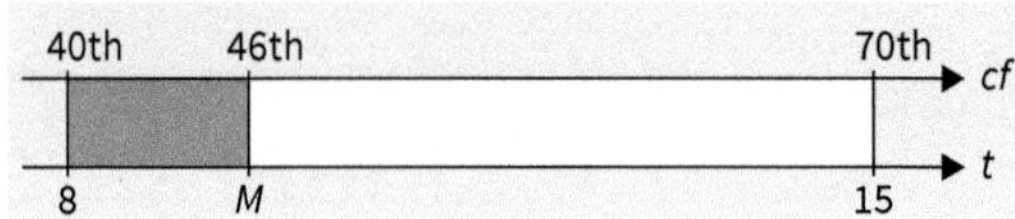

Figure 7.25: Estimating the median time

46 is $\frac{6}{30}=\frac{1}{5}$ of the way from 40 to 70, so M is $\frac{1}{5}$ of the way from 8 to 15.

ii Given that a calculated estimate of the upper quartile is 14 minutes 46 seconds, calculate estimates of the lower quartile and the interquartile range.

Let the lower quartile be Q_1.

Q_1 is the $\frac{92}{4}=23$rd value, which lies between 3 and 8; class interval is $8-3=5$.

Class boundaries have cf values 15 and 40; class frequency is $40-15=25$.

$$\frac{Q_1-3}{8-3}=\frac{23-15}{40-15}$$

$$\frac{Q_1-3}{5}=\frac{8}{25}$$

$$Q_1=3+\frac{8}{25}\times 5$$

$$Q_1=4.6$$

$$Q_1=4\,\text{min}\ 36\,\text{sec}$$

The cf-axis from 15 to 40 is aligned with the t-axis from 3 to 8, as shown in Figure 7.26.

Figure 7.26: Estimating the lower quartile

Estimate for the interquartile range is
14 min 46 sec – 4 min 36 sec = 10 min 10 sec.

23 is $\frac{8}{25}$ of the way from 15 to 40, so Q_1 is $\frac{8}{25}$ of the way from 3 to 8.

2 All of the players that took part in ten football matches last Saturday were monitored, and the distance covered by each of them was recorded in Table 7.37.

Table 7.37: Distances covered by footballers

Distance (d km)	No. players (cf)
$d<0$	0
$d<1$	20
$d<3$	40
$d<6$	66
$d<8$	100
$d<10$	220

A calculated estimate of the 85th percentile is 9.45 km.

i Calculate estimates of the 15th percentile and the range of the middle 70% of the distances covered.

Let the 15th percentile be P.

P is the $\frac{15}{100}\times 220 = 33$rd value, which lies between 1 and 3; class interval is $3-1=2$.

Class boundaries have cf values 20 and 40; class frequency is $40-20=20$.

$$\frac{P-1}{3-1}=\frac{33-20}{40-20}$$

$$\frac{P-1}{2}=\frac{13}{20}$$

$$P=1+\frac{13}{20}\times 2$$

$$P=2.3\text{ km}$$

The cf-axis from 20 to 40 is aligned with the d-axis from 1 to 3, as shown in Figure 7.27.

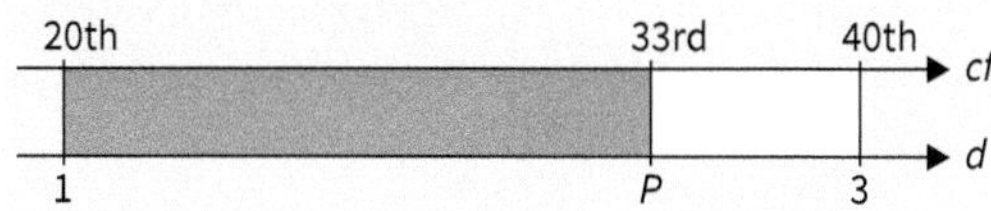

Figure 7.27: Estimating the 15th percentile

33 is $\frac{13}{20}$ of the way from 20 to 40, so P is $\frac{13}{20}$ of the way from 1 to 3.

Estimate for the range of the middle 70% of the distances is $9.45-2.3=7.15$ km.

One of the players was Raheem, who covered a distance of 9.25 km.

ii Calculate an estimate of the number of players that covered a shorter distance than Raheem.

Let the distance covered by Raheem be in the Rth position.

9.25 km is in the class $8\le d<10$, which has an interval of 2 and a frequency of 120.

$$\frac{R-100}{220-100}=\frac{9.25-8}{10-8}$$

$$\frac{R-100}{120}=\frac{1.25}{2}$$

$$R=100+\frac{1.25}{2}\times 120$$

$$R=175$$

The cf-axis from 100 to 220 is aligned with the d-axis from 8 to 10, as shown in Figure 7.28.

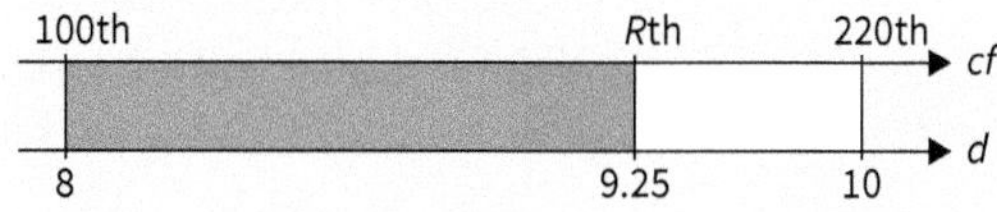

Figure 7.28: Estimating numbers covering less than Raheem

9.25 is $\frac{1.25}{2}=\frac{5}{8}$ of the way from 8 to 10, so R is $\frac{5}{8}$ of the way from 100 to 220.

We estimate that 174 players covered a shorter distance than Raheem.

Exercise 7E

1 **i** Calculate, by linear interpolation, an estimate of the median value of W, X, Y and Z shown in the cumulative frequency tables in Tables 7.38–7.41. Give exact answers where possible; otherwise give them correct to 2 decimal places.

a Table 7.38: Cumulative frequency table for W

W	cf
$W < 0$	0
$W < 20$	10
$W < 40$	35
$W < 60$	55
$W < 80$	75
$W < 100$	90
$W < 120$	100

b Table 7.39: Cumulative frequency table for X

X	cf
$X < 0$	0
$X < 10$	25
$X < 20$	75
$X < 30$	115
$X < 40$	155
$X < 50$	190
$X < 60$	200

c Table 7.40: Cumulative frequency table for Y

Y	cf
$Y < 0$	0
$Y < 50$	80
$Y < 110$	170
$Y < 180$	249
$Y < 210$	303
$Y < 270$	372
$Y < 300$	400

d Table 7.41: Cumulative frequency table for Z

Z	$Z < 0$	$Z < 4$	$Z < 8.5$	$Z < 11.4$	$Z < 15$	$Z < 20$
cf	0	44	89	159	199	240

ii Calculate, by linear interpolation, estimates of the lower quartiles and the upper quartiles of the variables W, X, Y and Z shown in part **i**. Hence find estimates for the interquartile ranges of the values in each distribution.

2 The cumulative frequency table in Table 7.42 summarises the heights, h cm, of a group of 140 students.

Table 7.42: Students' heights

Height (h cm)	$h < 140$	$h < 148$	$h < 156$	$h < 160$	$h < 168$	$h < 180$
No. students (cf)	0	16	48	98	126	140

i Calculate an estimate of the lower and upper quartiles of the heights.

ii Write down your estimate of the interquartile range.

Seventy-two of these students are shorter than Diego.

iii Calculate an estimate of Diego's height.

3 During a cricket match, two fast bowlers were monitored and the speed, s km/h, at which they delivered each ball, was recorded. Results for bowler A and for bowler B are summarised in the cumulative frequency table in Table 7.43.

Table 7.43: Bowlers' delivery speeds

Speed (s km/h)	Bowler A No. deliveries (cf)	Bowler B No. deliveries (cf)
$s < 110$	0	0
$s < 120$	48	56
$s < 130$	138	120
$s < 140$	212	164
$s < 150$	240	200

i Calculate an estimate of the median speed for bowler A and for bowler B.
ii Calculate an estimate of the interquartile range of the speeds for bowler A and for bowler B.
iii Make two comparisons between A and B regarding their bowling speed and its consistency.

4 The masses, m grams, of the 3760 guavas harvested by a farmer are summarised in Table 7.44.

Table 7.44: Guava masses

Mass (m grams)	$m < 160$	$m < 165$	$m < 170$	$m < 180$	$m < 200$
No. guavas (cf)	0	1410	2424	3414	3760

The probability that a randomly selected guava is less than x grams is 0.75.

i Find an estimate for x, and state the statistical name used for the value of x in this case.

The co-operative where the guavas are sold rejects all guavas under y grams.

ii Given that 15% of this farmer's guavas were rejected, calculate an estimate of the value of y.

5 The times taken by 140 cyclists to complete a 91.9 km race are summarised in Table 7.45.

Table 7.45: Cycle race times

Time (t hours)	$t < 5.0$	$t < 5.10$	$t < 5.25$	$t < 5.50$	$t < 5.60$
No. cyclists (cf)	0	34	87	123	140

i By finding the 35th and 65th percentiles, calculate an estimate of the range of the middle 30% of the times, giving your answer in minutes and seconds.
ii Calculate an estimate of the median *speed* of the cyclists.

6 Readings of a variable, X, were taken and it was discovered that $8 \leq X < 40$. A cumulative frequency polygon illustrating the readings is a straight line. Calculate an estimate of:

i the median value of X,
ii the range of the middle 90% of the values of X,
iii the percentage of the readings for which $X < 16$,
iv the 30th percentile.

7 A ballroom dance marathon was organised in which 100 couples danced for as long as possible.

The lengths of time for which they danced, to the nearest hour, are summarised in Table 7.46.

Table 7.46: Dance marathon times

Dance time (hours)	10–24	25–36	37–40	41–50
Number of couples (*f*)	3	48	30	19

i Draw up a cumulative frequency table for the data.
ii Show that a calculated estimate of the median is 36 hours and 15 minutes.
iii Calculate the 70th percentile of the dance times, giving your answer in hours and minutes.

After x hours, 37 couples had stopped dancing.

iv Calculate an estimate of the value of x.

7.5 Standard Deviation and Variance

Standard deviation is a widely used measure of dispersion that is calculated using all of the values in a distribution.

The variance of a distribution is the difference between two squared quantities:

- the mean of the squares of the values
- the square of the mean of the values.

The standard deviation is the positive square root of the variance.

$$\text{Variance} = \text{Mean of squares} - \text{Square of mean}$$
$$\text{Standard deviation} = +\sqrt{\text{Variance}}$$

For a set or list of N numbers, denoted X:

$$\text{Standard deviation} = \sqrt{\frac{\Sigma X^2}{N} - \left(\frac{\Sigma X}{N}\right)^2} \quad \text{where the mean } \overline{X} = \frac{\Sigma X}{N}$$

Example

1 **A set of numbers is 5, 7, 11, 14, 18. Find the variance and the standard deviation.**

$$\text{Mean of squares} = \frac{5^2+7^2+11^2+14^2+18^2}{5} = \frac{715}{5} = 143$$

$$\text{Mean} = \frac{5+7+11+14+18}{5} = \frac{55}{5} = 11$$

$$\text{Variance} = 143 - 11^2 = 22$$

$$\text{Standard deviation} = \sqrt{22} = 4.69 \text{ (3 significant figures)}$$

For an ungrouped frequency distribution of X, with frequencies f:

$$\text{Standard deviation} = \sqrt{\frac{\Sigma fX^2}{\Sigma f} - \left(\frac{\Sigma fX}{\Sigma f}\right)^2} \quad \text{where the mean } \overline{X} = \frac{\Sigma fX}{\Sigma f}$$

Example

2 Find the standard deviation of the variable X shown in Table 7.47.

Table 7.47: Frequency distribution of X

X	10	20	30	
f	3	11	6	$\Sigma f = 20$

The frequency table is extended to find the necessary totals, as in Table 7.48.

Table 7.48: Extended frequency table for X

fX	30	220	180	$\Sigma fX = 430$
fX^2	300	4400	5400	$\Sigma fX^2 = 10100$

Standard deviation $= \sqrt{\frac{\Sigma fX^2}{\Sigma f} - \left(\frac{\Sigma fX}{\Sigma f}\right)^2} = \sqrt{\frac{10100}{20} - \left(\frac{430}{20}\right)^2} = 6.54$ (3 significant figures)

Alternative formulae for finding the standard deviation are:

(i) A set or list of N numbers

$$\sqrt{\frac{\Sigma(X-\overline{X})^2}{N}}$$

(ii) An ungrouped frequency distribution

$$\sqrt{\frac{\Sigma f(X-\overline{X})^2}{\Sigma f}}$$

Note that $\overline{X}$ is subtracted from all the values in the distribution; this is not very convenient, unless $\overline{X}$ is an integer.

Example

3 The five numbers 7, 9, 13, 59 and 67 have a mean of 31.

$$\text{Standard deviation} = \sqrt{\frac{(7-31)^2 + (9-31)^2 + (13-31)^2 + (59-31)^2 + (67-31)^2}{5}}$$

$$= \sqrt{692.8}$$

$$= 26.3$$

For grouped data, we are only able to calculate estimates of the standard deviation and variance. The same formulae are used as for an ungrouped frequency distribution, but class mid-values, M, are used instead of X.

Estimate of standard deviation $= \sqrt{\frac{\Sigma fM^2}{\Sigma f} - \left(\frac{\Sigma fM}{\Sigma f}\right)^2}$, where the estimated mean is $\frac{\Sigma fM}{\Sigma f}$

Class mid-values for grouped data should be calculated carefully, especially when the values have been given to a certain degree of accuracy. Mid-values may not be the same as they appear in the rounded data, as the following example illustrates.

Example

4 The ages, in completed years, of 20 children are given in the grouped frequency table in Table 7.49.

Table 7.49: Children's ages

Age (years)	5–9	10–14	15–19
No. children (f)	7	8	5

The children's ages are written with the actual class boundaries so that mid-values can be found, as shown in Table 7.50.

Table 7.50: Age classes

Actual age (A years)	f	Mid-value (M)	fM	fM^2
$5 \leq A < 10$	7	7.5	52.5	393.75
$10 \leq A < 15$	8	12.5	100	1250
$15 \leq A < 20$	5	17.5	87.5	1531.25
	$\Sigma f = 20$		$\Sigma fM = 240$	$\Sigma fM^2 = 3175$

Class mid-values are 7.5, 12.5 and 17.5, not 7, 12 and 17.

Estimate of mean $= \frac{\Sigma fM}{\Sigma f} = \frac{240}{20} = 12$ years

Estimate of standard deviation $= \sqrt{\frac{\Sigma fM^2}{\Sigma f} - \left(\frac{\Sigma fM}{\Sigma f}\right)^2} = \sqrt{\frac{3175}{20} - \left(\frac{240}{20}\right)^2} = \sqrt{14.75}$

$= 3.84$ years or approximately 3 years 10 months.

How would the use of incorrect mid-values affect your calculated estimate of the mean and the standard deviation?

Features of the measures of dispersion

When selecting a measure of dispersion to represent the spread of a distribution, some thought must be given to the appropriateness of each measure. Depending on the characteristics of the data and their context, one measure is likely to be more suitable to use than the others. A selection of their features is given in Table 5.38.

Table 5.38: Features of the measures of dispersion

Range	Simple to calculate Easily used to compare spread between similar sets of data Informative for minimum and maximum values Based on only two values in a set of data Easily affected by extreme values
Interquartile range	Unlikely to be affected by extreme values Can be calculated without accurately recording all the data Dependant on the median being an appropriate average Only based on two values in a set of data

Standard deviation	Takes into account all the values in a set of data Can be used in further calculations Has applications when values deviate from the mean due to chance Dependant on the mean being an appropriate average Easily affected by extreme values and errors in recording

Exercise 7F

1 For each if these sets of numbers calculate:

a the mean, **b** the variance, **c** the standard deviation

i 5, 9, 12, 14 **ii** 11, 16, 23, 27, 32 **iii** 1, 2, 2, 2, 3, 89

iv 10, 45, 63, 77, 83, 85, 90 **v** 3, 7, 16, 22, 25, 25, 31, 32 **vi** 5, 1, 4, 5, 4, 1, 5, 4, 1, 2

2 The masses of six men are 65.2 kg, 66.0 kg, 68.3 kg, 70.8 kg, 71.4 kg, and 73.5 kg.

i Calculate their mean mass and the standard deviation of their masses.

ii Explain why the mean and standard deviation that you have calculated are actually estimates.

3 A ranger at a game park recorded the number of animals that visited a watering hole each day for a week.

The numbers were: 16, 21, 33, 19, 27, 22 and 25.

i Find, to the nearest integer, the mean number of animals that visited the watering hole per day.

ii Using the exact value of the mean, calculate the standard deviation, correct to 3 significant figures.

4 Use the frequency distributions of the variables *A*, *B*, *C*, *D* and *E* given in Tables 7.51–7.55 to calculate:

a the mean, **b** the variance, **c** the standard deviation.

i Table 7.51: Frequency distribution for *A*

A	10	20	30
f	6	9	5

ii Table 7.52: Frequency distribution for *B*

B	13	14	15	16
f	4	7	9	5

iii Table 7.53: Frequency distribution for *C*

C	*f*
11	15
12	24
13	30
14	25
15	6

iv Table 7.54: Frequency distribution for *D*

D	*f*
1.0	8
1.5	11
2.0	17
2.5	3
3.0	1

v Table 7.55: Frequency distribution for *E*

E	*f*
5.2	13
5.5	19
5.8	28
6.1	42
6.4	39
6.7	23
7.0	21

5 The number of half-day absences of each of a group of 50 workers last year is given in Table 7.56.

Table 7.56: Half-day absences

No. half-day absences	0	1	2	3	4	5	6	7	8	9	10
No. workers (f)	2	3	4	7	3	8	9	3	7	1	3

i Calculate the mean number of half days' absence per worker.
ii Find the standard deviation.
iii Convert your answer from part **ii** to minutes, given that a working day is 8 hours long.

6 A survey revealed that, of 300 students, 145 had read no novels; 84 had read one novel; 63 had read two novels; 7 had read three novels; and 1 student had read six novels in the past year.

i Illustrate these data in a table as an ungrouped frequency distribution.
ii Calculate the mean number of novels read by the students in the past year.
iii Calculate, to 3 significant figures, the standard deviation.
iv The mean number of novels read by 300 teachers was 4.5 and the standard deviation was 1.2. Make two meaningful comments comparing the reading habits of the students and the teachers.

7 A set of thirteen numbers is: 8, 8, 8, 8, 8, 8, 8, 9, 9, 9, 9, 9, 9.

i Which two measures of dispersion will have the same value for these data? State that value. A fourteenth number, x, is added to this set.
ii If $x = 10$, explain what will happen to each of the measures in your answer to part **i**.
iii If $x = 0$, what will happen to the measure that did not appear in your answers to part **i**?

8 A student was tasked with recording the times taken for 25 athletes in a long distance race.

She started her stopwatch as the race began and retired to the shade, where she promptly fell asleep. On waking, she found that x athletes had already finished the race, but she did manage to record the times of all the remaining athletes.

State the possible value(s) for x, if she was able to reliably calculate:

i the standard deviation, **ii** the interquartile range.

9 A woman employs six young men to work at her distribution centre, and each is paid a monthly salary from \$1400 to \$1500. The owner pays herself no less than \$7500 per month.

The range, interquartile range and standard deviation of their monthly salaries are calculated.

i Write down these three measures in the order – from best to worst – in which they highlight the fact that the owner earns much more than her employees.
ii Justify why you have ranked the measures in this way.

10 The grouped frequency table in Table 7.57 shows data for a continuous variable X.

Table 7.57: Grouped frequency table for X

X	$0 \le X < 10$	$10 \le X < 20$	$20 \le X < 30$	$30 \le X < 40$
Frequency (f)	8	12	6	4

i Calculate an estimate of the mean value of X.
ii Showing all your working, calculate an estimate of the standard deviation of X.

11 The capacities of 85 containers were recorded and are shown in Table 7.58.

Table 7.58: Container capacities

Capacity (C litres)	No. containers (f)
$20 \le C < 24$	7
$24 \le C < 28$	15
$28 \le C < 30$	29
$30 \le C < 32$	22
$32 \le C < 35$	12

i Calculate an estimate of the mean capacity.
ii Showing all working, calculate an estimate of the standard deviation in litres. Give your final answer correct to the nearest 10 millilitres.

12 The heights of 200 male students and 100 female students are summarised in the grouped frequency table in Table 7.59.

Table 7.59: Students' heights

Height (x cm)	$145 \le x < 155$	$155 \le x < 170$	$170 \le x < 185$	$185 \le x < 120$
No. males (f)	37	102	59	2
No. females (f)	24	66	10	0

i Calculate an estimate of the standard deviation of the heights of:
a the males, **b** the females.

The mean height of the 300 students is $163\frac{73}{120}$ cm, and the mean of the squares is $26855\frac{47}{48}$ cm^2.

ii Find the standard deviation of the heights of all 300 students.
iii Show that your answer to **ii** is not a weighted average of your answers to **i a** and **b**.

13 A fun-day event where some games were organised was attended by 168 children. The children were divided equally into six groups according to their ages in completed years.

The age groups were 2–5, 6–8, 9–10, 11–12, 13 and 14–16 years.

i Construct, using actual class boundaries, a grouped frequency table to illustrate the data given above.
ii Calculate an estimate of the mean age.
iii Calculate an estimate of the standard deviation, giving your answer to the nearest month.

14 As part of her school agriculture project, a student planted 350 tomato seeds and recorded the time that each of them took to germinate. The results, for the seeds that germinated, are given in Table 7.60.

Table 7.60: Germination times

Time taken (hours)	24–26	26–30	30–35	35–50	50–60	60–72
No. seeds (f)	1	3	7	72	192	55

i For the seeds that germinated, calculate:
a an estimate of the mean time taken, **b** an estimate of the standard deviation.
ii What difficulty would be encountered if you were asked to calculate an estimate of the standard deviation of the times taken to germinate by all 350 seeds?

15 The altitudes, X metres, of a random sample of 100 peaks are summarised in Table 7.61.

Table 7.61: Altitudes of peaks

Altitude (X metres)	1200–1400	1400–1800	1800–2000	2000–2300
No. peaks (f)	3	59	23	15

i Calculate an estimate of the mean $\overline{X}$ and the standard deviation σ.
ii Use linear interpolation to calculate estimates of Q_1 and Q_3, the lower and upper quartiles.
iii Find, correct to 2 decimal places, the value of k when each of Q_1 and Q_3 is expressed as $\overline{X} + k\sigma$.

7.6 Measures of Dispersion for Combined Sets of Data

When calculating the mean value for combined sets of data, we need to find the sum of all the values in both sets and also the total number of values in those sets.

Similarly, when calculating the standard deviation for combined sets of data, we need to find the sum of all the squares in both sets.

For two sets of data, A and B, which are combined:

$$\text{Standard deviation of } A \text{ and } B = +\sqrt{\text{Mean of the squares of } A \text{ and } B - \text{Square of the mean of } A \text{ and } B}$$

Examples

1 X and Y represent two sets of numbers.

The 10 numbers in set X add up to 50, and the squares of these numbers add up to 300.

The 20 numbers in set Y add up to 160, and the squares of these numbers add up to 1200.

For set X, we have: $N = 10, \Sigma X = 50$ and $\Sigma X^2 = 300$.

For set Y, we have: $N = 20, \Sigma Y = 160$ and $\Sigma Y^2 = 1200$.

The mean of set X and Y combined $= \frac{50+160}{10+20} = 7$.

The mean of the squares of set X and Y combined $= \frac{300+1200}{10+20} = 50$.

Standard deviation of set X and Y combined $= \sqrt{\frac{300+1200}{10+20} - \left(\frac{50+160}{10+20}\right)^2} = \sqrt{50-7^2} = 1$

2 30 boys and 25 girls were each asked how many pets they owned.

Using B and G to represent the numbers of pets owned by the boys and by the girls, the following results were obtained: $\Sigma B = 56$, $\Sigma B^2 = 152$, $\Sigma G = 50$, $\Sigma G^2 = 154$.

Find the standard deviation of the number of pets owned by the 55 children.

$$\text{Standard deviation} = \sqrt{\frac{\Sigma B^2 + \Sigma G^2}{30+25} - \left(\frac{\Sigma B + \Sigma G}{30+25}\right)^2} = \sqrt{\frac{152+154}{30+25} - \left(\frac{56+50}{30+25}\right)^2} = 1.36 \text{ pets.}$$

3 Two researchers, *P* and *Q*, investigated the masses of adult chaffinches in two locations. Their findings are presented in Table 7.62. Find the standard deviation for the combined results of the two researchers.

Table 7.62: Chaffinch masses

Mass (g)	*M* mid-value	Researcher *P* frequency (*f*)	*fM*	*fM*²	Researcher *Q* frequency (*f*)	*fM*	*fM*²
16–18	17	5	85	1445	39	663	11271
18–19	18.5	84	1554	28749	48	888	16428
19–21	20	11	220	4400	38	760	15200
	Totals	100	1859	34594	125	2311	42899

Standard deviation for *P* and *Q* combined $= \sqrt{\frac{34594 + 42899}{100 + 125} - \left(\frac{1859 + 2311}{100 + 125}\right)^2} = 0.964\,\text{g}$.

Exercise 7G

1 **i** Data collected for two variables, *P* and *Q*, yielded the following results: $\Sigma P = 420$ and $\Sigma Q = 1290$.

Given that 25 values of *P* and 75 values of *Q* were used in obtaining the totals above, find:

a the mean of *P*, **b** the mean of *Q*,

c the mean when the values of *P* and *Q* are combined.

ii Given further that $\Sigma P^2 = 9000$ and $\Sigma Q^2 = 25000$, calculate for the values in *P* and *Q* combined:

a the variance, **b** the standard deviation.

2 Twelve values of each of the variables *C* and *D* yielded the following results:

$\Sigma C = 72$, $\Sigma D = 240$, $\Sigma C^2 = 2400$ and $\Sigma D^2 = 24720$.

Find:

i the mean of *C* and *D* combined, **ii** the standard deviation of *C* and *D* combined.

3 Fifteen observations of each of two variables, *Y* and *Z*, yielded the following data:

$\Sigma Y = 104$, $\Sigma Y^2 = 950$, $\Sigma Z = 32$, and $\Sigma Z^2 = 72$.

Calculate the standard deviation of the distribution of *Y* and *Z* combined.

4 The data in Table 7.63 were obtained for two variables, *P* and *Q*.

Table 7.63: Data for variables *P* and *Q*

	Number of values	Sum of values	Mean	Sum of squares	Variance	Standard deviation
P	56	2352	*a*	100 800	*b*	*c*
Q	44	*d*	53.5	*e*	49	*f*

i Calculate the values of *a*, *b*, *c*, *d*, *e* and *f* used in Table 7.69.

ii For the combined distribution of *P* and *Q*, find:

a the mean, **b** the variance.

5 The data in Table 7.64 were obtained for the two variables M and N.

Table 7.64: Data for variables M and N

	Number of values	Sum of values	Mean	Sum of squares	Variance	Standard deviation
M	40	p	−1.2	208.144	q	r
N	80	48	s	t	u	2.4

i Calculate the values of p, q, r, s, t and u in Table 7.70.

The distributions of the two variables M and N are combined.

ii For the combined distribution, find:

a the mean, **b** the standard deviation.

6 A variable X has 10 values such that $\Sigma X = 640$ and $\Sigma X^2 = 41000$. A variable Y has 20 values such that $\Sigma Y = 800$. Given that the values of x and y combined have a standard deviation of 14, find:

i the value of ΣY^2, **ii** the standard deviation of Y.

7 An artist has been given 400 squares of card for painting watercolours.

The total area of the cards is 500 000 cm^2 and the total of the perimeters of the cards is 56 000 cm.

i Find the mean length of the sides of the cards.

ii Calculate the standard deviation of the lengths of the sides of the cards.

8 Data on the masses, in grams, of two consignments of diamonds are summarised in Table 7.65.

Table 7.65: Diamond masses

	Consignment 1	Consignment 2
Number of diamonds	125	225
Sum of masses (g)	132.25	238.95
Sum of squares of masses (g^2)	725	1033

i Calculate the mean and standard deviation of the masses in:

a consignment 1, **b** consignment 2.

ii Use your answers from **i** to make comparisons between the consignments.

iii Find the variance of the masses of all 350 diamonds.

9 Twenty pupils at a school were each awarded a mark out of ten for punctuality and helpfulness, as shown in Table 7.66.

Table 7.66: Punctuality and helpfulness marks

Mark	4	5	6	7	8	9
Punctuality: No. pupils (f)	1	1	4	5	9	0
Helpfulness: No. pupils (f)	0	8	6	3	2	1

i Show that the variance for each set of marks is less than 1.4.

ii Calculate the variance when the marks for punctuality and helpfulness are combined.

10 A jeweller received a delivery of 75 sapphires in two colours. Their masses, to the nearest 0.1 grams, are summarised in Table 7.67.

Table 7.67: Sapphire masses

	Number of sapphires	
Mass (g)	**Green**	**Blue**
0.8–1.2	2	18
1.2–1.8	3	16
1.8–2.4	12	12
2.4–2.8	8	4

Calculate an estimate of the standard deviation of the masses of all 75 sapphires.

11 For two days Percy recorded the number of cars that drove past his house every hour for eight hours.

On the first day the range of his data was 0 and the mean number of cars per hour was 2.

i Calculate the standard deviation for the first day.

On the second day the range of his data was 40 and the mean number of cars per hour was 5.

ii Calculate the standard deviation for the second day.
iii Find the standard deviation of the number of cars during Percy's 16 hours of observation.

12 The ages, correct to the nearest year, of 12 girls and 18 boys are given in Table 7.68.

Table 7.68: Children's ages

Age (nearest year)	8	9	10–11	12
Number of girls (f)	5	1	1	5
Number of boys (f)	1	8	8	1

i Without calculation, state which group has the largest standard deviation. Explain how you arrived at your answer.
ii Calculate the variance of the ages of the combined group of 30 children. Include the units for the variance in your answer.

8 Linear Transformation of Data

Learning Objectives

In this chapter you will learn:

- How one distribution can be derived from another using a linear transformation
- About the effect a linear transformation has on the measures of central tendency and the measures of dispersion
- How to scale a set of data to a given mean and standard deviation
- Why and how scaling is used to compare performances in different activities

Introduction

If asked, you could easily find a measure of central tendency and a measure of dispersion for the ages of four friends, but will those measures be the same or different in five years' time?

What happens to the mean and standard deviation of employees' salaries if they all receive a 10% pay rise?

Once questions such as these have been answered, we will turn our attention to comparing performances in different activities. Should we only consider actual scores when comparing performances in two tests or are there other factors that need be taken into consideration?

Linear transformation is a process by which one set of numbers is ***mapped*** onto another set of numbers by addition and/or multiplication.

For example, the linear function or equation $y = 3x + 2$ maps the values $x = \{1, 2, 3\}$ onto the values $y = \{5, 8, 11\}$. The distribution 5, 8, 11 has been **derived** from the distribution 1, 2, 3.

8.1 Measures of Central Tendency for Derived Distributions

If the measures of central tendency of a distribution are known, then the measures of central tendency for a distribution derived by a combination of addition and/or multiplication can be found directly.

Example

1 From an original distribution of 5, 8, 20, 35, many others can be derived.

Some examples are shown in Table 8.1.

Table 8.1: Derived distributions

Derived distribution	Operation(s) required
6, 9, 21, 36	Adding 1
3, 6, 18, 33	Subtracting 2 (adding −2)
10, 16, 40, 70	Multiplying by 2
1.25, 2, 5, 8.75	Dividing by 4 (multiplying by $\frac{1}{4}$)
11, 17, 41, 71	Multiplying by 2 and adding 1
6.25, 10, 25, 43.75	Increasing by 25% (multiplying by 1.25)
1.6, 2.56, 6.4, 11.2	Reducing by 68% (multiplying by 0.32)

Identical operations must be performed on all the values in the original distribution.

Note that a percentage change in all the values of a distribution is achieved by multiplication, not by addition or subtraction.

- Percentage increase is the result of multiplication by a number that is greater than 1
- Percentage decrease is the result of multiplication by a number that is between 0 and 1

Examples

2 The distribution of $X = \{4, 12, 12, 14, 20, 22, 28\}$ has mode = 12, median = 14, mean = 16.

i $X + 30 = \{34, 42, 42, 44, 50, 52, 58\}$ is derived from X and has mode = 42, median = 44 and mean = 46 (see Figure 8.1).

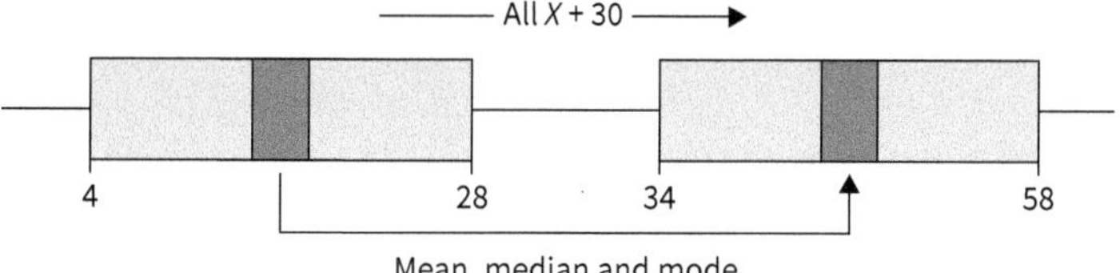

Figure 8.1: Distributions of X and $X + 30$

All values in X are increased by 30, and the three measures of central tendency all increase by 30.

ii $\frac{X}{2} = \{2, 6, 6, 7, 10, 11, 14\}$ is derived from X and has mode = 6, median = 7 and mean = 8.

All values of X are divided by 2 (multiplied by $\frac{1}{2}$), and the three measures of central tendency are all halved.

3 The frequency distribution of a variable K is shown in Table 8.2.

Table 8.2: Frequency distribution of K

K	5	6	7	8	9	
f	12	15	16	5	1	$\Sigma f = 49$

K has: mode = 7, median (25th) = 6, mean = $\frac{311}{45}$ = 6.35 (3 significant figures).

The distribution $2K + 3$ is derived from K with identical frequencies, as shown in Table 8.3.

Table 8.3: Frequency distribution of $2K+3$

$2K+3$	13	15	17	19	21	
f	12	15	16	5	1	$\Sigma f = 49$

$2K+3$ has: mode $= (2\times 7)+3 = 17$, median (25th) $= (2\times 6)+3 = 15$, mean $= \left(2\times\frac{311}{49}\right)+3 = 15.7$.

All three measures of central tendency have been multiplied by 2 and further increased by 3.

- All three measures of central tendency are affected by the same operations that are used to derive a distribution, whether that is multiplication or addition or a combination of these. Identical operations must be performed on all of the original values.

Exercise 8A

1 The set of integers $\{p, 13, 18, 29, 29\}$ has mode $= 29$, mean $= 20$ and median $= 18$. Without calculating the value of p, find the three measures of central tendency of the following derived distributions.

i $(p+2)$, 15, 20, 31, 31 **ii** $(p-5)$, 8, 13, 24, 24 **iii** $2p$, 26, 36, 58, 58

iv $\frac{p}{2}$, 6.5, 9, 14.5, 14.5 **v** $(2p-1)$, 25, 35, 57, 57 **vi** $\frac{p+1}{2}$, 7, 9.5, 15, 15

2 The variable Q has mode $= 6$, mean $= 8$ and median $= 7$. Find:

i the mode of $2Q$, **ii** the mean of $Q+18$, **iii** the median of $3Q+6$.

3 The variable G has mode $= 6.2$, mean $= 5.6$ and median $= 5.85$. Find:

i the mean of $\frac{G}{5}-1$, **ii** the median of $2(G+5)$, **iii** the mode of $1.7+1.5G$.

4 The variable H has a mean of 18. Find the new mean when all values in H are increased by 10%.

5 The variable T has a median of 2.6. Find the new median when all the values of T are decreased by 15%.

6 A distribution with a mean of 30.8 was derived from the distribution of P by decreasing all the values in P by 12%. Find the mean value of P.

7 The variable R shown in Table 8.4 has a mean of 4.8. The variables W and V in Tables 8.5 and 8.6 are derived from R.

Table 8.4: Frequency table for R

R	3	4	5	6
f	a	b	c	d

Table 8.5: Frequency table for W

W	7	9	11	13
f	a	b	c	d

Table 8.6: Frequency table for V

V	2.0	2.5	3.0	3.5
f	a	b	c	d

i Find the mean value of W.
ii Find the mean value of V.

8 A boy calculated the mean mass of the students in his class to be 57.2 kg. He later discovered that the weighing machine had given readings that were 10% above the correct mass of each student.

What was the actual mean mass of the students in his class?

9 The ungrouped distribution of P shown in Table 8.7 has a mean value of 17.4.

Table 8.7: Distribution of P

P	6	14	22	30	38
f	a	b	c	d	e

Calculate an estimate of the mean value of the grouped distributions of variables W, X and Y shown in Tables 8.8–8.10.

Table 8.8: Distribution of W

W	5–13	13–21	21–29	29–37	37–45
f	a	b	c	d	e

Table 8.9: Distribution of X

X	$0 \le X < 4$	$4 \le X < 8$	$8 \le X < 12$	$12 \le X < 16$	$16 \le X < 20$
f	a	b	c	d	e

Table 8.10: Distribution of Y

Y	6.0–8.4	8.4–25.2	25.2–27.6	27.6–44.4	44.4–46.8
f	a	b	c	d	e

10 A police officer recorded the speeds of vehicles passing a checkpoint. The mean speed of the vehicles was found to be 100.8 km/h.

Back at the station, he discovered that the device was underestimating each vehicle's speed by 4%.

What was the actual mean speed of the vehicles?

8.2 Measures of Dispersion for Derived Distributions

How are the measures of dispersion affected when one distribution is used to derive another? Are they all affected in the same way as the measures of central tendency?

Examples

1 The smallest value in a distribution is 5, and the largest value is 11, so the range is 6.

If all values are increased by 20, the smallest will be 25 and the largest will be 31 (see Figure 8.2).

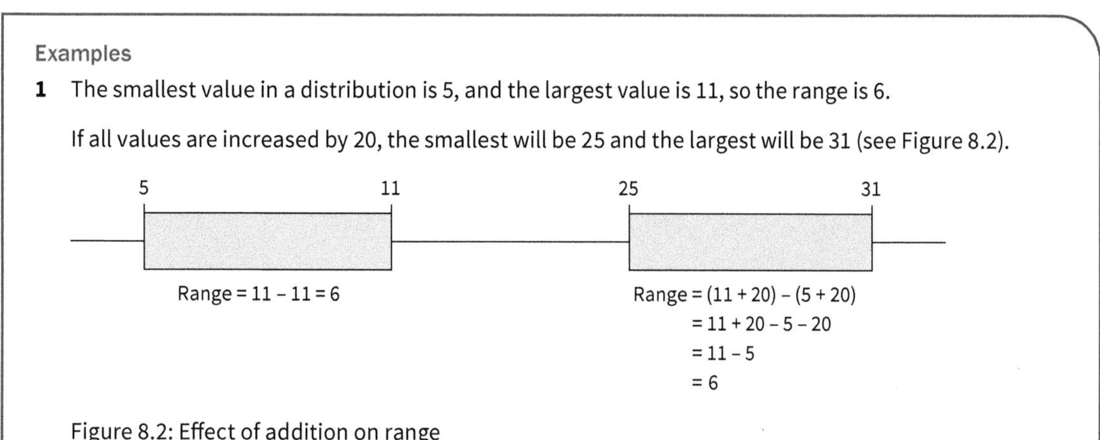

Figure 8.2: Effect of addition on range

The range is unaffected if we add the same amount to each value; this is also true if all the values are reduced by the same amount.
If the values in the original distribution above were each reduced by 4, the range would be $(11 - 4) - (5 - 4) = 6$.

2 The smallest value in a distribution is 5 and the largest value is 11, so the range is 6.
If all values are multiplied by 4, the smallest will be 20 and the largest will be 44 (see Figure 8.3).

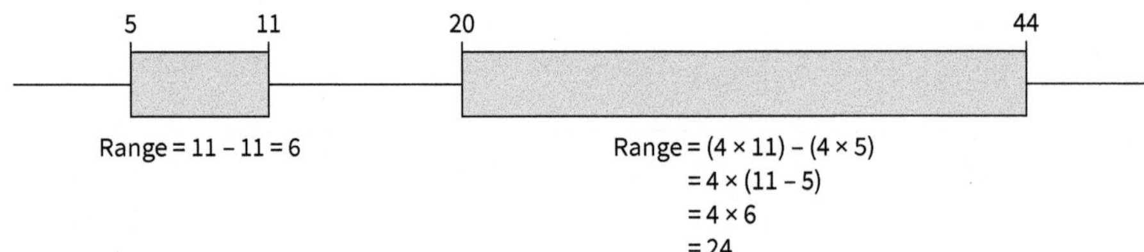

Range = 11 − 11 = 6

Range = (4 × 11) − (4 × 5)
= 4 × (11 − 5)
= 4 × 6
= 24

Figure 8.3: Effect of multiplication on range

The range of the derived distribution is four times larger than the range of the original distribution.
If all the values are divided by 4 then the range will be $\frac{11}{4} - \frac{5}{4} = \frac{6}{4}$ or 1.5, which is $\frac{1}{4}$ of the original range.

3 Table 8.11 shows the frequency distribution of a variable, X, and the derived distribution $3X + 1$.
If the standard deviation is affected in the same way as the range, we would expect the standard deviation of $(3X + 1)$ to be three times the standard deviation of X.

Table 8.11: Frequency distribution of X

X	f	fX	fX^2
3	4	12	36
4	7	28	112
5	6	30	150
	$\Sigma f = 17$	$\Sigma fX = 70$	$\Sigma fX^2 = 298$

$3X + 1$	$f(3X + 1)$	$f(3X + 1)^2$
10	40	400
13	91	1183
16	96	1536
	$\Sigma f(3X + 1) = 227$	$\Sigma f(3X + 1)^2 = 3119$

Standard deviation of X

$= \sqrt{\left(\frac{298}{17}\right) - \left(\frac{70}{17}\right)^2}$

$= \sqrt{0.5743944637...}$

$= 0.758$ (3 sig. figs)

Standard deviation of $(3X + 1)$

$= \sqrt{\left(\frac{3119}{17}\right) - \left(\frac{227}{17}\right)^2}$

$= \sqrt{5.169550173...}$

$= 2.274$ (4 sig. figs)

By checking that $3 \times 0.758... = 2.274...$, we can confirm that the standard deviation of $(3X + 1)$ is three times the standard deviation of X.
By checking that $3^2 \times 0.5743944637... = 5.169550173...$, we can state that the variance of $(3X + 1)$ is 3^2 times the variance of X.

All measures of dispersion are:

- Unaffected by addition (and by subtraction)
- Affected by multiplication (and by division), and by the same factor.

Examples

4 The distribution of a variable X has a range of 25 and a standard deviation of 7.2. The following distributions are derived from X.

i $X+5$

All values in X are increased by 5.
Measures of dispersion are not affected by addition.
The range of the derived distribution will remain at 25, and the standard deviation will remain at 7.2.

ii $0.5X$

All values in X are multiplied by 0.5.
Measures of dispersion are affected by multiplication and by the same factor.
The range of the derived distribution will be $0.5 \times 25 = 12.5$, and the standard deviation will be $0.5 \times 7.2 = 3.6$.

iii $4X-1$

All values in X are multiplied by 4 and then reduced by 1.
The measures of dispersion are only affected by multiplication here.
The range of the derived distribution will be $4 \times 25 = 100$, and the standard deviation will be $4 \times 7.2 = 28.8$.
The variance of $(4X-1)$ will be $4^2 \times 7.2^2 = 829.44$.

Exercise 8B

1 The distribution of a variable T has a range of 12, and a standard deviation of 6.3. Find the range and the standard deviation of the following derived distributions:

i $T+7$ ii $T-2$ iii $2T$

iv $3T+4$ v $\frac{1}{4}T-1$ vi $\frac{T+6}{3}$

2 Each value in a distribution is reduced by 25%. If the standard deviation was originally 4.4, what will it be after the percentage reduction in the values?

3 The masses of a group of children have a mean of 46.7 kg and a standard deviation of 9.1 kg. Find the new mean and the new standard deviation, if each child in the group reduces his or her mass by:

i 900 g, ii 5%, iii 900 g, and then by 5%.

4 The distribution of a particular variable has an interquartile range of 8.0. All values in this distribution are decreased by 3 and then further decreased by 20%. Find the interquartile range of the resulting distribution.

5 The variable P shown in the frequency table in Table 8.12 has a standard deviation of 6.6.

Table 8.12: Frequency table for P

P	10	14	18	22	26
f	p	q	r	s	t

i Find the standard deviation of each of the variables A and B shown in Tables 8.13 and 8.14.

Table 8.13: Frequency table of A

A	15	19	23	27	31
f	p	q	r	s	t

Table 8.14: Frequency table of B

B	25	35	45	55	65
f	p	q	r	s	t

ii Calculate an estimate of the standard deviation of the grouped distribution of the variable T shown in Table 8.15.

Table 8.15: Distribution of T

T	5–	7–	9–	11–	13–15
f	p	q	r	S	t

6 The number of books owned by the boys in a group has a standard deviation of 3.4.

i If each boy in the group receives one new book at Christmas:

a What will the standard deviation of the number of books be after Christmas?

b What will the variance be after Christmas?

ii What would each boy need to do so that the standard deviation increases from 3.4 to 6.8?

7 Each value in a distribution is increased by 15% and the standard deviation changes to 5.29.

What was the standard deviation of the original distribution?

8 The set of numbers 6, 10, t, 14, 15 has a mean of m and a standard deviation of d. Use this information to find, in terms of m and d, the mean and standard deviation of the following sets of numbers:

i 10, 14, $(t+4)$, 18, 19 **ii** 18, 30, $3t$, 42, 45 **iii** 2, 4, $(0.5t-1)$, 6, 6.5.

9 A distribution, whose smallest and largest values are 10 and 18, is used to derive another distribution. The smallest value of the derived distribution is 9 and its range is 4. If the standard deviation of the derived distribution is 1.3, find the variance of the original distribution.

10 The monthly salaries of the employees at Grindtech last year had a mean of \$4600 and a standard deviation of \$750. In January this year, each employee received a 6% pay increase plus a bonus of \$500. Calculate the mean and standard deviation of their monthly salaries, including bonuses, for January this year.

8.3 Scaling

Scaling is a linear transformation of one set of numbers to another set of numbers that have a chosen mean and a chosen deviation (the standard deviation is commonly used). This process can be used to compare, amongst other things, performances in different activities, such as examinations and athletics races.

For example, George scored 60% in a chemistry exam and Georgina scored 60% in a physics exam. Pablo came third in a 400-metre race and Paulina came third in an 800-metre race. How should we measure the performance of each pair to decide who performed better?

To do this fairly, we must measure their performances against everyone else that wrote the exams or competed in the races. Their actual scores and running times are expressed in terms of the mean and the standard deviation of everyone involved in the activities, and then scaled to a chosen mean and standard deviation. By doing this, we are taking into consideration the level of difficulty of both exams, and the quality of the competition in both races.

In the examples and exercises that follow:

- The raw mean of a set of values is denoted by $\overline{X}$,and the raw standard deviation by σ_X.
- The scaled mean is denoted by $\overline{Y}$, and the scaled standard deviation by σ_Y.

Standard Scores

In an exam, a student's raw score is expressed as a standard score in terms of $\overline{X}$ and σ_X for all the candidates that took the exam:

$$\text{Candidate's standard score} = \overline{X} + N \times \sigma_X$$

N is the number of raw standard deviations above or below the mean:

$$N = \frac{\text{raw score} - \overline{X}}{\sigma}$$

A **scaled** mark is then obtained by substituting the chosen values $\overline{Y}$ and σ_Y into the candidate's standard score:

$$\text{Candidate's scaled score} = \overline{Y} + N \times \sigma_Y$$

Example

1 In a test, the raw mean was $\overline{X} = 60$ and the raw standard deviation was $\sigma_X = 10$.

A raw mark of 50 has a standard score of $\overline{X} - \sigma_X \left[N = \frac{50-60}{10} = -1 \right]$.

A raw mark of 80 has a standard score of $\overline{X} + 2\sigma_X \left[N = \frac{80-60}{10} = +2 \right]$.

These raw marks are to be scaled using a mean $\overline{Y} = 65$ and a standard deviation $\sigma_Y = 12$.

The raw mark of 50 = $\overline{X} - \sigma_X \xrightarrow{\text{scaled}} \overline{Y} - \sigma_Y = 65 + (-1 \times 12) = 53$.

The raw mark of 80 = $\overline{X} + 2\sigma_X \xrightarrow{\text{scaled}} \overline{Y} + 2\sigma_Y = 65 + (+2 \times 12) = 89$.

Alternatively, a raw score X can be transformed to a scaled score Y without finding the value of N:

$$(N =) \frac{Y - \overline{Y}}{\sigma_Y} = \frac{X - \overline{X}}{\sigma_X}$$

For the previous example, these equivalent fractions are:

$$\frac{\text{scaled score} - 65}{12} = \frac{50-60}{10} \Rightarrow \text{scaled score} = 65 - \frac{12}{10} \times (50-60) = 53$$

$$\frac{\text{scaled score} - 65}{12} = \frac{80-60}{10} \Rightarrow \text{scaled score} = 65 + \frac{12}{10} \times (80-60) = 89$$

The scaled scores of 53 and 89 have been derived from the raw scores of 50 and 80.

Notice that the difference between the two raw scores is equal to $3\sigma_X$, and the difference between the two scaled scores is equal to $3\sigma_Y$.

Example

2 In a 400-metre race, the mean time was 80 seconds and the standard deviation was 16 seconds. In an 800-metre race, the mean time was 174 seconds and the standard deviation was 36 seconds. Pablo ran the 400-metre race in 72 seconds, and Paulina ran the 800-metre race in 147 seconds. The times are to be scaled with a mean of 100 seconds and a standard deviation of 20 seconds. Find the scaled time for Pablo and for Paulina, and decide who performed better.

Pablo: $\frac{Y-100}{20}=\frac{72-80}{16} \longrightarrow Y=100+\frac{72-80}{16}\times 20=90$

Paulina: $\frac{Y-100}{20}=\frac{147-174}{36} \longrightarrow Y=100+\frac{147-174}{36}\times 20=85$

Pablo's scaled time is 90 seconds and Paulina's scaled time is 85 seconds.
Given the quality of the competition in their races, Paulina performed better than Pablo.

Exercise 8C

1 Given $\bar{X}=60$ and $\sigma_X=8$, write each of the following raw values in terms of $\bar{X}$ and σ_X:

i 68, **ii** 52, **iii** 72, **iv** 44, **v** 80, **vi** 34.

2 The marks in a chemistry exam had a mean of 60 and a standard deviation of 20. The scores are to be scaled with a mean of 40 and a standard deviation of 16. Find the scaled score of each of the following candidates whose raw marks are as indicated.

i Enrique 70 **ii** Maria 20 **iii** Phenyo 10
iv Wazeem 85 **v** Maatla 26 **vi** Dick 48

3 In a geography examination, the mean of the raw scores was 50 and the standard deviation was 16. The teacher scaled the scores with a mean of 40 and a standard deviation of 24.

The raw scores of seven students and the scaled scores of two students are given in Table 8.16.

Table 8.16: Geography examination results

Student	Raw mark	Standard score (using 50 & 16)	Scaled mark (using 40 & 24)
Patrick	66	$\bar{X}+\sigma_X$	$40+24=64$
Meesha	34		a
Caleb	50		b
Jane	42		c
Fatima	58		d
Basil	90		e
George	26		f
Pontso	g		$=46$
Ludwig	h		$=70$

Work out the scaled scores and the raw scores represented by the letters ***a*** to ***g***.

4 A biology exam consists of two written papers, 1 and 2. Boi scored 70% on paper 1 and 54% on paper 2. On paper 1 the mean was 65% and the standard deviation was 20%; on paper 2 the mean was 50% and the standard deviation was 12%. The scores for both papers are to be scaled with a mean of 60% and a standard deviation of 18%.

i Find Boi's scaled mark on:

a paper 1, **b** paper 2.

ii Given the level of difficulty of the two papers, on which one did Boi perform better? Give a reason for your answer.

5 In the past year, Elena has taken part in two chess tournaments – one in Italy and one in Sri Lanka. In the Italy tournament she scored $6\frac{1}{2}$ points, and in the Sri Lanka tournament she scored 6 points. In both tournaments the mean score of all the competitors was $4\frac{2}{3}$. The standard deviation in Italy was $2\frac{7}{24}$ and in Sri Lanka it was $1\frac{3}{5}$.

i Scale Elena's score in the Italy tournament and in the Sri Lanka tournament with a mean of 5 and a standard deviation of 3.

ii Given the strength of the competition, in which of these tournaments was Elena least successful? Justify your answer.

6 Kevin and Josh are athletes who participate in both track and field events. Kevin runs in 3000-metre races and takes part in the triathlon; Josh runs in 200-metre races and takes part in the high jump. Both athletes took part in a recent competition where they were each involved in their two events.

Table 8.17 gives the mean and the standard deviation of all the raw measurements taken in each event. Kevin's and Josh's race times, Kevin's triathlon score and Josh's best high jump are given in the last two columns.

Table 8.17: Track and field performance

	Mean	Standard deviation	Kevin	Josh
3000 m	506 seconds	36.8 seconds	496.8 seconds	—
Triathlon	1294 points	240 points	1240 points	—
200 m	25.5 seconds	3.25 seconds	—	26.8 seconds
High jump	1.88 metres	0.05 metres	—	1.88 metres

Recorded measurements for each of the four events are to be scaled with a mean of 0 and a standard deviation of 1.

i Find:

a Kevin's scaled time in the 3000-metre race, **b** Kevin's scaled points score in the triathlon,

c Josh's scaled time in the 200-metre race.

ii In which of the three events in part **i** did either Kevin or Josh perform best, given the strength of the competition? Explain your reasoning.

Josh's recorded high jump is identical to the mean in that competition.

iii Why would it not be appropriate to scale this measurement to 0?

7 Three prizes were awarded for the best combined performance in art and drama. The mean raw score in art was 62 and the standard deviation was 8. The mean raw score in drama was 48 and the standard deviation was 16. The raw scores of the three prize winners are shown in Table 8.18.

Table 8.18: Art and drama scores

Student	Art	Drama
Danielle	62	64
Petros	74	44
Quincy	58	72

To decide the prize winners, scores were scaled with a mean of 55 and a standard deviation of 12.

i Calculate the scaled marks in each subject for each of the three students.
ii By finding the total of the scaled scores, find which student was awarded each of the prizes.

8 Table 8.19 shows some raw scores and scaled scores for students who took three science examinations. The mean and the standard deviation for each subject are given.

Table 8.19: Science examination results

	Raw scores			**Scaled scores**		
Student	**Chemistry**	**Physics**	**Biology**	**Chemistry**	**Physics**	**Biology**
April	40	68	55	*a*	74	46
Lucky	45	44	73	*c*	*d*	*e*
Ketan	*f*	*g*	*h*	38	76	62
Mean	40	52	64	58	58	58
Standard deviation	15	12	9	*b*	*b*	*b*

The scores for all subjects were scaled with a mean of 58 and a standard deviation of *b*.

i Find the values of the letters *a* to *h* that appear in the table.
ii Find the total of the three scaled scores, and state which of these students performed best overall.

9 The raw mean in a test was 56, and the scores are to be scaled with a mean of 60. The scaled deviation is to be made equal to half the raw deviation. Find the scaled score of a student who scored 30 in the test.

10 The mean scores on papers 1 and 2 of a biology examination were 64 and 48, respectively. The standard deviation for paper 1 was 8, and the standard deviation for paper 2 was 20. The scores for both papers are to be scaled with a standard deviation of 10, and a mean such that a student who scored 60 on both papers is awarded a scaled score for paper 1 that is half her scaled score for paper 2. Find the scaled mean that is necessary to achieve this.

Probability and Expectation 9

Learning Objectives

In this chapter you will learn:

- To distinguish between mutually exclusive, independent and dependent events and calculate probabilities accordingly
- To use a variety of techniques to find probabilities for selections made with or without replacement
- To apply your knowledge of expectation to expected profit and loss in simple games of chance
- About probability distributions for discrete variables

Introduction

The probability of a single event occurring may be theoretical or based on observations of what has happened in the past. The same is true in regard to two or more events, whether we investigate the probability of either of them occurring, or of both of them occurring; this is something that is of great interest to insurance and risk management companies, stock market investors, and so on. You may know your chances of passing a maths exam and a statistics exam separately, but how does this relate to your chances of passing just one of them, either of them, or both of them?

Once such probabilities have been found, they can be applied to expectation in situations where the results depend on chance.

9.1 Mutually Exclusive Events

When looking at the possible results of an experiment, it may be useful to know the probability that *either this or that* occurs. This is the probability of event A or event B, written P(A or B).

In simple cases, we can use the addition rule: P(A or B) = P(A) + P(B). However, this rule applies only if A and B are **mutually exclusive**. Mutually exclusive events have no common favourable outcomes, i.e. the two events cannot occur at the same time.

Examples

1 Table 9.1 gives the numbers of animals on Edwin's farm.

Table 9.1: Farm animals

	Sheep	Goats	Totals
Male	5	8	13
Female	14	22	36
Totals	19	30	49

If one animal is selected at random, find the probability that it is:

i a sheep or a goat, **ii** female or a goat, **iii** male or a sheep.

i There are 19 sheep and 30 goats, and there are $19+30=49$ animals that are a sheep or a goat. Being a sheep and being a goat are mutually exclusive; no animal can be a sheep and a goat.

$$\text{P(a sheep or a goat)} = \text{P(sheep)} + \text{P(goat)} = \frac{19}{49}+\frac{30}{49}=\frac{49}{49}=1$$

The selected animal is *certain* to be a sheep or a goat.

ii There are 36 females and 30 goats, but there are not $36+30=66$ animals that are female or a goat. The 22 female goats have been counted twice. Being female and being a goat are not mutually exclusive.

$$\text{P(female or a goat)} = \text{P(female)} + \text{P(goat)} - \text{P(female goat)} = \frac{36}{49}+\frac{30}{49}-\frac{22}{49}=\frac{44}{49}$$

iii There are 13 males and 19 sheep, but there are not $13+19=32$ animals that are male or a sheep. The 5 male sheep have been counted twice. Being male and being a sheep are not mutually exclusive.

$$\text{P(male or a sheep)} = \text{P(male)} + \text{P(sheep)} - \text{P(male sheep)} = \frac{13}{49}+\frac{19}{49}-\frac{5}{49}=\frac{27}{49}$$

Find the probability that the selected animal is:

iv female or a sheep,

v male or a goat,

vi neither female nor a sheep.

2 From the six cards in Figure 9.1, find the probability of randomly selecting a card that is square or black.

  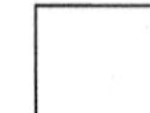 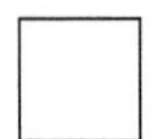 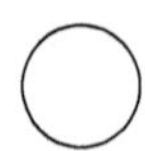 

Figure 9.1: Card selection

No. square or black cards = No. square cards + No. black cards − No. square black cards

$$= 4+3-2=5$$

$$\text{P(square or black)} = \text{P(square)} + \text{P(black)} - \text{P(square and black)} = \frac{4}{6}+\frac{3}{6}-\frac{2}{6}=\frac{5}{6}$$

3 The five cards shown in Figure 9.2 are laid face down on a table and one card is selected at random.

1 2 4 5 9

Figure 9.2: Number cards

Consider the two events:

A: an odd number is selected, which has 3 favourable outcomes (1, 5 and 9),

B: a prime number is selected, which has 2 favourable outcomes (2 and 5).

The probabilities are $P(\mathbf{A}) = \frac{3}{5}$ and $P(\mathbf{B}) = \frac{2}{5}$.

Selecting the card with a '5' on it is favourable to both **A** and **B**.

Events **A** and **B** are not mutually exclusive, so $P(\mathbf{A} \text{ or } \mathbf{B}) \neq P(\mathbf{A}) + P(\mathbf{B})$.

$P(\mathbf{A} \text{ or } \mathbf{B}) = P(\mathbf{A}) + P(\mathbf{B}) - P(\mathbf{A} \text{ and } \mathbf{B}) = \frac{3}{5} + \frac{2}{5} - \frac{1}{5} = \frac{4}{5}$

Summarising, we have:

$$P(\mathbf{A} \text{ or } \mathbf{B}) = P(\mathbf{A}) + P(\mathbf{B}) - P(\mathbf{A} \text{ and } \mathbf{B}).$$
If **A** and **B** are mutually exclusive then
$$P(\mathbf{A} \text{ and } \mathbf{B}) = 0$$

Venn Diagrams

Venn diagrams use regions to represent sets of outcomes that are favourable to particular events. Outcomes favourable to a particular event are shown inside the region labelled for that event. Outcomes favourable to both events are shown in the region where the events overlap. Outcomes favourable to neither event are shown in the region outside the sets. $\mathscr{E}$ is the region containing the set of exhaustive outcomes, and is called the *universal* set.

The first Venn diagram in Figure 9.3 shows two sets, **A** and **B**.

A represents the set of outcomes favourable to event **A**. **B** represents the set of outcomes favourable to event **B**.

The shaded region in the second diagram in Figure 9.3 represents the outcomes favourable to **A** or **B**, and is called the *union* of the sets, $\mathbf{A} \cup \mathbf{B}$.

The shaded region in the third diagram in Figure 9.3 represents the outcomes favourable to both **A** and also **B**, and is called the *intersection* of the sets, $\mathbf{A} \cap \mathbf{B}$.

The shaded region in the fourth diagram in Figure 9.3 represents the outcomes favourable to neither **A** nor **B**, and is called the *complement* of the union, $(\mathbf{A} \cup \mathbf{B})'$.

Using set notation, the rule for finding the probability of **A** or **B** is:

$$P(\mathbf{A} \cup \mathbf{B}) = P(\mathbf{A}) + P(\mathbf{B}) - P(\mathbf{A} \cap \mathbf{B})$$
If **A** and **B** are mutually exclusive then
$$P(\mathbf{A} \cap \mathbf{B}) = 0 \text{ because } \mathbf{A} \cap \mathbf{B} = \varnothing$$

- $\mathbf{A} \cup \mathbf{B}$ is equivalent to **A** or **B**
- $(\mathbf{A} \cup \mathbf{B})'$ is equivalent to neither **A** nor **B**
- $\mathbf{A} \cap \mathbf{B}$ is equivalent to **A** and **B**
- $(\mathbf{A} \cap \mathbf{B})'$ is equivalent to not both **A** and **B**

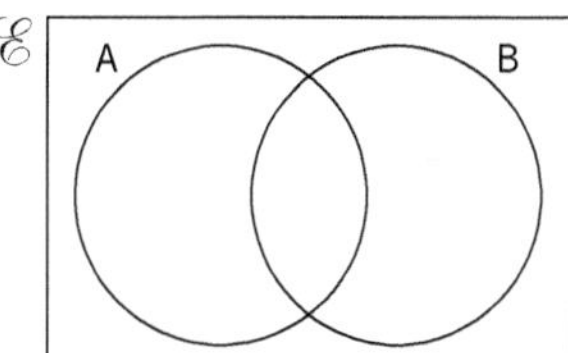

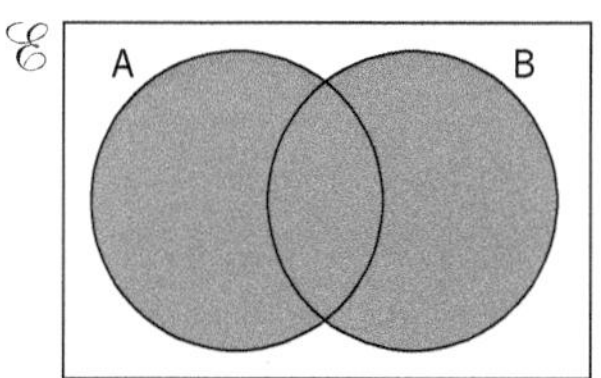

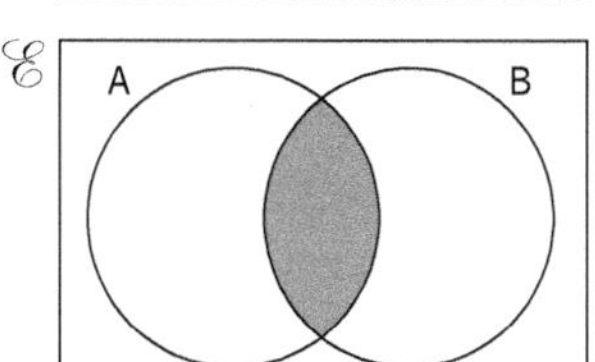

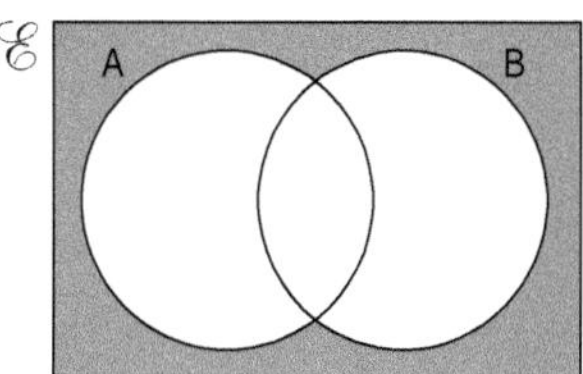

Figure 9.3: Venn diagrams for event **A** and event **B**

Examples

1 There are six possible outcomes when a normal six-sided die is rolled.

Consider the events:

A: a multiple of 3 is rolled, which has 2 favourable outcomes (3 or 6)

B: a square number is rolled, which has 2 favourable outcomes (1 or 4)

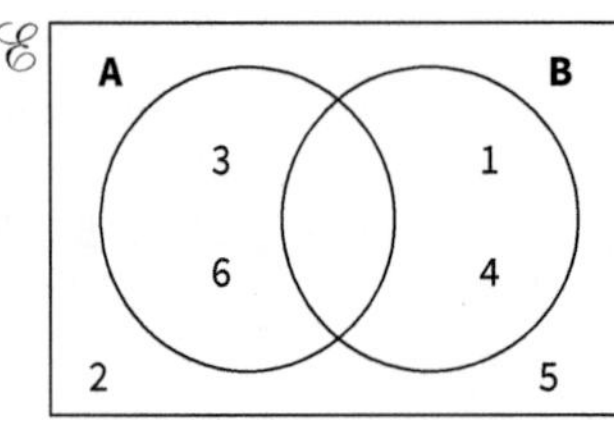

Figure 9.4: Event **A** and event **B**

A and **B** are shown in Figure 9.4.

A and **B** have no common favourable outcomes,

so **A** and **B** are mutually exclusive, and P(**A** and **B**) = 0.

P(**A** or **B**) = P(**A**) + P(**B**) − P(**A** and **B**)

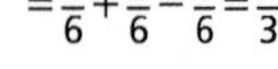

$$=\frac{2}{6}+\frac{2}{6}-\frac{0}{6}=\frac{2}{3}$$

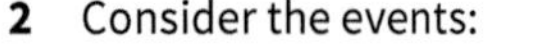

2 Consider the events:

A: a multiple of 3 is rolled, which has 2 favourable outcomes (3 or 6)

Z: an odd number is rolled, which has 3 favourable outcomes (1, 3 or 5)

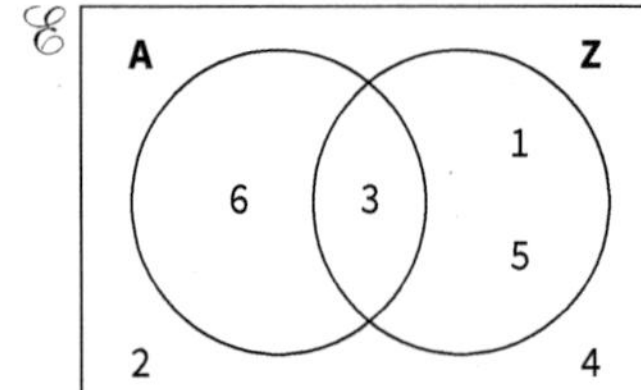

Figure 9.5: Event **A** and event **Z**

A and **Z** are shown in Figure 9.5.

There is one common favourable outcome (3), so **A** and **Z** are not mutually exclusive, and P(**A** and **Z**) $\neq$ 0

P(**A** or **Z**) = P(**A**) + P(**Z**) − P(**A** and **Z**)

$$=\frac{2}{6}+\frac{3}{6}-\frac{6}{6}=\frac{2}{3}$$

3 A class has 30 pupils: 20 study biology (**B**), 15 study history (**H**) and 12 study both of these subjects.

To make use of a Venn diagram, we label the appropriate regions with the numbers given in each set – see Figure 9.6.

a represents the number that study biology but not history,

b represents the number that study history but not biology,

c represents the number that study neither biology nor history.

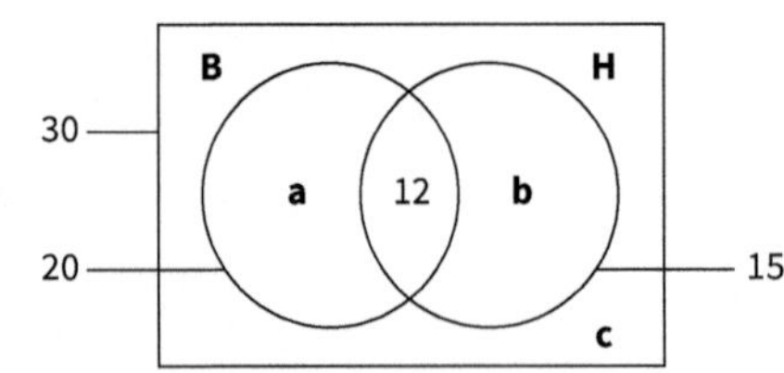

Figure 9.6: Event **B** and event **H**

From the diagram:

a + 12 = 20

12 + **b** = 15

a + 12 + **b** + **c** = 30

So, **a** = 8, **b** = 3 and **c** = 7

If one student is selected at random, find the probability that the student:

i studies either biology or history:

$$P(\mathbf{B} \cup \mathbf{H}) = P(\mathbf{B}) + P(\mathbf{H}) - P(\mathbf{B} \cap \mathbf{H}) = \frac{20}{30} + \frac{15}{30} - \frac{12}{30} = \frac{23}{30}$$

ii does not study biology:

$$P(B') = \frac{3}{30} + \frac{7}{30} = \frac{1}{3}$$

4 Table 9.2 shows the number of students that were present or absent in a class on Monday.

Table 9.2: Class attendance

	Absent	Present	Totals
Boys	2	18	20
Girls	1	14	15
Totals	3	32	35

A student's name from the class is selected at random. Find the probability that the selected student is:

i **A**bsent or a **B**oy

$$P(\mathbf{A} \cup \mathbf{B}) = P(\mathbf{A}) + P(\mathbf{B}) - P(\mathbf{A} \cap \mathbf{B})$$

$$= \frac{3}{35} + \frac{20}{35} - \frac{2}{34} = \frac{21}{35}$$

ii **P**resent or a **G**irl

$$P(\mathbf{P} \cup \mathbf{G}) = P(\mathbf{P}) + P(\mathbf{G}) - P(\mathbf{P} \cap \mathbf{G})$$

$$= \frac{32}{35} + \frac{15}{35} - \frac{14}{35} = \frac{33}{35}$$

5 **G** and **H** are two events, and it is given that $P(\mathbf{G}) = 0.5$, $P(\mathbf{H}) = 0.3$, and $P(\mathbf{G} \cup \mathbf{H}) = 0.7$. Find:

i $P(\mathbf{G} \cap \mathbf{H})$

ii $P(\mathbf{G} \cup \mathbf{H})'$

iii $P(\mathbf{G} \cap \mathbf{H})'$

A Venn diagram is used to solve the problem:

$P(\mathbf{G}) = \mathbf{a} + \mathbf{c} = 0.5$ [1]

$P(\mathbf{H}) = \mathbf{b} + \mathbf{c} = 0.3$ [2]

$P(\mathbf{G} \cup \mathbf{H}) = \mathbf{a} + \mathbf{b} + \mathbf{c} = 0.7$ [3]

[3] − [2] gives $\mathbf{a} = 0.4$

[3] − [1] gives $\mathbf{b} = 0.2$, so $\mathbf{c} = 0.1$ and $\mathbf{d} = 0.3$

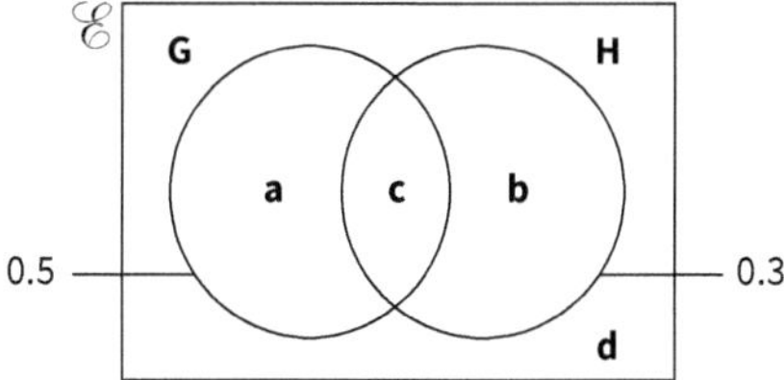

Figure 9.7: Event **G** and event **H**

i $P(\mathbf{G} \cap \mathbf{H}) = P(\mathbf{G} \text{ and } \mathbf{H})$

$= \mathbf{c} = 0.1$

ii $P(\mathbf{G} \cup \mathbf{H})' = P(\text{neither } \mathbf{G} \text{ nor } \mathbf{H})$

$= \mathbf{d} = 0.3$

iii $P(\mathbf{G} \cap \mathbf{H})' = P(\text{not both } \mathbf{G} \text{ and } \mathbf{H})$

$= 1 - \mathbf{c} = 0.9$

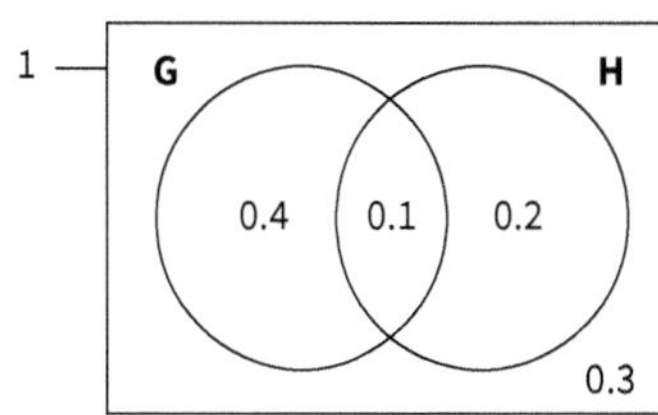

Figure 9.8: Solved Venn diagram for **G** and **H**

Exercise 9A

1 Table 9.3 gives information on the results of an examination taken by 80 students.

Table 9.3: Examination results

	Pass	Fail	Totals
Boys	32	4	36
Girls	39	5	44
Totals	71	9	80

i If one student is selected at random, find the probability that the student:
a passed, **b** is a boy, **c** passed or is a boy.
ii If a girl is selected at random, what is the probability that she failed?
iii If a student that passed is selected at random, what is the probability that it is a boy?

2 The letters A, B, B, B, C, D, D, E are each written onto squares of card and placed in a bag. If one card is randomly selected, find the probability that the letter written on the card is:

i A, **ii** in the word CADET,
iii not in the word TABLE, **iv** a vowel or in the word DONKEY.

3 Table 9.4 gives details of the numbers of items that a boy is carrying in a box.

Table 9.4: Box contents

	Pens	Pencils	Sweets
Blue	12	5	3
Red	7	9	2
Green	4	4	4

i Write down the fraction of the items in the box that is:
a a red pencil, **b** blue or a pen, **c** neither green nor a sweet.
ii If a pencil is selected at random, what is the probability that it is red?
iii If a blue item is randomly selected, what is the probability that it is not a pencil?

4. In a group of 25 boys, 9 are members of the chess club (**C**), 8 are members of the drama club (**D**) and 10 are members of neither of these clubs.

i Find the values of a, b and c in Figure 9.9.
ii If one boy is selected at random, find:
a $P(C \cap D)$,
b the probability that he is a member of just one of these clubs.

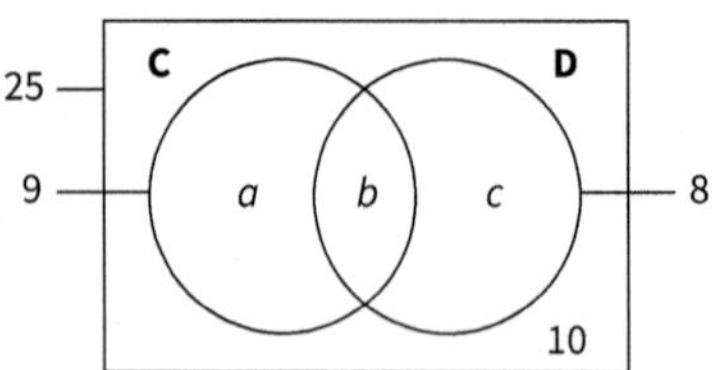

Figure 9.9: Venn diagram for **C** and **D**

5 A group of 40 boys were each asked whether or not they had read the novels *Bleak House* or *Great Expectations*. Their responses are shown in the Venn diagram in Figure 9.10.

If one boy is selected at random, find the probability that he has read:

i both novels,
ii neither of the novels,
iii just one of the novels.

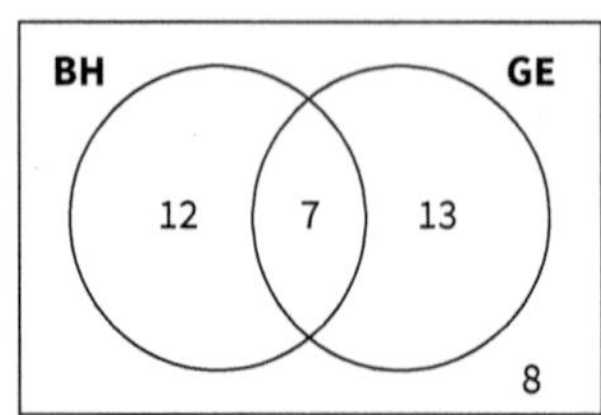

Figure 9.10: Readers of *Bleak House* and *Great Expectations*

6 A service station repaired 132 vehicles last month. The numbers of these vehicles requiring electrical, mechanical and bodywork repairs are shown in the Venn diagram in Figure 9.11.

i If one of these vehicles is randomly selected, find the probability that it required:

a mechanical repair,
b no bodywork repair,
c just one type of repair,
d just two types of repair.

ii If one of the vehicles that needed electrical repair was selected at random, find the probability that it required:

a bodywork repair,
b no mechanical repair,
c just one other type of repair.

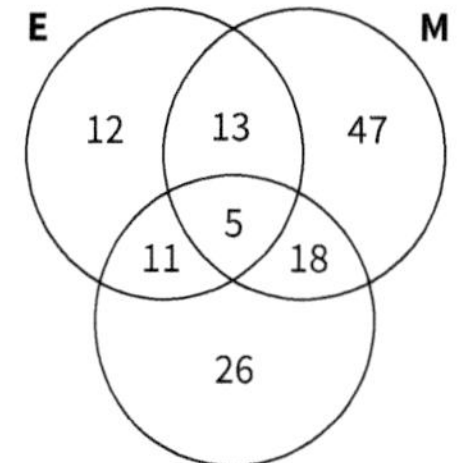

Figure 9.11: Electrical, mechanical and bodywork repairs

7 The 100 students at a technical college must study at least one subject from pure mathematics (**P**), statistics (**S**), and mechanics (**M**).

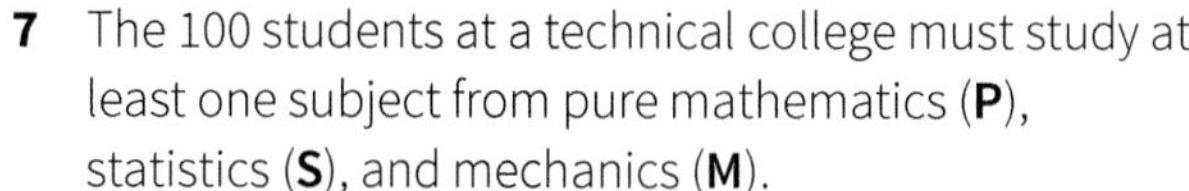

The numbers studying each subject are shown in the Venn diagram in Figure 9.12.

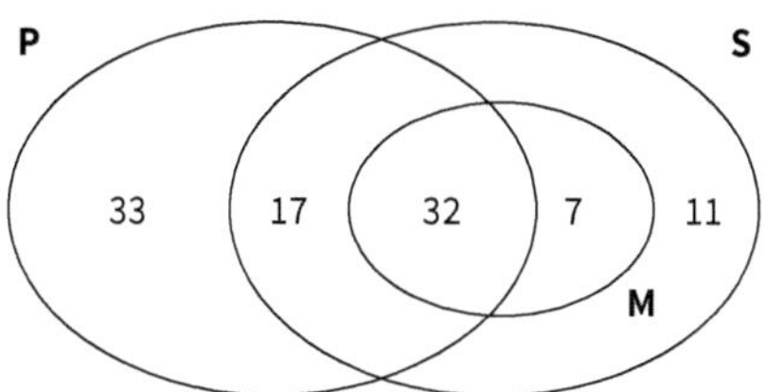

Figure 9.12: Students of mathematics, statistics and mechanics

i Who does the number 17 in Figure 9.12 refer to?
ii Find the probability that a randomly selected student studies just two of the three subjects.
iii If a statistics student is randomly selected, what is the probability that the student does not study mechanics?

8 Five events, A to E, that may occur when rolling a normal die are given.

A: even number	B: odd number	C: multiple of 3
D: prime number	E: square number	

State whether each of the following pairs of events is mutually exclusive or not.

i A and B	**ii** A and C	**iii** B and D
iv A and D	**v** C and E	

9 Two events are X and Y, where $P(X) = 0.5$, $P(Y) = 0.6$ and $P(X \cap Y) = 0.2$.

i State, with a reason, whether X and Y are mutually exclusive events.
ii Use a Venn diagram to find $P(X \cup Y)$.
iii What is the probability that either X or Y, but not both, occurs?

10 A, B and C are three events: $P(A) = 0.3$, $P(B) = 0.4$, $P(C) = 0.3$, $P(A \cap B) = 0.12$, $P(A \cap C) = 0$ and $P(B \cap C) = 0.1$.

i State, with a reason, which pair(s) of events (from A, B and C) are mutually exclusive.
ii Use a Venn diagram to find $P(A \cup B \cup C)'$, the probability that neither A nor B nor C occurs.

11 When Jayasree plays a game of chess with her brother, the probability that she does not win is 0.5, and the probability that she does not draw is 0.8. Find the probability that she loses against her brother.

12 A square board measuring 30 cm by 30 cm has two rectangular cards attached to it, as shown in Figure 9.13.

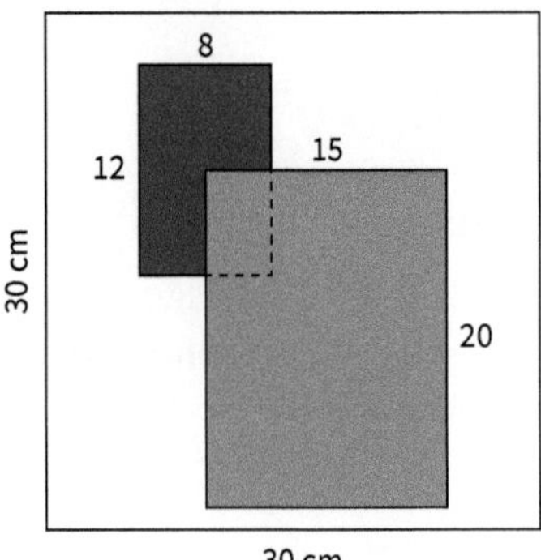

Figure 9.13: Cards attached to board

The small card measures 8 cm by 12 cm, and the large card, which hides exactly one-quarter of the small card, measures 15 cm by 20 cm.

A dart is randomly thrown so that it sticks within the perimeter of the square board.

Use areas to calculate the probability that the dart pierces:

i the large card, **ii** both cards, **iii** the large card only,
iv the small card only, **v** neither card,
vi both cards, given that it pierces at least one of them.

13 Given that $P(A) = 0.4$, $P(B) = 0.7$ and that $P(A \cap B) = 0.3$, find:

i $P(A \cup B)$ **ii** $P(A \cup B)'$

9.2 Combined Events

Experiments produce events that can be studied in combination. A combination of events may arise as the result of one or more experiments.

Combined events are either **independent** of one another, or **dependent** upon one another. Identifying the way in which selections are made – with or without replacement – will often determine whether they are independent or dependent.

Independent Events

If one event can occur without being affected by another event, then the two events are independent of one another. This is typically when selections are made *with* replacement.

Examples of experiments that will produce mutually independent events are:

- Selecting a card from a pack, replacing it, and then selecting another card from the same pack
- Selecting a ball from a bag and rolling a die
- Tossing a coin and rolling a die
- Tossing two coins
- Rolling three dice.

The multiplication rule for two independent events, **A** and **B**, is:

$$P(\mathbf{A} \text{ and } \mathbf{B}) = P(\mathbf{A}) \times P(\mathbf{B}) \text{ or}$$
$$P(\mathbf{A} \cap \mathbf{B}) = P(\mathbf{A}) \times P(\mathbf{B})$$

This rule can be extended to any number of mutually independent events.

$$P(\mathbf{A} \text{ and } \mathbf{B} \text{ and } \mathbf{C} \text{ and } \ldots) = P(\mathbf{A}) \times P(\mathbf{B}) \times P(\mathbf{C}) \times \ldots$$

Knowing how many outcomes are favourable to a combined event is vital and, if those outcomes are equally likely, can greatly reduce the amount of working required to solve a problem.

Examples

1 If two dice are rolled, there are two methods of obtaining a total of 11: (5 and 6) or (6 and 5).

P(total of 11) = P(5 and 6) + P(6 and 5)

$$= \left[\frac{1}{6} \times \frac{1}{6}\right] + \left[\frac{1}{6} \times \frac{1}{6}\right] = \frac{1}{18}$$

Two equally likely methods, each with a probability of $\frac{1}{36}$, gives P(total of 11) $= 2 \times \frac{1}{36} = \frac{1}{18}$.

2 If three dice are rolled, there are three methods of obtaining a total of 4: (1, 1, 2), (1, 2, 1) or (2, 1, 1).

P(total of 4) = P(1, 1, 2) + P(1, 2, 1) + P(2, 1, 1)

$$= \left[\frac{1}{6} \times \frac{1}{6} \times \frac{1}{6}\right] + \left[\frac{1}{6} \times \frac{1}{6} \times \frac{1}{6}\right] + \left[\frac{1}{6} \times \frac{1}{6} \times \frac{1}{6}\right] = \frac{1}{72}$$

Three equally likely methods, each with a probability of $\frac{1}{216}$, gives P(total of 4) $= 3 \times \frac{1}{216} = \frac{1}{72}$.

Note that the equally likely outcomes in the previous examples are mutually exclusive. Results that are favourable to a particular combined event can be found by listing, using two-way tables or tree diagrams.

Two-way tables are useful when dealing with a combination of just two events. All the equally likely outcomes for one event are used as row headings, and all the equally likely outcomes for the other event are used as column headings. Such a table, with r rows and c columns, shows $(r \times c)$ equally likely outcomes, each having a probability of $\frac{1}{(r \times c)}$.

Examples

3 A normal die is rolled and a fair coin is tossed. The possible outcomes are shown in Table 9.5.

Table 9.5: Two-way table for coin and die

Coin						
Head (H)	1, H	2, H	3, H	4, H	5, H	6, H
Tail (T)	1, T	2, T	3, T	4, T	5, T	6, T
Die	**1**	**2**	**3**	**4**	**5**	**6**

The 12 equally likely outcomes are shown in the grid, and each has a probability of $\frac{1}{12}$.

i P(square number and a tail)

Two of the 12 outcomes are favourable: (1, T) or (4, T).

P(square number and a tail) $= 2 \times \frac{1}{12} = \frac{1}{6}$

ii P(odd number and a head)

Three of the 12 outcomes are favourable: (1, H) or (3, H) or (5, H).

P(odd number and a head) $= 3 \times \frac{1}{12} = \frac{1}{4}$.

Probabilities can be found by counting the number of favourable outcomes in a two-way table *if and only if* the outcomes for each experiment shown in the table are equally likely.

Examples

4 Two normal dice are rolled. The 36 equally likely outcomes are shown in Table 9.6.

Table 9.6: Two-way table for two dice

2nd						
6	1, 6	2, 6	3, 6	4, 6	5, 6	6, 6
5	1, 5	2, 5	3, 5	4, 5	5, 5	6, 5
4	1, 4	2, 4	3, 4	4, 4	5, 4	6, 4
3	1, 3	2, 3	3, 3	4, 3	5, 3	6, 3
2	1, 2	2, 2	3, 2	4, 2	5, 2	6, 2
1	1, 1	2, 1	3, 1	4, 1	5, 1	6, 1
	1	2	3	4	5	6 1st

We simply count the number of these 36 outcomes that are favourable to various combined events.

i P(both numbers are odd) $= \frac{9}{36} = \frac{1}{4}$ **ii** P(sum of numbers is 9) $= \frac{4}{36} = \frac{1}{9}$

iii P(sum of numbers is 6 or 7) $= \frac{11}{36}$ **iv** P(numbers are the same) $= \frac{6}{36} = \frac{1}{6}$

5 Every Saturday, Fred goes jogging (J), cycling (C), sailing (S) or walking (W). He is equally likely to do any of these activities independently of what he does on any other Saturday.

For any two Saturdays, the 16 equally likely outcomes are shown in Table 9.7.

Table 9.7: Two-way table for Saturday activities

2nd				
W	JW	CW	SW	WW
S	JS	CS	SS	WS
C	JC	CC	SC	WC
J	JJ	CJ	SJ	WJ
	J	C	S	W 1st

Probabilities for any combination of events are found by counting those that are favourable.

i Probability that he does the same activity on two consecutive Saturdays $= \frac{4}{16} = \frac{1}{4}$.

ii Probability that he goes sailing just once on any two Saturdays $= \frac{6}{16} = \frac{3}{8}$.

iii Probability that he does not go jogging on any two Saturdays $= \frac{9}{16}$.

Tree diagrams are a means of showing the outcomes of combined events and their probabilities.

The possible outcomes of each experiment are shown at the ends of branches, and probabilities shown on the branches. The first experiment is shown at the left side, and successive experiments to the right.

Example

6 A bag contains three red buttons (R) and two blue buttons (B).

A button is randomly selected, replaced, and then another button is randomly selected.

All the possible outcomes are shown on the tree diagram in Figure 9.14.

1st		2nd		
$\frac{3}{5}$ R	$\frac{3}{5}$	R	Red and Red	$P(RR) = \frac{3}{5} \times \frac{3}{5} = \frac{9}{25}$
	$\frac{2}{5}$	B	Red and Blue	$P(RB) = \frac{3}{5} \times \frac{2}{5} = \frac{6}{25}$
$\frac{2}{5}$ B	$\frac{3}{5}$	R	Blue and Red	$P(BR) = \frac{2}{5} \times \frac{3}{5} = \frac{6}{25}$
	$\frac{2}{5}$	B	Blue and Blue	$P(BR) = \frac{2}{5} \times \frac{2}{5} = \frac{4}{25}$

Figure 9.14: Tree diagram for red and blue buttons

i Probability of selecting buttons of the same colour = P(RR) + P(BB) = $\frac{9}{25} + \frac{4}{25} = \frac{13}{25}$.

ii Probability of selecting buttons of different colours = P(RB) + P(BR) = $\frac{6}{25} + \frac{6}{25} = \frac{12}{25}$.

iii Probability of selecting at least one red button = P(RR) + P(RB) + P(BR) = $\frac{9}{25} + \frac{6}{25} + \frac{6}{25} = \frac{21}{25}$.

All of the outcomes except BB are favourable to selecting at least one red button, which gives a shortcut to the solution for part **iii**:

Probability of selecting at least one red button = 1 − P(BB) = $1 - \frac{4}{25} = \frac{21}{25}$.

Tree diagrams can become complicated if an experiment has many possible outcomes, or if many experiments take place.

Matters are often simplified if outcomes are thought of simply as *successes* or *failures*.

Suppose a bag contains ten balls, where one is pink (P), two are red (R), three are green (G) and four are blue (B), and the first of several experiments is to select a ball at random.

Depending on the question, it may not be necessary to show all four colours on the tree diagram, but rather use one of the initial choices shown in Figure 9.15 instead.

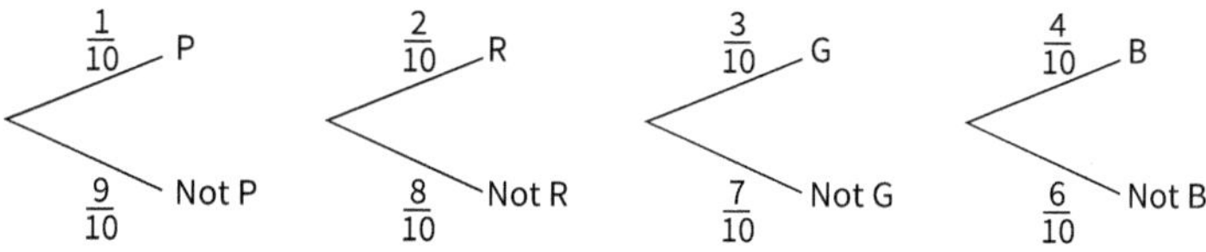

Figure 9.15: Combining initial outcomes

Example

7 Two dice are rolled. Find the probability of obtaining at least one 3.

We are only interested in whether or not a 3 is rolled with each die.

On a tree diagram, we can reduce the possible outcomes for each die to a success (3) or a failure (X) – see Figure 9.16.

$P(3) = \frac{1}{6}$ and $P(X) = \frac{5}{6}$

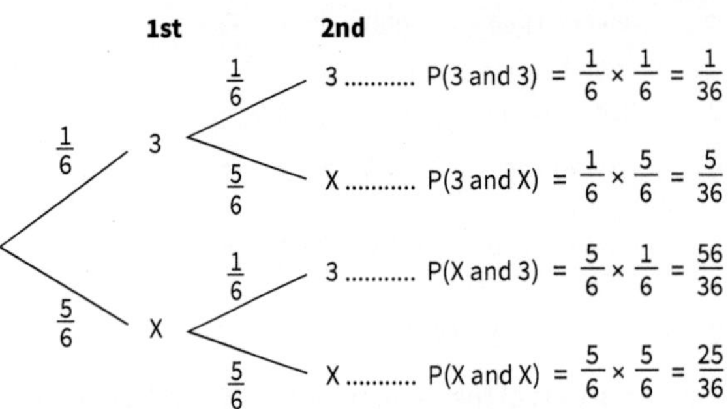

Figure 9.16: Rolling threes with two dice

The three favourable outcomes are (3 and 3), (3 and X) or (X and 3).

P(rolling at least one 3) $= \frac{1}{36} + \frac{5}{36} + \frac{5}{36} = \frac{11}{36}$.

8 The probability that it rains on any particular day in November in a certain town is 0.3.

Let R represent rain and let X represent no rain, so P(R) = 0.3 and P(X) = 0.7.

The tree diagram in Figure 9.17 shows all the possible outcomes and their probabilities for any three days in November.

Use the tree diagram to find the probability that, on any three particular days in November, it rains on:

i all of them, **ii** none of them, **iii** exactly one of them,
iv just two of them, **v** at least one of them.

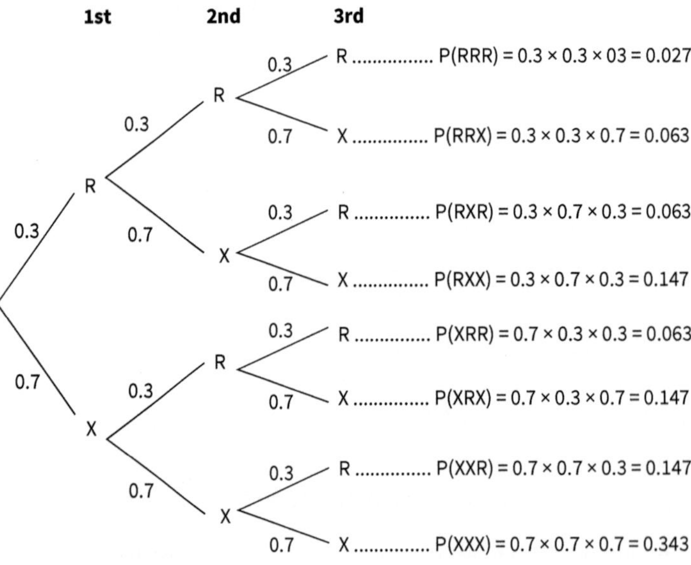

Figure 9.17: Probability of rain

9 A bag contains eight red balls, four blue balls and three green balls. One ball is randomly selected, replaced, and then another ball is selected. How, and in how many ways, can exactly one red ball be selected?

There are two ways to approach this problem:

i Four ways that are not equally likely: see Table 9.8.

Table 9.8: Not equally likely outcomes

1st ball	Red	Red	Blue	Green
2nd ball	Blue	Green	Red	Red

So, P(exactly one red ball) $= P(RB) + P(RG) + P(BR) + P(GR)$

$$= \left[\frac{8}{15} \times \frac{4}{15}\right] + \left[\frac{8}{15} \times \frac{3}{15}\right] + \left[\frac{4}{15} \times \frac{8}{15}\right] + \left[\frac{3}{15} \times \frac{8}{15}\right]$$

$$= \frac{112}{225}$$

ii Two ways, that are equally likely: see Table 9.9.

Table 9.9: Equally likely outcomes

1st ball	Red	Not Red
2nd ball	Not Red	Red

So, P(exactly one red ball) $= P(RX) + P(XR)$

$$= \left[\frac{8}{15} \times \frac{7}{15}\right] + \left[\frac{7}{15} \times \frac{8}{15}\right] \text{ or simply } 2 \times \left[\frac{8}{15} \times \frac{7}{15}\right]$$

$$= \frac{112}{225}$$

Note that the working is much simplified when the blue and green balls are thought of as *not red*.

Exercise 9B

1 A boy tosses two fair coins. Find the probability that he obtains:

i two heads, **ii** two tails,
iii one head and one tail, **iv** at least one head.

2 A girl tosses a fair coin and rolls a normal die. Find the probability that she obtains:

i a head and a 2, **ii** a tail and an odd number, **iii** a head and neither a 5 nor a 6,
iv a tail and a square number, **v** a head and a factor of 12.

3 A bag contains six coloured balls of equal size: one is green, two are blue and three are red. One ball is randomly selected, replaced, and then another ball is randomly selected.

i Calculate the probability that both balls are:
a red, **b** blue, **c** green.
ii Find the probability that the balls are:
a the same colour, **b** different colours.

4 A fair die, numbered from 1 to 6, is rolled three times. The three scores are added to obtain the total.

i Find how many ways there are to obtain a total of:
a 3, **b** 4, **c** 5, **d** 15.
ii Calculate the probability of obtaining each of the totals in part **i**.

5 Dorcus and Sarah each roll a normal six-sided die. Find the probability that:

i they do not roll the same number,
ii the absolute difference between the numbers they roll is 1.

6 A fair blue die is in the shape of a cube, and it is numbered 2, 3, 3, 5, 6, 7.

A fair red die is a regular tetrahedron in shape, and it is numbered 3, 7, 7, 8.

Each die is rolled once.

i Find the probability that:
a both dice score 3, **b** just one of the dice scores 3, **c** neither of the dice scores 3.
ii Find the probability that the sum of the two numbers obtained is:
a 5, **b** 10,
c more than 13, **d** at least 6.
iii Find the probability that the blue die scores more than the red die.

7 The probabilities that Abel, Betty and Yu are late for school on any particular day are 0.02, 0.04 and 0.05, respectively.

i Giving your answers as exact decimals, find the probability that:
a Abel is late on two consecutive days, **b** Yu is not late on any two consecutive days.
ii Find, as an exact decimal, the probability that, on any particular day:
a Abel and Betty are both late, **b** Betty is the only one of the three who is not late,
c only Abel is late.

8 A child presses one of the numbered buttons on a telephone (see Figure 9.18) and then presses a second button, both at random. When two buttons are pressed it makes a two-figure number.

7	8	9
4	5	6
1	2	3
	0	

Figure 9.18: Telephone keypad

Find, as an exact decimal, the probability that the two-figure number is:

i 15, **ii** 27 or 72, **iii** greater than 95,
iv a multiple of 11, **v** a multiple of 13, **vi** an odd number.

9 Ester plays a game of tennis and a game of golf each weekend. A game of tennis cannot be drawn, but a game of golf can be drawn.

The probability that she wins at tennis is 0.6.

The probability that she does not win at golf is 0.55, and she has a 70% chance of not drawing at golf.

i Construct a tree diagram showing the six possible outcomes for Ester in these two games.
ii Find the probability that she:
a loses at golf, **b** loses at tennis, **c** wins at tennis and draws at golf,
d wins just one of the two games, **e** wins at least one of the two games.

10 A bag contains five brown fuses and three pink fuses. A box contains six brown fuses and four pink fuses. An electrician randomly selects a fuse from the bag and a fuse from the box. Find the probability that:

i a particular fuse is selected from the bag, **ii** a particular pink fuse is selected from the box,
iii both selected fuses are brown, **iv** the two selected fuses are the same colour,
v at least one of the selected fuses is pink.

11 The probability that the 6 a.m. bus departs on time on any particular day is 0.2.

i What is the probability that the 6 a.m. bus does not depart on time on any particular day?
ii Find the probability that, in the next three days, the 6 a.m. bus departs on time:
a on all three days, **b** on just one day, **c** on exactly two days.

12 Letters and parcels delivered by a courier can take up to two days to arrive at their destinations. Table 9.10 shows the percentages of each particular type of item arriving.

Table 9.10: Delivery times

	Arriving		
Item	**Same day**	**After one day**	**After two days**
Letter	15%	50%	35%
Parcel	6%	24%	70%

i Find the probability that for Nico, who posted two letters on Monday, the letters:
a both arrive on Monday, **b** both arrive on Wednesday,
c arrive on the same day as each other.
ii Find the probability that for Sunil, who posted two parcels on Friday:
a one arrives on Friday and the other arrives on Saturday, **b** neither arrives on Friday.
iii Find the probability that for Emanuel, who posted one letter and one parcel on Thursday:
a the items arrive on the same day as each other, **b** the letter arrives the day before the parcel.

13 Amos plays one game of chess with each of his three friends Bashi, Cedric and Dilip. Table 9.11 gives the probabilities of some of the possible results for Amos.

Table 9.11: Chess results

	Result		
Opponent	**Win**	**Draw**	**Lose**
Bashi	0.65	0.05	
Cedric	0.42		0.44
Dilip		0.26	0.62

Use Table 9.12 to find, as an exact decimal, the probability that Amos:

i wins against Bashi and against Cedric, **ii** loses all three games,
iii fails to win a game, **iv** draws just one of the games,
v wins at least one of the games.

14 Amrit and Tawanda each have a set of three numbered cards (see Figure 9.19), which they place face down on a table.

Figure 9.19: Numbered cards

Each boy randomly turns over a card, and the winner is the one who turns over the largest number.

Find the probability that:

i Amrit wins the first game,
ii one of Amrit or Tawanda wins the first game,
iii Tawanda's first win is in the second game,
iv neither wins until the third game.

15 Ankit has a fair coin. He has tossed it nine times, and each time it has landed on heads. What is the probability that it lands on tails when he tosses it for the tenth time?

16 In attempting to qualify for a first-aid award, any of three types of certificate can be awarded to a candidate that passes. Table 9.12 gives the percentage of each type awarded in the past.

Table 9.12: First-aid awards

Gold	Silver	Bronze	No certificate
8%	20%	42%	30%

Two past candidates are selected at random.

i Find, as an exact decimal, the probability that:
  a both were awarded silver certificates,
  b neither was awarded a gold certificate,
  c just one of them was awarded a certificate.

Three past candidates are randomly selected.

ii Find, as an exact decimal, the probability that they were awarded:
  a the same type of certificate,
  b three different types of certificate.

17 A hockey team can win, lose or draw a game. If a particular team has a 20% chance of drawing any game, use Table 9.13 to find the probability that the team draws just one out of three games.

Table 9.13: Hockey result probabilities

1st game	Draw	X	X
2nd game	X	Draw	X
3rd game	X	X	Draw

Dependent Events and Conditional Probability

If one event cannot occur without being affected by another event, then the two events are dependent upon one another. Probabilities in such cases are '**conditional**', as they depend on the outcome of another event. This is typically when selections are made *without* replacement.

Examples of experiments that will produce mutually dependent events are:

- Selecting a card from a pack, not replacing it, then selecting another card from the same pack
- Selecting two balls from a bag at the same time, or one after the other
- Selecting two students from a class.

Examples

1 A bag contains three discs: two are black and one is white. One disc is randomly selected, not replaced, and a second disc is randomly selected.

Figure 9.20 shows the bag before the first selection is made.

P(black) $=\frac{2}{3}$ and P(white) $=\frac{1}{3}$

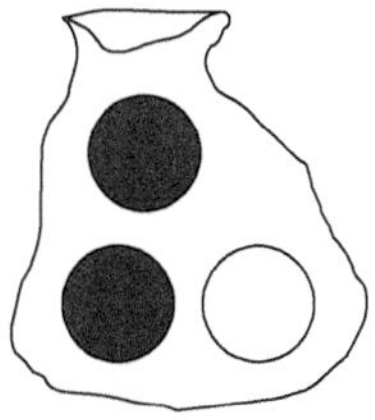

Figure 9.20: Before first selection

After the first selection, the bag could contain either

two black discs (Figure 9.21) or one black disc and one white disc (Figure 9.22).

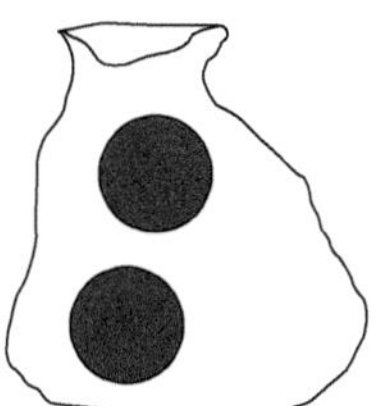

Figure 9.21: Two black discs remain

In this case, for the second selection P(black) = 1 and P(white) = 0.

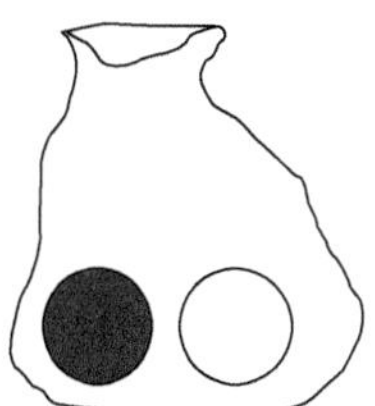

Figure 9.22: One of each remains

In this case, for the second selection P(black) $=\frac{1}{2}$ and P(white) $=\frac{1}{2}$.

We have a situation where P(second disc is black) $=\frac{1}{2}$ or 1

and P(second disc is white) $=\frac{1}{2}$ or 0.

The probabilities for the second selection depend on the outcome of the first selection.

For example, we have:

P(2nd disc is black, given that 1st is black) $=\frac{1}{2}$

In short, this is written P(black | black) $=\frac{1}{2}$, and so on.

The tree diagram in Figure 9.23 shows the possible outcomes and their probabilities.

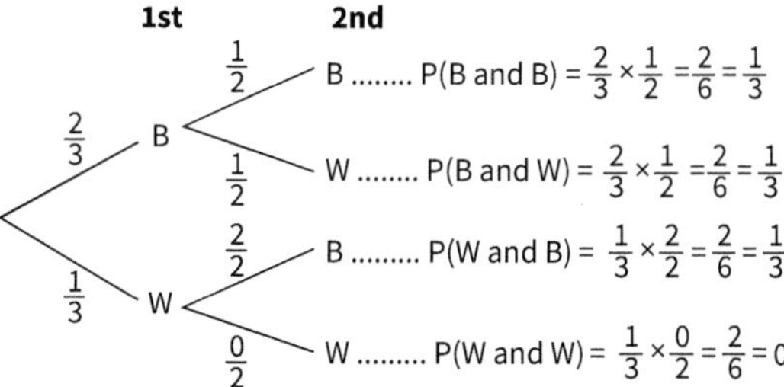

Figure 9.23: Tree diagram for discs in a bag

If **A** and **B** are mutually dependent events then:

P(**A** and **B**) = P(**A**) × P(**B**, given that **A** has already occurred), written as

$$P(\mathbf{A} \text{ and } \mathbf{B}) = P(\mathbf{A}) \times P(\mathbf{B} \mid \mathbf{A})$$

To solve problems involving mutually dependent events, we still have the option of listing favourable outcomes, using two-way tables or tree diagrams.

Examples

2 In a particular street, there are 12 houses: 7 of type A, 3 of type B and 2 of type C.

If two houses are selected at random, find the following probabilities:

i P(both are type A) $= \text{P(A and A)} = \text{P(A)} \times \text{P(A} \mid \text{A)} = \frac{7}{12} \times \frac{6}{11} = \frac{7}{22}$

ii P(they are the same type) = P(A and A) + P(B and B) + P(C and C)

$$= \left[\frac{7}{12} \times \frac{6}{11}\right] + \left[\frac{3}{12} \times \frac{2}{11}\right] + \left[\frac{1}{12} \times \frac{0}{11}\right] = \frac{4}{11}$$

iii P(one of each type) = P(A and not A) + P(B and not B) + P(C and not C)

$$= \left[\frac{7}{12} \times \frac{5}{11}\right] + \left[\frac{3}{12} \times \frac{9}{11}\right] + \left[\frac{2}{12} \times \frac{10}{11}\right] = \frac{41}{66}$$

3 A bag contains two red discs (R) and three green discs (G). Two discs are selected without replacement.

This combination of events can be investigated using a two-way table (see Table 9.14), but we need to distinguish between the two red discs and between the three green discs, because no one individual disc can be selected twice. We label the red disks R_1 and R_2, and the green discs G_1, G_2 and G_3. The five discs are equally likely to be selected.

Table 9.14: Two-way table for red/green disc selection

2nd disc					
G_3	RG	RG	GG	GG	—
G_2	RG	RG	GG	—	GG
G_1	RG	RG	—	GG	GG
R_2	RR	—	GR	GR	GR
R_1	—	RR	GR	GR	GR
	R_1	R_2	G_1	G_2	G_3 **1st disc**

The dashes in the table indicate that none of the five discs can be selected twice.

The table shows 20 equally likely outcomes and, by simply counting, we can see that:

P(two red) $= \frac{2}{20} = \frac{1}{10}$

P(two green) $= \frac{6}{20} = \frac{3}{10}$

P(one red and one green) $= \frac{12}{20} = \frac{3}{5}$

Explain why the sum of these three probabilities is equal to 1.

4 Two students are randomly selected from a class of 18 girls (G) and 22 boys (B). The possible outcomes are shown in the tree diagram in Figure 9.24.

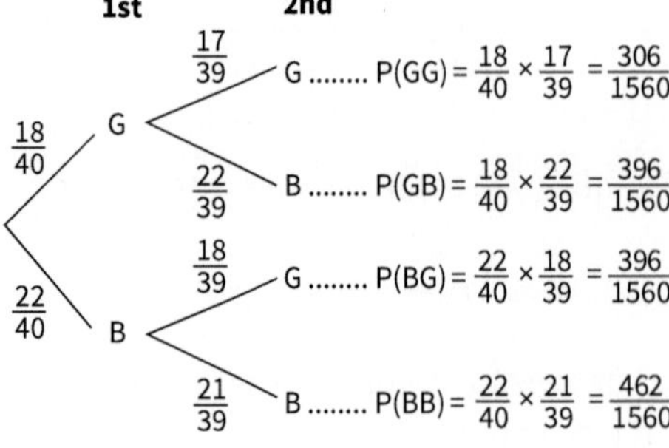

Figure 9.24: Tree diagram for boy/girl selection

ii Find the probability of selecting two students who are:

a the same gender:

$$P(GG) + P(BB) = \left[\frac{18}{40} \times \frac{17}{39}\right] + \left[\frac{22}{40} \times \frac{21}{39}\right] = \frac{306}{1560} + \frac{462}{1560} = \frac{32}{65}$$

b different genders:

$$P(GB) + P(BG) = \left[\frac{18}{40} \times \frac{22}{39}\right] + \left[\frac{22}{40} \times \frac{18}{39}\right] = \frac{369}{1560} + \frac{396}{1560} = \frac{33}{65}$$

iii Find the probability that one particular student, Shruti, is selected.

Shruti can be selected first or, if not, second.

P(Shruti is selected) = P(selected 1st) + P(selected 2nd | not selected 1st)

$$= \frac{1}{40} + \left[\frac{39}{40} \times \frac{1}{39}\right] = \frac{1}{20}$$

Note that each student, just like Shruti, has a 1 in 20 chance of being selected.

Exercise 9C

1 A box contains five green apples and three red apples. One apple is randomly taken from the box, and a second apple is to be randomly selected.

i Write down the probability that the second apple is green, given that:
a the first was green, **b** the first was red.

ii Write down the probability that the second apple is red, given that:
a the first was green, **b** the first was red.

2 A bag contains five coins of equal size: three are silver and two are bronze. One coin is selected at random and, without replacement, a second coin is randomly selected.

i Find, as a simple fraction, the probability that:
a two silver coins are selected, **b** two bronze coins are selected,
c coins of the same type are selected, **d** coins of a different type are selected.

ii Show that the outcomes described in **i c** and **d** are exhaustive.

3 Two children are randomly selected from a group of 10 boys and 18 girls. Find the probability of selecting:

i a particular child, **ii** a particular boy, **iii** two boys,
iv children of the same gender, **v** at least one girl.

4 Arnold has three tins of beans and six tins of peas. The tins are identical in shape and size, but all the labels have been removed, so he doesn't know what is in any of the tins.

If he opens two tins at random, find the probability that:

i both contain beans, **ii** neither contains beans, **iii** just one contains peas.

5 Charlene has bought a bag of 12 mixed peppers: 3 are red, 4 are yellow and 5 are green.

i If she randomly selects two peppers from the bag, find the probability that:
a both are red, **b** exactly one is green.

ii If she randomly selects three peppers from the bag, find the probability that:
a none of them are red, **b** at least one is red.

6 A box contains four toffee sweets and eight chocolate sweets. Two sweets are randomly selected.

i Find the probability that:
a two toffees are selected, **b** two chocolates are selected, **c** one of each type is selected.

ii Find the probability that:
a the second sweet is toffee, **b** the second sweet is chocolate.

7 The heights, h cm, of 40 children are summarised in Table 9.15.

Table 9.15: Children's heights

Height (h cm)	$150 \le h < 155$	$155 \le h < 160$	$160 \le h < 165$	$165 \le h < 170$	$170 \le h < 175$
No. children (f)	6	13	15	5	1

If two of these children are selected at random, find the probability that:

i both are less than 155 cm, **ii** both are 170 cm or more, **iii** at least one is less than 155 cm.

8 Table 9.16 shows the flavours, sizes and numbers of fruit drinks that a boy has in his cool box.

Table 9.16: Fruit drinks

	Orange	**Lemon**	**Totals**
Small	5	4	9
Large	3	8	11
Totals	8	12	20

i If two drinks are randomly selected, find the probability that:
a both are small lemon, **b** both are orange, **c** one of each size is selected.

ii If two small drinks are selected, find the probability that they are the same flavour.

9 At a conference, there are 25 delegates. Twelve are from Belgium, eight from Chile and five from Denmark.

i If one delegate is randomly selected, find the probability that they are not from Chile.

ii If two delegates are selected at random, find, as a simple fraction, the probability that:
a both are from Belgium, **b** neither is from Denmark,
c one is from Chile and one is from Belgium.

iii If two delegates that are not from Belgium are selected, find the probability that they are both from Denmark.

10 All of the 150 students studying their first year of A Levels at Goodhope College come from one of four secondary schools. Table 9.17 gives the numbers of each.

Table 9.17: A Level students

	Axeter	**Bolton**	**Chase**	**Drumly**	**Totals**
Boys	26	16	13	25	80
Girls	6	14	23	27	70
Totals	32	30	36	52	150

i If two students are selected at random, find, as a simple fraction, the probability that:

a both are from Bolton, **b** both are girls,

c both are boys from Chase, **d** at least one is a boy from Drumly.

ii For which of the eight categories of student are gender and school of origin independent? Explain your answer.

11 A school sports coach assembles a group of 55 students who play volleyball or softball or both.

In the group there are 36 students who play volleyball, 15 boys who play softball, 19 girls who play volleyball and 31 softball players.

Two of the students are chosen at random.

Find the probability that both the chosen students play both sports.

12 Samson sometimes goes to the gym before eating supper in the evening, and the probability that he goes to the gym on any particular evening is 0.65.

The probability that he has chips for supper after going to the gym is 0.2, and the probability that he has chips for supper after not going to the gym is x.

This information is shown in the tree diagram in Figure 9.25.

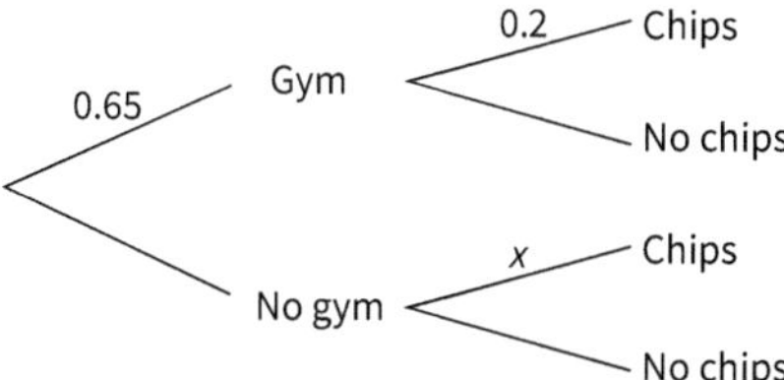

Figure 9.25 Exercise and diet

i If the probability that he has chips for supper on any particular evening is 0.27, find the value of x.

ii If Samson had chips for supper yesterday, find, as a simple fraction, the probability that he had been to the gym.

13 The number of students in each of 21 classes at a school is given in Table 9.18.

Table 9.18: Numbers of students

No. students	31	32	33	34	35	36
No. classes (f)	2	3	5	8	2	1

i If two classes are randomly selected, find the probability that both contain more than 34 students.

ii Find the total number of students in these 21 classes.

iii If two students are randomly selected, find the probability that they both belong to a class that has at least 34 other students in it.

14 On average, Pavithra eats breakfast on four mornings per week, and she is three times as likely to eat a cooked breakfast as she is to eat an uncooked breakfast. Find the probability that Pavithra eats a cooked breakfast tomorrow morning.

15 The histogram in Figure 9.26 shows the masses of 290 apples.

If two apples are selected at random, find an estimate of the probability that:

i both are less than 164 grams,
ii both are 155 grams or more,
iii at least one is at least 182 grams.

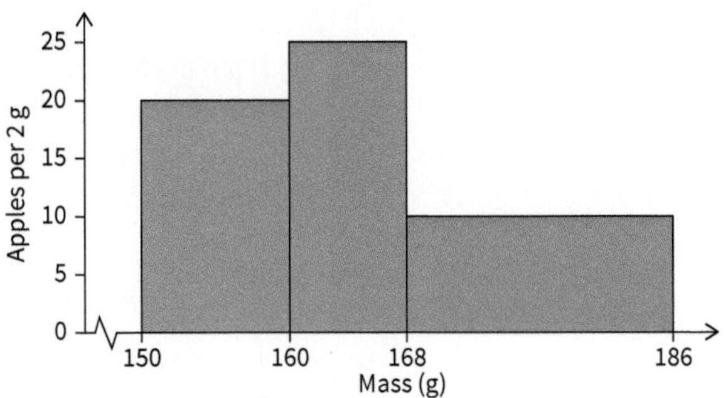

Figure 9.26: Apple masses

16 The Venn diagram in Figure 9.27 shows the number of girls (**G**) and the number who like singing (**S**) in a class of 40.

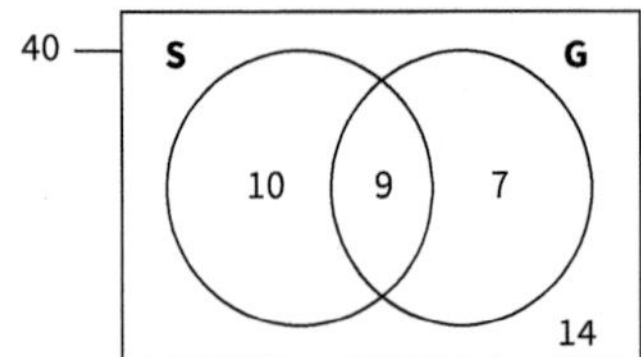

Figure 9.27: Girls and singing

If two children are randomly selected from this class, find the probability that:

i both are girls,
ii neither likes singing,
iii just one is a boy that likes singing.

Exercise 9D (mixed combined events)

1 A bag contains nine cards numbered 1 to 9, and a box contains 26 cards lettered A to Z.

i If a card is selected from the bag and a card is selected from the box, find the probability that:
  a the number 7 is selected, **b** the letter D is selected,
  c an even number and either a P or a Q are selected,
  d a factor of 12 and a letter in the word LIVERPOOL are selected.

ii If all the cards are placed in a tub and two are randomly selected, find the probability of selecting:
  a a number and a letter, **b** two letters,
  c two numbers, **d** at least one letter that is in the word DESUETUDE.

2 The species and continent of origin of the animals kept at a zoo are given in Table 9.19.

Table 9.19: Animal origins

	Africa	Asia	America	Europe
Cat	8	2	3	0
Reptile	6	4	9	1
Rodent	1	3	7	11
Bird	9	15	16	5

i If two animals are randomly selected, find the probability that:
  a a particular animal is selected, **b** a particular cat is selected, **c** both are birds,
  d both originate in Africa, **e** neither is a rodent.

ii If two Asian animals are randomly selected, find the probability that:
  a both are reptiles, **b** at least one is a bird,
  c at most one is a cat, **d** they are the same species.

3 The probability that it will rain on any particular day in a certain town in June is estimated to be 0.4.

i Find the probability that it will rain on at least two of the first three days in June.
ii Find, as a percentage to 3 significant figures, the probability that it will not rain at all during the month of June.

4 A and B are two events such that $P(A) = 0.65$, $P(B) = 0.40$ and $P(A \cap B) = 0.23$.

i Giving reasons for your answers, state whether or not A and B are:
a mutually exclusive, **b** independent.
ii Using a Venn diagram, or otherwise, find the probability that:
a A does not occur, **b** B occurs, but A does not, **c** neither A nor B occurs.

5 One hundred new houses in three styles, *A*, *B* and *C*, have been built. All of the houses have their front doors facing north, south, east or west. Table 9.20 gives the number of each.

Table 9.20: House styles

	North	South	East	West	Totals
Style *A*	16	11	5	6	38
Style *B*	10	7	8	4	29
Style *C*	4	22	5	2	33
Totals	30	40	18	12	100

i Find the probability that a randomly selected house is:
a in style *B* and faces north, **b** in style *C*,
c not facing south, **d** facing west, given that it is in style *A*.
ii If two houses are randomly selected, find the probability that they are:
a facing the same direction, **b** in the same style.
iii If three north-facing houses are selected at random, find the probability that they are in three different styles.

The number of bedrooms in each style of house is: $A = 4$, $B = 3$, $C = 2$.

The occupant of one randomly selected bedroom is to be interviewed.

iv Find the probability that the interviewee lives in a house that is neither type *B* nor faces west.

6 In a cycling proficiency test, any of three classes of certificate are awarded to an entrant that passes.

Table 9.21 summarises the awards given in the past.

Table 9.21: Cycling proficiency awards

No certificate	2nd class	1st class	Distinction
28%	21%	27%	24%

i If two past entrants are selected at random, find the probability that:
a both received a distinction,
b both received a distinction, if it is known that they were both awarded a certificate,
c neither received a 1st or 2nd class award,
d they were awarded the same class of certificate.

Three past entrants who did not receive distinctions are selected at random.
ii Find the probability that none of them was awarded a certificate.

7 Celine has two mobile phones with two different numbers. One is black and one is white.

When she leaves home to go to work, she is equally likely to take the black phone or the white phone; 20% of the time she forgets to take either, but she never takes both.

If she is carrying a phone that rings on the way to work, there is a 50% chance that she will answer it.

Arthur randomly selects one of Celine's two numbers and calls it when she is on her way to work.

By constructing a tree diagram, or otherwise, find the probability that Celine:

i answers Arthur's call on the black phone,
ii does not answer Arthur's call,
iii is unaware of Arthur's call.

8 Gigi has a bag containing four pink discs and five orange discs. By selecting two discs at random, both with and without replacement of the first disc, she wishes to compare the probabilities of selecting discs of different colours.

Express, as a simple ratio, the probabilities of using these two methods of selection.

9.3 Expectation

When an experiment is repeated N times (N trials), we expect event A to occur $N \times P(A)$ times.

This leads naturally to studying games of chance where scores, points or prizes are awarded.

The expected score in a game can be found using each possible score and its probability.

For all the possible scores that can be obtained: Expected score $= \Sigma[\text{score} \times P(\text{score})]$

Examples

1 Find the expected score when a normal die, numbered 1, 2, 3, 4, 5 and 6, is rolled.

The possible scores of 1, 2, 3, 4, 5, 6 are equally likely; each has a probability of $\frac{1}{6}$.

$$\text{Expected score} = [1 \times P(1)] + [2 \times P(2)] + [3 \times P(3)] + [4 \times P(4)] + [5 \times P(5)] + [6 \times P(6)]$$

$$= \left[1 \times \tfrac{1}{6}\right] + \left[2 \times \tfrac{1}{6}\right] + \left[3 \times \tfrac{1}{6}\right] + \left[4 \times \tfrac{1}{6}\right] + \left[5 \times \tfrac{1}{6}\right] + \left[6 \times \tfrac{1}{6}\right]$$

$$= \tfrac{1}{6} \times (1+2+3+4+5+6)$$

$$= \tfrac{1}{6} \times 21 = 3.5$$

When rolling a normal die, the expected score is 3.5.

2 An unbiased square spinner is numbered 1, 5, 7, 5 (see Figure 9.28). Find the expected score when it is spun once.

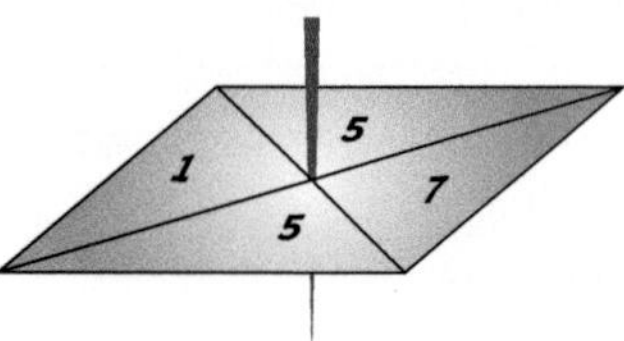

Figure 9.28: Square spinner

$$\text{Expected score} = [1 \times P(1)] + [5 \times P(5)] + [7 \times P(7)]$$

$$= \left[1 \times \tfrac{1}{4}\right] + \left[5 \times \tfrac{2}{4}\right] + \left[7 \times \tfrac{1}{4}\right]$$

$$= \tfrac{1}{4}\,[1 + 10 + 7] = 4.5$$

The expected score from one spin is 4.5.

- The expected score is equal to the mean of all the equally likely possible scores.

In Example 1, we have $\frac{1+2+3+4+5+6}{6} = 3.5$, because the six possible scores are equally likely.

In Example 2, we have $\frac{1+5+7+5}{4} = 4.5$, because the four possible scores are equally likely.

Examples

3 The two square spinners in Figure 9.29 are each spun once. Find the expected total if the scores from the two spinners are added together.

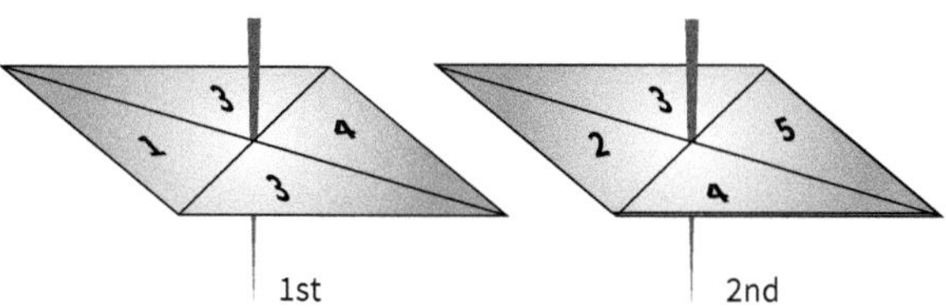

Figure 9.29: Two square spinners

There are seven possible total scores (3, 4, 5, 6, 7, 8, 9) which are not equally likely.

There are 16 possible outcomes which are equally likely, and they are shown in Table 9.22.

Table 9.22: Equally likely outcomes for two spinners

2nd				
5	6	8	8	9
4	5	7	7	8
3	4	6	6	7
2	3	5	5	6
	1	**3**	**3**	**4** **1st**

Probabilities for each total score from 3 to 9 are found from Table 9.22.

$$\text{Expected total} = 3\times P(3) + 4\times P(4) + 5\times P(5) + 6\times P(6) + 7\times P(7) + 8\times P(8) + 9\times P(9)$$

$$= \left[3\times\frac{1}{16}\right] + \left[4\times\frac{1}{16}\right] + \left[5\times\frac{3}{16}\right] + \left[6\times\frac{4}{16}\right] + \left[7\times\frac{3}{16}\right] + \left[8\times\frac{3}{16}\right] + \left[9\times\frac{1}{16}\right]$$

$$= \frac{1}{16}[3+4+15+24+21+24+9]$$

$$= 6\frac{1}{4}$$

The expected score with the 1st spinner is $\frac{1+3+3+4}{4} = 2\frac{3}{4}$.

The expected score with the 2nd spinner is $\frac{2+3+4+5}{4} = 3\frac{1}{2}$.

The two spinners are independent, so the expected total with both spinners is $2\frac{3}{4} + 3\frac{1}{2} = 6\frac{1}{4}$

Exercise 9E

1 Calculate the expected score with one roll of a fair six-sided die that is numbered:

i 0, 2, 4, 6, 8, 10 **ii** 1, 3, 7, 8, 9, 14 **iii** 2, 2, 3, 5, 5, 5.

2 A normal six-sided die, numbered from 1 to 6, is rolled twice. Find the expected total when the two numbers rolled are added together.

3 Find the expected total score when the two numbers rolled on the dice in question **1.i** and **ii** are added together.

4 A biased six-sided die is numbered from 1 to 6. The probability of rolling a 6 is equal to 0.5 and the other five possible scores are equally likely. Find the expected score when it is rolled once.

5 A biased six-sided die is numbered 1 to 6, and is such that rolling an odd number is twice as likely as rolling an even number. Find the expected score with each roll of the die.

6 Two fair spinners, which are both regular polygons, are shown in Figure 9.30; each is spun once.

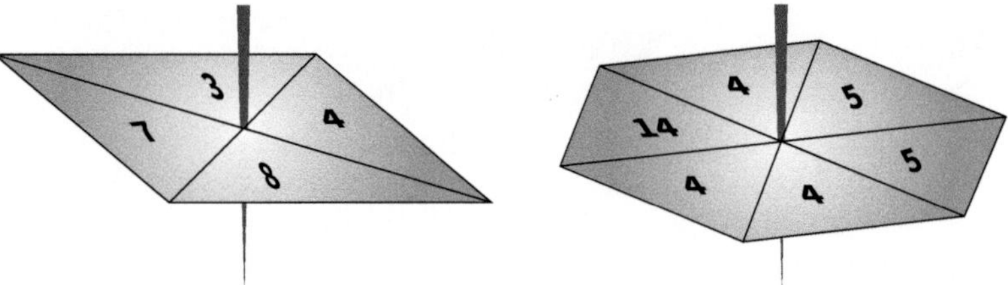

Figure 9.30: Two spinners

i Find the expected score with each spinner.
ii Find the expected total if the scores on the two spinners are:
a added together, **b** multiplied together.

7 A spinner is in the shape of an equilateral triangle and is numbered 22, 25 and X.
Find the value of X if the expected score on the spinner is 26.

8 The three sides of an equilateral triangle spinner are numbered 3, 4, 5. The spinner is spun twice and the two scores are added together to give the total.

i Write down the smallest and the largest possible totals that can be obtained.
ii Construct a two-way table showing the nine equally likely outcomes and the five possible totals.
iii Find the expected total.

9 A game consists of tossing two fair coins, for which the following points are awarded:

- 10 points for two heads
- 5 points for two tails
- 6 points for a head and a tail.

Find the expected number of points awarded when the two coins are tossed.

10 A square spinner, numbered 1, 1, 4, 6, is spun twice and the two scores added together to give the total. Find, by use of a two-way table or otherwise, the expected total.

11 The rotating disc shown in Figure 9.31 is divided into eight sectors with equal areas.

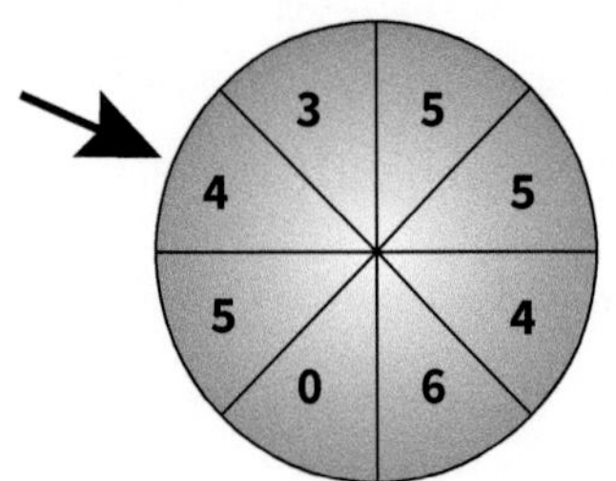

Figure 9.31: Rotating disc

The disc is spun and the score to which the fixed arrow points when it stops is awarded.

i What is the most likely score with one spin?
ii Find the expected score with one spin.

In a game, the disc is spun twice and the two scores are added together to give the total score.

iii Given that the first and second spins are independent of one another, find the expected total score.

12 A biased four-sided spinner is numbered 1, 2, 3, 4.

On any spin, P(1) = 0.3, P(2) = 0.45 and P(3) = 0.15.

i Find the probability of scoring 4 with one spin.
ii Find the expected score with one spin.
The spinner is spun twice and the two scores are added together.

iii Calculate the probability of scoring:
a the lowest possible total, **b** the highest possible total.
iv Find the expected total score with two spins.

Probability Distributions

When all the possible values of a discrete variable and their corresponding probabilities are tabulated, this is referred to as a probability distribution.

If the values of the variable occur by chance, the variable is referred to as a *discrete random variable*.

The probabilities for all the possible values of a variable are exhaustive and their sum is therefore 1.

From a probability distribution, we can find the expected value or expectation of a variable.

The expectation of the variable X is commonly written E(X).

The variable is denoted by an upper case letter and its possible values by the same letter in lower case.

Examples

1 Table 9.23 shows all the possible scores when rolling a fair die numbered 1, 1, 1, 2, 2, 3.

The variable, which is the score, X, has three possible values: $x = \{1, 2, 3\}$.

Table 9.23: Die scores

Possible score, $X = x$	1	2	3
Probability, $P(X = x)$	$\frac{3}{6}$	$\frac{2}{6}$	$\frac{1}{6}$

Expectation of X, $E(X) = [1 \times P(1)] + [2 \times P(2)] + [3 \times P(3)]$

$$= \left[1 \times \tfrac{3}{6}\right] + \left[2 \times \tfrac{2}{6}\right] + \left[3 \times \tfrac{1}{6}\right] = 1\tfrac{2}{3}$$

For a discrete variable, X, with possible values, x: Expectation of X, $E(X) = \Sigma\left[x \times P(X = x)\right]$

Examples

2 The probability distribution of a variable, Y, which has values $y = \{5, 6, 7, 8, 9, 10\}$, is given in Table 9.24.

Table 9.24: Probability distribution of Y

y	5	6	7	8	9	10
$P(Y = y)$	0.15	0.23	0.18	$2a$	0.08	a

All possible values of Y are shown, so the sum of the probabilities is 1.

i $0.15 + 0.23 + 0.18 + 2a + 0.08 + a = 1$

$$3a = 0.36$$

$$a = 0.12$$

ii Expectation of Y:

$E(Y) = (5 \times 0.15) + (6 \times 0.23) + (7 \times 0.18) + (8 \times 0.24) + (9 \times 0.08) + (10 \times 0.12) = 7.23$

3 There are two red apples and three green apples in a bag. Mary randomly selects two apples. Let the variable R be the number of red apples that Mary selects.

The possible values of R are $r = \{0, 1, 2\}$.

$P(r = 0) = P(GG) = \frac{3}{5} \times \frac{2}{4} = \frac{6}{20}$

$P(r = 1) = P(RG) + P(GR) = \left[\frac{2}{5} \times \frac{3}{4}\right] + \left[\frac{3}{5} \times \frac{2}{4}\right] = \frac{12}{20}$

$P(r = 2) = P(RR) = \frac{2}{5} \times \frac{1}{4} = \frac{2}{20}$

The probability distribution of R is tabulated in Table 9.25.

Table 9.25: Probability distribution of R

r	0	1	2
$P(R = r)$	$\frac{6}{20}$	$\frac{12}{20}$	$\frac{2}{20}$
or $P(R = r)$	30%	60%	10%

Mary's expectation is to select $\left[0 \times \frac{6}{20}\right] + \left[1 \times \frac{12}{20}\right] + \left[2 \times \frac{2}{20}\right] = \frac{4}{5}$ or 0.8 red apples.

Expectation is the 'long-term average' value of a variable, and can be thought of as the average value of a variable over a very large number of trials.

If Mary in the previous example repeatedly selects two apples from the five apples in the bag then, on average, she will select:

- 0 red apples 30% of the time
- 1 red apple 60% of the time
- 2 red apples 10% of the time.

The expectation, 0.8, is a weighted average of 0, 1 and 2 with weights of 30, 60 and 10.

Exercise 9F

1 The probability distributions of three discrete variables are given in Tables 9.26–9.28. Find the expectation of each of Q, R and S.

i Table 9.26: Probability distribution of Q

q	1	2	3
$P(Q = q)$	0.2	0.5	0.3

ii Table 9.27: Probability distribution of R

r	1	3	5	7
$P(R = r)$	0.1	0.3	0.4	0.2

iii Table 9.28: Probability distribution of S

s	0	0.35	0.62	0.84	0.97
$P(S = s)$	0.3	0.24	0.22	0.18	0.06

2 Probability distributions of three variables, X, Y and Z, are given in Tables 9.29–9.31.

For each variable, find:

a the value of a in the table, **b** the expectation of the variable.

i Table 9.29: Probability distribution of X

x	1	2	3	4	5
$P(X=x)$	0.13	0.15	0.32	$3a$	$2a$

ii Table 9.30: Probability distribution of Y

y	2.6	3.2	3.8	4.6	5.1	6.7
$P(Y=y)$	0.03	0.07	0.12	0.45	a^2	0.17

iii Table 9.31: Probability distribution of Z

z	0	5	10	15	20	25	30
$P(Z=z)$	$\frac{a}{35}$	$\frac{2a}{35}$	$\frac{3a}{35}$	$\frac{4a}{35}$	$\frac{5a}{35}$	$\frac{6a}{35}$	$\frac{7a}{35}$

3 Two equilateral triangular spinners are spun and the two numbers on which the spinners rest are added together. The first spinner is numbered 1, 2, 3, and the second spinner is numbered 2, 3, 4. The two-way table in Table 9.32 describes the outcomes.

Table 9.32: Outcomes for two spinners

2nd			
4	5	6	c
3	4	b	6
2	a	4	5
	1	**2**	**3** 1st

i Find the values of a, b and c in Table 9.32.

ii Use Table 9.32 to draw up the probability distribution for the total score, S.

iii Find the expected value of S.

4 The probability distribution of the variable X is given in Table 9.33.

Table 9.33: Probability distribution of X

X	7	12	19	q
$P(X=x)$	0.1	0.27	0.39	0.24

Given that the expectation of X is 19.27, find the value of q.

5 Two normal dice, both numbered from 1 to 6 are rolled. The score, D, is the absolute difference between the two numbers rolled. For example, if a 3 and a 5 are rolled, then $D=2$.

i By constructing a table showing all 36 possible outcomes, or otherwise, draw up a probability distribution for the variable, D.

ii Calculate the expected value of D.

6 A bag contains five red discs and four black discs of the same shape and size. Yvonne randomly selects two discs from the bag.

i List the values that the variable, R, the number of red discs selected, can take.

ii Show that $P(R=0)=\frac{1}{6}$.

iii Draw up a probability distribution for the variable, R.
iv Calculate the expectation of R.
v Without further calculation, state the value of $E(B)$, where B is the number of black discs selected.

7 Hamza has eight classical CD's in his collection, two of which are Beethoven string quartets.

He decides to donate two of his classical CD's, selected randomly, to a local charity.

Find the number of Beethoven string quartets that he can expect to donate.

8 Visitors to an art exhibition are each given a box of sweets with four éclairs, five bonbons and six toffees.

Salvador randomly selects three sweets from his box.

i List the values that the variable, T, the number of toffees selected, can take.
ii Draw up a probability distribution for the variable, T.
iii Calculate the number of toffees that Salvador should expect to select.
iv Given that the expected number of bonbons is exactly 1, find the expected number of éclairs.

Fair Games and Expected Winnings

Two friends may invent a game with prizes that they give to each other, or a player may pay to enter a game that offers prizes. Any money paid to enter a game is the *stake*, which is not returnable, and the money won or lost is the *winnings*.

The prize money that a player can expect to win each time s/he plays a game is known as the expected winnings.

A game is **fair** if the expected winnings of the two players involved are the same, or if the stake paid to enter the game is equal to the expected winnings.

For all prizes offered: Expected winnings $= \Sigma[\text{Prize} \times \text{P(winning prize)}]$

Examples

1 Ellen and Richard play a game with five cards numbered 1, 2, 3, 4 and 5. The cards are laid face down on a table and Ellen turns over one card at random.

If the number on the card is even, Richard gives Ellen \$6.

If the number on the card is odd, Ellen gives Richard \$4.

Probability that Ellen wins \$6 prize $=$ P(even number) $= \frac{2}{5}$.

Probability that Richard wins \$4 prize $=$ P(not even number) $= \frac{3}{5}$.

Ellen's expected winnings $= \$6 \times \text{P(win \$6)} = \$6 \times \frac{2}{5} = \$2.40$.

Richard's expected winnings $= \$4 \times \text{P(win \$4)} = \$4 \times \frac{3}{5} = \$2.40$.

Their expected winnings are the same, so the game is fair.

2 Ariel and Miranda play a game in which Miranda rolls two normal dice, both numbered 1, 2, 3, 4, 5, and 6.

If the sum of the two numbers is greater than 7, Ariel gives her \$4.20, or if the sum of the two numbers is less than 4, Ariel gives her \$3.

If the sum of the numbers is 4, 5, 6 or 7, then Miranda gives Ariel $\$q$.

Find the value of q if the game is known to be fair.

Probability that Miranda wins \$4.20 = P(sum on dice > 7) $= \frac{15}{36} = \frac{5}{12}$.

Probability that Miranda wins \$3 = P(sum on dice < 4) $= \frac{3}{36} = \frac{1}{12}$.

Miranda's expected winnings $= \$\left(4.20 \times \frac{5}{12}\right) + \left(3 \times \frac{1}{12}\right) = \$2$.

Probability that Ariel wins $\$q$ = P(sum on dice is 4, 5, 6 or 7) $= 1 - \left(\frac{5}{12} + \frac{1}{12}\right) = \frac{1}{2}$.

Ariel's expected winnings $= \$q \times \frac{1}{2} = \$\frac{q}{2}$.

The game is fair, so $\frac{q}{2} = 2$, giving $q = 4$.

Exercise 9G

1 Brian tosses a fair coin once. If the coin lands heads up, Susie gives him \$4. Calculate Brian's expected winnings for one game.

2 Fergie rolls a normal six-sided die, and is given \$ 12 by Charles if she rolls a square number. If Fergie does not roll a square number, she gives Charles \$ 5.

i Calculate Fergie's expected winnings for one game.
ii State, with a reason, whether or not the game is fair.

3 Angela and Bridget each have three cards numbered 1, 2 and 3. The cards are laid face down and each girl randomly selects a card then turns it over.

If the cards show the same number, Angela gives Bridget \$6, but if the cards show different numbers, Bridget gives Angela $\$x$.

Find the value of x which makes this a fair game.

4 Craig and Edward play a game that involves tossing three coins.

Craig tosses the coins and if he obtains three heads or three tails, Edward gives him \$ 7, otherwise Craig gives Edward \$ 2.

i Find the expected winnings for Craig and for Edward.
ii State which of the players is disadvantaged in this unfair game.

5 Jason and Kylie each have a fair four-sided die in the shape of a tetrahedron.

Jason's die is numbered 3, 6, 9 and 12, and Kylie's die is numbered 2, 7, 7 and 10.

Jason and Kylie roll their dice together and each notes the number that lands face down.

If the sum of the two numbers is more than 11, Kylie gives Jason \$ 4, otherwise Jason gives Kylie $\$y$.

Find the value of y, if this game is known to be fair.

6 Candy and Uma play a game using a bag containing ten discs: six are red, three are blue and one is white.

Uma randomly selects two discs from the bag. If the two discs are the same colour then Candy gives Uma \$ 3, but if they are different colours then Uma gives Candy \$ 2.

With evidence for your answer, find out whether or not this game is fair.

7 Karen rolls a normal six-sided die in a game. Her father gives her \$3 if she rolls a 6 or \$4 if she rolls a prime number. If she fails to roll a 6 or a prime number then she gives her father \$$x$.

Find the values of x for which Karen will have an advantage in this game.

8 Oscar and Fifi play a game using a dart and a rectangular board that has three playing cards fixed to it, as shown in Figure 9.32. The board measures 12 cm by 15 cm and each playing card measures 3.6 cm by 5 cm.

Fifi, who is blindfolded, throws a dart at the board: if it sticks in to the spade card (♠), Oscar gives her \$5 or if it sticks into a club card (♣) Oscar gives her \$4.50. If the dart sticks into any other part of the board, Fifi gives Oscar \$$p$.

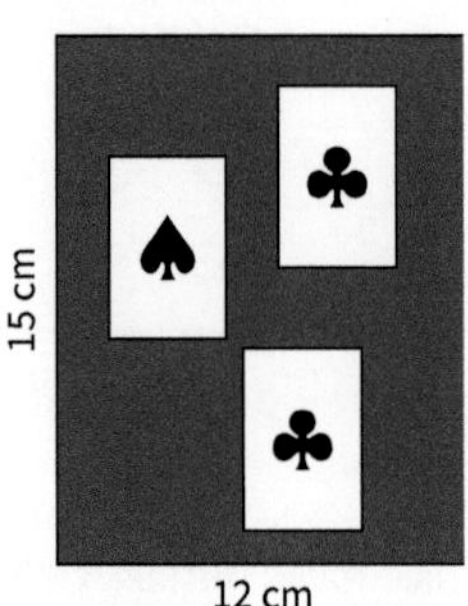

Figure 9.32: Cards on a board

i Find the area of:

  a each of the playing cards, **b** the board that is not covered by the playing cards.

ii Calculate Fifi's expected winnings with each throw of the dart.

iii Find the value of p, if Oscar's expected winnings are exactly half of Fifi's expected winnings.

9 Figure 9.33 shows a game board on which a player moves his or her counter from 'Start' according to the score obtained by rolling a normal die.

If at any time a player's counter lands on an empty square, it is moved back to the start.

Start →	1		3		5	6	7			10	11			14		16	17	18

Figure 9.33: Game board

i Find the probability that a player's counter is:

  a moved back to the start after the first roll of the die,

  b on square 1 after rolling the die twice,

  c on square 18 after rolling the die three times.

After a player has rolled the die three times, the organiser awards the following prizes:

- \$54 if a player's counter is on 16
- \$81 if a player's counter is on 17.

ii Find the probability that a player wins:

  a the \$54 prize, **b** the \$81 prize.

iii Hence, calculate a player's expected winnings in this game.

iv What would a fair stake for this game be if the organiser also awarded a prize of \$50 to a player whose counter was on square 1 after rolling the die three times?

10 i A biased spinner is in the shape of an irregular quadrilateral. The sides of the spinner are numbered with scores of 2, 4, 5 and 6. The shape of the spinner is such that the probability of obtaining a score of 5 with each spin is 0.4 and the probabilities of obtaining the other scores are proportional to the scores themselves.

a Write down the values of p, q and r used in Table 9.34, which shows the possible scores with one spin and their probabilities.

Table 9.34: Results of one spin

Score	2	4	5	6
Probability	p	q	0.4	r

b Hence, calculate the expected score with one spin.

ii A game is organised using this biased spinner. A player, who pays an entry fee, spins the spinner once and is awarded a number of dollars ($) equal to her score if her score is a prime number, otherwise she is awarded nothing.

a Write down the scores for which a player will not be awarded a prize.

b Calculate a fair stake for playing this game.

iii Another game is organised using this biased spinner for which an entry fee must also be paid. The spinner is spun twice and the two numbers obtained are added together to give the total score.

A prize of $5 is awarded to a player who obtains a total score of 10 or more.

a Write down the lowest possible total score and the highest possible total score.

b Write down the probability of obtaining a total score of 5.

c Show that the probability of obtaining a total score of 10 is equal to 0.28.

d Calculate the stake that is charged if a player's expected loss is $0.25 per game.

10 Bivariate Data

Learning Objectives

In this chapter you will learn:

- To identify situations where correlation between two sets of data is likely to exist
- How to describe, in simple terms, the correlation between two variables
- How to investigate the degree of correlation by drawing a scatter diagram
- To use the method of calculating averages and semi-averages to draw a line of best fit
- How to find the equation of a line of best fit and how to use it to estimate and predict values
- To be aware of the limited accuracy of the estimates and predictions that you make

Introduction

Data connecting two variables are referred to as **bivariate** data. The values in two sets may or may not be related. If they are, there may be a simple rule that connects the values in one set with the values in the other.

When an employee decreases his effort at work, what happens to his chances of promotion?

As summer approaches and the amount of daylight increases, what changes occur in the growth rate of a plant?

Although there are limitations to its use, a rule connecting two sets of values can be used to make estimates and predictions of values within or outside the range of values that are already known.

10.1 Correlation

Correlation is a description of the relationship between variables. Some variables are related, some are not.

- Are girls' shoe sizes related to their heights?
- Are the amounts of hair on men's heads related to their ages?

These two questions are asking, 'Are the two variables correlated in any way?'

- What will happen to students' test marks if they spend more time revising?
- How do the amounts of fruit produced by apple trees change as the trees get older?

These two questions are asking, 'How are the two variables correlated?'

The type of correlation depends on how the value of one variable changes as the value of the other variable changes.

Examples

1 Tall girls usually take a larger shoe size than short girls.
As one variable, height, increases, the other variable, shoe size, increases.
The variables are correlated, and the correlation is positive.

2 Older men generally have less hair on their heads than younger men.
As one variable, age, increases, the other variable, amount of hair on head, decreases.
The variables are correlated, and the correlation is negative.

10.2 Scatter Diagrams

The type of correlation that exists between two variables is found by plotting pairs of corresponding values onto a graph, which is called a scatter diagram or scatter graph.

Figure 10.1 shows sketches of possible scatter diagrams for the two examples above.

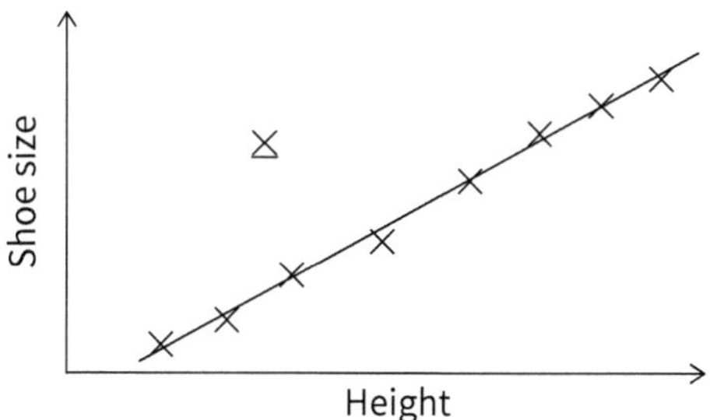

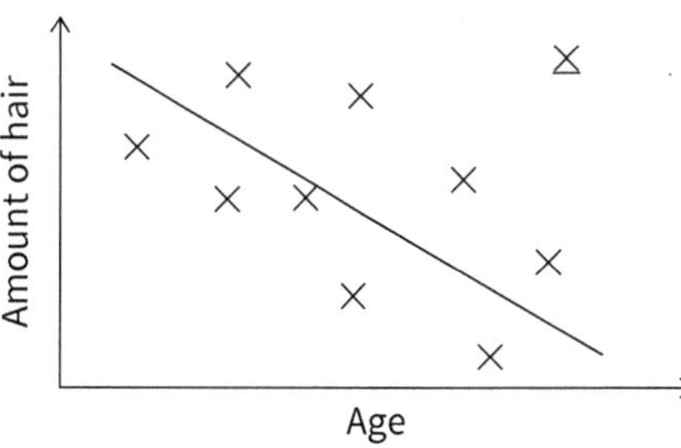

Figure 10.1: Scatter diagrams for Examples 1 and 2

A line of best fit has been drawn onto each scatter diagram, which helps to describe the correlation.

Example 1 shows strong positive linear correlation, as the points lie very close to a line with a positive gradient.

Example 2 shows weak negative linear correlation, as the points lie quite far from a line with a negative gradient.

Not everyone conforms to expectation; each scatter diagram has one *rogue point*.

The first rogue point represents a short girl who has big feet and the second rogue point represents an old man who has a lot of hair on his head.

Some variables may be correlated in a non-linear way, or not correlated at all, as the examples in Figure 10.2 show.

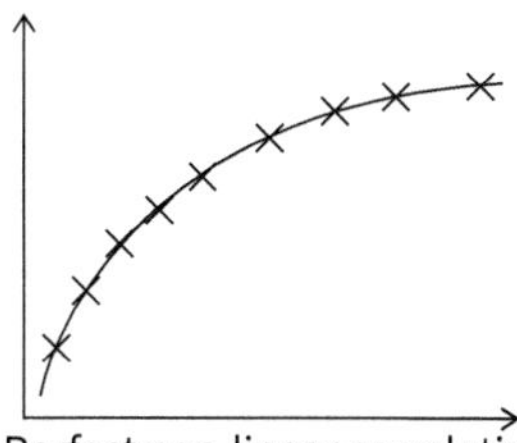
Perfect non-linear correlation

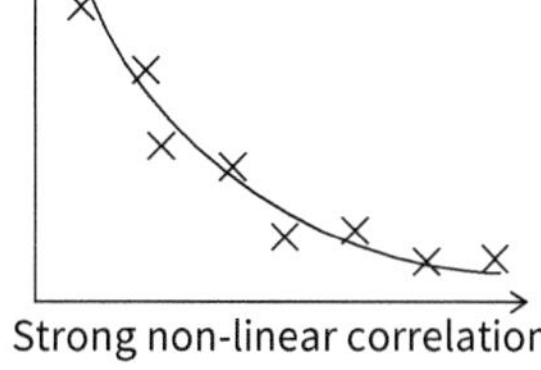
Strong non-linear correlation

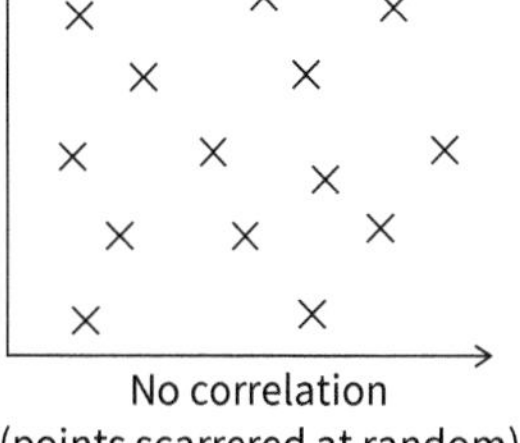
No correlation
(points scarrered at random)

Figure 10.2: Non-linear correlation and uncorrelated data

Interpolation and Extrapolation

A line (or curve) of best fit can be used to estimate or predict values of the variables by:

- **Interpolation**: estimating a value within the range of values that are already known,
- **Extrapolation**: estimating a value that is outside the range of values that are already known.

Extrapolation is less reliable than interpolation because correlation may not continue outside the range of known values.

It is important to know how to draw an accurate line of best fit by calculation, but for initial practice the line can be drawn carefully by eye through the points that you have plotted.

Independent and Dependent Variables

If two variables are correlated then the value of one of them will usually be controlled by the value of the other. The variable that is in control is the independent variable and the variable that is controlled is the dependent variable.

It is conventional to plot the independent variable on the horizontal axis of a scatter diagram.

Examples

1 Garden waste decays as time passes; time does not pass because people's garden waste is rotting. Time is independent of how decayed the garden waste is.

2 The quality of maize produced by a farmer depends largely on the weather; the sun does not hide because the farmer's maize is small and tasteless.
The weather is independent of the quality of a farmer's maize.

3 As people age, they tend to have fewer teeth; they do not age because their teeth fall out.
People's ages are independent of the number of teeth they have.

4 Men's hat sizes depend on how large their heads are; their heads do not grow because they decide to put on a big hat.
The size of men's heads is independent of the hat size they wear.

Exercise 10A

1 The variables in six bivariate distributions were measured. The values obtained were plotted onto the scatter diagrams in Figure 10.3.

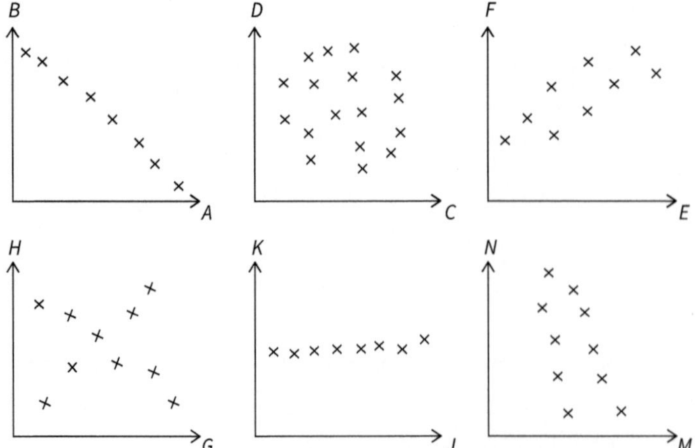

Figure 10.3: Scatter diagrams

Write down the pair(s) of variables that have:

i no correlation, **ii** positive correlation,
iii negative correlation, **iv** strong correlation,
v weak correlation.

2 Readings of two variables X and Y are given in Table 10.1.

Table 10.1: Values of variables X and Y

X	8	3	11	7	2	10	4
Y	6	4	8	6	3	7	5

i Draw and label an X-axis from 0 to 15, and a Y-axis from 0 to 10.
ii Plot the seven points given in the table, and draw a line of best fit through them by eye.
iii Describe the correlation between the two variables.
iv Use your line of best fit to predict:
  a the value of Y when $X = 0$,
  b the value of Y when $X = 6$,
  c the value of X for which $Y = 9$.
v Which of your answers in **iv** do you think is the most reliable? Give a reason for your answer.

3 Nine students (A to I) took tests in mathematics and in history that were both marked out of 10. Their scores are shown in Table 10.2.

Table 10.2: Mathematics and history test scores

Student	A	B	C	D	E	F	G	H	I
Score in mathematics	7	3	6	10	8	1	9	3	4
Score in history	2	6	4	1	9	8	2	7	5

i Draw axes for both variables from 0 to 10, using the horizontal axis for the scores in mathematics.
ii Plot one point to represent the marks of each student and draw a line of best fit by eye.
iii Name the rogue student, and explain what quality she has that makes her different from the others.

4 Values of two variables P and Q were obtained in an experiment, and are shown in Table 10.3.

Table 10.3: Experimental results for P and Q

P	3	7	1	2	8	4	6	2.5
Q	5	8	0	2.5	8.5	6.5	7.5	3.5

i Draw and label a horizontal axis for P, and a vertical axis for Q, both from 0 to 12.
ii Plot the eight points given in the table, and draw a curved line of best fit through them by eye.
iii Use your curved line of best fit to predict the value(s) of:
  a Q when $P = 5$, **b** Q when $P = 12$, **c** P at which $P = Q$.
iv Which of your answers in **iii** do you think is the least reliable? Give a reason for your answer.

Line of Best Fit and its Equation

A line of best on a scatter diagram shows how the bivariate data are correlated. It can also be used to estimate or predict values of either variable by interpolation or extrapolation. However, its use is often limited, especially if we are extrapolating, because we have to assume that the correlation continues outside the range of the values that we already know.

To draw a line of best fit, three averages for the values of X and Y are calculated. This is carried out by following the steps detailed below:

1 Find the arithmetic means $\overline{X}$ and $\overline{Y}$, which give the average point $(\overline{X},\overline{Y})$
2 Order the pairs of values in ascending values of X, then divide the pairs into two equal groups, group 1 and group 2, discarding the middle pair if there are an odd number of pairs.
3 Find the arithmetic means $\overline{X}_1$ and $\overline{Y}_1$, for group 1 to obtain the lower semi-average point, $(\overline{X}_1,\overline{Y}_1)$
4 Find the arithmetic means, $\overline{X}_1$ and $\overline{Y}_1$, for group 2, to obtain the upper semi-average point, $(\overline{X}_2,\overline{Y}_2)$,
5 Plot the average point $(\overline{X},\overline{Y})$ and the two semi-average points and $(\overline{X}_1,\overline{Y}_1)$ and $(\overline{X}_2,\overline{Y}_2)$, onto the scatter diagram
6 Draw, with a ruler, the line of best fit through $(\overline{X},\overline{Y})$, passing as closely as possible to $(\overline{X}_1,\overline{Y}_1)$ and $(\overline{X}_2,\overline{Y}_2)$

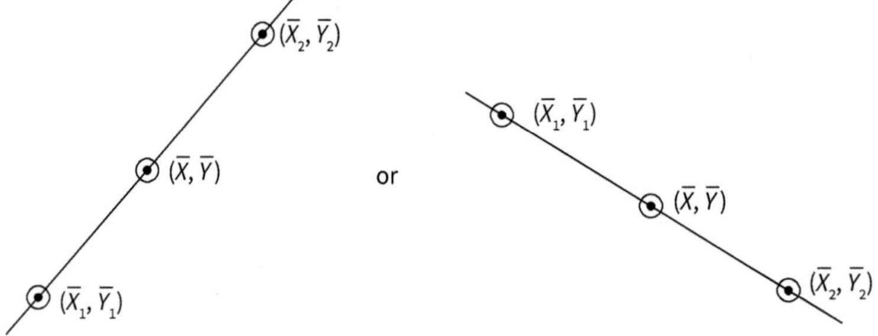

Figure 10.4: Drawing a line of best fit

The equation of a straight line for the variables X and Y is $Y = mX + c$.

- Y is the dependent variable and X is the independent variable.
- m is the gradient of the line.
- c is the Y-intercept (the value of Y at which $X = 0$).

Whenever possible the gradient should be found using $(\overline{X},\overline{Y})$and one other point, say (a, b), which is known to be on the line of best fit: $m = \frac{\overline{Y}-b}{\overline{X}-a}$.

The Y-intercept can often be found by observation from the graph, by common sense or calculated by substituting the values of $\overline{X}$ and $\overline{Y}$ into the equation after the gradient has been found.

If $Y = mX + c$, then substituting the average point $(\overline{X},\overline{Y})$ gives $\overline{Y} = m\overline{X} + c$.

Making c the subject, we obtain $c = \overline{Y} - m\overline{X}$.

Examples

1 A straight line has a gradient of 4 and passes through the point (1, 7). Find its equation.

As $m = 4$, we know that the equation is $y = 4x + c$.

Substituting $x = 1$ and $y = 7$ gives $c = 7 - (4 \times 1) = 3$.

The equation is $y = 4x + 3$.

2 Variables X and Y are such that $(\overline{X},\overline{Y}) = (12, 25)$, and the line of best fit also passes through the point (8, 19). Find the equation of the line.

The gradient of the line, $m = \frac{25-19}{12-8} = \frac{3}{2}$ or 1.5, so the equation is $Y = 1.5X + c$.

Substituting the averages $\overline{X} = 12$ and $\overline{Y} = 25$ into $Y = 1.5X + c$ gives $c = 25 - (1.5 \times 12) = 7$.

Equation is $Y = 1.5X + 7$ or $Y = \frac{3X}{2} + 7$.

3 The percentage scores of 8 students (A to H) in mathematics (X) and in art (Y) are given in the table.

Table 10.4: Mathematics and art scores

Student	A	B	C	D	E	F	G	H
Mathematics (X%)	56	67	33	84	15	48	63	90
Art (Y%)	62	48	79	31	83	60	54	23

The average values are: $\overline{X} = \frac{56+67+33+84+15+48+63+90}{8} = \frac{456}{8} = 57$

$$\overline{Y} = \frac{62+48+79+31+83+60+54+23}{8} = \frac{440}{8} = 55$$

This gives the average point $(\overline{X},\overline{Y}) = (57, 55)$.

The pairs of values are now ordered in ascending values of X and divided into two equal groups.

Table 10.5: Scores ranked by mathematics

Student	E	C	F	A		G	B	D	H
X	15	33	48	56		63	67	84	90
Y	83	79	60	62		54	48	31	23

Mean scores for Group 1 are: $\frac{15+33+48+56}{4} = 38$ and $\frac{83+79+60+62}{4} = 71$.

Mean scores for Group 2 are: $\frac{63+67+84+90}{4} = 76$ and $\frac{54+48+31+23}{4} = 39$.

The two semi-average points are $(\overline{X}_1,\overline{Y}_1) = (38, 71)$ and $(\overline{X}_2,\overline{Y}_2) = (76, 39)$.

A point is plotted with a cross to represent the two scores of each student.

The average point and the two semi-average points are then plotted, and a line of best fit is drawn across the scatter diagram, through $(\overline{X},\overline{Y})$, and as close as possible to the two semi-average points.

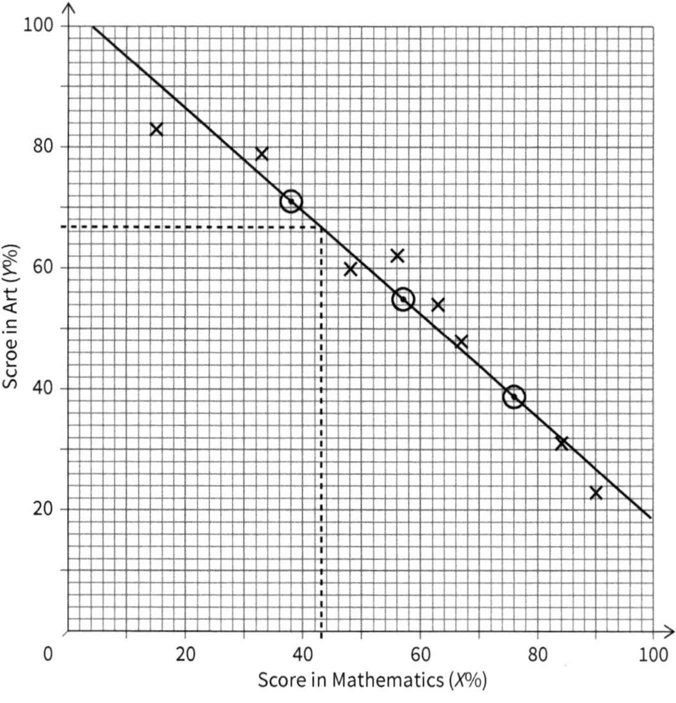

Figure 10.5: Calculated line of best fit

The points lie fairly close to the line of best fit, which has a negative gradient, so the two variables have a fairly strong negative linear correlation.

This can be interpreted as, 'the higher the score in mathematics, the lower the score in art'.

The broken line drawn onto the scatter diagram allows us to interpolate from the line of best fit: we expect a student who scores 43% in mathematics to score about 67% in art.

The equation of the line of best fit can also be used to interpolate or extrapolate.

Using the average point (57, 55) and either semi-average point, the line's gradient is

$m = -\frac{16}{19}$ or -0.842.

$c = \overline{Y} - mX$

$c = 55 - (-\frac{16}{19} \times 57) = 103$

The equation of this line is $Y = 103 - \frac{16}{19}X$ or $Y = 103 - 0.842X$.

Substituting a mathematics score of $X = 43$ gives us an art score of $Y = 67\%$, confirming what we found by reading from the graph.

Exercise 10B

1 Given the gradient, m, and the coordinates of one point that the line passes through, find the equation of the following lines, using x as the independent variable and y as the dependent variable:

i $m = 5$, through (28, 150) **ii** $m = 17$, through (12, 200) **iii** $m = 2.5$, through (13, 40)
iv $m = -9$, through (10, 10) **v** $m = 0.35$, through (120, 14) **vi** $m = -\frac{7}{5}$, through (35, 1).

2 Find the gradient of the straight line that passes through the following pairs of points:

i (15, 27) and (27, 51), **ii** (69, 105) and (205, 173), **iii** (13, 72) and (46, 61),
iv (74, 83) and (54, 38), **v** (2, 64) and (41, 97), **vi** (24, –15) and (–48, 87).

3 For variables X and Y, write down the equation of the line of best fit that has a gradient of 0.023 and that intersects the Y-axis at (0, –3.06).

4 Find the equation of the line of best fit passing through:

i (3.4, 0.75), with $\overline{X} = 45$ and $\overline{Y} = 16.35$, **ii** (1.8, 1.9), with $\overline{X} = 61.8$ and $\overline{Y} = 6.1$,
iii (11.8, 3.866), with $\overline{X} = 20.3$ and $\overline{Y} = 3.05$.

5 A line of best fit passes through the average point (13.8, 12.5), and both of the semi-average points (18.12, 1.70) and (10, q). Find the value of q.

6 The line of best fit for variables T and P has a gradient of 0.5. The average value of T is 6 and the average value of P is 7. If P is the dependent variable, find:

i the equation of the line in the form $P = mT + c$, **ii** the coordinates of the P-intercept,
iii the value of P when $T = -8$.

10.3 Scatter Diagrams in Context

Everyday variables obey certain natural laws and their possible values are in some way limited by their **context**:

- Lengths of objects, times taken and numbers of people cannot take negative values.
- Masses of dogs and students' percentage marks in a test have a limited range of values.
- A farmer who has no chickens on his farm will get no chickens' eggs.
- If you spend no money in a shop, then you can buy no groceries in that shop.

If the gradient of a line is calculated using the average point $(\overline{X},\overline{Y})$ and (0, 0), then the gradient will give a value for the 'average of Y per average of X', as the gradient $m = \frac{\overline{Y}-0}{\overline{X}-0} = \frac{\overline{Y}}{\overline{X}}$.

The gradient of any line of best fit gives an average ratio of 'units of Y per unit of X'.

Examples

1 If a scatter diagram has 'cost of items' on the vertical axis and 'number of items purchased' on the horizontal axis, the line of best fit must go through the point (0, 0) and the gradient will give a measure of the average cost per item.

2 If a scatter diagram has 'number of employees' on the vertical axis, 'number of shops' on the horizontal axis, and its gradient is 7, this tells us that there are, on average, 7 employees per shop.

Exercise 10C

1 Students took two examinations in science. The percentage marks for ten students are shown in Table 10.6.

Table 10.6: Science examination marks

Student	A	B	C	D	E	F	G	H	I	J
Paper 1 (X%)	54	40	74	62	80	38	36	44	84	68
Paper 2 (Y%)	52	32	68	62	68	52	30	38	72	56

i On graph paper, draw axes for X and for Y from 0 to 100, using 1 cm to represent a mark of 10%.

ii Draw a scatter diagram for the data.

iii Showing your working, calculate the average point $(\overline{X},\overline{Y})$, and the two semi-average points.

iv Plot the three average points onto your scatter diagram, and draw a line of best fit through them.

v Use the average point $(\overline{X},\overline{Y})$, and one other point on the line to find the gradient of the line.

vi Find, to the nearest integer, the Y-intercept and write down the equation of the line of best fit.

The point for student F is furthest from the line.

vii What does this tell you about student F?

2 An experiment gave the pairs of values for two variables, R and W, shown in Table 10.7.

Table 10.7: Experimental values for R and W

R	5.00	3.25	2.25	5.75	4.50	4.00	2.75	3.60
W	6.20	4.20	0.80	6.60	5.60	5.00	2.80	p

i Assuming that R is the independent variable, draw a scatter diagram to illustrate these data with the axis for the dependent variable from 0 to 10.
ii Draw a curved line of best fit by eye through the points that you have plotted.
iii Use your line to estimate, to 1 decimal place, the unknown value p in the table.

It was discovered that the values of W have an upper boundary.

iv Estimate this upper boundary value of W.

3 Sybil manages a sanctuary for abandoned horses. For each of the past eight weeks she has recorded the number of horses at the sanctuary and the number of bags of horse feed that she had to buy for them – see Table 10.8.

Table 10.8: Bags of horse feed bought

Week	1	2	3	4	5	6	7	8
Number of horses (H)	9	5	16	10	7	4	11	14
Number of bags (B)	14	7	23	16	10	6	16	20

i State, giving a reason, which is the independent variable.
ii On a sheet of graph paper, draw axes for the number of horses using 1 cm per unit, and for the number of bags using 4 cm for 5 units.
iii Plot the eight points from the table.
iv Calculate the coordinates of the average point for these data, and plot it onto the scatter diagram.
v Explain why the line of best fit should pass through the point (0, 0).
vi Draw the line of best fit.
vii Find, to 2 decimal places, the gradient of the line of best fit, and explain its meaning in the context of this question.
viii Write down the equation of the line of best fit.

Each of the bags that Sybil bought contained 40 kg of horse feed, and each bag cost $35.

ix Showing your working, use your equation in **viii** to estimate the average daily cost of feeding one horse at the sanctuary.

4 The recommended daily dose, in milligrams, of deworming powder for domestic cats is given in Table 10.9.

Table 10.9: Deworming powder dosage

Mass of cat (M kg)	0.5	1.0	1.5	2.0	2.5	3.0	3.5	4.0	4.5	5.0
Daily dose (D mg)	2.0	3.0	4.0	5.0	6.0	8.0	9.0	10.0	11.5	12.0

i Which is the independent variable? Give a reason for your answer.
ii On graph paper, draw axes for mass from 0 kg to 8 kg, and for daily dose from 0 mg to 16 mg.
iii Draw a scatter diagram for these data.
iv Find the coordinates of the average point.
v Explain why the line of best fit should pass through the point (0, 0).
vi Plot the average point onto the scatter diagram, and draw a line of best fit.
vii Calculate the gradient of the line, giving your answer to 2 decimal places, and write down the equation of the line.
viii Interpret the value of the gradient in the context of this question.
ix Use your equation to find the value of D when $M = 50$.
x Explain why the answer that you have obtained in **ix** has no practical meaning.

5 A group of tourists from Bahrain visited Brazil on a holiday in June.

The visitors exchanged different amounts of Bahraini dinars (BD) at various banks in Brazil.

The amount that each exchanged, in dinars, and the amount that each received, in Brazilian reais (R $), are shown in Table 10.10.

Table 10.10: Exchanging dinars for reais

Tourist	Faiza	Abdul	Emile	Fifi	Wazim	Hamza	Marie	Aziz	Anouar	Hassan
Reais (R $)	2800	4610	7150	11 240	15 000	4960	5700	12 945	10 300	13 600
Dinars (BD)	400	650	1000	1530	2000	700	820	1780	1440	1860

i Draw an axis for the independent variable using 1 cm to represent 100 units, and an axis for the dependent variable, using 1 cm to represent 500 units.
ii Draw a scatter diagram to illustrate the data.
iii By calculating and plotting appropriate average values, draw a line of best fit.
iv Describe the correlation.
v Calculate the gradient of your line, and explain its meaning in the context of this question.
vi Calculate an estimate of the number of dinars that was needed to purchase R$58 000 in June.
vii If the numbers in the table above showed how many reais where exchanged by a group of Brazilian tourists at various banks in Bahrain, then, without drawing a new diagram:
  a briefly explain how you would construct the scatter diagram differently,
  b calculate, correct to 2 decimal places, what the gradient of the line of best fit would be.

6 A student wants to find out if there is any correlation between the morning temperatures and the numbers of absentees at her school.

She has calculated the mean weekly temperature at 7 a.m. for nine weeks, and found the total number of absentees during each of these weeks from school records, as shown in Table 10.11.

Table 10.11 Absentees and temperature

No. absentees (*A*)	33	26	28	20	45	50	36	43	51
Mean temperature (*T* °C)	+3.0	+6.4	+5.3	+9.0	−1.0	−2.3	+2.7	+0.2	−3.5

i Draw axes for temperature from −4 °C to 12 °C and for number of absentees from 0 to 60, with the independent variable on the horizontal axis.
ii Draw a scatter diagram for the student's data.
iii By calculating and plotting the average point and the semi-average points, draw a line of best fit.
iv Use your line of best fit to predict the number of absentees when the average temperature is 8 °C.
v Find, to 1 decimal place, the gradient of the line of best fit.
vi Find, to the nearest integer, the value of A when $T = 0$, and use it to write down the equation of the line of best fit.
vii Use your equation to find A when $T = 18$. Use the value you have obtained as a basis for comment on the relationship between these two variables in the context of this question.

7 The masses and volumes of 13 specimens of stone, collected from a dry river bed, are given in Table 10.12.

Table 10.12: Stone specimens

Specimen	A	B	C	D	E	F	G	H	I	J	K	L	M
Mass (*M* g)	26.0	17.0	14.0	8.0	14.0	29.0	23.5	35.0	10.0	45.5	29.5	51.5	25.0
Volume (*V* cm³)	15.0	22.0	7.5	11.0	18.0	16.0	30.5	20.0	14.0	25.0	38.5	29.0	33.5

i Draw axes for volume horizontally from 0 cm^3 to 40 cm^3, and for mass vertically from 0 g to 60 g.
ii Draw a scatter diagram to illustrate these data.
iii Suggest a practical reason to explain why the points fall into two distinct groups.
iv Find the coordinates of the average point for each group, and plot these onto the diagram.
v Draw a line of best fit for each of the two groups of points.
vi Write down the coordinates of the point where the lines intersect, and explain its significance.
vii Calculate, correct to 2 decimal places, the gradients of the two lines, and explain their meaning in the context of the data given in this question.

8 Eight variables, each relating to the 40 students in a class, are given below:

P: their heights
Q: their shoe sizes
R: their average test marks in mathematics
S: their years of birth
T: their ages
U: their average test marks in science
V: the daily distances that they travel to school
W: the amount of time they spend studying in the evenings.

i What type of correlation, if any, could be expected to exist between:
ii Give an example of a different variable that is likely to be:
a positively correlated with *V*, **b** negatively correlated with *W*.

Time Series

11

Learning Objectives

In this chapter you will learn:

- To investigate variation and trends in sets of data by drawing time series graphs
- About seasonal variation and how to identify situations in which it occurs
- To show, by calculating centred moving averages, the trend in a set of data, and how to describe it
- How to calculate mean seasonal variation
- How to calculate estimates and predictions using seasonal components
- To appreciate the limited accuracy of the predictions that you make

Introduction

Time is a particularly important variable because so many others depend on it. At what time of day and on which day of the week would you advise a company to advertise its product on the radio? How would you expect the sales of umbrellas to vary from one **season** to the next?

Values of many variables depend on the time of year, or on some other time period. There may be a pattern in the way values vary over time, and if that pattern has some regularity to it then estimates and predictions can be made.

A time series is made up of measurements or readings of a variable taken at regular intervals of time.

The time intervals may be hourly, daily, weekly, monthly, seasonally or quarterly, termly, yearly, and so on.

The data is shown in a *time series graph*, which shows how the value of a variable has changed over a period of time. Time, as always, is the independent variable, so the time intervals are shown horizontally – usually along the longest side of the graph paper – and measurements or readings of the variable are shown vertically. Points are plotted and joined consecutively by ruled lines.

11.1 Variation and Trend

Variation refers to the changes in values from one time period to another, which are emphasised by the ruled lines that join the points on a time series graph.

If a pattern in the variation can be seen, it is perhaps best investigated by looking at changes in consecutive values of the variable; do they go up, down or remain constant?

The **trend** is a description of whether the value of the variable is increasing, decreasing or remaining constant over the whole period of time for which the readings have been taken.

You should not expect patterns in the variation to be perfectly regular.

Examples

1 Readings of a variable, X, are shown for 16 consecutive time periods in Table 11.1.

Table 11.1: Readings of X

Time period	1st	2nd	3rd	4th	5th	6th	7th	8th	9th	10th	11th	12th	13th	14th	15th	16th
Value of X	25	31	37	22	19	24	29	35	21	17	23	27	33	19	15	22

Looking at changes in values (U = up, D = down), we find the following: UUDDUUUDDUUUDDU

This seems to have no pattern until it is broken down: UUDDU / UUDDU / UUDDU.

The pattern in the variation repeats after every five time periods.

Now we can investigate the trend by looking at sequences of every 5th reading.

The sequence for the 1st, 6th, 11th and 16th readings is: 25, 24, 23, 22, . . .

The sequence for the 2nd, 7th and 12th readings is: 31, 29, 27, . . ., and so on.

We can see that the values of X are decreasing.

2 Each term for four years, a student recorded her end-of-term examination mark in English – see Table 11.2.

Table 11.2: English examination marks

Year	2013			2014			2015			2016		
Term	1	2	3	1	2	3	1	2	3	1	2	3
Mark (%)	30	60	55	40	70	65	50	80	75	60	90	85

The data are shown in the time series graph in Figure 11.1.

Several important observations can be made from the graph:

- Her marks in English improved over time – this is the 'trend' shown by the data.
- The pattern in the variation of marks repeats every three terms, i.e. yearly.
- Marks were lowest in term 1 and highest in term 2 every year.

The variation and the trend allow us, by extrapolation, to predict what may happen in the future.

In doing this, we are assuming that the trend and variation continue in the same way.

By studying her marks, and assuming that the trend continues, we can predict her marks for 2017.

If her marks are set out in line with the pattern of variation, as in Table 11.3, the trend is clear to see.

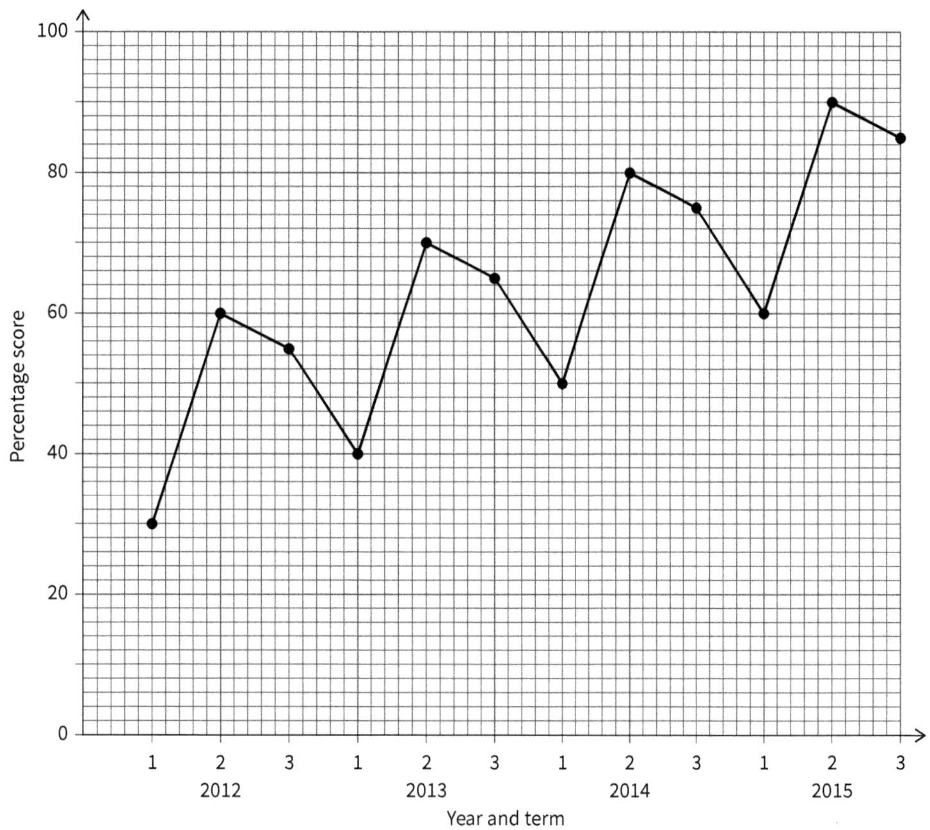

Figure 11.1: Time series graph of examination marks

Table 11.3: Alternative view of examination marks

	2013	2014	2015	2016
Term 1	30	40	50	60
Term 2	60	70	80	90
Term 3	55	65	75	85

Prediction for 2017
≈ 70
≈ 100
≈ 95

These predictions may not come true for any number of practical reasons, for example:

- Scoring 100% in an examination is highly unlikely.
- The student could fall sick at some point in time and perform badly.
- An examination could be cancelled.

Exercise 11A

1 The values of a variable *V* were recorded for ten time periods – see Table 11.4.

Table 11.4: Recorded values of *V*

Time period	1st	2nd	3rd	4th	5th	6th	7th	8th	9th	10th
V	2	5	3	6	4	7	5	8	6	9

i Draw a time series graph for the data, using 1 cm between time periods and 1 cm for 1 unit of *V*.
ii Describe the trend.
iii After how many time periods does the pattern in the variation repeat?
iv Study your graph and the table, and predict the value of *V* in the 11th and 12th time periods.

2 The values of a variable *Y* were recorded for 16 time periods – see Table 11.5.

Table 11.5: Recorded values of *Y*

Time period	1st	2nd	3rd	4th	5th	6th	7th	8th	9th	10th	11th	12th	13th	14th	15th	16th
Y	28	30	20	18	10	23	27	19	16	8	20	25	17	15	5	18

i Draw a time series graph for these data, using 1 cm between time periods and 2 cm for 5 units of *Y*.
ii Describe the trend.
iii After how many time periods does the pattern in the variation repeat?
iv Estimate the value of *Y* in the 17th and 18th time periods.

3 The consumption of electrical energy, in kilowatt-hours (kWh), at a bakery for each of the four seasons in a year for a period of $2\frac{3}{4}$ years is given in Table 11.6.

Table 11.6: Electricity consumption of bakery

Year	Season	Consumption (kWh)
2013	I	27 500
	II	22 500
	III	15 000
	IV	25 000
2014	I	28 000
	II	22 000
	III	15 500
	IV	24 000
2015	I	27 000
	II	23 000
	III	14 500
	IV	

i On graph paper with the longest side horizontal, draw and label an axis for time, using 2 cm between successive seasons, and an axis for energy consumed from 10 000 kWh to 30 000 kWh using 4 cm to represent 5000 kWh.
ii Use the data in the table to draw a time series graph.
iii Describe the trend in electricity consumption at the bakery.
iv During which season of each year does the bakery consume the greatest amount of electrical energy?
v By studying your graph and the table:
  a estimate the number of kilowatt-hours of electrical energy consumed in season IV of 2015,
  b suggest a practical reason why the estimate that you have made in **a** could be quite inaccurate.

4 Records from a hotel were used to calculate the percentage of its rooms that were occupied each night over ten six-month periods which, for each year, are April to September (summer) and October to May (winter). The data are presented in Table 11.7.

Table 11.7: Hotel occupancy

Year	2011		2012		2013		2014		2015	
Six-month period	Apr–Sep	Oct–May	Apr–Sep	Oct–May	Apr–Sep	Oct–May	Apr–Sep	Oct–May	Apr–Sep	Oct–May
Average occupation (%)	58	28	61	21	65	15	70	10	76	6

i Draw and label a horizontal axis for time with 2 cm between successive six-month periods and a vertical axis from 0% to 80%.
ii Plot the ten points from the table and draw a time series graph for the data.
iii Describe the variation shown in your graph.

The hotel manager predicts that the variation and trend will continue for at least five more years.

iv Give two reasons why the hotel manager's prediction cannot possibly come true.

11.2 Seasonal Variation

Variation is described as **seasonal** if the pattern in the variation repeats at regular time intervals of one year or less.

Some examples of variation that would be described as seasonal are:

- Daily sales figures which show a pattern that repeats each week.
- Hourly temperature readings which show a pattern that repeats each day.
- Monthly rainfall measurements which show a pattern that repeats each year.

11.3 Trend Line and Moving Averages

Predictions or estimates for future values of a variable are made by extrapolating from a trend line, and the predictions that we make are quite limited – we have to assume that the variation and trend will continue into the future.

A trend line is a line of best fit that passes through a set of calculated moving averages.

Moving averages are values that represent the trend at times when readings were taken; they should not fall between these times, but must be centred on them.

Centred moving averages, or general trend values, effectively **eliminate** the variation by averaging out groups of recorded values onto a straight line.

The trend in the data can be seen by observing the gradient of the trend line.

Calculation of moving averages depends on the type of variation shown by the variable.

Is the variation 2-point, 3-point, 4-point, 5-point, . . . ?

N-point moving averages are calculated by finding the mean of *N* consecutive values of the variable.

Examples

Readings of a variable, Z, were recorded every four months, where a period of four months represents one-third of a year, or one term – see Table 11.8.

Table 11.8: Readings of Z

	Year 1			Year 2			Year 3			Year 4		
Four-month period	1st	2nd	3rd	1st	2nd	3rd	1st	2nd	3rd	1st	2nd	3rd
Z	9	4	4	10	4	6	11	6	7	12	6	8

Although not completely regular, the pattern in the variation is reasonably clear.

Using U = up, D = down and a dash for no change, we have: D–U / DUU / DUU / DU . . .

Z has three-termly (or three four-monthly) seasonal variation.

Calculations of three-termly moving averages are simplified if values are tabulated vertically – see Table 11.9.

Table 11.9: Retabulated readings of Z

	Term	Z	Three-termly totals	Three-termly moving averages
Year 1	1st	9	—	—
	2nd	4	$9+4+4=17$	5.67
	3rd	4	$4+4+10=18$	6.00
Year 2	1st	10	$4+10+4=18$	6.00
	2nd	4	$10+4+6=20$	6.67
	3rd	6	$4+6+11=21$	7.00
Year 3	1st	11	$6+11+6=23$	7.67
	2nd	6	$11+6+7=24$	8.00
	3rd	7	$6+7+12=25$	8.33
Year 4	1st	12	$7+12+6=25$	8.33
	2nd	6	$12+6+8=26$	8.67
	3rd	8	—	—

The first moving average is the mean of the first three values of Z, which are 9, 4 and 4.

The second moving average is the mean of the second three values of Z, which are 4, 4 and 10.

The mean of each group of three values is written centred on the middle value used in the calculation.

- The first moving average is centred on the 2nd term of year 1.
- The tenth and final moving average is centred on the 2nd term of year 4.

Moving averages (marked ×) are centred on times when the readings were taken, so they represent the trend and can be plotted onto the graph (see Figure 11.2). A trend line is drawn through them.

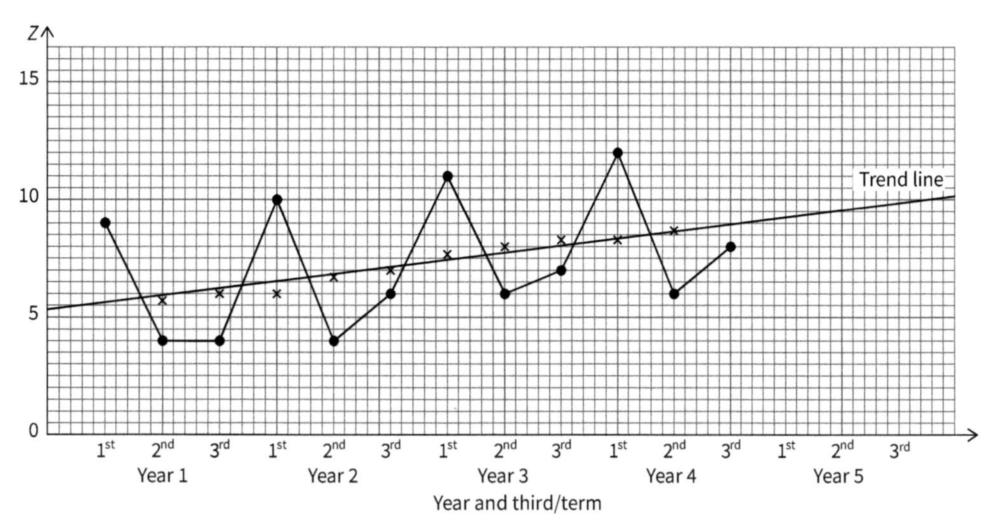

Figure 11.2: Time series and trend for Z

From the positive gradient of the trend line it can be seen that values of Z are increasing as time passes.

11.4 Centred Moving Averages

When variation is odd-pointed, all the moving averages will be automatically centred on a time when readings were taken, and so they represent the trend at those times.

When variation is even-pointed, none of the moving averages will be centred on a time when the readings were taken, and so they do not represent the trend at those times.

Even-pointed moving averages must be centred by further calculation. To do this, we find the mean of each successive pair of moving averages. Each centred moving average will then represent the trend at a time when the readings were taken.

Examples of variation where moving averages are not automatically centred are:

- four-quarterly seasonal
- 12-monthly seasonal
- two-half-yearly seasonal
- six-bimonthly seasonal

Examples

Readings of a variable P, which has four-quarterly seasonal variation, were taken at three-monthly intervals over a period of $3\frac{1}{2}$ years.

Each four-quarterly total shown in Table 11.10 is the sum of four consecutive readings.

Each four-quarterly moving average is the mean of four consecutive readings.

Each centred four-quarterly moving average is the mean of two consecutive four-quarterly moving averages.

$295+130+75+240=740$ is the first four-quarterly total; $\frac{740}{4}=185$ is the first four-quarterly moving average.

$130+75+240+235=680$ is the second four-quarterly total; $\frac{680}{4}=170$ is the second four-quarterly moving average.

$\frac{185+170}{2}=177.5$ is the first centred four-quarterly moving average.

Table 11.10: Readings and moving averages for *P*

Year	Quarter	Value of *P*	Four-quarterly total	Four-quarterly moving average	Centred four-quarterly moving average
Year 1	1st	295			
			—	—	
	2nd	130			—
			740	185	
	3rd	75			177.5
			680	170	
	4th	240			167.0
			656	164	
Year 2	1st	235			163.5
			652	163	
	2nd	106			160.0
			628	157	
	3rd	71			153.0
			596	149	
	4th	216			146.5
			576	144	
Year 3	1st	203			143.5
			572	143	
	2nd	86			140.5
			552	138	
	3rd	67			135.5
			532	133	
	4th	196			131
			516	129	
Yr 4	1st	183			—
			—	—	

Values of *P* are plotted and joined to give the time series graph in Figure 11.3.
Centred four-quarterly moving averages are plotted, and a line of best fit is drawn through them to give the trend line.

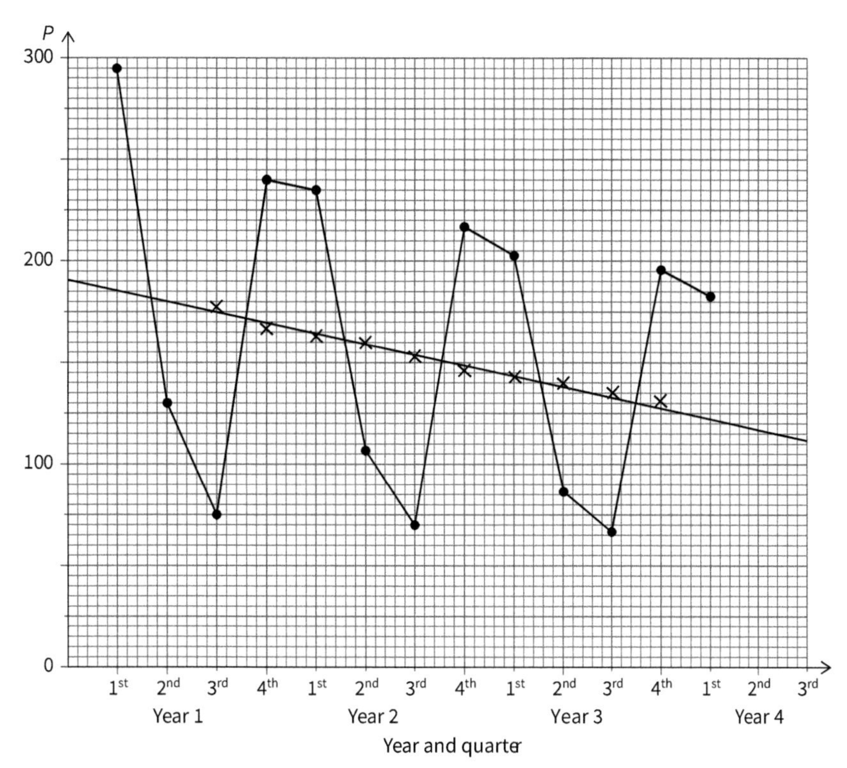

Figure 11.3: Readings, moving averages and trend for P

The trend line has a negative gradient, so it is clear that the values of P are decreasing as time passes.

If the variation and trend continue, then we should expect the values of P to continue decreasing.

Exercise 11B

1 From the list of values of the variable X in Table 11.11, calculate a set of 12 centred three-point moving averages.

Table 11.11: Values of X

Time period	1st	2nd	3rd	4th	5th	6th	7th	8th	9th	10th	11th	12th	13th	14th
X	98	89	74	101	95	80	107	98	98	116	101	98	119	107

2 From the list of values of the variable Y in Table 11.12, calculate a set of 11 centred five-point moving averages.

Table 11.12: Values of Y

Time period	1st	2nd	3rd	4th	5th	6th	7th	8th	9th	10th	11th	12th	13th	14th	15th
Y	26	75	50	45	35	29	82	57	51	41	33	93	67	58	49

3 From the list of values of the variable Z in Table 11.13, calculate a set of ten centred seven-point moving averages. Give all values correct to 1 decimal place.

Table 11.13: Values of Z

Time period	1st	2nd	3rd	4th	5th	6th	7th	8th	9th	10th	11th	12th	13th	14th	15th	16th
Z	14	56	76	91	88	70	81	22	61	83	111	103	75	89	68	73

4 For the readings of the variable P given in Table 11.14, find the value of the three centred two-point moving averages a, b and c. One two-point total and one moving average are included in the table.

Table 11.14: Readings and moving averages for P

Season	P	Two-point total	Two-point moving average	Centred two-point moving average
I	15			
II	29			a
		46	23	
III	17			b
IV	35			c
I	23			

5 For the readings of the variable Q given in Table 11.15, find the value of the four centred four-point moving averages d, e, f and g. One four-point total and one moving average are included in the table.

Table 11.15: Readings and moving averages for Q

Week	Q	Four-point total	Four-point moving average	Centred four-point moving average
1	56			
2	76			
		284	71	
3	88			d
4	64			e
5	84			f
6	104			g
7	112			
8	92			

6 For the readings of the variable R given in Table 11.16, find the value of the three centred six-point moving averages j, k and l. One six-point total and one moving average are included in the table.

Table 11.16: Readings and moving averages for R

Months	R	Six-point total	Six-point moving average	Centred six-point moving average
May–Jun	97			
Jul–Aug	119			
Sep–Oct	127			
Nov–Dec	107			j
Jan–Feb	121			k
		792	132	
Mar–Apr	149			l
May–Jun	157			
Jan–Feb	131			
Mar–Apr	199			

7 The quarterly numbers of telephone units used by an advertising agency over a four-year period are displayed in Table 11.17.

Table 11.17: Telephone usage

	Quarter			
Year	**1st**	**2nd**	**3rd**	**4th**
2013	1196	1276	1148	1028
2014	1164	1408	1284	1176
2015	1288	1520	1432	1332
2016	1448	1568	1490	1490

i Draw axes using 1 cm between quarters along the short side of the graph paper horizontally, and from 1000 to 1600 using 2 cm for 50 units vertically.

ii Plot the 16 points in the table and draw a time series graph for the data.

iii Use the figures in the table to calculate a set of ten centred four-quarterly moving averages. Plot them onto the graph and draw a trend line.

iv For which quarters do the number of telephone units used fall consistently:

a above the trend line, **b** below the trend line.

v Why do the data in the table not give a true reflection of the use that the advertising agency made of the telephone company's services?

8 The numbers of traffic violations in a town exhibit four-point seasonal variation. The numbers of violations in each season is given in Table 11.18 for a period of 45 months.

Table 11.18: Traffic violations

Year and quarter		No. traffic violations	Four-point totals	Four-point moving average	Centred four-point moving average
2012	I	100	—		
				—	
	II	120			—
			720	180	
	III	300			185.0
			760	190	
	IV	200			197.5
			820	205	
2013	I	140			a
			900	225	
	II	180			232.5
			960	240	
	III	380			252.5
			1060	265	
	IV	260			277.5
			1160	290	
2014	I	240			297.5
			1220	b	
	II	280			315.0
			1300	325	
	III	440			335
			1380	345	
	IV	c			355.0
			1460	365	
2015	I	320			w
			y	x	
	II	360			
	III	z			

i Find the values of a, b, and c in Table 11.18.

ii Draw axes using 1 cm between seasons for 15 seasons horizontally, and from 100 to 500 using 4 cm for 100 units vertically.

iii Plot the centred four-point moving averages and draw a trend line.

iv Use your trend line to estimate w, the moving average that will be centred on the 1st quarter of 2015.

v Use the value of w found from the trend line to estimate the values of x, y and z in Table 11.18.

11.5 Seasonal Adjustment

Once a best-fitting trend line has been drawn across a time series graph, we can predict, by calculation, estimates for future values of the variable. The first step is to obtain a general trend value for a particular time in the future by extrapolating from the trend line. This value can then be adjusted by the addition of a calculated seasonal component.

Seasonal Components and Mean Seasonal Variation

A seasonal component is the mean of the variations from the general trend values at related points on a time series graph. These variations are also referred to as deviations.

If, for example, a variable has four-quarterly seasonal variation, there will be four seasonal components altogether; one for each of the four quarters. The 1st quarter seasonal component will be the mean deviation from the trend line of all the known 1st quarter values of the variable.

A variable with 12-monthly seasonal variation will have 12 seasonal components; one for each month.

$$\text{Predicted value} = \text{general trend value} + \text{seasonal component}$$

A seasonal component can be positive, negative or equal to zero, and a set of seasonal has a sum of zero.

$$\sum \text{Seasonal components} = 0$$

Examples

1 **i** A variable has four-quarterly seasonal variation.

Over a period of five years, the season I readings were: 250, 280, 285, 330 and 370.

The general trend values at these points in time were: 160, 180, 205, 235 and 280.

Let the next season I general trend value be y and the mean of the season I deviations be z – see Table 11.19.

Table 11.19: Season I values

Season I reading	250	273	288	309	335	x	
General trend value	160	180	200	220	240	y	
Deviation	+90	+93	+88	+89	+95	z	$\sum$Deviations = +455

Mean of the season I deviations is $+\frac{455}{5} = +91$, so the season I component is $z = +91$.

Now suppose $y = 260$.

We add the seasonal component of $z = +91$ to $y = 260$ to give an estimate for the next season I reading.

x = general trend value (y) + season I component (z)

$x = 260 + 91 = 351$

Our prediction is that the next season I reading will be 351.

ii Table 11.20 gives the components for seasons I, II, III and IV of this same variable. Find the season IV component, p.

Table 11.20: Four seasons' values

Season	I	II	III	IV
Seasonal component	+91	−107	+35	p

The sum of the seasonal components is zero, so $+91-107+35+p=0$, which gives $p=-19$.

The season IV component is −19.

2 Four readings for the month of April are given in Table 11.21 for a variable with 12-monthly seasonal variation. General trend values and deviations are included in the table.

Table 11.21: April readings

Year	2013	2014	2015	2016	2017	
April readings	54	62	70	48	x	
April general trend values	80	82	84	86	y	
Deviations	−26	−20	−14	−38	z	ΣDeviations = −98

Seasonal component for April = mean of deviations for April, which is $z=-\frac{98}{4}=-24.5$.

Suppose the general trend value from the trend line for April 2017 is $y=88$. Then we estimate the reading for April 2017 to be:

$x=y+z$

$x=88+(-24.5)$

$x=63.5$

Exercise 11C

1 Find the missing seasonal component, x, in each of Tables 11.22–11.25.

i Table 11.22: Seasonal variation

Season	I	II	III	IV
Seasonal component	13.6	−47.7	29.5	x

ii Table 11.23: Seasonal variation

Two-month period	1st	2nd	3rd	4th	5th	6th
Seasonal component	6.9	x	−11.4	3.8	4.1	5.9

iii Table 11.24: Seasonal variation

Term/third of a year	1st	2nd	3rd
Seasonal component	x	$-14\frac{3}{8}$	$9\frac{1}{3}$

iv Table 11.25: Seasonal variation

Six-month period	1st	2nd
Seasonal component	+16.2	x

2 A variable, Q, has four-point seasonal variation with the seasonal components shown in Table 11.26.

Table 11.26: Seasonal components of Q

Season	I	II	III	IV
Seasonal component	14.0	−21.7	9.5	1.8

The general trend values for Q in the four seasons of 2016 were found to be 128.9, 67.1, 43.0 and 100.

Calculate an estimate of the actual values of Q for each of the four seasons of 2016.

3 The 1st quarter readings of a variable P and the general trend values for those quarters are given in Table 11.27.

Table 11.27: First quarter readings for P

First quarter of year	2012	2013	2014	2015	2016
General trend value	52	60	68	76	84
Reading	72	84	90	94	100

i Use the figures in the table to calculate the 1st quarter seasonal component for P.
ii The general trend value for the 1st quarter of 2017 is 92. Use your answer to **i** to predict the value of P in the 1st quarter of 2017.
iii Write down two assumptions that you are making about the variation in the values of P.

4 The variable X has two-point seasonal variation. Readings of X are given in Table 11.28, along with general trend values, for six six-month periods.

Table 11.28: Readings and trend of X

Year	2013		2014		2015	
Six-month period	Jan–Jun	Jul–Dec	Jan–Jun	Jul–Dec	Jan–Jun	Jul–Dec
General trend value	1018	955	893	846	798	742
Reading	700	1280	560	1172	480	1060

i Find the mean deviation from the general trend values for the six-month periods from:
  a January to June,
  b July to December.
ii The general trend values for the two six-month periods in 2016 are 700 and 650, respectively. Use your answers to part **i** to predict the value of X in the six-month period from:
  a January to June 2016,
  b July to December 2016.

5 Electricity bills are sent to a school at the end of each term. The bills from term 1 of 2012 to term 3 2015 are shown in the time series graph in Figure 11.4. A trend line for the data is also shown on the graph.

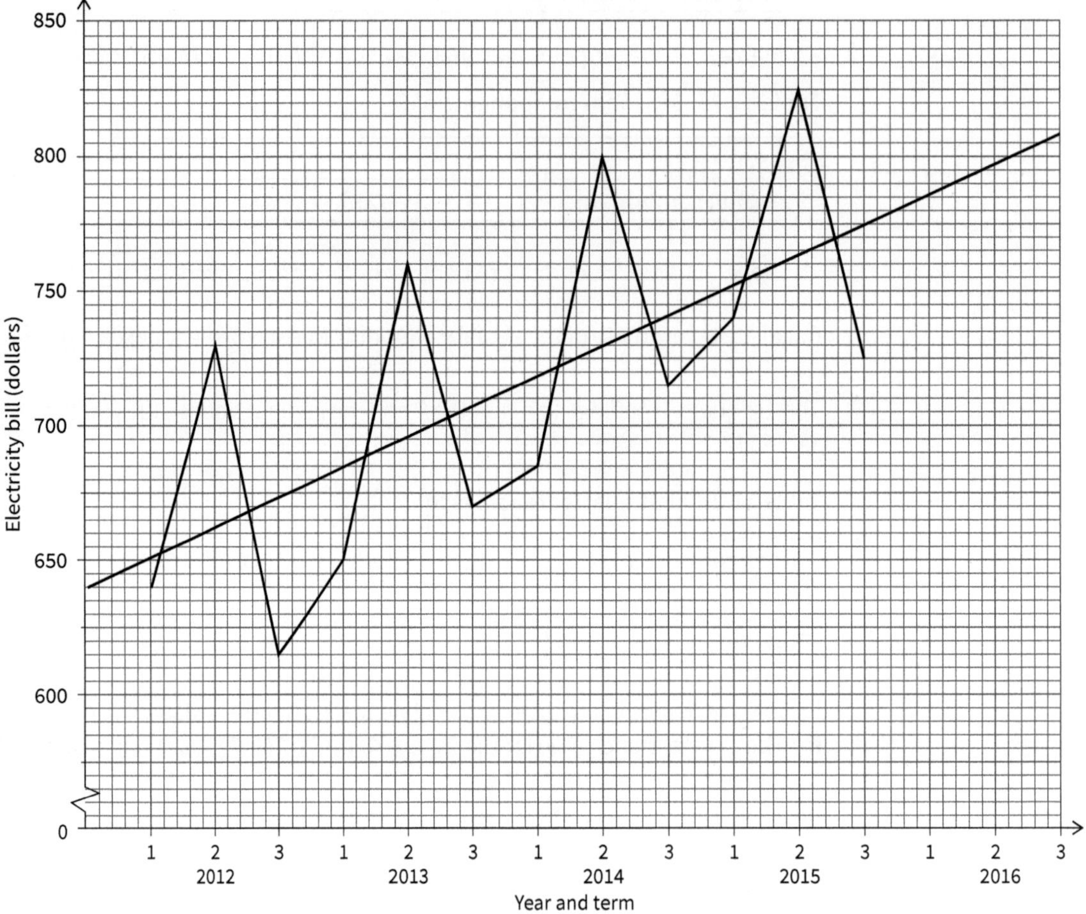

Figure 11.4: Time series and trend for school electricity bills

i Explain briefly why it was not necessary to centre the moving averages used to draw the trend line for this set of data.

ii Describe the trend in the context of this question.

Table 11.29 shows the four general trend values for term 1 of each of the four years.

Table 11.29: Four-year trend values

Term 1 of year	2012	2013	2014	2015
General trend value	650	685	718	753

iii Use these figures and values from the graph to calculate the mean variation (deviation) from the general trend values for the term 1 electricity bills.

iv Use your answer to **iii** and the trend line to estimate, to the nearest dollar, the value of the electricity bill sent to the school at the end of term 1 of 2016.

v Suggest, in the context of this question, a practical reason why your estimate may be inaccurate.

6 Table 11.30 gives the sales figures (in \$10 000s) for a company manufacturing and selling ice cream. The sales figures have four-point seasonal variation.

Table 11.30: Ice cream sales

Year	Season	Sales (\$10 000s)	Four-point moving average	Centred four-point moving average
2013	I	5.86		
	II	11.64		
			10.25	
	III	17.42		10.205
			10.16	
	IV	6.08		10.34
			10.52	
2014	I	5.50		10.7875
			11.055	
	II	13.08		11.05
			11.045	
	III	19.56		10.99
			10.935	
	IV	6.04		11.2725
			11.61	
2015	I	5.06		11.955
			12.3	
	II	15.78		12.295
			12.29	
	III	22.32		12.28
			12.27	
	IV	6.00		12.325
			12.38	
2016	I	4.98		
	II			

i Using 2 cm between seasons horizontally and 2 cm for \$50 000 vertically, draw a time series graph and trend line onto the same diagram for these data.

ii Describe the trend in sales for:

a season II and season III, **b** season I and season IV.

iii What evidence is there to suggest that sales are increasing?

iv Calculate the season II component for the ice cream sales.

v Write down the general trend value for season II of 2016.

vi Use your answers to parts **iv** and **v** to estimate the sales in season II of 2016.

vii Suggest one practical reason why your estimate for the sales in season II of 2016 might be much lower than the actual sales.

7 Figure 11.5 shows the trend line for the variable P, which is a measure of the size of the population of puffins on a remote island. P has been observed to have four-quarterly seasonal variation.

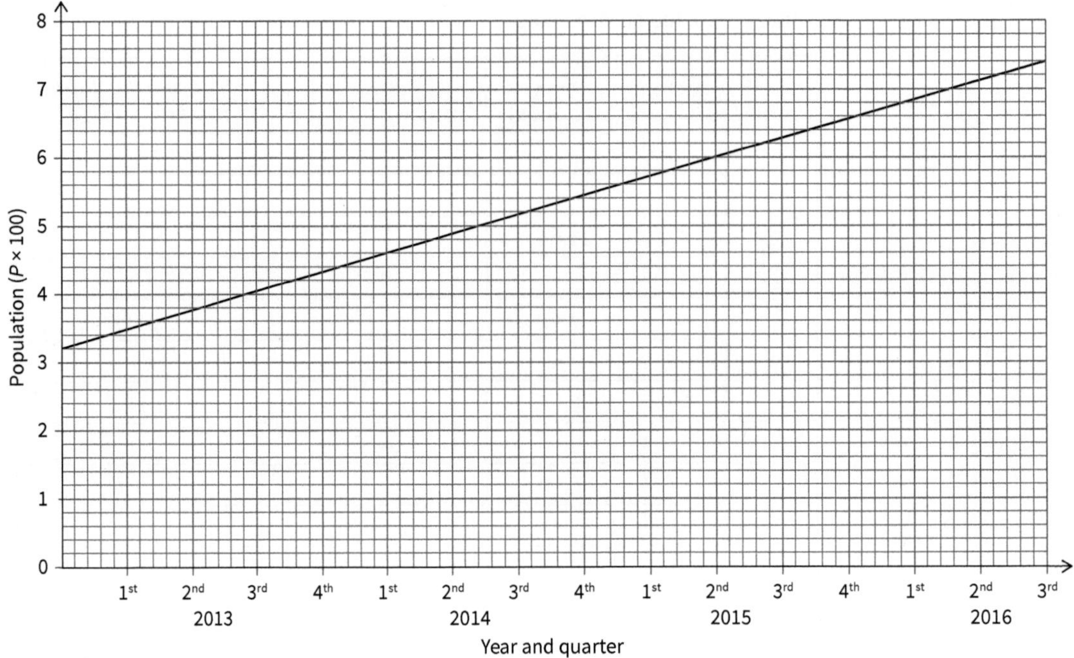

Figure 11.5: Puffin population trend

Seasonal components for P are given in Table 11.31.

Table 11.31: Seasonal variation of puffin population

Season/quarter	1st	2nd	3rd	4th
Seasonal component	−11	x	+27	−29

i Find the value of x.
ii Estimate the population size in the 2nd quarter of 2016.

8 The numbers of births at a hospital over a five-year period from 2011 show six-bimonthly seasonal variation. After analysing the data, the seasonal components are shown in Table 11.32.

Table 11.32: Seasonal components for births

Two-month period	1st	2nd	3rd	4th	5th	6th
Seasonal component	−22	−5	+12	y	+4	−15

i Find the value of y.
ii Given that the general trend values for the 4th and 6th two-month periods of 2016 are 143 and 84, estimate how many more births there will be in the 4th than the 6th two-month period of 2016.

The general trend value for the 1st two-month period is three times that of the 3rd two-month period in 2016.

iii Given that the same numbers of births are expected in these two two-month periods, find the total number of births that are expected in these two two-month periods.

9 Three university students are working on projects which involve them carrying out calculations that illustrate the use of moving averages.

The students and the calculations that each has to carry out are given below:

- Jack: Twelve-monthly moving averages on the monthly sales of new cars for a motorcar dealer.
- Kenny: Three-termly moving averages on pupil attendances at a school.
- Ludo: Four-quarterly moving averages on the quarterly electricity consumption at a factory.

i Which one of the three students will find that it is not necessary to centre the moving averages?
ii Explain why centring the moving averages will not be necessary for this student.

10 A soft drinks manufacturer recorded its seasonal sales (in \$10 000s) over a period of $3\frac{1}{2}$ years, as shown in Table 11.33.

Table 11.33: Soft drink sales

Year	Season	Sales (× \$10 000)
2	I	2.6
0	II	5.2
1	III	5.7
2	IV	4.7
2	I	2.4
0	II	4.8
1	III	5.5
3	IV	4.5
2	I	2.2
0	II	4.4
1	III	5.3
4	IV	4.3
2	I	2.0
0	II	4.0
1	III	
5	IV	

i Using 1 cm between seasons and 2 cm to represent \$10 000, draw a time series graph to illustrate these data.
ii Calculate an appropriate set of centred moving averages.
iii Plot the centred moving averages onto the graph, and draw a trend line.
iv Write down the general trend value for season III of 2015.
v By calculating the mean variation for season III, and using it as a seasonal component, predict the value of the sales, in \$, in season III of 2015.

11 Table 11.34 shows the profits, in \$100s, of a clothing manufacturer over a four-year period.

Table 11.34: Clothing profits

	Season			
Year	**I**	**II**	**III**	**IV**
2012	752	333	577	622
2013	680	301	513	590
2014	584	261	457	558
2015	512	221	401	526

i Calculate an appropriate set of centred moving averages for the data.
ii Calculate the seasonal component for season II.
iii Given that the season II general trend value for 2016 is 375, predict the profit, in dollars, for season II of 2016.

12 Figure 11.6 shows the number of new customers opening accounts at a bank over a period of 33 months. A straight line illustrating the trend is also shown.

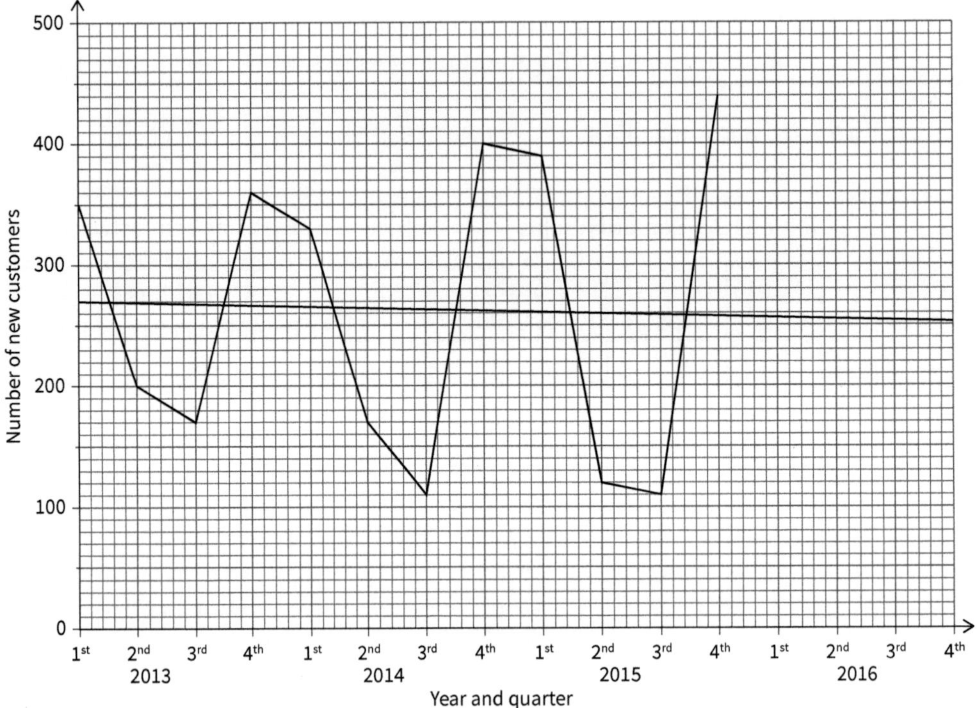

Figure 11.6: New bank customers

i Describe the trend in the context of this question.
ii Describe the variation shown in the time series graph.

The mean of the 4th quarter deviations shown in Figure 11.6 is +139.8.

iii Calculate an estimate of how many fewer new customers will open accounts at the bank in the 4th quarter of 2016 than did in the 4th quarter of 2015.
iv Why is it not possible to use the data presented in Figure 11.6 to determine the trend in the number of customers that have accounts at the bank?

Exam-Style Questions

1 Five items, A to E, are described:

A: The possible height of a tree
B: The types of ticket that can be purchased for a train journey
C: The possible length of time taken, to the nearest hour, for an aeroplane to complete a flight
D: The number of letters in the phrase 'brown ducks fly'
E: The possible number of empty chairs in a restaurant.

Write down the letter of the item that:

i is not a variable, **ii** describes a qualitative variable,
iii describes a discrete quantitative variable.

2 Each of the following statements refers to a measure of central tendency. Write down the name of the measure referred to in each case.

i A teacher calculates a measure for the test marks of the students in his class, so that he can see who came in the top half of the class.
ii Janice calculates the amount of money that she and each of her three friends should contribute so that the cost of a meal is shared equally.
iii Iqbal writes down a measure for a qualitative variable.

3 Arsène and José are playing a game using a fair coin and a fair six-sided die numbered 1, 2, 3, 4, 5 and 6. Arsène tosses the coin and rolls the die.
They have agreed that if the coin lands heads up and the die shows an odd number, or if the die shows a 6, José will pay Arsène \$3.50.
However, if Arsène obtains neither of these results then he must pay José \$$x$.

Calculate the value of x, if this game is known to be fair.

4 Data for a quantitative variable are classified consecutively as having values 2–5, 6–8 or 9–12.

For the class given as 6–8:

i Find the class interval, if the values are the number of wheels on each of the vehicles in a large parking area.
ii Write down the lower class limit and upper class limit, if the values are the masses, to the nearest gram, of a sample of birds' eggs.
iii Find the class mid-value, if the values are the number of complete sentences served by inmates at various prisons in the past month.

5 Table ESQ.1 summarises the ages, to the nearest year, of the final-year students at a college.

Table ESQ.1: Students' ages

Age (nearest year)	20–21	22–25	26–29
Number of students (f)	y	36	30

A histogram is to be drawn to illustrate these data, in which the 22–25 class will be represented by a column of height 9 cm.

i Explain why the actual interval of the 22–25 class is 4 years.

ii Find:

a the correct column height for the 26–29 class,

b the value of y, given that the 20–21 class will be represented by a column of height 8 cm.

6 Two events are **A** and **B**, where P(**A**) = 0.4, P(**B**) = 0.65 and P(**A** ∩ **B**) = 0.26.

i Use Figure ESQ.1 to find the probability that neither **A** nor **B** occurs.

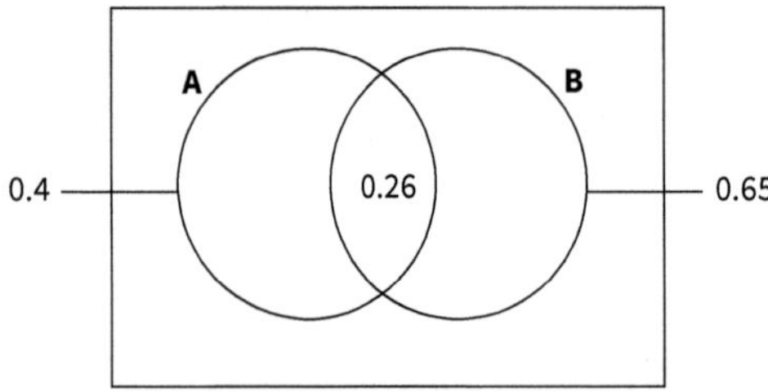

Figure ESQ.1: Venn diagram for events **A** and **B**

ii State, giving a reason for each of your answers, whether events **A** and **B** are:

a mutually exclusive, **b** independent.

7 A company produces four materials, A, B, C and D, used in the manufacture of electronic components. The percentage bar chart in Figure ESQ.2 represents its total current stock of 4000 grams of these materials.

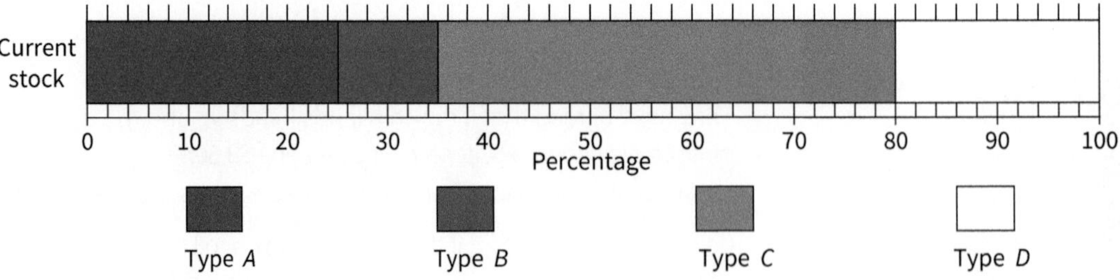

Figure ESQ.2: Manufacturing material stocks

i Calculate the number of grams of material C that the company has in stock.

The value of each of the materials is given, in dollars per gram, in Table ESQ.2.

Table ESQ.2: Manufacturing material values

Type of material	A	B	C	D
Value per gram ($)	5.40	13.50	3.00	6.75

ii Calculate the total value of the 4000 grams of material.

The total value of the materials is to be illustrated in a pie chart, with one sector representing the value of each type of material.

iii Describe, but do not draw, the pie chart.

8 A researcher is devising a questionnaire about a new electronic reading device. She has studied the market and has classified it by gender and age, as shown in Table ESQ.3.

Table ESQ.3: Electronic reading device market

	Under 18	18 to 25	25 to 50	50 and over
Male (%)	1	5	21	4
Female (%)	3	6	45	15

i Write down the percentage of the market that the researcher expects to be:
a in the under 18 age group, **b** female.

The researcher considers giving the questionnaire to a sample of 600 people, stratified by gender and age.

ii Find the number of each of the following that should be in the sample:
a females in the 18 to 25 age group, **b** males.

The questionnaire was actually given to 75 people in each of the eight classes shown in the table.

iii State a likely undesirable result of doing this.
iv Write down one advantage of using open questions in a questionnaire.

9 Twenty-six adults were asked to catch a tennis ball, fired at various speeds from a machine. Each adult attempted to catch the ball 100 times. The numbers of successful catches are shown in the back-to-back stem-and-leaf diagram in Figure ESQ.3.

Men		Women
	1	9
5 1	**2**	3 5 9
8 2 0	**3**	0 2 6 7 8 9
4 4 3 3 2	**4**	3 4
0 0	**5**	1
	6	
9	**7**	

Key: 1 | **2** | 3 represents 21 catches for a man and 23 catches for a woman

Figure ESQ.3: Number of catches

i Find the range for the men and for the women.
ii Find the median number of catches made by the women.

The interquartile range for the women is 14.

iii Find the interquartile range for the men.
iv Explain why the interquartile range would be a better measure of dispersion to use than the range in comparing the data for the two groups

10 A variable, P, was measured at regular intervals over a period of 60 months up to the end of the year 2015. It was found that P has four-monthly seasonal variation.

i Explain what is meant by *seasonal variation*.

Seasonal components for P over the 60-month period are given in Table ESQ.4.

Table ESQ.4: Seasonal components of *P*

Four-month period	1st	2nd	3rd
Seasonal component	+152.2	x	−96.6

ii Find the value of the missing seasonal component, x.

iii Calculate the sum of the deviations between the general trend values and the values of P for the 1st four-month periods over these 60 months.

iv Describe briefly and in general terms the calculations that must be performed so that a trend line can be drawn onto a time series graph.

The general trend value for the 3rd four-month period of 2016 is 541.

iv Estimate the value of P for the 3rd four-month period of 2016.

11 People applying to a computing school are given an aptitude test.

Those who are accepted take a progress test three months after the course has begun.

Table ESQ.5 gives the aptitude test scores, X, and the progress test scores, Y, for a random sample of eight students, A to H.

Table ESQ.5: Aptitude and progress test scores

	A	*B*	*C*	*D*	*E*	*F*	*G*	*H*
Aptitude, *X*	36	28	34	31	35	42	38	40
Progress, *Y*	22	16	26	19	21	30	27	35

For these data: $\Sigma X = 284,\ \Sigma Y = 196,\ \Sigma X^2 = 10230,\ \Sigma Y^2 = 5072.$

i Show that the mean of the combined aptitude and progress test scores is equal to 30.

ii Calculate, correct to 2 decimal places, the standard deviation of the combined aptitude and progress test scores.

iii What type of correlation, if any, would you expect between the students' aptitude test scores and their progress test scores? Give a reason for your answer.

12 Seminars on information technology (IT) and public relations (PR) were each held on three consecutive days, and were attended by a total of 133 delegates. No delegate attended more than one of the six seminars. The numbers attending are illustrated in Table ESQ.6.

Table ESQ.6: Seminar attendees

	Monday		Tuesday		Wednesday	
	Women	**Men**	**Women**	**Men**	**Women**	**Men**
Information technology (IT)	12	8	10	8	12	5
Public relations (PR)	15	14	13	14	9	13

i How many more delegates attended the PR seminar than the IT seminar over the three-day period?
ii What proportion of those that attended on Wednesday were men at the PR seminar?
iii If one delegate is randomly selected, find the probability that they are either a woman or attended the PR seminar on Monday.
iv If two delegates that attended a seminar on Tuesday are selected at random, find the probability that both are women that attended the IT seminar.

13 A clock in the centre of a town is set to chime four times each hour. Table ESQ.7 shows when the chimes begin, and their duration.

Table ESQ.7: Clock chimes

Begin	On the hour	Quarter past the hour and quarter to the hour	Half past the hour
Duration	60 seconds	25 seconds	30 seconds

i Find the mean duration of the four hourly chimes.
ii Calculate the standard deviation of these durations.

The clock is serviced every Monday by Marius, who may arrive at any random time, day or night.

iii On how many of the 52 Mondays of the year do you expect the clock to be chiming at the moment Marius arrives to service it?

For exactly seven days of February last year, the clock did not chime because of a broken spring, which took Marius some time to repair.

iv Find the mean of the duration of the chimes for all the 28 days of February last year.
v State whether the standard deviation of the durations was greater, the same or less in February than in all the other months last year.

14 A group of students are testing a new product designed to improve the growth rate of fruit trees. The students prepare two seed beds and treat one of them with the product. They plant 100 apple seeds in each bed, and after five days the heights of the 200 seedlings are measured. Their results are summarised in the cumulative frequency diagram in Figure ESQ.4.

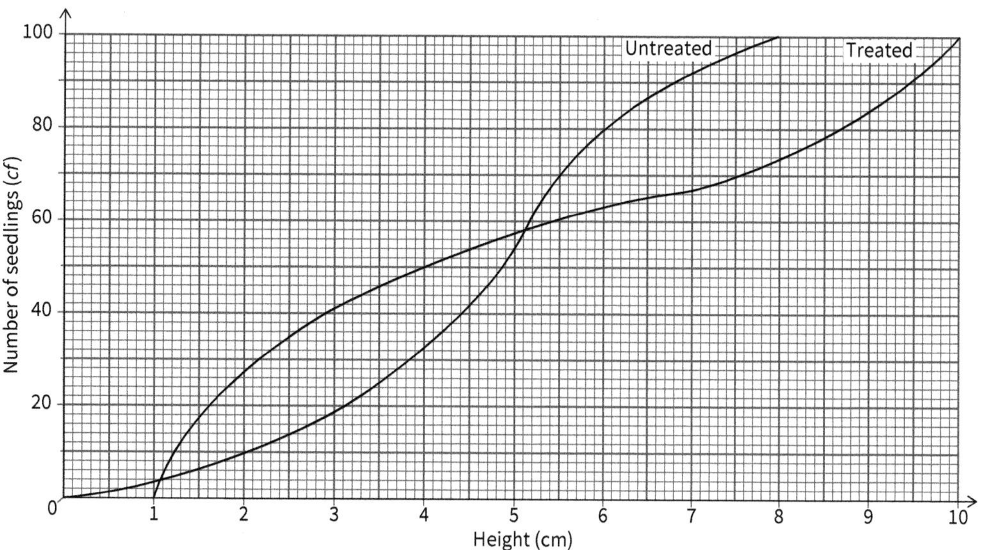

Figure ESQ.4: Seedling heights

i How many seedlings in the untreated bed had grown to heights of less than 3 cm?
ii How many seedlings in the treated bed had grown to heights of 7 cm or more?
iii Find the median height of the seedlings in each of the two beds.
iv In which of the beds were the heights of the seedlings most dispersed?
v The *N*th percentiles of the heights in the two beds are the same. Find the value of *N*.
vi If one of the 200 seedlings is selected at random, find the probability that its height is 6.6 cm or more.

15 The labels on jars of peanut butter advertise that each contains 350 grams.

The cumulative frequency table in Table ESQ.8 summarises the results of a survey conducted on the actual contents of 520 jars.

Table ESQ.8: Peanut butter jar contents

Mass of peanut butter (*m* grams)	Number of jars (*cf*)
$349.0 \le m < 349.6$	60
$349.6 \le m < 350.4$	140
$350.4 \le m < 350.9$	300
$350.9 \le m < 352.0$	520

i How many jars contained between 349.6 g and 350.4 g of peanut butter?
ii Calculate, by linear interpolation, giving exact answers, an estimate of:
a the median mass of peanut butter in these jars, **b** the 85th percentile of the masses.
iii Calculate an estimate of the number of jars that did not contain less than the advertised mass of peanut butter.

16 i Wayne and Irina plan to participate in the first round of a talent contest. To reach the next stage of the contest, they must qualify in two or more categories from singing, dancing and acting.

Estimates of their chances of qualifying in each category are shown in Table ESQ.9.

Table ESQ.9: Qualifying chances

	Singing	Dancing	Acting
Wayne	$\frac{1}{2}$	$\frac{2}{3}$	$\frac{3}{5}$
Irina	$\frac{1}{3}$	$\frac{1}{9}$	$\frac{1}{6}$

Assuming that these estimates are accurate, find the probability that:

a Wayne qualifies in all three categories,
b Irina qualifies in none of the three categories,
c Wayne reaches the next stage of the contest.

ii The raw scores of the eight finalists, A to H, are recorded in Table ESQ.10.

Table ESQ.10: Raw scores in final

Contestant	A	B	C	D	E	F	G	H
Raw score in category X	74	37	35	61	31	76	69	49
Raw score in category Y	62	45	46	61	43	64	60	51

a Show that the mean of the raw scores for the finalists in the two categories are equal.

The mean raw scores for the four lowest scoring finalists are represented on a scatter diagram by a point plotted at (38, 46.25).

b Find the coordinates of the point that can be plotted to represent the mean of the raw scores for the four highest scoring finalists.

c Using any two of the three average points, find, in the form $Y = mX + c$, the equation of the line of best fit that would be drawn onto the scatter diagram.

d Write down the letters A to H in descending order of their total raw scores.

iii In what situation would it be appropriate and fair to award prizes to the finalists in the order that you have written them down in part **ii d**?

17 A heavy industry has three classes of employee, X, Y and Z. Information about the numbers of employees and accidents last year at two companies, P and Q, is given in Table ESQ.11. Accident rates are given to the nearest whole number per 1000 employees; standard population figures apply to the whole industry.

Table ESQ.11: Industrial accidents

	Company P			Company Q			
	Employees	Accidents	Crude rate	Employees	Accidents	Crude rate	Standard population
X	48	6	125	36	4	a	10%
Y	104	16	154	112	17	b	30%
Z	256		199	260	45	c	60%

i Show that there were a total of 73 accidents at company P last year.

ii Calculate, to the nearest whole number, the crude accident rates, a, b and c, at company Q.

iii Find to the nearest whole number the crude accident rate at each of the two companies.

iv The standardised accident rate at company Q is 160.5; find the standardised rate at company P.

v What evidence suggests that employment with company Q is safer than with company P?

vi What additional information would you ask the companies to provide, if you were asked to make a fair report on the comparative safety at P and Q?

Answers to Exercises and Exam-style Questions

Chapter 1 Ungrouped Data

Exercise 1A

1 **i** 73 **ii** $\frac{27}{100}$ **iii** $\frac{7}{10}$

iv **a** 75% **b** 70% **v** Boys

2 **i**

	S	M	L	
R	20	23	32	75
Y	15	14	16	45
	35	37	48	120

ii **a** $\frac{3}{8}$ **b** $\frac{37}{120}$ **iii** $\frac{32}{75}$

iv 42.9%

3 **i**

	CF	OW	
S	5	8	13
M	10	7	17
	15	15	30

ii $\frac{1}{6}$ **iii** 10

4 **i**

	Stew	Hot pot	
Tart	26	18	44
Ice	32	24	56
	58	42	100

ii $\frac{9}{50}$

5 **i** 40% **ii** $\frac{10}{31}$ **iii** 62.5% **iv** Saloons

6 **i**

	Black	White	
Plastic	9	20	29
Wooden	15	16	31
	24	36	60

ii $\frac{17}{20}$ or 85%

7 **i** 20 **ii** 10 **iii** 11 **iv** 32

v Impossible to have more employed adults than adults in a house.

8 **i** 53 **ii** 28 **iii** 27 **iv** 18

v Came by taxi today, but will come by bus tomorrow.

vi Today's and tomorrow's numbers could represent a completely different set of people.

9 **i**

	Last year		This year	
	Pass	**Fail**	**Pass**	**Fail**
Paper 1	310	*12*	*310*	*35*
Paper 2	303	*19*	*311*	*34*
Paper 3	305	*17*	*294*	*51*

ii 34 **iii** 0

10 **i** 90 **ii** 76 **iii** 9 **iv** $\frac{5}{7}$

v 65% **vi** $\frac{4}{11}$ **vii** 40%

Exercise 1B

1 **i**

X	f	fX
0	2	0
1	2	2
2	3	6
3	7	21
4	4	16
5	2	10
6	0	0
7	1	7
	21	62

ii 21 is the number of school days in June; 62 is the number of late arrivals in June.

iii **a** 3 **b** 14 **c** 3 **d** $\frac{1}{3}$ or 33.3%

iv 19 (21 – 2 days of 0 late arrivals)

2 **i**

No. children (X)	No. doctors (f)	fX
0	7	0
1	6	6
2	6	12
3	3	9
4	2	8
5	1	5
	25	40

ii These *25* female doctors have ***40*** children altogether.

iii 11

3 **i** **a** 14 yrs **b** 30 **c** $\frac{1}{15}$ or 6.67%
d 8 **e** 10%
ii 129 yrs **iii** 424 yrs

4 **i** 130 **ii** **a** 50 **b** 67
iii $\frac{1}{10}$ **iv** 20% **v** $\frac{79}{99}$

5 **i** 8 **ii** 4 **iii** 233 **iv** 20%

6 **i** 3 **ii** 120 **iii** $\frac{19}{40}$ or 47.5%
iv Frequency = sector angle ÷ 3 **v** 124

Text example questions

i 4:3 **ii** 70.7%

Exercise 1C

1 **i** **a** Football **b** Badminton
c $\frac{2}{9}$ **d** 8.89%
ii Some play more than one sport **iii** 4:13

2 **i** Any representing 2, 4, 8 or 16 items
ii 264 **iii** $\frac{2}{11}$ **iv** 30.3%

3 **i** Any sixth of it can easily be drawn and will be clearly understood.
ii 12 **iii** 3 **iv** 114 **v** $\frac{1}{3}$

Text example questions

i 30 **ii** $\frac{7}{30}$ **iii** 90%

Text example question

i 28 **ii** 32 **iii** $\frac{9}{14}$ **iv** 35.7%

Exercise 1D

1 **i** Car **ii** 8 **iii** 8:5
iv 7.4% **v** $\frac{5}{9}$

2 **ii** 166 **iii** Thursday and Friday
iv No; numbers of potatoes not given.

3 **i** 5 **ii** 1 **iii** 25%
iv 55 **v** 6

4 **i**

No. texts	No. children (f)
0	5
1	9
2	3
3	2
4	1

ii 25

5 **ii** 26 **iii** 59

6 **i**

No. unsuccessful throws	No. men (f)
0	4
1	14
2	20
3	18
4	10

ii 148
iii **a** 4 **b** 38 **c** 48

Exercise 1E

1 **ii** $\frac{4}{15}$ or 26.7% **iii** $\frac{1}{3}$

2 **i**

	1	2	3	4	5	6	
A	2	4	12	16	14	7	55
B	4	7	10	9	14	6	50
C	3	5	14	11	14	3	50
	9	16	36	36	42	16	155

ii **a** 155 **b** Week 5 **c** 5 and 6
iii 11:10:10 **iv** 32.3%

3 **i** 13:4, 77:23 and 38:11
ii 2015 **iii** 23%

4 **i** 20 **ii** 27
iii X: 24 and 36; Z: 27 and 24; X and Z: 9 and 20

Text example questions

ii Kim
iii Glenda

Exercise 1F

1 **i** 10, 11 and 17 **ii** **a** $\frac{5}{19}$ **b** 28.9%

iii **b** 18.3% **iv** Valley road

2 **i**

	Truck	Car	Motorbike	
Mike's	25	80	15	120
Jomo's	15	70	15	100

ii Jomo's 15% (Mike's 12.5%)

iii Mike's \$16 750; Jomo's \$13 050

iv 43.8%

3 **i** 30 **ii** 16 **iii** 4 **iv** 16.7%

v 11.1% to 13.3% to 7.69% described

4 **ii** 3A **iii** 3B **iv** 4:3 **v** 3A

Exercise 1G

1 **i** **a** 30% **b** 65% **c** 67.8%

2 **i** With 22%, 52%, 16%, 10% sections

ii 26% **iii** 57

3 **i** **a** Soup = 5000; Beans = 4000; Tomatoes = 1000

b 42% **c** S: 42%, 36%, 22%; T: 15%, 60%, 25%

ii **a** North = 3450; South = 4050; West = 2500

b 10% **c** W: 44%, 46%, 10%

4 **i** 112, 128 and 80

ii **a** 520 **b** 31.5%

5 A: Necessarily true B: Necessarily false

C: Not necessarily false D: Not necessarily true

6 A: Not necessarily false B: Necessarily true

C: Necessarily false D: Not necessarily true

7 **i**

	C&B	C&M	B&M
1st year	33	63	54
2nd year	54	81	45

ii

	C	M	B
1st year	96	117	87
2nd year	135	126	99

iv It shows the trades separately and the actual numbers of trainees

Text example questions

i 117 **ii** 713 **iii** $\frac{10}{117}$ or 8.55%

iv 12.0% **v** $\frac{1}{5}$

Exercise 1H

2 **i** 14 **ii** 2009 and 2010

iii 94 **iv** 5 and 6

v S/he was late every day that week.

3 **i** 5 **ii** 3

iii \$ or bags on vertical axis

iv \$0 (they did not collect on that day)

4 **ii** 2008 and 2009 **iii** 2.5%, 2.33%, 2.17%

iv 117.5%

v By numbering the profit axis starting at 1 (million), rather than 0.

Exercise 1I

1 **i** 216°, 126° and 18° **ii** 60%, 35%, 5%

2 68°, 102°, 124°, 66° with 18.9%, 28.3%, 34.4%, 18.3%

3 **i** 42% **ii** **a** 29 400 **b** 588

4 **i** 18°, 54°, 162°, 63°, 45°, 18°

iii **a** 108 **b** 12 **c** 240

5 7.2 cm

6 9.8 cm

7 10 625

8 **i** \$21 870 **ii** 8.48 cm

9 **i** 11.25 cm **ii** 600

10 **i** 201 cm^2 **ii** 8.00 cm **iii** 7.65 cm **iv** 139 cm^2

11

F. Act.	G	B
Sport	162	150
Lessons	144	55
Lunch	54	45
	360	250

Exercise 1J

1 **i** $x=3$ **ii** 4 **iii** 2 **iv** 60%

2 **i** 3, 5, 4, 2 **ii** 3

3 **i** 25 **ii** Worked in radio and TV but not on stage. **iii** 15 **iv** 7

4 **i** 10 **ii** 9 **iii** 28%

5 **i** 8 **ii** 44 **iii** 185 **iv** $\frac{3}{5}$ **iv** 43.5%

6 **i** $x = 12$

ii

No. continents	No. Americans (f)
0	12
1	22
2	14
3	2
	50

Chapter 2 Basic Probability

Exercise 2

1 **i** **a** $\frac{1}{2}$ **b** $\frac{1}{5}$ **c** $\frac{7}{10}$
ii **a** 9 **b** $\frac{1}{3}$

2 **i** 35 **ii** $\frac{1}{35}$ **iii** $\frac{1}{35}$ **iv** $\frac{3}{7}$ **v** A girl

3 **i** $\frac{1}{3}$ **ii** $\frac{2}{3}$ **iii** $\frac{1}{3}$ **iv** $\frac{1}{3}$ **v** 0 **vi** 1

4 **i** $\frac{1}{2}$ **ii** $\frac{1}{4}$ **iii** $\frac{3}{13}$ **iv** $\frac{1}{26}$ **v** $\frac{3}{4}$ **vi** $\frac{2}{13}$

5 **i** 0.34 **ii** 124

6 **i** $\frac{2}{3}$ **ii** 12

7 **i** $\frac{1}{11}$ **ii** $\frac{5}{11}$ **iii** 24, 4 and 16

8 **i** $\frac{1}{12}$ **ii** $\frac{1}{12}$
iii **a** $\frac{1}{4}$ **b** $\frac{1}{3}$ **c** $\frac{5}{12}$ **d** $\frac{3}{4}$ **e** $\frac{2}{3}$ **f** $\frac{7}{12}$

9 **i** **a** 20% **b** 30% **c** 50% **d** 50% **e** 80% **f** 70% **g** 0% **h** 100%
ii **a** 20 **b** 12 **c** 32

10 **i** $\frac{1}{20}$ **ii** $\frac{9}{40}$ **iii** $\frac{1}{8}$ **iv** $\frac{1}{2}$ **v** $\frac{3}{8}$

11 **i** 20 **ii** 60 **iii** 40 **iv** 80 **v** 80 **vi** 100

12 **i** **a** $\frac{1}{8}$ **b** $\frac{3}{8}$ **c** $\frac{5}{8}$
ii **a** 50 **b** 250 **c** 300
iii 640 or more

13 **i** **a** $\frac{5}{6}$ **b** 5 **ii** 10 **iii** 30

14 **i** $\frac{1}{33}$ **ii** $\frac{1}{33}$ **iii** $\frac{6}{11}$

15 **i** $\frac{1}{19}$ **ii** $\frac{3}{19}$ **iii** $\frac{1}{19}$ **iv** $\frac{5}{19}$ **v** $\frac{1}{19}$ **vi** $\frac{11}{19}$

Chapter 3 Data Collection

Exercise 3A

1 **i** Young people wearing similar footwear
ii Allow them try out the shoes
iii Are they comfortable/attractive/reasonably priced?

2 **i** Agree 50%, Don't know 40%, Disagree 10%
iii Not visited since building works completed
iv **a** 5:1 **b** 5:1 **c** 5:1

3 **i** 44° **ii** 86% **iii** 12.0 cm

4 **i** **a** Everyone said yes
b 14 yes; 6 no
c 15 yes; 15 no
d at least 15 people were in that group
e The summed score was an even number between 22 and 30, inclusive
ii *C* must be; *A*, *B* and *D* could be

5 **i** It is not viewed as a negative opinion.
ii 4000
iii Average resident = +2. His/her response is (halfway) between 'fairly good' and 'average'.
iv **a** 2811
b No; Average resident's response is still between 'fairly good' and 'average'.

Exercise 3B

1 **i** Only 4 numbers are under 40
ii Only 4 different numbers under 40
iii 24, 17, 02, 31, 36

2 **i** 21, 50, 10, 35, 47 **ii** 30, 17, 41, 29, 06, 43
iii 08, 18, 28, 38, 48

3 **i** 07, 20, 37, 22 **ii** 41, 03, 26, 19, 37

iii 03, 13, 23, 33, 43, 53

4 **i** **a** 81, 97 and the second 45 **b** 13, 36, 45, 06, 27

c They are all women

ii **a** 03 or 10 **b** both have 3 women and 2 men

iii Split into 2 groups (< 47 and > 46); 3 women (04, 17, 37) and 2 men (48, 77)

5 **i** 10% **ii** Stratifying is unnecessary

iii **a** 20, 51, 13, 28, 07, 18

b 92 is too big; 51 cannot appear twice

iv **a** 00 and 09 **b** 05, 15, 25, 35, 45, 55

v **a** 3 beach, 2 cruise, 1 weekend break

b 56, 07, 33, 26, 12, 47

6 **i** **a** Use 18, 29, 04, 88, 93, 35, 06 (88 & 93 discarded); Ayanda, Yash, Pierre, Vijay, Dodi.

b it contains no girls

ii **a** Tefo, Rudy, Debbie, Fred

b Dodi, Ayanda, Lisa

c Stella, Nazeem, Chloe, Victor, Jip, Julia.

7 **i** 3 **ii** 406 and 637 **iii** 026, 386, 626

8 13 boys and 17 girls

9 **i** 949, 580, 271

ii Use MoT computer and registration numbers

10 **i** 24 **ii** 31

iii

	M	F	
Track	17	14	31
Field	9	10	19
	26	24	50

iv Not to be stratified by their continent of origin.

11 **i** 2.5%

ii He took 250 containers instead of 250 litres.

iii Take 500 containers of any flavour from any supermarket (sugar is being tested, not juice)

12 **i** $\frac{1}{5}$ **ii** $\frac{4}{17}$

iii Seniors constitute a greater proportion of the membership than juniors

iv JB = 3, JG = 2, SB = 6, SG = 5

13 C is correct.

14 **i** **a** 3 boys, 2 girls **b** Stratified (by gender)

ii **a** 2655 **b** 2784

iii **a** Ignoring the 2 (thousands), the girls' numbers only go up to 655, so 0.673 cannot be used

b 2143, 2772, 2081, 2219, 2500

15 Should include those that do not buy regularly/It will give a value that is much higher than the true average/Not all villagers drive a car.

Chapter 4 Grouped Data

Exercise 4A

1 **i** Shapes, attitudes, hairstyles

ii Heights, altitudes, volumes, duration

2 Discrete

3 **i** Discrete **ii** Continuous

4 *W*, *X* and *Z* are discrete; *Y* is continuous

5 Discrete

6 *A* is qualitative, *C* is not a variable, *D* is continuous

7 **i** Both quantitative: *C* discrete, *D* continuous

ii Both qualitative: *E* continuous, *F* discrete

8 **i** Gold, silver and bronze. **ii** Time taken and speed.

9 **i** 5 **ii** Uncountable **iii** 8

iv 4 **v** 9

10

	Discrete	Continuous
Quantitative	*D* *H**	*A*
Qualitative	*G**	*B* *F*
Not a variable	*D** *C*	*H* *E*

*D** if you are in a one-room building

*G** the digits carry no quantitative significance

H if it is a specific number, but *H** if you plan to read 5 or 6

Text example questions

i 16 **ii** 31 **iii** 30%

Exercise 4B

1 **i** Frequencies: 5, 6, 7, 8, 7, 4, 3

ii **a** 18 **b** $\frac{7}{20}$ **c** 55%

2 **i** 2–6, 7–9, 10–16, 17–20; all frequencies = 13

ii 6, 9, 16, 20

3 **i** 25999.5 and 34999.5

ii 23 499.5, 30 499.5, 42 499.5, 58 749.5 **iii** 945 000

iv 29 406 740

v 132 000 (the same [minimum number of] people at each match)

4 **i** 104 **ii** 12 : 13 **iii** 77.5%

iv Cannot see how many were born in each month.

5 **i** Frequencies: 4, 8, 7, (1)

ii **a** each class interval is 4 **b** 1.5, 5.5, 9.5, 13.5

6 **i** Because they are grouped with those who scored 11, 12, 13 and 14 goals.

ii 17

iii 0–14 goals with angle 236°; 15–29 goals with angle 124°

iv $r = 4.18$ cm

7 **i** 35 **ii** 44

8 **i** 12 500 **ii** 13 499

9 **i** \$1050 **ii** **a** \$10 500 **b** \$11 499.90

10 **i** 25 **ii** 104 **iii** 45 and 65

iv **a** 1145 **b** 1620

11 **i** 50 **ii** 949

iii Class interval = 300, mid-value = 499.5 **iv** 6176

Exercise 4C

1 **i** 18 **ii** 8 **iii** 20%

iv **a** 30–39 **b** 10–19

2 **i**

0	1 2 3 3 4 4 5 6 7 8 9
1	0 1 2 3 3 5 6
2	0 6

ii 6 **iii** 40%

3 **i** 88

iii *D* applies best, but *B* also applies; Equal numbers of passengers appear 3 times, but there is no way of telling whether they were carried on the same day(s).

4 **i**

Batsman *P*		Batsman *Q*
	2	3 4
8 7 7 6	**3**	1 6
8 7 4 1 1	**4**	2 5 8
9 7 3 2	**5**	1 2 6 7
1 0	**6**	4 8
	7	1 7

ii **a** *Q*; scored more runs (higher average)
b *P*; scores are less varied

5 **i** **a** 251 **b** 480

ii 5 (maximum is 7 boys in a row)

Exercise 4D

1 **i** 370

ii Upper boundaries: (7, 8), 9, 10, 11, 12; cf: (0), 2, 10, 21, 37, 40

iii **a** 37 **b** 19 **c** 27

2 **i**

Mark	3	4	5	6	7	8	9
f	2	3	5	6	4	3	1

ii 10 **iii** cf: (0), 2, 5, 10, 16, 20, 23, 24

iv **a** $\frac{1}{3}$ **b** $\frac{7}{12}$

3 **i** Frequencies: (0, 1, 5), 11, 14, 10, 6, 5, 2, (1)
ii **a** 8 **b** 30 **iii** $\frac{5}{7}$

4 **i** 69 **ii** 45

iii cf: (0), 4, 8, 14, 24, 41, 55, 63, 69

iv 10 **v** 20.3%

vi No; they could have listened to the news at other times of day.

5 **i**

Number of unsuccessful attempts (*u*)	$u \le 0$	$u \le 1$	$u \le 2$	$u \le 3$	$u \le 4$	$u \le 5$
Number of children (*cf*)	3	8	16	26	37	50

ii **a** 3 **b** 13 **c** 18

6 **i** It is not possible to select 0 or 5 red balls.

ii cf: (0), 5, 20, 34, 40 **iii** 29

7 **i** **a** 1 **b** 21 **c** 17 **ii** 20%

Exercise 4E

1 **i** 169.5 cm **ii** 149.5 cm **iii** 10 cm
iv 154.5 cm, 164.5 cm, 174.5 cm

2 **i** 5 min **ii** 105 min
iii 50 min **iv** 30, 30, 40 min

3 **i** Nearest 100 m **ii** 4050 m
iii 6050 m **iv** 3650 m

4 **i a** 3.45 cm **b** 3.95 cm **c** 0.5 cm
ii a 3800 **b** 5%

5 **i** 6.25 m, 12.75 m **ii** 6.5 m **iii** 9.5 m

6 **i** 2 yr **ii** 1 yr **iii** 8 yr

7 **i a** Continuous **b** Discrete **c** Continuous
ii a 6.5 and 13.5 **b** 7 and 13 **c** 7 and 14

8 **i a** 49.5 **b** 50 **c** 49.5
ii a Discrete **b** Continuous **c** Discrete

9 **i** A game with no goals.
ii All the players are childless.
iii Admission is free.

10 Boy: 2 Nov 2005 & 1 Nov 2006; Sister: 2 May 2008 & 1 May 2009.

Exercise 4F

1 **i** 70 **ii** 1 kg **iii** 2.5 kg **iv** 290
v 24.1% **vi** 55 **vii** 6 kg

2 **ii a** 155 **b** 160 **c** 185 **d** 25

3 **ii a** 71 **b** 58 **c** 61 **d** 51

4 **i** Boundaries: 175, 225, 275, 325, 375, 425
ii a 21 **b** 13 **c** 2.5%

5 **i** Boundaries: 1150, 1750, 2350, 2950
ii 44.8% **iii** 18

6 **i** 9 full pots; 3 full pots (270 and 90 litres)
ii a 9 **b** 32 **c** 12 **d** 43

7 **i** Region A; total frequency = 30 days
ii Jane; Maximum for A = 98 hr + the missing day, Minimum for B = 138 hr

8 **i** 50 **ii** 48 kg
iii Lower boundary = 8 kg; all chickens < 8 kg

iv

Mass	f
8–16	10
16–24	10
24–32	10
32–40	10
40–48	10

9 They slept longer and lost weight.

Exercise 4G

1 **i** 6, 8, 5 watermelons per kg
iii a 3 **b** 10

2 **i** 4, 8,6 vehicles per hour
iii a 12 **b** 12

3 **ii a** 310 **b** 360
c 90 **d** 22.2%

4 **i** 205 **ii** Frequencies: 40, 120, 45
iii a 100 **b** 33 **c** 50
iv a $\frac{4}{41}$ **b** $\frac{6}{41}$

5 **i** Densities: 100, 700, 600, 300 patients per °C
ii a 320 **b** 310 **iii** 18%

6 **i** 161 **ii** 43

7 **i** 0.08 m **ii** 8 cm
iii 3, 3, 5, 3.5 men per centimetre or 300, 300, 50, 350 men per metre
iv 6 **v** 1.93 m

8 **i** Boundaries: 105 cm, 125 cm, 165 cm, 195 cm; Densities: 2, 1.5, 1 children per cm
ii 76.9% **iii** 26

9 **i** Boundaries are 20.5 and 24.5 hours.
ii Boundaries: 20.5, 24.5, 28.5, 33.5, 39.5, 47.5, 50.5; Densities: 30, 40, 26, 14, 20, 10 seeds per hour
iii a 345 **b** 180 **c** 81.0%

10 **i** 11.5 mm and 12.5 mm
ii Densities: 35, 60, 85, 15
iii a 95 **b** 30 **c** 175 **iv** 35%

11 **i** 134 **ii a** 64.2% **b** 14.2%
iii Departed less than 5 minutes late.

12 **i** Densities: 2, 3.2, 6.2, 5, 0.8 vehicles per km/h
ii 112 **iii** $5750

13 **i** 3.6 cm **ii** 95 and 59

14 **i** \$1.625 **ii** Heights: (8.3 cm), 2.2 cm, 4.8 cm, 6.4 cm

iii 180 days

15 **i** **a** 312 **b** 48 mins

ii **a** 68 **b** 59 **c** 103

16 **i** $a = 18, b = 13.5, c = 11, d = 3.8$ **ii** 6.5 cm

17 **i** $p = 14, q = 25, r = 18$ **ii** $T = 24$

18 **i**

Wind speed (knots)	Locations per 0.4 knots (Density)	Number of locations (Frequency)
(2–4)	(0.6)	3
(4–8)	3.2	32
(8–16)	(2.0)	(40)
16–24	1.4	28
24–28	3.0	(30)
28–30	5.8	29
		$\Sigma f = 162$

ii **a** 55 **b** 33

iii 25.6 knots or more.

Exercise 4H

1 **i** 610 **ii** 990 **iii** 1100

iv 500 **v** 490

2 **i** **a** 52 **b** 28 **c** 48

d 32 **e** 69 **f** 21

3 **i** 144

ii $a = 7.6, b = 9.4, c = 36, d = 131$

iii **a** 33 **b** 11.25 pieces of rope per metre

4 **ii** **a** 20 **b** 50 **c** 54

d 16 **e** 34

5 **ii** **a** ≈ 44 **b** ≈ 136 **c** ≈ 168

d ≈ 121 **e** ≈ 124

6 **i** (0, 0) can be plotted

ii **a** 6.5 and 7.0 **b** 4.0 and 6.5

iii 90

7 **i** cf: (0), 14, 78, 125, 165, 191, (200)

ii **a** GE **b** TS **c** FS **d** BE

8 **i** $a = 16, b = 18, c = 20, d = 22$

ii **a** 22 and 92 **b** 39 and 75 **c** 58 and 56

d 79 and 35 **e** 102 and 12

9 **i** cf: (0), 10, 26, 56, 76, 90

ii **a** 38 **b** 36 **c** 49

10 **i** Interval to frequency ratio is constant (1 : 12) **ii** 312

	A	B	C	Totals
1–2 p.m.	150	(800)	(50)	1000
2–3 p.m.	(80)	390	(30)	500
3–4 p.m.	70	(210)	20	300
4–5 p.m.	(85)	540	(75)	700
Totals	385	1940	(175)	(2500)

ii 1–2 p.m. and 4–5 p.m.; initial enthusiasm and last minute decisions to enter

iii $\frac{1}{485}$

Chapter 5 Measures of Central Tendency

Exercise 5A

1

	Mean	Median	Mode
i	42	41	17
ii	109.75	111	98 and 115
iii	10.3	3.5	1.0
iv	0	0	none/all
v	11.44	11	10
vi	17	17	none/all
vii	38.7	39	40
viii	5.79	5.75	5.7

2 **i** 3000 g **ii** 5100 g **iii** 8100 g **iv** 162 g

3 **i** 232.5 cm **ii** 118.5 cm **iii** 7.9 cm

4 **i** 2120% **ii** 66.25%

5 **i** 6 **ii** 200 **iii** 5 **iv** **a** 988 **b** 4.94

6 $N = 15$

7 Sum = 136.5

8 $q = 49$

9 2.67 m

10 95.6 kg

11 1 hr 19 m and 1 hr 29 m

12 $x = 29$

13 **i** **a** Mode **b** 11

ii **a** Median **b** 25 **iii** $p = 38$

14

X	0	1	2	3	4
f	6	12	8	4	2

ii 1 **iii** 1 **iv** 1.5

15 **i** 40 **ii** 120

16 **i** 31 **ii** 23 **iii** 22.5

17 **i** **a** 90.5% **b** 93%

ii The girl who scored 92%

18 $p = 7$

19 **i** 2 **ii** 9 **iii** **a** 13 **b** 23

20 **i** 4 **ii** 3 **iii** 3 **iv** A positive integer

21 **i** p **ii** $p+1$

22 $y = 26$

Exercise 5B

1 **i** **a** 15 cm **b** 23.6 kg **c** 42.775 km/h

d 32.8 sec **e** 1137 m

ii **a** $10\text{cm} \le V < 20\text{cm}$ **b** $20\text{kg} \le W < 28\text{kg}$

c $40\text{km/h} \le X < 55\text{km/h}$ **d** 30–39 sec

e 1100–1300 m

2 **i** 53.9 cm **ii** $60\text{cm} \le L < 70\text{cm}$

3 **i** 172

ii

Mean no. people per hour	15–18	18–23	23–25	25–31
No. polling stations	48	40	24	60

iii 22.5 **iv** 61 888

4 **i** 62.5 min **ii** 59 min 59 sec

iii It has the highest density (2.8 rowers per min)

5 **i** 24–36

ii 6–24

iii 21.252

6 **i** Actual boundaries are 1 and 5 laps

ii **a** \$2608 **b** 6.52

7 **i** 11.5 **ii** 14.5 **iii** 13.25

Text example question

i $\approx 97.9\,°\text{F}$ **ii** 154 **iii** $176 - 154 = 22$

Text example question

i Shape unaffected

ii Correct diagram will be translated by $\begin{pmatrix} -0.5 \\ 0 \end{pmatrix}$

iii Incorrect diagram will give lower median value

Exercise 5C

1 **i** 20 **ii** 173.2 cm **iii** 6

2 **iii** 1.8 **iv** **a** 67 **b** 30

3 **iii** 163.3 g **iv** **a** 84 **b** 19 **c** 21

4 **i** **a** 188 **b** \$460

ii **a** \$1145 **b** 24 **c** 132

5 **iii** **a** 720 hours **b** 64 **c** 24

6 **iii** **a** 15.3 min **b** 38 **c** 31

d 41.5% to 42% **e** 72

7 **i** 1.5 m and 5.5 m

v **a** 16.5 m **b** 37 **c** 7

vi $X = 14.4$ m **vii** $Y \approx 1878$ cm

8 25.25

9 **i** 12.65 and 13.15 volts **iv** **a** 12.80 volts

b 12.08 volts **c** 49 or 50 **d** 51

10 **i** **c** 21 yr 10 mths

ii **b** Ascotta: it has more people in the appropriate age range from which to select its team/Median age on Ascotta is lower than on Zollora.

11 **iii** **a** 350 **b** 44 **c** 92

iv $t < 0.67$ sec

Exercise 5D

1 Mode

2 A mode, B mean, C mean, D median

3 Find the median.

4 Mean; affected by the extreme value

5 Mode

6 **i** 1

ii 0; it is the smallest value and not central

iii $z = 14$ (class mid-value is 10)

7 The variable is continuous/The raw data (masses) have been rounded off.

Chapter 6 Weighted Averages

Exercise 6A

1 18

2 3.184

3 53.9%

4 59.2%

5 **i a** Daniel 52 **b** Eva 64

ii Aesop 48 **iii** 100

6 **i** 9 km **ii** 45 min **iii** 9.33 km/h

7 **i a** 11.2 g and 14 cm^3 **b** 0.8 g/cm^3

ii a 10.8 g and 16 cm^3 **b** 3.02 g/cm^3

8 Weight is 7

Exercise 6B

1 $A = 125$, $B = 110$, $C = 150$, $D = 200$, $E = 95$, $F = 102.5$

2 $P =$ \$20.00, $Q =$ \$17.50, $R =$ \$32.00, $S =$ \$22.00, $T =$ \$14.80

3 **i** \$88 **ii** \$92

4 **i a** 105 **b** 91 **ii** \$875

5 **i a** 98 **b** 114.5 **ii** \$89.60 **iii** 95

6 **i** Price relatives are based on 2006 prices

ii Price of diesel was the same in those two years

iii \$2.10 **iv** \$0.72 **v** \$4.86 or \$4.85

Exercise 6C

1 120

2 113

3 **i** \$5100 **ii** \$6175 **iii** 121.1

iv She still has 3 tortoises, 7 cats and 25 fish.

4 **i a** 117.4375 **b** 134.125

ii 114.2 **iii** \$4.02

Exercise 6D

1 **i** 107.63 **ii** 112.30 **iii** 103.87

2 $x = 37$

3 **i** 120, 112 and 96 **ii** 110.8

4 **i** 8 : 2 : 1 **ii** 109, 113, 98 **iii** 108.73

iv \$149 500 (\$149 503.75 using 108.73)

v Number of staff, amount of equipment or amount of maintenance work may change.

5 **i a** 24 : 25 : 24

b 4 : 5 : 6

ii a 95, 103, 102.5

b 100.2

c 100.7

6 **i a** \$3360 **b** \$960 **ii** 1 : 7 : 2

iii 112, 97, 108 **iv** 100.7 **v** \$561.90

7 **i** 104, $107\frac{1}{3}$, 96 **ii** 10 : 9 : 8

iii 102.74 **iv** 1.36%

8 **i** 23 : 20 : 57 **ii** 135, 87.5, 124 **iii** 119.23

iv The quantity of fuel used (or the car) may not be the same

Exercise 6E

1 7.5‰ 2 112 3 16 800

4 **i** 637 500 **ii** 640 050

5 102

6 25

7 **i** 80 **ii** 99.0 **iii** 97.6

8 **i** 373, 59, 100 **ii** Drivers; rates are 48, 0, 50

9 Increased by exactly 0.1%

10 $a = 1$, $b = 20$, $c = 83\frac{1}{3}$, $d = 200$, $e = 62.5$, $f = 128$

Exercise 6F

1 **i** 8.76‰ **ii** 24.7‰ **iii** 16.283‰

2 **i a** 45 000 **b** 378 **c** 8.4‰

d $p = 4.5$ **e** 7.325‰

ii a $x = 3.5, y = 88, z = 7000$ **b** 8.4‰

c Crude death rates **d** 8.425‰

e Westwood: lower standardised rate.

3 **i** 11.6‰ **ii** 11.85‰ **iii** 12.2‰ **iv** 11.95‰

v Southlake; lower standardised rate

4 **i** Environments are equally healthy.

ii Redville has a higher proportion of elderly than Greenwood.

5 **i** Pinkerton

ii Pinkerton has a higher proportion of elderly than Blueflat.

6 **i** $a = 9, b = 7500, c = 66$ **ii** 25.625‰

iii 22.74‰ **iv** 1025 **v** 42.81‰

7 **ii** $225 + 1092 + 959 + 171 = 2447$ **iii** 96.72‰

iv $+2447 - 759$ gives increase of 1688

8 **i** $a = 120, b = 15, c = 150, d = 40\%$

ii 128‰ **iii** 162.5‰

iv a Mechanics are mainly responsible for all breakdowns.

b Yes; standardised rate at Megahaul > standardised rate at Grab-a-Line

v Megahaul vehicles may be old or unreliable models/spare parts may be of low quality

9 **i** $a = 86.9‰, b = 59.2‰, c = 154.6‰, d = 24.4‰$

ii 80.5‰

iii $p = 2005, q = 303, r = 11, s = 1$; 82.0‰

iv $A = 84.7‰, B = 82.6‰$

v Krassimir B: crude rate for foundry workers is lower; Ivan A: crude rate for surface workers is lower.

vi Petko B: standardised accident rate is lower at mine B, so it is a safer place at which to work.

10 **i** $12 + 2 + 6 = 20$ **ii** $275 + 105 + 160 = 540$

iii both $44\frac{4}{9}$‰

iv 0.465, 0.30, 0.235 or equivalent

v 42.65‰ and 47.4125‰

vi 'proportion/fraction' and 'worsened' or equivalent.

vii There is no information on the seriousness of the accidents.

Chapter 7: Measures of Dispersion

Exercise 7A

1 **i** 17 **ii** 15 **iii** 40

2 **i** 3 **ii** 4 **iii** 25

3 **i** 5 **ii** 3 **iii** 7

4 3 minutes and 11 minutes

5 **i** 30 cm **ii** 9 g **iii** 0.6 sec

6 $94.99

Exercise 7B

1 **i a** 11 **b** 31 **c** 20

ii a 6 **b** 25 **c** 19

iii a −2 **b** 14 **c** 16

iv a 4 or 3.5 **b** 22 or 24 **c** 18 or 20.5

v a 60 or 59 **b** 98 or 101 **c** 38 or 42

vi a 15 or 14.75 **b** 37 or 38.5 **c** 22 or 23.75

2 **i** 15th and 45th **ii** 40

3 **i** 99 **ii** 3, 6 and 3

4 **i** 32.5th and 97.5th

ii 1.25 and 1.5

iii 0.25

5 **i** 4 and $5\frac{1}{4}$ **ii a** $\frac{11}{49}$

b $\frac{12}{49}$ **c** $\frac{26}{49}$

6 **i a** 2 **b** 1

ii a

No. children	0	1	2	3	4	5	6
No. men (f)	4	72	99	44	23	13	4

b 583 **c** 2

Exercise 7C

1 **i** $98 - 23 = 75\%$ **ii** 54% **iii** $72 - 38 = 34\%$

2 **i** 22 **ii** 18 and 29; 11

3 **i** 106 and 150 **ii** 23

iii More women on average; numbers of women less varied

4 i

0	5 5 6 6 6 7 7 7 7 8 8 8 9 9
1	1 1 1 2 2 2 3 4 5 6 6 8
2	2 2 3 4

Key **1** | 1 represents $110

ii $45

iii Max is $244.99 because amounts are to the nearest $10.

iv $110 **v** $80

5 i Key: 8 | **0** | 7 represents 8 beds sold at branch *A* and 7 beds sold at branch *B*.

Branch *A*		Branch *B*
8 8	**0**	7 8
9 9 8 8 7 7 7 6 5 4 4 4 2 1	**1**	0 1 1 1 1 1 2 2 2 3 3 3 4 7
7 6 5 3 2 1 1 0	**2**	0 1 5 6
3	**3**	0 3 4 5 6 9

ii *A*: 18.7, 18, 17; *B* 18.7, 13, 11 (mean, median, mode)

iii Obtain data on takings or profit.

6 i a 5.3 **b** 2.8

ii a 2.35 **b** 1.6

iii a 20.4 **b** 13.6

7 i

	Min	Max	LQ	Med	UQ	R	IQR
A	−0.8	4.7	1.0	2.6	3.7	5.5	2.7
B	−1.3	5.9	−0.8	0.2	2.2	7.2	3.0

ii Station *A*; higher average temperature/more consistent temperature.

8 i 8, 11, 13, 17, 22 at 0 cm, 3 cm, 5 cm, 9 cm, 14 cm

ii 21, 27, 36.6, 43, 51 at 0 cm, 3 cm, 7.8 cm, 11 cm, 15 cm

iii 7.5, 38.3, 48.3, 55.9, 69.5 at 0 cm, 5.2 cm, 7.7 cm, 9.6 cm, 13 cm

9 3.8, 39.8, 46.3, 77.3, 81.3 at 0 cm, 7.2 cm, 8.5 cm, 14.7 cm, 15.5 cm

9.7, 11, 13, 16, 21 at 0 cm, 4 cm, 6 cm, 9 cm, 14 cm

10 −30, 220, 330, 440, 600 at 0 cm, 5 cm, 7.2 cm, 9.4 cm, 12 cm

11 i 32 **ii** 11

iii 13, 27, 32, 38, 45 at 0 cm, 7 cm, 9.5 cm, 12.5 cm, 16 cm

12 ii a 0.50 **b** 0.23

iv $0.775 - 0.315 = 0.46$ g/cm^3

v 0.32, 0.42, 0.50, 0.65, 0.77 at 0 cm, 2 cm, 3.6 cm, 6.6 cm and 9 cm

13 i 46 **ii** 28.5

14 i a $21 500 **b** $22 500

ii $20 300 and $22 200

iii Females at 0 cm, 4.6 cm, 7 cm, 8.4 cm, 12 cm; Males at 1 cm, 6.6 cm, 9 cm, 11.4 cm, 13.6 cm

iv Males have higher and more dispersed salaries.

Exercise 7D

1 i a 5.8 hr **b** 9.1 hr **c** 3.3 hrs **d** 11.3/11.4 hr

ii 282/283 days **iii** $\frac{1}{3}$ **iv** 3.3 hrs

2 ii *X*: **a** 3.5 to 3.2 **b** 9.5 to 9.3

Y: **a** 24.3 to 25.0 **b** 33.6 to 34.0

Z: **a** 7.77 to 7.75 **b** ≈ 61.75

3 iii a ≈ 2.97 m **b** ≈ 20.39 m

iv a ≈ 19.17 m **b** Median

v 22.25 m

vi a 16 **b** 26

4 iv a ≈ 3.65 cm **b** ≈ 0.124 cm

c 0.75 **d** 12 or 13

e ≈ 0.22 cm

5 iv a ≈ 9.83 min **b** ≈ 46.15 min

v ≈ 47.8 min

vi Boys slower on average, but their times are less dispersed.

6 i 18 and 26

iv a ≈ 38.2 yr **b** ≈ 8.0 yr

c ≈ 35.6 yr **d** 104

7 19 litres (3.8 containers)

8 i a 20 cm b 147

iii a ≈ 267.5 cm b 97

9 i a 0.30 sec b 0.37 sec

c 0.66 sec

ii 0.52 sec iii 0.15 sec

10 i 22.5 − 2.0 = 20.5 ii 13.5 − 8.0 = 5.5

iii 2.0 … 8.0 … 10.0 … 13.5 … 22.5 with own scale

11 i 800 ii 4 hours

iii Women; lower range and lower IQR

iv a $p = 64, q = 72, r = 84, s = 100, t = 320$ b 2.5 up to 5

Exercise 7E

1 i a 55 b 26.25 c 136.58 d 9.78

ii a 32 and 80; 48 b 15 and 38.75; 23.75

c $63\frac{1}{3}$ and $208\frac{1}{3}$; 145 d 5.6 and 13.29; 7.69

2 i 152.75 cm and 162 cm

ii 9.25 cm iii 158 cm

3 i $A = 128$; $B = 126.875$ km/h ii $A = 14.3$; $B = 17.9$ km/h

iii A is faster, but less consistent.

4 i $x = 174$ g; Upper quartile ii $y = 162$ g

5 i 5h 16m 40s − 5h 8m 33s = 8 m 7 s

ii $17\frac{2}{3}$km/h (91.9 ÷ median t)

6 i 24 ii 28.8 iii 25% iv 17.6

7 i Upper boundaries: (9.5), 24.5, 36.5, 40.5, 50.5

ii $24.5 + \frac{47}{48} \times 12$ iii 39 hr 2 min iv $x = 33$

Text example question

Mean: too small (by 0.5); Standard deviation the same.

Exercise 7F

1 i a 10 b 11.5 c 3.39

ii a 21.8 b 56.56 c 7.52

iii a 16.5 b 1051.6 c 32.4

iv a 64.7 b 70 c 26.5

v a 20.125 b 99.1 c 9.96

vi a 3.2 b 2.76 c 1.66

2 i 69.2 kg and 2.97 kg ii Rounded to nearest 100 g.

3 i 23 ii 5.20

4 A: a 19.5 b 54.75 c 7.40

B: a 14.6 b 0.96 c 0.980

C: a 12.83 b 1.3011 c 1.14

D: a 1.725 b 0.236875 c 0.487

E: a 6.17 b 0.258 c 0.508

5 i 5.08 ii 2.61 half-days iii 626 min

6 ii 0.79 iii 0.909

iv (On average) the teachers read more books than the students, but the number of books that the teachers read is more varied/dispersed.

7 i Range and IQR; Equal to 1

ii Range increases; IQR stays the same

iii Standard deviation increases

8 i $x = 0$

ii $x = \{0, 1, 2, 3, 4, 5, 6\}$

9 i Range; Standard deviation; IQR

ii Range > St. Dev > IQR

or 6000 ≤ Range ≤ 6100; 2099.55 ≤ St. Dev ≤ 2134.56; 0 ≤ IQR ≤ 100

10 i 17 ii 9.80

11 i 29.0 litres ii 3.08 litres or 3080 millilitres

12 i a 9.92 cm b 7.60 cm ii 9.40 cm

iii Weighted average of **a** and **b** is 9.15

13 i All frequencies are 28

ii 10.4 yr iii 3 yr 10 m

14 i a 53.3 hr b 8.45 hr

ii No upper boundary for the 20 seeds that failed to germinate in less than 72 hours.

15 i 1742.5 m and 220 m

ii 1549 m and 1913 m

iii $k = -0.88, k = 0.77$

Exercise 7G

1 i a 16.8 b 17.2 c 17.1

ii a 47.59 b 6.90

2 i 113 ii 31

3 3.676

4 **i** **a** $a = 42, b = 36, c = 6, d = 2354, e = 128095, f = 7$
ii **a** 47.06 **b** 74.3064

5 **i** $p = -48, q = 3.7636, r = 1.94, s = 0.6, t = 489.6, u = 5.76$
ii **a** 0 **b** 2.411

6 **i** 34 000 **ii** 10

7 **i** 35 cm **ii** 5 cm

8 **i** **a** 1.058 g and 2.16 g **b** 1.062 g and 1.86 g
ii Diamonds in consignment 2 are heavier and masses are less dispersed.
iii 3.90 g^2

9 **i** Var(P) = 1.3 and Var(H) = 1.39 **ii** Var(P & H) = 1.5475

10 0.566 g

11 **i** 0 **ii** 13.2 **iii** 9.47

12 **i** Girls; high frequencies at extreme values. **ii** 1.9525 years^2

Chapter 8 Linear Transformation of Data

Exercise 8A

1

	Mode	Mean	Median
i	31	22	20
ii	24	15	13
iii	58	40	36
iv	14.5	10	9
v	57	39	35
vi	15	10.5	9.5

2 **i** 12 **ii** 26 **iii** 27

3 **i** 0.12 **ii** 21.7 **iii** 11

4 19.8

5 2.21

6 35

7 **i** 10.6 **ii** 2.9

8 52 kg

9 $(W = P + 3)$ 20.4; $(X = 0.5P - 1)$ 7.7; $(Y = 1.2P)$ 20.88

10 105 km/h

Exercise 8B

1 **i** 12 and 6.3 **ii** 12 and 6.3
iii 24 and 12.6 **iv** 36 and 18.9
v 3 and 1.575 **vi** 4 and 2.1

2 3.3

3 **i** 45.8 and 9.1 kg **ii** 44.365 and 8.645 kg
iii 43.51 and 8.645 kg

4 6.4

5 **i** A is 6.6; B is 16.5 **ii** T is 3.3

6 **i** **a** 3.4 **b** 11.56
ii Double the number he owns

7 4.6

8 **i** $m + 4; d$ **ii** $3m; 3d$ **iii** $0.5m - 1; 0.5d$

9 6.76

10 \$5376 and \$795

Exercise 8C

1 **i** $\bar{X} + \sigma_X$ **ii** $\bar{X} - \sigma_X$ **iii** $\bar{X} + 1.5\sigma_X$
iv $\bar{X} - 2\sigma_X$ **v** $\bar{X} + 2.5\sigma_X$ **vi** $\bar{X} - 3.25\sigma_X$

2 **i** Enrique 48 **ii** Maria 8 **iii** Phenyo 0
iv Wazeem 60 **v** Maatla 12.8 **vi** Dick 30.4

3 $a = 16, b = 40, c = 28, d = 52, e = 100, f = 4, g = 54, h = 70$

4 **i** **a** 64.5 **b** 66
ii Paper 2; his scaled mark was higher than on paper 1.

5 **i** Italy 7.4; Sri Lanka 7.5
ii In Italy; her scaled score was lower.

6 **i** **a** −0.25 **b** −0.225 **c** +0.4
ii Kevin in 3000 m; It is the only one of the three that is better than the average.
iii Only his best jump was recorded.

7 **i**

	Art	Drama
Danielle	55	67
Petros	73	52
Quincy	49	73

ii 1st Petros; Joint 2nd Danielle and Quincy

8 **i** $a = 58, b = 12, c = 62, d = 50, e = 70, f = 15, g = 70, h = 67$
ii Lucky

9 47 **10** 16

Chapter 9 Probability and Expectation

Text example questions

iv $\frac{41}{49}$ **v** $\frac{5}{7}$ **vi** $\frac{8}{49}$

Exercise 9A

1 **i** **a** $\frac{71}{80}$ **b** $\frac{9}{20}$ **c** $\frac{15}{16}$ **ii** $\frac{5}{44}$ **iii** $\frac{32}{71}$

2 **i** $\frac{1}{8}$ **ii** $\frac{5}{8}$ **iii** $\frac{3}{8}$ **iv** $\frac{1}{2}$

3 **i** **a** $\frac{7}{50}$ **b** $\frac{31}{50}$ **c** $\frac{33}{50}$
ii $\frac{1}{2}$ **iii** $\frac{3}{4}$

4 **i** $a = 7, b = 2, c = 6$ **ii** **a** $\frac{2}{25}$ **b** $\frac{13}{25}$

5 **i** $\frac{7}{40}$ **ii** $\frac{1}{5}$ **iii** $\frac{5}{8}$

6 **i** **a** $\frac{83}{132}$ **b** $\frac{6}{11}$ **c** $\frac{85}{132}$ **d** $\frac{7}{22}$
ii **a** $\frac{16}{41}$ **b** $\frac{23}{41}$ **c** $\frac{24}{41}$

7 **i** Students that study pure and statistics, but not mechanics.
ii $\frac{6}{25}$ **iii** $\frac{28}{67}$

8 **i** Yes **ii** No **iii** No
iv No **v** Yes

9 **i** Not mutually exclusive; $P(X \cap Y) \neq 0/P(X) + P(Y) > 1$
ii 0.9 **iii** 0.7

10 **i** A and C; P(A and C) = 0 **ii** 0.22

11 0.3

12 **i** $\frac{1}{3}$ **ii** $\frac{2}{75}$ **iii** $\frac{23}{75}$ **iv** $\frac{2}{75}$
v $\frac{44}{75}$ **vi** $\frac{2}{29}$

13 **i** 0.8 **ii** 0.2

Text example question

i 0.027 **ii** 0.343 **iii** 0.441
iv 0.189 **v** 0.973

Exercise 9B

1 **i** $\frac{1}{4}$ **ii** $\frac{1}{4}$ **iii** $\frac{1}{2}$ **iv** $\frac{3}{4}$

2 **i** $\frac{1}{12}$ **ii** $\frac{1}{4}$ **iii** $\frac{1}{3}$ **iv** $\frac{1}{6}$
v $\frac{5}{12}$

3 **i** **a** $\frac{1}{4}$ **b** $\frac{1}{9}$ **c** $\frac{1}{36}$
ii **a** $\frac{7}{18}$ **b** $\frac{11}{18}$

4 **i** **a** 1 **b** 3 **c** 6 **d** 10
ii **a** $\frac{1}{216}$ **b** $\frac{1}{72}$ **c** $\frac{1}{36}$ **d** $\frac{5}{108}$

5 **i** $\frac{5}{6}$ **ii** $\frac{5}{18}$

6 **i** **a** $\frac{1}{12}$ **b** $\frac{5}{12}$ **c** $\frac{1}{2}$
ii **a** $\frac{1}{24}$ **b** $\frac{1}{4}$ **c** $\frac{1}{6}$ **d** $\frac{23}{24}$
iii $\frac{1}{8}$

7 **i** **a** 0.0004 **b** 0.9025
ii **a** 0.0008 **b** 0.00096 **c** 0.01824

8 **i** 0.01 **ii** 0.02 **iii** 0.04 **iv** 0.09
v 0.07 **vi** 0.5

9 **ii** **a** 0.25 **b** 0.4 **c** 0.18 **d** 0.51
e 0.78

10 **i** $\frac{1}{8}$ **ii** $\frac{1}{10}$ **ii** $\frac{3}{8}$ **iv** $\frac{21}{40}$
v $\frac{5}{8}$

11 **i** 0.8 **ii** **a** 0.008 **b** 0.384 **c** 0.096

12 **i** **a** 2.25% **b** 12.25% **c** 39.5%
ii **a** 2.88% **b** 88.36%
iii **a** 37.4% **b** 38.6%

13 **i** 0.273 **ii** 0.08184 **iii** 0.17864 **iv** 0.34266
v 0.82136

14 **i** $\frac{1}{3}$ **ii** $\frac{2}{3}$ **iii** $\frac{2}{9}$ **iv** $\frac{2}{27}$

15 $\frac{1}{2}$

16 **i** **a** 0.04 **b** 0.8464 **c** 0.42
ii **a** 0.0826 **b** 0.04032

17 0.384

Text example question

Exhaustive/one is certain to occur

Exercise 9C

1 **i** **a** $\frac{4}{7}$ **ii** **a** $\frac{3}{7}$
b $\frac{5}{7}$ **b** $\frac{2}{7}$

2 **i** **a** $\frac{3}{10}$ **b** $\frac{1}{10}$ **c** $\frac{2}{5}$ **d** $\frac{3}{5}$
ii $\frac{2}{5}+\frac{3}{5}=1$

3 **i** $\frac{1}{14}$ **ii** $\frac{1}{14}$ **iii** $\frac{5}{42}$ **iv** $\frac{10}{21}$
v $\frac{37}{42}$

4 **i** $\frac{1}{12}$ **ii** $\frac{5}{12}$ **iii** $\frac{1}{2}$

5 **i** **a** $\frac{1}{22}$ **b** $\frac{35}{66}$ **ii** **a** $\frac{21}{55}$ **b** $\frac{34}{55}$

6 **i** **a** $\frac{1}{11}$ **b** $\frac{14}{33}$ **c** $\frac{16}{33}$
ii **a** $\frac{1}{3}$ **b** $\frac{2}{3}$

7 **i** $\frac{1}{52}$ **ii** 0 **iii** $\frac{73}{260}$

8 **i** **a** $\frac{3}{95}$ **b** $\frac{14}{95}$ **c** $\frac{99}{190}$ **ii** $\frac{4}{9}$

9 **i** $\frac{17}{25}$ **ii** **a** $\frac{11}{50}$ **b** $\frac{19}{30}$ **c** $\frac{8}{25}$
iii $\frac{5}{39}$

10 **i** **a** $\frac{29}{745}$ **b** $\frac{161}{745}$ **c** $\frac{26}{3725}$ **d** $\frac{137}{447}$
ii Boy from Bolton; $\frac{80}{150}\times\frac{30}{150}=\frac{16}{150}$

11 $\frac{2}{45}$

12 **i** $x=0.4$ **ii** $\frac{13}{27}$

13 **i** $\frac{1}{70}$ **ii** 701
iii $\frac{106}{701}\times\frac{105}{700}=\frac{159}{7010}$ or 0.0227

14 $\frac{3}{7}$

15 **i** 0.267 **ii** 0.684 **iii** 0.133

16 **i** $\frac{2}{13}$ **ii** $\frac{7}{26}$ **iii** $\frac{5}{13}$

Exercise 9D

1 **i** **a** $\frac{1}{9}$ **b** $\frac{1}{26}$ **c** $\frac{4}{117}$ **d** $\frac{35}{234}$
ii **a** $\frac{234}{595}$ **b** $\frac{65}{119}$ **c** $\frac{36}{595}$ **d** $\frac{32}{119}$

2 **i** **a** $\frac{1}{50}$ **b** $\frac{1}{50}$ **c** $\frac{1}{5}$ **d** $\frac{46}{825}$
e $\frac{91}{150}$
ii **a** $\frac{1}{46}$ **b** $\frac{20}{23}$ **c** $\frac{275}{276}$ **d** $\frac{5}{12}$

3 **i** 0.104 **ii** 0.124%

4 **i** **a** Not mutually exclusive; $P(A\cap B)\neq 0$ or $A\cap B\neq\varnothing$
b Not independent; $P(A\cap B)\neq P(A)\times P(B)$
ii **a** 0.35 **b** 0.17 **c** 0.18

5 **i** **a** $\frac{1}{10}$ **b** $\frac{33}{100}$ **c** $\frac{3}{5}$ **d** $\frac{3}{19}$
ii **a** $\frac{239}{825}$ or 0.290 **b** $\frac{1637}{4950}$ or 0.331
iii $6\times\frac{16}{609}=\frac{32}{203}$ or 0.158 **iv** $\frac{38}{61}$ or 0.623

6 **i** **a** 0.0576 **b** $\frac{1}{9}$
c 0.2704 **d** 0.1746
ii 0.050

7 **i** 0.1 **ii** 0.8 **iii** 0.6

8 8:9

Exercise 9E

1 **i** 5 **ii** 7 **iii** $3\frac{2}{3}$

2 7

3 12

4 4.5

5 $3\frac{1}{3}$

6 **i** 5.5 and 6
ii **a** 11.5 **b** 33

7 31

8 **i** 6 and 10 **iii** 8

9 6.75

10 6

11 **i** 5 **ii** 4
iii 8

12 **i** 0.1 **ii** 2.05
iii **a** 0.09 **b** 0.01 **iv** 4.1

Exercise 9F

1 **i** 2.1 **ii** 4.4 **iii** 0.4298

2 **i** **a** $a=0.08$ **b** 3.15
ii **a** $a=0.4$ **b** 4.783
iii **a** $a=1.25$ **b** 20

3 **i** $a=3, b=5, c=7$

ii

s	3	4	5	6	7
$P(S=s)$	$\frac{1}{9}$	$\frac{2}{9}$	$\frac{3}{9}$	$\frac{2}{9}$	$\frac{1}{9}$

iii 5

4 $q=33$

5 **i**

d	0	1	2	3	4	5
$P(D = d)$	$\frac{6}{36}$	$\frac{10}{36}$	$\frac{8}{36}$	$\frac{6}{36}$	$\frac{4}{36}$	$\frac{2}{36}$

ii 194 or $1\frac{17}{18}$

6 **i** $r = \{0, 1, 2\}$

iii

r	0	1	2
$P(R = r)$	$\frac{12}{72}$	$\frac{40}{72}$	$\frac{20}{72}$

iv $1\frac{1}{9}$

v $\frac{8}{9}$

7 0.5

8 **i** $t = \{0, 1, 2, 3\}$

ii

t	0	1	2	3
$P(T = t)$	$\frac{504}{2730}$	$\frac{1296}{2730}$	$\frac{810}{2730}$	$\frac{120}{2730}$

iii 1.2

iv $3 - 1 - 1.2 = 0.8$

Exercise 9G

1 \$2

2 **i** \$4 (or \$0.67 if expected loss is included)

ii Not fair; Fergie Exp win < Charles Exp win

3 \$3

4 **i** Craig \$1.75; Edward \$1.50 **ii** Edward

5 \$8.80

6 Fair; both exp win = \$1.20

7 $x < 7.50$

8 **i** **a** 18 cm² **b** 126 cm² **ii** \$1.40 **iii** \$1.00

9 **i** **a** $\frac{1}{3}$ **b** $\frac{1}{18}$ **c** 0

ii **a** $\frac{1}{54}$ **b** $\frac{1}{108}$; **iii** \$1.75 **iv** \$4.99

10 **i** **a** $p = 0.1, q = 0.2, r = 0.3$ **b** 4.8

ii **a** 4 and 6 **b** \$2.20

iii **a** 4 and 12 **b** 0 **d** \$3.30

Chapter 10 Bivariate Data

Exercise 10A

1 **i** *C* and *D*, *G* and *H* **ii** *E* and *F*, *J* and *K*

iii *A* and *B*, *M* and *N*

iv *A* and *B*, *J* and *K*

v *E* and *F*, *M* and *N*

2 **iii** Fairly strong positive correlation

iv **a** $Y \approx 2.2$ **b** $Y \approx 5.3$ **c** $X \approx 13$

v Answer **(b)**; within known values

3 **iii** Student E; Scored well in both tests.

4 **iii** **a** $Q \approx 7$ **b** $Q \approx 9$

c $P \approx 1.5$ and $P \approx 8.5$

iv Answer **(b)**; Correlation may not continue beyond $P = 8$.

Exercise 10B

1 **i** $y = 5x + 10$ **ii** $y = 17x - 4$

iii $y = 2.5x + 7.5$ **iv** $y = 100 - 9x$

v $y = 0.35x - 28$ **vi** $y = -\frac{7}{5}x + 50$

2 **i** 2 **ii** $\frac{1}{2}$ **iii** $-\frac{1}{3}$

iv $\frac{9}{4}$ or $2\frac{1}{4}$ or 2.25

v $\frac{11}{13}$ or 0.846

vi $-\frac{17}{12}$ or $-1\frac{5}{12}$ or -1.42

3 $Y = 0.023X - 3.06$

4 **i** $Y = 0.375X - 0.525$ or $Y = \frac{3}{8}X - \frac{21}{40}$

ii $Y = 0.07X + 1.774$ or $Y = \frac{7}{100}X - \frac{887}{500}$

iii $Y = 4.9988 - 0.096X$ or $Y = 5 - 0.096X$

5 Equation $Y = 47 - 2.5X$; $q = 22$

6 **i** $P = 0.5T + 4$ **ii** (0, 4) **iii** $P = 0$

Exercise 10C

1 **iii** (58, 53), (42.4, 40.8), (73.6, 65.2)

v $\frac{61}{78}$ or 0.782

vi 8; $Y = 0.782X + 8$

vii Performed better than expected on paper 2 / Performed worse than expected on paper 1.

2 **iii** $p \approx 4.6$ **iv** 8 to 9

3 **i** *H*: the number of bags that she needs to buy depends on the number of horses at the sanctuary.

iv (9.5, 14)

v No bags of feed needed if there are no horses.

vii 1.47; Average number of bags bought per horse per week.

viii $B = 1.47H$

xi \$7.35

4 **i** M: Dose depends on the mass/size of the cat.

iv (2.75, 7.05)

v Zero mass means there is no cat, so no de-wormer is required.

vii 2.56; $D = 2.56M$

viii Average number of milligrams per 1 kg of cat

ix $D = 128$

x Domestic cats do not grow to 50 kg.

5 [BD is the independent variable]

iii (1218, 8830.5) and through (0, 0)

iv Strong positive (linear)

v 7.25: Average exchange rate/Average number of reais received for BD1

vi BD8000

vii **a** Reais will be the independent variable / Switch axes/ Reflect in $y = x$ / Inverse function

b 0.14

6 **iii** (2.2, 36.9); (–1.65, 47.25); (5.925, 26.75)

iv 21 absentees

v –2.7

vi $A = 43$: $A = 43 - 2.7T$

vii $A = -5.6$; Correlation does not continue beyond the range of known values or is not valid when $T > 15.9$°C

7 **iii** Two types of stone were collected.

iv (18.75, 33.50) and (23.9, 18.1)

vi (0, 0); Stones with no volume have no mass.

vii 1.79 and 0.76: the two types of stone have average densities of 1.79 g/cm^3 and 0.76 g/cm^3.

8 **i** **a** Positive **b** None **c** None **d** Positive **e** Negative **f** none

ii **a** Time taken to travel to school, etc.

b Amount of time spent watching TV etc.

Chapter 11 Time Series

Exercise 11A

1 **ii** Value of V is increasing **iii** Two **iv** 7 and 10

2 **ii** Value of Y is decreasing **iii** Five

iv 21 to 24; 14 to 16

3 **iii** Consumption is fairly constant (decreasing slightly)

iv Season I **v** **a** ≈ 23 000 kWh

b Bakery burns down/Workers on strike/Use different type of fuel/Closed for refurbishment/etc.

4 **iii** Two-point (half-yearly) seasonal

iv Winter rate will reach 0% and summer rate will reach 100% well before 2020.

Exercise 11B

1 87, 88, 90, 92, 94, 95, 101, 104, 105, 105, 106, 108

2 46.2, 46.8, 48.2, 49.6, 50.8, 52, 52.8, 55, 57, 58.4, 60.0

3 68.0, 69.1, 69.9, 70.9, 73.7, 75.9, 76.6, 77.7, 84.3, 86.0

4 $a = 22.5, b = 24.5, c = 27.5$

5 $d = 74.5, e = 81.5, f = 88.0, g = 94.5$

6 $j = 125, k = 131, l = 138$

7 **iii** 1158, 1170.5, 1204, 1239.5, 1273.5, 1303, 1335.5, 1373.5, 1413, 1439, 1452.25, 1479.25

iv **a** 2nd quarters **b** 4th quarters

v There is no data on incoming calls.

8 **i** $a = 215, b = 305, c = 340$ **iv** $w = 370$

v $x = 375, y = 1500, z = 480$

Exercise 11C

1 **i** $x = 4.6$ **ii** $x = -9.3$ **iii** $x = 5\frac{1}{24}$ **iv** $x = -16.2$

2 Q1 = 142.9, Q2 = 45.4, Q3 = 52.5, Q4 = 101.8

3 **i** +20 **ii** $P = 112$

iii That it is seasonal and continues into 2017.

4 **i** **a** –323 **b** +323

ii **a** 377 **b** 973

5 **i** They are automatically centred/Variation is three-point.

ii The school's electricity bills are increasing.

iii –23 to –18

iv $762 to $767

v School may install/remove air conditioners, so bills will increase/decrease more than expected, etc.

6 **ii** **a** Increasing **b** Decreasing

iii Gradient of trend line is positive

iv +2.4 to +2.6

v 12.5 to 13.0

vi $149000 to $156000

vii May have been a very hot quarter/Competitor went out of business.

7 **i** $x = +13$ **ii** 723

8 **i** $y = +26$ **ii** 100 **iii** 58

9 **i** **a** Kenny

b Automatically centred/3 is an odd number

10 **ii** 4.525, 4.45, 4.375, 4.325, 4.275, 4.2, 4.125, 4.075, 4.025, 3.95

iv 3.60 to 3.8

v Average deviation 1.2 to 1.3; \$48000 to \$51000

11 **i** 562, 549, 537, 525, 509, 492, 480, 469, 456, 442, 430, 419

ii −210 **iii** \$16 500

12 **i** The number of new customers opening accounts at the bank each quarter is decreasing.

ii Four-point (quarterly) seasonal

iii ≈ 47

iv There is no information on how many customers are closing accounts.

Exam-Style Questions

1 **i** *D* **ii** *B* **iii** *E*

2 **i** Median

iii Mean

iv Mode

3 \$2.50

4 **i** 3 **ii** 5.5 and 8.5 **iii** 7.5

5 **i** Boundaries are 21.5 and 25.5

ii **a** 7.5 cm **b** $y = 16$

6 **i** 0.21

ii **a** No; $A \cap B \neq \varnothing$ or $P(A \text{ and } B) \neq 0$ etc.

b Yes; $P(A \text{ and } B) = P(A) \times P(B)$

7 **i** 1800 g **ii** \$21 600

iii 4 sectors with equal angles (90°)

8 **i** **a** 4% **b** 69%

ii **a** 36 **b** 186

iii Sampling error

iv Responses are not restricted.

9 **i** Men 58, Women 32

ii 36 **iii** 16

iv The extreme value of 79 affects the range but not the IQR

10 **i** Pattern in variation repeats at regular time intervals of one year or less.

ii $x = -55.6$ **iii** 761

iv Moving averages that must be centred

v 444.4

11 **ii** 7.51

iii Positive; those with good aptitude scores will make good progress.

12 **i** 23 **ii** $\frac{1}{3}$ **iii** $\frac{85}{133}$ **iv** $\frac{1}{22}$

13 **i** 35 sec **ii** 14.6 sec **iii** Twice **iv** 26.25 sec

v Greater

14 **i** 19 **ii** 33

iii Treated 4 cm; Untreated 4.85 cm

iv Treated

v $N = 58$ **vi** 0.23

15 **i** 80 **ii** **a** 350.775 g **b** 351.61 g

iii 420

16 **i** **a** $\frac{1}{5}$ **b** $\frac{40}{81}$ **c** $\frac{19}{30}$

ii **b** (70, 61.75)

c $Y = \frac{31}{64}X + \frac{891}{32}$ **d** *F*, *A*, *G*, *D*, *H*, *B*, *C*, *E*.

iii If the standard deviations for *X* and *Y* were equal.

17 **i** $0.199 \times 256 \approx 51$ **ii** $a = 111, b = 152, c = 173$

iii 179 and 162 **iv** 178.1

v *Q* has a lower standardised accident rate.

vi Any relating to the seriousness of the accidents.

Glossary

Absolute: a non-negative value.
Aggregate: a whole formed by combining several separate elements.
Approximated: rounded off to a certain degree of accuracy.
At random: due entirely to chance.
Average: any of the measures of central tendency – mean, median or mode.

Bias: showing prejudice towards or against a certain type of person, item or group.
Bivariate: involving two variables.

Class: a group of numerical values into which the data are organised.
Class boundary: a boundary that lies half-way between the upper class limit of one class and the lower class limit of the next class in grouped discrete data.
Class interval: the difference between the lower and upper class boundary values; the width of a column in a histogram.
Class limit: either of the lowest or highest actual value that can exist in a class of data.
Class mid-value: the mean of the lower and upper class boundaries.
Closed question: a question to which only one of a limited number of answers is acceptable.
Conditional: dependent upon another event.
Context: a specific situation.
Continuous: without gaps between possible values.
Correlation: a relationship between the values of two variables.
Crude: not processed; raw.
Cumulative frequency: the number of values of a variable that are less than the upper boundary value of a class.

Decile: the value below which a given tenth of the values in a set of data fall.
Dependent: affected by another event.
Derived: generated by performing consistent operations on each value in a distribution.
Deviation: the amount by which a single measurement differs from a fixed value, such as the mean.
Discrete: with gaps between possible values.
Dispersion: the degree to which values are spread out.
Dual: showing information for two sets of data.

Eliminate: to effectively cancel out by the use of average values.
Equally likely: having the same chance of occurring.
Estimate: an approximate calculation of the value of something.
Event: something that can occur due to an outcome or, more commonly, a combination of outcomes.
Exhaustive: describing or accounting for everything that can possibly occur.
Expectation: a statement of what is expected to happen during a trial, including the number of times an event is expected to occur.
Experiment: an action that takes place which has at least one possible result.
Extrapolation: a method of estimating a value outside the range of values that are already known.
Extreme value: a value in a set of data that is not typical of the majority of the values.

Fair game: one in which two players have equal chances of winning, and their expected profit is zero.

Favourable outcome: one that leads to a particular event occurring.
Frequency: the number of times that a particular value occurs in a set of data.
Frequency density: a measure of the frequency per standard interval of a variable.
Frequency distribution: a table showing how many times each value or class of values occurs.
Frequency polygon: a statistical diagram consisting of line segments, whose end points are the mid-values of classes of data.

Grouped: put into classes of values.

Histogram: a statistical diagram in which column area is proportional to class frequency.

Independent: not affected by another event.
Index: an indicator of relative size or value.
Inter-: between.
Interpolation: a method of estimating a value within the range of values that are already known.
Interquartile range: the spread of the middle half of a set of ordered values.

Linear transformation: a conversion or mapping of one set of numbers to another by multiplication and/or addition.

Mean: the sum of a set of values divided by the number of values.
Median: the middle value in an ordered set of data.
Modal class: the class of values in a distribution with the highest frequency density.
Mode: the most frequently occurring value.
Mutually exclusive: refers to two events where, if either one of them occurs, then the other cannot.

Open question: a question to which any answer is acceptable.
Outcome: any of the possible results of an experiment.

Percentile: the value below which a given percentage of the values in a set of data fall.
Population: the whole from which a sample is selected.
Prediction: an estimate of a value at some time in the future.
Probability: a measure of how likely it is that an event occurs.
Proportional: having a constant ratio to another quantity.

Quarter: a period of approximately three.
Quartile: any of the three values (lower, middle and upper) that divide a distribution into four parts with an equal number of values in each part.

Range: the difference between the largest and smallest value.
Raw data: data that has not yet been processed.
Relative: compared to another (fixed) value.
Representative: closely reflecting the characteristics of a population.

Sample: part of a population.
Sampling error: the differences between sample and population characteristics.
Sampling frame: a (numbered) list of names that specifies the individuals or items in a sample.
Scaled: adjusted by a consistent method.
Season: one of the four quarters of a year.
Seasonal: dependent on the time of year.
Sectional: divided into sections to show the parts that make up the whole.
Standard deviation: a measure of the deviations from the mean.
Standard interval: a quantity used as a standard unit for a set of unequal class intervals.
Standardised: weighted by standard population figures.

Tabulated: any method of summarising data in a table.
Trend: a description of whether values are increasing, decreasing or remaining constant as time passes.
Trial: a set of repeated experiments.

Ungrouped: not put into classes of values; existing individually.

Variable: an observed, counted or measured item, which can take more than one value.
Variation: changes in values.

Weight: a measure of significance or importance.
Weighted average: a mean value calculated with the significance of each item or set of items taken into account.

Index